# TO
# ISTANBUL

MELISSA SHALES

EYEWITNESS TRAVEL

Left **Gate of Felicity, Topkapı Palace** Centre **Mehter Band** Right **Blue Mosque**

LONDON, NEW YORK,
MELBOURNE, MUNICH AND DELHI
www.dk.com

Produced by Coppermill Books
55 Salop Road, London E17 7HS

Printed and bound in China
by Leo Paper Products Ltd

First published in Great Britain in 2007
by Dorling Kindersley Limited
80 Strand, London WC2R 0RL
A Penguin Company

13 14 15 16 10 9 8 7 6 5 4 3 2 1

**Copyright 2007, 2013 © Dorling
Kindersley Limited, London**

**Reprinted with revisions 2009, 2011, 2013**

MIX
Paper from
responsible sources
FSC
www.fsc.org   FSC™ C018179

# Contents

## Istanbul's Top 10

Cover: Front – **4Corners:** SIME/Anna Serrano main; **DK Images:** Tony Souter bl. Spine – **DK Images:** Linda
Whitwam b. Back – **DK Images:** Tony Souter tl; Linda Whitwam tc; Francesca Yorke tr.

Left **Grand Bazaar** Centre **Dolmabahçe Palace** Right **View from Sülemaniye Mosque**

Contents

Left **Deesis Mosaic, South Gallery, Haghia Sophia** Right **Fortress of Asia**

# ISTANBUL'S
## TOP 10

ISTANBUL'S TOP 10

# Highlights of Istanbul

*Istanbul is one of the greatest cities the world has ever known. Inhabited for at least 5,000 years, it was capital of two of the world's most powerful empires – those of the Byzantines and the Ottomans – and its every stone is steeped in history. The highlights are easy; you can cover the major attractions in the first couple of days. But after that, the choice can be overwhelming, especially as this ancient city is reinventing itself once more as a modern centre for nightlife, food and shopping. The only answer is to come back again – and again. If you do, this endlessly fascinating city will certainly reward you.*

### Topkapı Palace
A palace fit for a sultan, several wives, hundreds of concubines and thousands of retainers, the Topkapı was not only a royal residence, but also the Ottoman Empire's centre of government *(see pp8–11)*.

### Haghia Sophia
One of the greatest icons of the Christian church, Haghia Sophia has stood for 1,500 years – a miraculous feat of design and engineering that has survived fire, war and earthquake, and outlived two great empires *(see pp12–13)*.

### Blue Mosque
Sultan Ahmet I's great mosque is one of the world's most famous religious buildings – "blue" on account of the delicately patterned İznik tiles which adorn the interior *(see pp14–15)*.

### Archaeological Museum
Turkey's world-class national collection, which remarkably was begun only in the mid-19th century, contains ancient treasures from across the length and breadth of the Ottoman Empire and beyond, including artifacts from Babylon, Syria, Egypt, Greece, Rome and Persia *(see pp16–17)*.

### Grand Bazaar

More mall than market since its last restoration, the Grand Bazaar remains a true Turkish delight, a shopaholic's colourful fantasy that is also a photographer's dream. Whether you are after a Hereke carpet or a pair of silk slippers, you will be satisfied here – in the bazaar at the western end of the Silk Road *(see pp18–19)*.

Map labels: Balat, Fener, Edirnekapı, Karagümrük, Keçeciler Cad, Fatih, Findıkzade, Saraç, Haseki, Aks

### 6 Süleymaniye Mosque
Sultan Süleyman I, the Ottomans' greatest emperor, and Sinan, the empire's most talented architect, created more than 400 buildings together. This imposing mosque is their masterwork (see pp20–21).

### 7 Church of St Saviour in Chora
With more than 100 profoundly beautiful early-14th-century mosaics and frescoes of biblical scenes, this church is one of the greatest of Istanbul's many Byzantine treasures (see pp22–3).

750 ⌐——— yards ⌐ 0 ⌐ metres ———⌐ 750

### 8 Çemberlitaş Baths
The perfect way to recuperate from an overdose of sightseeing is to steam gently beneath the marble domes of a traditional Turkish bath before allowing an attendant to massage those aching feet. The experience is cleansing, cultural and reviving (see pp24–5).

### 10 Bosphorus Cruise
Take to the water on a ferry trip up the Bosphorus, and enjoy a fabulously lazy day off. The air is clean, the pace unhurried and, best of all, sightseeing can be done from the deck, with the promise of a great lunch ahead (see pp28–9).

### 9 Dolmabahçe Palace
This 19th-century Occidental fantasy was a key component in the downfall of the Ottoman Empire. Sultan Abdül Mecit's decision to build a lavishly opulent European-style palace almost bankrupted the Treasury, and in the end could be financed only by foreign loans (see pp26–7).

# ⑩ Topkapı Palace

*Fresh from his conquest of Constantinople, Mehmet II built Topkapı Sarayı as his main residence in 1459–65. He planned it as a series of pavilions in four courtyards – a tribute in stone to the tent encampments of his nomadic forebears. Mehmet's palace was also the seat of government, and contained a college for training officials and soldiers. While government moved across the road to the Sublime Porte in the 16th century, Topkapı continued as the sultan's palace until Abdül Mecit I moved to Dolmabahçe Palace in 1856.*

*Imperial Gate*

⭐ Book your ticket for the Harem as soon as you arrive, and see the rest of the palace while waiting for your time-slot.

◯ There is a café in the first courtyard and a good (if expensive) restaurant, Konyalı, for lunch in the fourth. This is a good place to try Ottoman court cuisine, but it can be crowded. You can book a table in advance on (0212) 513 96 96.

- Babıhümayun Cad
- Map S3
- (0212) 512 04 80
- Open 9am–5pm (7pm in summer) Wed–Mon
- 25 TL plus an additional 15 TL for entry to the Harem (tickets are available at the kiosk by the Harem entrance)
- www.topkapisarayi.gov.tr

## Top 10 Features

1. Imperial Gate
2. First Courtyard
3. Harem
4. Gate of Salutations
5. Kitchens
6. Throne Room
7. Third Courtyard
8. Imperial Wardrobe
9. Treasury
10. Imperial Sofa

### ① Imperial Gate (Bâb-ı Hümayun)

Built in 1478, this gate *(above left)* is the main entrance to the palace, with gatekeepers' quarters on either side. An apartment belonging to Mehmet II above the gate was destroyed by fire in 1866.

### ② First Courtyard (Alay Meydanı)

This vast outer courtyard takes in all of Gülhane Park, sweeping down the hill to Sirkeci and including the 6th-century church of Haghia Eirene (Aya İrini Kilisesi), the wooden houses of Soğukçeşme Sokağı and the imposing Archaeological Museum.

### ③ Harem

A maze of rooms and corridors, the Harem was a closed world occupied by the sultan's wives, concubines and children. A guided tour is a must.

### ④ Gate of Salutations (Bâb-üs Selâm)

At this elaborate gate *(left)*, built in 1524, visitors were greeted, and high officials who had upset the sultan were arrested and strangled. The gateway leads into the Second Courtyard (Divan Meydanı), where the Treasury now has a magnificent display of arms and armour.

➡ Don't miss the fascinating collection of priceless miniatures and manuscripts situated next to the Treasury.

### Kitchens

These huge kitchens once catered for 800–1,000 people a day. Now they display a marvellous collection of ceramics, crystal and silver, including the Chinese celadon ware favoured by early sultans because, supposedly, it changed colour when it came into contact with poison.

Entrance

### Throne Room (Arz Odası)

In the Throne Room *(right)*, the Sultan would consult his ministers and governors, welcome ambassadors and other dignitaries, and host smaller formal state occasions.

### Third Courtyard (Enderûn Meydanı)

The Gate of Felicity (Bâb-üs Saadet) leads to the Third Courtyard, containing the sultan's private quarters and those of the Harem's white eunuchs.

### Imperial Wardrobe (Seferli Koğuşu)

Fittingly, the Imperial Wardrobe is now the home of the costume museum, a sumptuous collection of some 3,000 elaborately embroidered royal robes *(above)*.

### Treasury (Hazine Koğuşu)

With exhibits including the jewel-encrusted Topkapı Dagger *(below)* and the amazing 86-carat Spoonmaker's Diamond, the Topkapı Treasury may be the most ostentatious collection of wealth ever gathered outside of the legendary Aladdin's cave.

### Imperial Sofa (Sofa-ı-Hümayun)

The Imperial Sofa was a place to relax, its gardens studded with pavilions built by successive sultans. The finest is the Baghdad Pavilion (Bağdat Köşkü), built by Murat IV in 1639 to celebrate his capture of the city of Baghdad the year before.

### Religious Relics

The Pavilion of the Holy Mantle (Hasoda Koğuşu) contains several of Islam's holiest relics. Exhibits include hairs from the Prophet's beard, one of his teeth, two of his swords and the sacred standard used during his military campaigns. The most important relic of all is the Holy Mantle, a plain black camel-hair cloak that the Prophet gave as a present to a poet. Once a year, it was displayed to high officials then doused in water; the drops squeezed from it were sent out as talismans against the plague.

Left **Imperial Baths** Centre **Salon of the Valide Sultan** Right **Imperial Hall**

# Features of the Topkapı Harem

## 1 Barracks of the Black Eunuchs

Apart from the sultan and his sons, the only men allowed into the Harem were the black eunuchs, up to 200 slaves from Sudan and Ethiopia. Their barracks lie on one side of the Courtyard of the Black Eunuchs, with its arcade of marble columns.

## 2 Courtyard of the Concubines

This colonnaded courtyard lies beside the Harem Baths. As many as 300 concubines lived in the Harem at a time.

## 3 Golden Cage

Mehmet III became sultan in 1595, following the murder of all but one of his 19 brothers. After that, heirs to the throne were kept in the "Golden Cage", a secure area of the Harem, until they were needed. As a result, many were weak, feeble-minded, and certainly ill-fitted for government when they took the throne.

Detail, the Golden Cage

## 4 Salon of the Valide Sultan

The valide sultan (sultan's mother) was by far the most powerful woman in the palace, and enjoyed the use of some of the best rooms in the Harem.

## 5 Sultan's Apartments

The sultan spent much of his off-duty time in his suite within the Harem. Look out for the gilded bedroom of Sultan Abdül Hamit I (1774–89), the Hall of Murat III (1574–95), and the beautiful Fruit Room (see p58).

## 6 Imperial Baths

Standing next to each other at the centre of the complex are the baths of the sultan and the valide sultan, both elegantly faced with marble.

## 7 Imperial Hall

In the Imperial Hall the sultan entertained his closest friends. Although the hall was within the Harem, only a few women – the sultan's mother, chief wife, favourites and daughters – were allowed entry.

## 8 Favourites' Apartments

*Haseki* (favourites) who bore a child received their own apartments and their freedom (if slaves). After the sultan's death, those who had borne only daughters were married out of the Harem or moved to the old palace, while those with sons remained in the palace.

**Courtyard of the Black Eunuchs**

*The guided tour of the Harem is extensive, covering around 40 rooms.*

### Wives' Apartments

The sultan's wives (under Islamic law, he was allowed to have up to four) also had their own apartments. While wives took formal precedence in the Harem hierarchy, the real power lay with the sultan's favourites and mother. Occasionally a sultan would marry a concubine – as in the case of Süleyman I, who married his beloved Roxelana (known in Turkish as Haseki Hürrem). Wives were often traded in political treaties.

### Golden Way

This long, dark passage is known as the Golden Way because on festivals the Sultan would scatter gold coins here for the members of the Harem.

## Top 10 Ottoman Women

1. Hafsa Sultan (mother of Süleyman I)
2. Roxelana (wife of Süleyman)
3. Nurbanu Sultan (wife of Selim II, daughter-in-law of Süleyman)
4. Mihrimah (daughter of Süleyman, wife of Grand Vizier Rüstem Paşa)
5. Safiye Sultan (mother of Mehmet III)
6. Handan Sultan (wife of Mehmet III)
7. Kösem Sultan (wife of Ahmet I)
8. Hatice Turhan Sultan (mother of Mehmet IV)
9. Nakşidil Sultan (mother of Mahmut II)
10. Bezmiâlem (wife of Mahmut II, mother of Abdül Mecit I)

Roxelana

## Life in the Harem

*Behind the doors of the Harem, life was far less exciting than it was portrayed to be in the breathless accounts of 19th-century European commentators. There was undoubtedly intrigue, and if a woman was fortunate enough to be one of the sultan's favourites she might well develop a taste for lavish comfort and lovely gifts, yet daily existence for most was mundane – even dully routine. The Harem was less a den of vice than a family home and girls' school. Of its 1,000 or so occupants, more than two-thirds were servants or royal children, while concubines – who usually arrived between the ages of 5 and 12 – spent years living in dormitories and undergoing a thorough education before being introduced to the sultan.*

**The Favourite Sultana** by Etienne Jeaurat – a European vision of Harem life.

The English word harem derives from the Arabic harãm ("forbidden").

# TOP 10 Haghia Sophia

*Haghia Sophia, the Church of Holy Wisdom (Ayasofya in Turkish), is an awe-inspiring expression of religious faith and one of the world's foremost architectural wonders. The first church on the site burned down in 404, the second was destroyed during the Nika Riots of 532, but the third – inaugurated by Emperor Justinian in 537 – stands firm today, despite countless wars and earthquakes, a blazing beacon to the faith of its creators. The church was converted into a mosque in 1453. Since 1934 it has been a museum.*

*Imperial Box*

🕐 After your visit, it's well worth coming back at night to see both Haghia Sophia and the Blue Mosque floodlit.

🚫 No refreshments are provided within the complex, but there are many options in Sultanahmet Square and Divanyolu Caddesi, a couple of minutes' walk away.

---

• Sultanahmet Meydanı
• Map R4
• (0212) 528 45 00
• Open 9am–6pm Tue–Sun in summer, 9:30am–4:30pm Tue–Sun in winter
• Adm 25 TL
• www.ayasofyamuzesi.gov.tr

## Top 10 Features

1 Exterior
2 Galleries
3 Weeping Pillar
4 Columns
5 Narthex
6 Coronation Square
7 Islamic Elements
8 Nave
9 Dome
10 Windows

### Exterior
Its deep red walls piled high with semidomes soaring up towards the vast central dome, the main building is much as it was in the 6th century – except for the buttresses added to secure the structure, which, unfortunately, partly obscure the original shape.

### Galleries
Women used the galleries for prayer. There are splendid mosaics in the south gallery: look out for Christ Pantocrator (Almighty) with John the Baptist and the Virgin Mary; and Mary holding the Infant Christ, flanked by Emperor John II Comnenus and Empress Irene *(below)*.

### Weeping Pillar
Emperor Justinian rested his aching head against the damp stone of this pillar *(above)* and was instantly cured. Ever since, visitors have queued to touch the miraculous spot.

### Columns
The Byzantines were great scavengers, and most of the columns in the Haghia Sophia were salvaged from pagan temples.

*The architects who created Haghia Sophia were two Greek mathematicians, Isidorus of Miletus and Anthemius of Tralles.*

### Narthex
There are doors leading into the nave from each bay of the narthex; the large central one, the Imperial Gate, was once reserved for the Emperor and the Patriarch. At the south end of the narthex, look back above the door as you exit into the Vestibule of the Warriors to see the wonderful 6th-century mosaic of Constantine and Justinian offering their city and church to the infant Christ *(above)*.

### Coronation Square
Set into the floor near the *minbar*, the site of the emperor's throne is marked in a square of patterned marble. In Byzantine times, this was considered to be the centre of the world *(omphalion)*.

### Islamic Elements
The conversion of the church into a mosque began in 1453. The mosaics were plastered over (and discovered only in the 1930s). The *mihrab* and *minbar* *(see p15)* were added by Sultan Murat III in the 16th century. Look up to see the calligraphic roundels *(above)* at the base of the dome.

### Nave
On entering the nave *(below)* the overwhelming impression is of the vast space enclosed by the dome. This sits on four arches rising out of four enormous marble piers, which frame double colonnades at either end.

### Dome
The soaring dome, 32 m (101 ft) in diameter, rises 56 m (183 ft) above the ground. Supported by 40 ribs made from special lightweight hollow bricks, it was and remains a miracle of engineering. The original design was even more ambitious – it survived for 21 years before being destroyed by an earthquake in 559.

### Windows
Banks of windows in the tympanum walls beneath the dome, as well as a circle of windows between the ribs of the dome, flood the church with light.

### Changing Faces
In the last bay of the south gallery, on the east wall, look for the superb mosaic of Christ enthroned, flanked by Empress Zoë and Emperor Constantine IX Monomachus. It is clear that the emperor's head has been altered. Historians believe that the figure was initially a portrait of Zoë's first husband, Romanos III Argyros, but after his death in 1034 it was replaced with the image of her second husband, Michael IV. After Michael died in 1041, the face of her third husband, Constantine, was added.

# 📕 Blue Mosque

*Sultan Ahmet I was only 19 when he commissioned this superb mosque, known in Turkish as the Sultanahmet Camii. So great was his enthusiasm for the project that at times he even worked alongside his labourers. With his architect, Mehmet Ağa, he wanted to surpass the Süleymaniye Mosque (the work of Ağa's teacher, Sinan) and Haghia Sophia. The result of their labours, completed in 1616, has become one of the most celebrated mosques in the world, known widely as the Blue Mosque because of the blue İznik tiles in the interior.*

*Prayer time*

🕐 To avoid prayer times, make the mosque your first stop in the morning, or visit in the midafternoon.

🍴 There are no places for refreshment inside the mosque complex, but Sultanahmet Square, Divanyolu Caddesi and the Arasta Bazaar offer plenty of possibilities.

• Sultanahmet Meydanı
• Map R5
• (0212) 518 13 19
• Open 9am–7pm daily, except during prayers
• Donations
• May–Sep: son-et-lumière performances each evening, with Turkish, English, French and German on different nights. Free

## Top 10 Features

1. The Setting
2. Entrance
3. Domes
4. Minarets
5. Ablutions Fountain
6. Courtyard
7. Tiles
8. Minbar and Mihrab
9. Sultan's Loge
10. Carpets

### The Setting

To underline the supremacy of Islam over Christian Byzantium, the Blue Mosque was built opposite Haghia Sophia *(above)*, on the site of the Byzantine royal palace.

### Entrance

The monumental main entrance to the mosque is rarely used. There are separate entrances for those going to pray and for tourists, around the side of the courtyard.

### Domes

Semidomes *(right)* surround the main dome, which is 23.5 m (77 ft) in diameter and 43 m (140 ft) high, and supported by four giant columns, each 5 m (16 ft) in diameter.

### Minarets

Legend has it that the sultan asked for a minaret capped with *altın* (gold), but the architect thought he had asked for *altı* (six) minarets. The sultan was pleased – no mosque apart from the great mosque in Mecca had six minarets.

➡ *Try to see the mosque by night at least once – it is beautiful at any time, but especially so when floodlit.*

### Ablutions Fountain
The fountain (left) at the centre of the mosque's courtyard is no longer used for ritual ablutions. Instead, the faithful use taps ranged along the outside of the courtyard. Washing the face, arms, neck, feet, mouth and nose is seen as an integral part of the act of prayer.

### Courtyard
The huge courtyard, which is faced with cool marble from the island of Marmara, has the same dimensions as the interior of the prayer hall. Look up for a splendid view of the mosque's cascade of domes and semidomes.

### Tiles
The majority of the blue İznik tiles (above) that give the mosque its name are too high on the interior walls to examine in detail. There are 20,143 tiles of 70 different styles – fulfilling the order put severe pressure on the İznik tile makers, and the sultan banned anyone else from placing orders until his was complete.

#### İznik Tiles
Ceramic production in İznik began during the Byzantine era. In the early years, the designs were based on Chinese models. Arabic motifs were added by Şah Kulu, one of 16 artists brought in from Tabriz by Sultan Selim I (1512–20). A rich turquoise was added to the traditional blue and white in the 1530s; purples, greens and coral reds came 20 years later. Master designer Kara Memi introduced swirling floral patterns, and by the time Ahmet I placed his order for the Blue Mosque, the İznik style was established.

### Minbar and Mihrab
At the front of the mosque are the minbar (left), the pulpit from which the imam delivers his sermons, and the mihrab (below), a niche that points towards Mecca.

### Sultan's Loge
To the left of the mihrab is the galleried box where the sultan prayed, its ceiling painted with arabesque designs.

### Carpets
The whole of the interior is laid with a modern carpet. Mosques have always had carpets, to cushion the knees and forehead during prayers.

For tips on Islamic etiquette See p39

# Archaeological Museum

*The national collection of one of the world's most ancient and enthralling countries naturally promises something special, and this fabulous museum does not disappoint. A world-class collection spanning 5,000 years, it was founded in 1881 by Osman Hamdi Bey, the son of a grand vizier, fuelled by the realization that European archaeologists and treasure-hunters were walking off with much of the Empire's heritage. There are three sections: the main museum, the Tiled Pavilion (Çinili Köşk) and the Museum of the Ancient Orient.*

*Façade*

🕐 It is not unusual to find some galleries closed due to staff shortages.

🍴 There is a fairly rudimentary drinks kiosk in the grounds.

• Osman Hamdi Bey Yokuşu, Topkapı Sarayı, Gülhane
• Map S3
• (0212) 520 77 40
• Open 9am–6pm Tue–Sun
• Adm 10 TL
• www.istanbularkeoloji.gov.tr

## Top 10 Features

1. Sidon Sarcophagi
2. Alexander Sarcophagus
3. Ishtar Gate
4. Hattuşaş Sphinx
5. Halikarnassos Lion
6. Treaty of Kadesh
7. Museum of the Ancient Orient
8. Tiled Pavilion
9. Istanbul Through the Ages
10. Anatolia and Troy Gallery

### Sidon Sarcophagi
**1** Osman Hamdi Bey discovered this remarkable group of 5th- and 4th-century-BC sarcophagi *(below)* in Sidon (modern Lebanon) in 1887.

### Alexander Sarcophagus
**2** Its high-relief frieze shows scenes of Alexander victorious in battle against the Persians, but the Alexander Sarcophagus, dating from the late 4th century BC, is in fact the tomb of King Abdalonymos of Sidon (died c. 312 BC). Faint traces remain of the gaudy colour that would once have covered it.

### Ishtar Gate
**3** The Ishtar Gate, built by King Nebuchadnezzar in 575 BC, was decorated with mosaic ceramic panels of dragons and bulls *(main image)*. The Processional Way through the gate was lined with 120 lions.

### Hattuşaş Sphinx
**4** This enigmatic 13th-century-BC stone feline was one of four discovered in the great Hittite city at Hattuşaş (Boğazkale) in Anatolia.

### Halikarnassos Lion
**5** The tomb of King Mausolus was one of the seven wonders of the ancient world – this simple lion *(left)* is a surviving relic.

*The tomb of Mausolus was so magnificent that his name has been enshrined for posterity in the word "mausoleum".*

### 6 Treaty of Kadesh

The world's oldest surviving peace treaty *(below)*, carved in stone in 1269 BC, was agreed by Egyptian Pharoah Ramses II and King Muwatalli of the Hittites after a battle in present-day Syria. It lays out the terms of the ceasefire and agrees the safe return of refugees.

### Key

| | |
|---|---|
| ▦ | Third floor |
| ▦ | Second floor |
| ▦ | First floor |
| ▦ | Ground floor |

### 7 Museum of the Ancient Orient

This section has well-preserved exhibits from Mesopotamia, Egypt and Babylon, including some of the world's first known writing – cuneiform clay tablets from 2700 BC.

### 8 Tiled Pavilion

Built in 1472 as a sports pavilion, this is the oldest secular building in Istanbul *(right)*. A masterpiece of İznik tiles itself, the pavilion also tells the story of Turkish ceramics, with displays from İznik and Kutahya.

### 9 Istanbul Through the Ages

This thoughtful exhibit provides a fascinating insight into the city, with maps, plans and drawings alongside exhibits such as the 14th-century bell from the Galata Tower.

### 10 Anatolia and Troy Gallery

Thousands of years of history are imaginatively timelined in this long gallery. On one side you can travel through Anatolia from the Stone Age to the Iron Age. On the other wall, follow the history of Troy from 3000 BC to the 1st century AD.

### Ancient Welcome

Visitors are greeted by an eclectic assortment of archaeological artifacts. In the entrance hall to the main museum stands a statue of the Egyptian god Bes. At the foot of the stairs to the Museum of the Ancient Orient are two basalt lions from Samal, dating from the 8th century BC. Outside the main museum are porphyry sarchophagi, from the 4th–5th century AD, thought to be those of Byzantine emperors. The portico itself is modelled on the 4th-century-BC Sarcophagus of the Mourning Women.

*Also worth a visit are galleries devoted to Byzantium, Cyprus and Syria-Palestine. There's a children's museum in the new wing.*

# 🔟 Grand Bazaar

*From the painted arches to the shopfronts gleaming with lanterns, piled with carpets or heaped with spices, the Kapalı Çarşı is a fantasy of Eastern opulence. Founded in 1461 by Sultan Mehmet II, the bazaar was designed as the trading heart of an empire. In addition to shops, banks, storerooms and cafés, it had travellers' accommodation, a bathhouse, mosques and a school. Destroyed several times by earthquake and fire, it has always bounced back. It offers a compelling and entertaining – if potentially expensive – day out.*

*Entrance to the Old Bazaar*

⊙ The hotels, school and bathhouse that were once part of the bazaar have gone; now the market has a police station, ATM machines, public toilets and other necessities for keeping its droves of visitors happy.

✿ There are small tea and coffee shops scattered throughout the market, as well as several good kebab shops, a couple of restaurants and a range of upmarket cafés.

• Map N3
• Open 8:30am–7pm Mon–Sat (surrounding street markets are usually open longer and on Sun)
• Free
• www.kapalicarsi.org.tr

## Top 10 Features

1. İç Bedesten
2. Jewellers' Street
3. Carpet Sellers
4. Outdoor Stalls
5. Street Names
6. Fountains
7. Sandal Bedesten
8. Gates
9. Zincirli Han
10. Valide Han

### İç Bedesten

This was the bazaar's first building, a Byzantine structure converted in 1461 into a sturdy lockup in which jewellery was traded and slaves were auctioned. Today it is used to sell precious goods such as antiques and rare icons.

### Jewellers' Street (Kalpakçılar Başı Caddesi)

The bazaar's widest street runs along the southern edge of the market, its shop windows piled high with jewels and precious metals. Around 100,000 kg (220,460 lb) of gold is traded in the bazaar each year. Gold jewellery is sold by weight, with a little added for craftsmanship.

### Carpet Sellers

The bazaar is home to Istanbul's finest carpet dealers, as well as lesser traders keen to sell you a hall runner or a bedside rug. Shops are scattered through out the market especially near the İç Bedesten on Halıcılar Çarşısı Caddesi.

### Outdoor Stalls
Surrounding the covered market is a maze of tiny lanes, with stalls selling carpets, souvenirs, clothes and vegetables. Locals shop here.

### Street Names
At one time, each part of the bazaar had its own specialism, as indicated by the street names. Look for the *terlikçiler* (slipper-makers), *aynacılar* (mirror-makers), *fesçiler* (fez-makers), *yorgancılar* (quilt-makers), *kazazcılar* (silk-thread-makers) and *kürkçüler* (fur-makers).

### Fountains
Two marble and copper fountains provided drinking water for the market traders before modern plumbing was installed. According to an 1880 survey, there were also 16 drinking-water posts, 1 fountain reservoir, and 8 wells for fire-fighters.

### Sandal Bedesten
In the southeast corner of the bazaar, the 15th-century Sandal Bedesten, its roof of 20 brick domes propped up by pillars, is the former antiques market. It now hosts a carpet auction every Wednesday at 1pm.

### Facts and Figures
The Grand Bazaar is one of the world's largest buildings, containing a network of 61 covered streets and enclosing an area of 307,000 sq m (3,305,000 sq ft). Every day in this teeming marketplace, as many as 30,000 traders in 4,500 shops befriend and haggle with up to 400,000 shoppers – both locals and visitors from all around the world. In business since its foundation in 1461, the bazaar is the world's oldest covered market.

### Zincirli Han
The *hans* provided accommodation, food and stables for travelling traders. This one, the oldest of 40 in the area, has been lovingly restored and is now occupied by Şişko Osman Halıcılık, a leading carpet dealer.

### Gates
Twenty-two gates lead into the covered bazaar from all directions. The Beyazıt Gate, rebuilt after an earthquake in 1894, is marked with the *tughra* (imperial sign) of Sultan Abdül Hamit II, and the happy assurance that "God loves tradesmen".

### Valide Han
Constructed in 1651, this building (the largest caravanserai in Istanbul) has been sadly neglected. Today it contains a mix of residential, gallery and workshop space.

Taxis near the Grand Bazaar have a bad reputation; some drivers charge up to ten times the going rate (see also p104).

# 🔟 Süleymaniye Mosque

*One of the finest creations of the Ottoman Empire's greatest architect, Sinan, Süleymaniye Camii was built in 1550–57 for Süleyman I. He established this magnificent hilltop mosque as a charitable foundation (külliye) as well as a place of worship – and it stands in a vast complex that includes medreses, a hamam, a hospital and a caravanserai. The mosque's towering domes dominate the skyline in a matchless display of imperial power, while its delicate calligraphy, stained-glass windows and decorative carvings add a lightness of touch. Süleyman and his wife Roxelana are buried in tombs in the courtyard.*

*Exterior view of mosque*

🍴 Take a few moments after exploring the mosque to visit the University's Botanic Gardens, next door.

☕ There are plenty of options for refreshment here, with the Darüzziyafe Restaurant *(see p71)* and Lalezar Café in the old soup kitchens, and a row of cafés right opposite the main entrance to the complex.

• Prof Siddik Sami Onar Cad
• Map M2
• (0212) 522 02 98
• Open 9am–7pm daily (closed at prayer times); Süleyman's tomb open 9:30am–4:30pm; Sinan's tomb open 9am–5pm Tue, Wed, Fri, Sun; hamam open 7am–midnight daily
• Free (adm charge for hamam).

## Top 10 Features

1. Sinan's Tomb
2. Süleyman's Tomb
3. Mosque Interior
4. Courtyard
5. Medreses
6. Addicts' Alley
7. İmaret
8. Hamam
9. Caravanserai
10. Views

### Sinan's Tomb
Sinan designed his own triangular mausoleum on the site of the house in which he lived while building the mosque, just beyond the northwest corner of the complex. It is a modest memorial to a prodigious talent.

### Süleyman's Tomb
Sultan Süleyman I, "the Magnificent", lies in a grandiose and highly decorated garden tomb *(above)*, with an ebony, mother-of-pearl and ivory door and a dome inlaid with tiny ceramic stars.

### Mosque Interior
The interior is simple and serene. The blue, white and gold dome *(above)* contains 200 stained-glass windows. The *mihrab* and pulpit are made from white marble decorated with İznik tiles.

### Courtyard
This great courtyard *(above)* is surrounded by a colonnade of porphyry, Marmara and pink Egyptian columns, said to be recycled from the Hippodrome.

➡️ *After visiting the tomb of Süleyman, take a look at that of his wife, Roxelana – one of the most formidable women in Turkish history.*

**Medreses**
Two of the six *medreses* (colleges) *(above)* – once part of the Imperial religious school providing theological and general education – house Süleyman's library of 110,000 manuscripts.

**Addicts' Alley**
The cafés of "Addicts' Alley" *(above)* – formally known as Prof Siddik Sami Onar Caddesi – once sold opium and hashish. It still has its cafés, but now the drug of choice is tobacco smoked in a water pipe *(nargile)*.

**İmaret**
The mosque kitchens not only fed the many workers, students, teachers and priests in the complex, but ran a soup kitchen for up to 1,000 people a day.

**Hamam**
This mosque's *hamam* is a mixed sex bathhouse, which makes it good for families. Somewhat alarmingly, it offers all visitors free life insurance during their bath!

**Caravanserai**
The mosque was a full-service complex – in the caravanserai, visitors and their animals could find food and lodging.

**Views**
The terraced gardens outside the main complex offer fine views *(below)* across the Golden Horn to the Galata Tower.

## Sinan

The incomparable Mimar Sinan, builder of 144 mosques and over 221 other buildings, never trained as an architect. He was born Greek Orthodox in 1489, and was conscripted to serve in the sultan's elite Janissary (New Army) Corps. He rose through the ranks to become Commander of the Infantry Cadet Corps, responsible for military engineering works, then in 1536 was appointed Architect of the Abode of Felicity by Süleyman. He held the post until his death aged 99 in 1588. Sinan considered the Selimiye Mosque in Edirne *(see p53)* his best work.

Climb to the gallery in the mosque's northeast corner for some of the finest views of Istanbul available anywhere in the city.

# Church of St Saviour in Chora

*The Church of St Saviour in Chora is home to one of the world's finest collections of Byzantine art: more than 100 magnificent mosaics and frescoes depicting biblical images. They were commissioned in 1315–21 by Byzantine statesman Theodore Metochites, who also restored the 11th-century church on the site. The church was converted into a mosque in 1511 and is known by locals as Kariye Mosque (Kariye Camii). Its works of art slipped into obscurity until they were rediscovered in 1860. Restoration began in 1948.*

*Exterior view*

📷 Photography is permitted, but flash is forbidden. Note that it is practically impossible to focus unless you use a tripod.

🍴 The Asitane Restaurant next door is a pleasant garden café, and one of the best places in Istanbul to eat traditional Ottoman cuisine.

• Kariye Camii Sok, Kariye Meydanı, Edirnekapı
• Map B2
• (0212) 631 92 41
• Open 9am–4:30pm (7pm in summer) Thu–Tue
• Adm 15 TL

## Top 10 Features

1. Exterior
2. Genealogy of Christ
3. Anastasis Fresco
4. Parecclesion
5. Ministry of Christ
6. Mosaic of Theodore Metochites
7. The Last Judgment
8. Life of the Virgin
9. Infancy of Christ
10. Dormition of the Virgin

### Exterior

Walk round the back of the church to experience the full impact of its architecture – with masonry of striped marble, six domes, layers of arches, undulating rooflines and, to one side, a minaret.

### Genealogy of Christ

The two domes of the inner narthex (western entrance) portray 66 of Christ's forebears. In one dome *(above)*, Christ is surrounded by ancestors including Adam, Abraham, Jacob and Jacob's 12 sons. In the other, the Virgin and Child survey the kings of the House of David.

### Anastasis Fresco

This resurrection fresco *(main image)* depicts Christ pulling Adam and Eve from their graves, while the gates of hell are broken and Satan lies bound at Christ's feet.

### Parecclesion

A funerary chapel south of the main church, this is a glory of frescoes depicting judgment and resurrection *(below)*. The unmarked tomb in the north wall may be that of Theodore Metochites.

➡ *There was an earlier (6th-century) church on this site, but nothing remains of it.*

### Ministry of Christ
The vaults of seven bays in the outer narthex and the south bay of the inner narthex detail the ministry of Christ *(above)*, including his temptation and miracles such as the wedding at Cana and the healing of the sick.

Outer narthex
Entrance to nave
Inner narthex
Entrance
Nave
Parececlesion

### Mosaic of Theodore Metochites
Over the door leading from the inner narthex to the nave is a superb mosaic *(above)* depicting Theodore Metochites in a large turban presenting his church to Christ, who raises a hand in blessing.

### Life of the Virgin
Twenty mosaics in the inner narthex depict the life of the Virgin Mary, based on the apocryphal 2nd-century Gospel of St James. They include images of Mary's first steps (at six months old), her time as a temple attendant (aged 3–13), and Joseph arriving home to find her pregnant.

### Infancy of Christ
Scenes from Christ's infancy are depicted in the semicircular panels of the outer narthex. Based on New Testament accounts, they include the Journey to Bethlehem, Mary and Joseph enrolling for taxation, the Nativity, and the terrible Massacre of the Innocents.

### The Last Judgment
In the main dome of the Paracclesion is a vision of the Last Judgment, with Christ in Majesty flanked by the Virgin Mary, John the Baptist and the Apostles. Adam and Eve kneel at Christ's feet.

### Dormition of the Virgin
This beautiful mosaic in the nave *(above)* shows Christ sitting beside his mother's coffin, cradling a baby that represents her soul. Above is Ashrael, the Angel of Death.

### Layout
You now enter through a side door, but the main entrance was originally by way of a long porch, the outer narthex, which leads into an inner narthex. In the alcoves of these two porches you find the majority of the mosaics. The inner narthex opens into the main body of the church (the nave). At the far end, the altar stands in front of the semicircular apse, flanked by the Prothesis (Communion chapel) and Diakonikon (vestry). To one side is a separate funerary chapel, the Pareeclesion.

# 🔟 Çemberlitaş Baths

*No stay in Istanbul would be complete without a bout of steaming, soaping, scrubbing and massaging in a Turkish bath (hamam). Çemberlitaş, built in 1584, is commonly hailed as one of the most beautiful. Designed by Sinan, it was commissioned by Selim II's wife Nur Banu as a way of providing financial support for the Atik Valide Sultan Mosque in Üsküdar (see p95), of which she was sponsor. Today Çemberlitaş is still used by Turks, but is most popular with tourists and photographers – it's a regular location for film and fashion shoots.*

A halvet *in the hot room*

🕐 If you are planning to stay in the *hamam* for any length of time, take a small bottle of water in with you.

⊖ The baths are sited halfway between the Grand Bazaar and Sultanahmet Square, and are an easy walk from either. The surrounding area is bursting with cafés, tea shops and restaurants – take your pick.

• Vezir Hanı Cad 8
• Map P4
• (0212) 522 7974
• Open 6am–midnight daily
• Adm 45 TL (69 TL with massage, 117 TL with oil massage)
• www.cemberlitas hamami.org

## Top 10 Features

1. Entrance
2. Men's Section
3. Women's Section
4. Dressing Room
5. Hot Room
6. Private Cubicles
7. Navel Stone
8. Cool Room
9. Oil Massage Room
10. Extras

### Entrance
At the ticket office, you are given a *pestemal* (a sarong-like garment, for modesty), a *kese* (a coarse mitt for scrubbing the body down) and tokens to give to the attendants. Men and women are then sent off to separate sections.

### Men's Section
Originally the *hamam* consisted of two identical suites of rooms, each with a separate entrance. The men's section of the baths is still exactly as envisaged by its creator, Sinan.

### Women's Section
The women's changing area was lost in 1868, when Divanyolu Caddesi was widened, so women now change in a corridor; but their hot room is unaltered.

### Dressing Room (Camekan)
Here *(below)*, an attendant will assign you a locker and give you a pair of slippers. Most people go nude under the *pestemal*, but wear a swimsuit if you wish to.

*Today, most baths operate separate hours for men and women. In Ottoman times, a breach of segregation was a capital offence.*

### Hot Room (Sıcaklık)
The hot room *(main image)* has a domed ceiling supported by 12 arches that rise from marble columns. The dome is pitted with glass "elephants' eyes", which channel the light through the steam to polka-dot the floor.

### Private Cubicles (Halvets)
Around the walls are a number of private cubicles with taps running cold, warm and hot water, which you can use to wash or cool down if the heat gets too much for you.

## Key

| | |
|---|---|
| ▦ | Men's Section |
| ▥ | Women's Section |

### Navel Stone (Göbek Taşı)
In the centre of the hot room is a large slab of marble *(left)*. Lie down and wait for the attendant. You will be covered in soap suds, and scrubbed all over with the *kese*. Then you will be lathered again, washed with a cloth, and soap-massaged *(below)*. Finally, your hair will be washed, and you will be vigorously rinsed with buckets of water.

### Cool Room (Soğukluk)
The cool room *(left)* is the place to sit and chat. The men's is as elegant as it was in Sinan's day; the women's a little less welcoming. Afterwards, head back to change, or go for your oil massage.

### Ancient Customs
The direct descendant of the Graeco-Roman bath, the *hamam* was eagerly adopted by Islamic invaders who really did believe that cleanliness is next to Godliness; the bath was a chance not only to cleanse the skin and detoxify the body, but also to restore the spirit. For women, time in the *hamam* was a welcome escape from the narrow world in which they spent their lives, as well as a place to check out potential daughters-in-law.

### Oil Massage Room
You will be one of several people being massaged *(right)* on a row of beds under bright lights. It's worth any discomfort you may experience – you'll feel great after.

### Extras
Take as much time as you like to return to the steam room or sit in the cool room. If you want the full works, the attendants will be happy to give you a manicure, pedicure or facial.

*It is customary to tip the attendants around 10 per cent.*

# TOP 10 Dolmabahçe Palace

*In 1843, Sultan Abdül Mecit, who wanted to reinvent the Ottoman Empire in a European image, employed Armenian architects Karabet and Nikoğos Balyan to build a luxurious new palace on the Bosphorus shore. Dolmabahçe Sarayı, completed in 1856, is the result. Luxurious it certainly is, with 46 reception rooms and galleries, and lavish decoration in gold and crystal that rivals the Palace of Versailles in France. Ironically, this extravagance hastened the end of the Empire, and the last emperor fled from here into exile in 1922.*

*The Swan Fountain in the Imperial Gardens*

## Top 10 Features

1. Gates
2. Waterfront Façade
3. Ceremonial Hall
4. Harem
5. State Rooms
6. Atatürk's Rooms
7. Crystal Staircase
8. Sultan's Bathrooms
9. Clock Tower
10. Gardens

🎫 Admission to the palace is by guided tour only. There are two itineraries: one of the Selamlık (the areas reserved for men, including the Ceremonial Hall); the other of the Harem (including the living quarters of the royal women, the sultan's private quarters, and Atatürk's bedroom, bathroom and study).

🍽 There is a café in the Clock Tower, and toilets near both entrances.

- Dolmabahçe Cad
- Map C5 • (0212) 236 90 00 • Tram: Kabataş, then a 5-minute walk
- Open 9am–4pm Tue, Wed, Fri–Sun (to 3pm, Oct–Feb) • Adm 30 TL for Selamlık, 20 TL for Harem, 40 TL for a combined ticket
- www.dolmabahce.gov.tr

### Gates
The palace had two ceremonial entrances, both highly ornamented: the Treasury Gate, which is now the main entrance, and the Imperial Gate *(above)*. Both gates still have a guard of honour.

### Waterfront Façade
The marble façade *(below)* is 284 m (930 ft) long. The State Rooms are on the left, the Ceremonial Hall in the centre, and the Harem on the right.

### Ceremonial Hall (Muayede Salonu)
The dome in this vast hall *(above)* is 36 m (118 ft) high. The crystal chandelier, a gift from Queen Victoria of England, has 750 lights and weighs 4.5 tonnes (more than 9,000 lb). It is the world's largest chandelier.

*If you only have time for one of the two tours, visit the Selamlık; the Ceremonial Hall and Crystal Staircase are unmissable.*

### Harem

A fascinating mix of East and West, the Harem has several apartments, furnished to various grades of luxury (for the sultan, his mother, wives, concubines, servants and guests) – also baths, a school, a maternity ward and a central salon *(left)* where the wives and concubines would meet for tea, chat and embroidery.

### State Rooms (Selamlık)

The rooms on the palace's seaward side were used by the Grand Vizier and ministers, while those on the landward side were administrative offices. They are all lavishly decorated and furnished.

### Crystal Staircase

This ornate double-horseshoe staircase has balusters of Baccarat crystal. It links the administrative offices with the ceremonial and function rooms upstairs.

### Sultan's Bathrooms

The Sultan had two bathrooms: one in the main palace, faced in marble; the other in the Harem, decorated in violet flowers and with a Murano glass mirror.

### Atatürk's Rooms

In the first years of the republic, Atatürk used the palace as his Istanbul base, keeping an office and bedroom *(above)* in the Harem. He died here, from cirrhosis of the liver, on 10 November 1938 – all the palace's clocks are set to 9:05am, the moment of his death.

### Atatürk

Born in 1881, Mustafa Kemal Paşa rose to prominence in 1915, leading Turkish forces to victory at Gallipoli. A leader of the Young Turks republican movement, he seized his moment following the end of World War I, abolishing the sultanate in 1922 and declaring a republic in 1923. As Turkey's first president, he Westernized the country – introducing the Latin alphabet, compulsory schooling, and rights for women. He is still idolized as the "Father of the Turks" (Atatürk); it is illegal in Turkey to criticize him publicly.

### Clock Tower

The four-storey tower, 27 m (90 ft) high, was added to the palace in 1890, during the reign of Sultan Abdül Hamit II *(see p89)*. The clock – which still keeps time – was built by the celebrated Parisian clockmaker Paul Garnier.

### Gardens

The palace and gardens stand on reclaimed land (the name Dolmabahçe means "Filled Garden"). In addition to the palace and its 16 external pavilions, the grounds once held a flour mill, pharmacy, aviary, glass factory and foundry.

*The former Crown Prince Pavilion, adjacent to Dolmabahçe Palace, now houses the Museum of Painting and Sculpture (see p92).*

# Bosphorus Cruise

*The Istanbul skyline is justifiably one of the most famous cityscapes in the world, and while there are many places from which to admire it, by far the best is the deck of a boat on the Bosphorus. After the bustle of the city centre, a trip up the Bosphorus gives you an entirely different perspective on the city. Give your lungs a break from breathing in traffic fumes and your feet a rest from trudging pavements. Take the local ferry for a modest fare, and spend a day floating serenely along the straits past magnificent shores and wooden villas.*

Bosphorus Bridge

🟢 The ferry journey to Rumeli Hisarı takes around 1 hour 45 minutes then goes straight back. There are only short stops en route, so take the local bus back if you'd like to visit any of the sights along the river (but be warned, it is slow).

🟢 Food is available on the ferry and there are various food facilities at the last stop on Anadolu Kavağı.

• Departs from Eminönü Boğaz Hattı Pier
• Map F4
• (0212) 444 18 51
• Departures daily, Apr–Nov: 1:35pm, Dec–Mar: 10:35am
• Fare 10 TL short circle cruise, 25 TL round trip (the full Bosphorus cruise)
• www.sehirhatlari.com.tr

## Top 10 Features

1. Eminönü Pier
2. Leander's Tower
3. Dolmabahçe Palace
4. Ortaköy
5. Bosphorus Bridge
6. Beylerbeyi Palace
7. Arnavutköy and Bebek
8. Fortress of Europe
9. Sarıyer
10. Anadolu Kavağı

### Eminönü Pier
The Bosphorus ferry departs from Eminönü port *(main picture)*, the city's busiest ferry terminal. Pick up a pretzel or fish sandwich from a street vendor.

### Leander's Tower (Kız Kulesi)
This tower on an island offshore from Üsküdar is a restaurant. Its Turkish name means "Maiden's Tower", after a legendary princess kept there; the English name refers to a hero of Greek myth *(see p95)*.

### Dolmabahçe Palace (Dolmabahçe Sarayı)
Sultan Abdül Mecit virtually mortgaged the Ottoman Empire to build this lavish palace *(above)* in the 1850s.

### Ortaköy
One of the prettiest villages on the straits, at the foot of the Bosphorus Bridge, Ortaköy *(above)* is a weekend retreat for İstanbullus.

### Bosphorus Bridge (Boğaziçi Köprüsü)
Completed in 1973, this 1,560-m (5,120-ft) long bridge, stretching between Ortaköy and Beylerbeyi, was the first to link Europe and Asia.

For more on the Dolmabahçe Palace See pp26–7

## Beylerbeyi Palace (Beylerbeyi Sarayı) (Asian Side)

This delightfully fussy palace *(above)* was built as a summer annexe to the Dolmabahçe. It had no kitchens, and food was rowed across as required.

### Arnavutköy and Bebek

The 19th-century wooden villas *(yalis)* that prettily line the waterfront along this central stretch of the Bosphorus are the city's most desirable real estate.

### Fortress of Europe (Rumeli Hisarı)

This castle *(above)* was built by Mehmet the Conqueror in 1452 prior to his attack on Constantinople. Across the water stands the Fortress of Asia (Anadolu Hisarı), built in the late 14th century.

### Sarıyer

This village *(right)* is the main fishing port on the Bosphorus. It has a historic fish market, as well as several good fish restaurants (with lovely views) near the shore.

### Anadolu Kavağı (Asian Side)

This is the last stop for the ferry, and the locals make a good living selling fish lunches and ice cream to the tourists. There is a wonderful view from a 14th-century fort, the Genoese Castle, on the hill above *(left)*.

## It's All a Myth

When Greek goddess Hera sent a swarm of gnats to plague the beautiful Io, her rival for the affections of the god Zeus, Io turned herself into a cow and swam across the straits to escape, giving the Bosphorus its name – the "Ford of the Cow". In another Greek myth, Jason and the Argonauts rowed up the Bosphorus in search of the Golden Fleece – perhaps an echo of the Black Sea tradition of using a lamb's fleece to trap the gold when panning.

For more on the Bosphorus and environs **See pp88–93**

Left **Florence Nightingale in Selimiye Barracks** Right **Atatürk reviews his troops**

# Moments in History

### 1 AD 330–95: Division of the Roman Empire

In 330, Constantine moved the capital of the Empire from Rome to the former Greek colony of Byzantium. It was initially called New Rome but later became Constantinople ("City of Constantine"). In 395, Theodosius divided the Empire between his sons, with the western half run from Rome and the eastern (Byzantine) half centred on Constantinople.

**Bust of Constantine**

### 2 1071: Battle of Manzikert

The Seljuk Turks from Persia defeated Byzantine forces at Manzikert and seized most of Anatolia. The Byzantines never recovered their eastern lands.

### 3 1204: Sack and Capture of Constantinople

The armies of the Fourth Crusade sacked Constantinople, driving the emperor into exile.

**The Capture of Constantinople in 1204**

Crusader rulers governed in Constantinople until 1261, when Byzantine Emperor Michael VIII Palaeologus recaptured the city.

### 4 1453: Birth of Istanbul

Following years of Ottoman encroachment into the Byzantine Empire, Sultan Mehmet II captured Constantinople, renaming it İslambol ("the City of Islam"). The last Byzantine emperor, Constantine IX, died fighting on the city walls.

### 5 1529: Siege of Vienna

The Ottoman Empire reached its maximum extent under Süleyman I. In 1526, he had taken control of southern Hungary. In the spring of 1529, he mustered a huge military force with the aim of consolidating his Hungarian gains and moving on to Vienna. A combination of serious flooding en route and a spirited defence led by a German mercenary, Niklas Graf Salm, sent the Turks packing and marked the end of Ottoman expansion in Western Europe.

### 6 1777: Turkish Delight

Ali Muhiddin Hacı Bekir, confectioner to the imperial court, invented a chewy sweet flavoured with rosewater and coated in icing sugar: *lokum* ("morsel of contentment"), better known as Turkish delight.

Preceding pages **Interior view of Haghia Sophia**

### 1853–6: Crimean War

**7** When Russia began to encroach on Ottoman territory, Britain and France weighed in on the side of the Turks. Florence Nightingale set up a hospital in Istanbul, defining modern nursing practice *(see p96)*.

### 1919–23: Birth of the Republic

**8** Mustafa Kemal Paşa – or Atatürk ("Father of the Turks") – led a bloodless revolution that abolished the sultanate, and fought a fierce war of independence. In 1923, as first president of the new Republic of Turkey, he moved the capital to Ankara, leaving Istanbul without political status for the first time in 1,600 years.

**Construction of the Bosphorus Bridge, 1972**

### 1973: Bosphorus Bridge

**9** The Bosphorus Bridge was opened between Ortaköy and Beylerbeyi, linking European Turkey to Asian Anatolia.

### 2010: Istanbul European Capital of Culture

**10** The city was chosen to be one of 2010's European Capitals of Culture. A programme of events showcased Istanbul's historic and traditional cultural heritage.

## Top 10 Notable Ottoman Emperors

**1 Osman Gazi (1299–1326)**
The Ottoman dynasty takes its name from that of its founder, Osman. In 1301, his forces won the first Ottoman victory against the Byzantine Empire at the Battle of Baphaeon.

**2 Orhan Gazi (1326–59)**
Orhan moved the Ottoman capital to Bursa and established Islam as the state religion.

**3 Murat I (1359–89)**
Murat founded the Janissary Corps, an elite group within the Ottoman army.

**4 Beyazıt I (1389–1402)**
Beyazıt began the Muslim colonization of Serbia.

**5 Mehmet II the Conqueror (1451–81)**
In 1453, Mehmet captured Constantinople from its Byzantine rulers. He laid out a new city on the rubble, and founded Topkapı Palace.

**6 Süleyman I the Magnificent (1520–66)**
A conqueror, lawmaker and patron of the arts, Süleyman presided over the golden age of Ottoman rule *(see p58)*.

**7 Mehmet III (1595–1603)**
Mehmet's mother had 18 of his 19 brothers strangled so that he could take the throne.

**8 Osman II (1618–22)**
The Janissaries raped and strangled Osman at Yedikule after his failed attempt to curb their power.

**9 Mahmut II (1808–39)**
Mahmut wiped out the Janissary Corps, slaughtering thousands in the purge.

**10 Mehmet VI (1918–22)**
The last of the Ottoman emperors fled into European exile in November 1922.

Left **Museum of Turkish and Islamic Arts** Centre **Rahmi Koç Museum** Right **Archaeological Museum**

# Museums and Galleries

### 1 Topkapı Palace (Topkapı Sarayı)

The buildings are spectacular, some of the collections are even more so – from the sea of Chinese porcelain in the kitchens to the Treasury, with its ostentatious display of jewellery, carved ivory and great rocks of emerald. Religious treasures include hair from the Prophet's beard *(see pp8–11)*.

### 2 Archaeological Museum (Arkeoloji Müzesi)

Don't miss the late-4th-century-AD marble tomb of Abdalonymus of Sidon, known as the "Alexander Sarcophagus". Its high-relief carving depicts Alexander the Great defeating the Persians at the Battle of Issus in 333 BC *(see pp16–17)*.

### 3 Military Museum (Askeri Müze)

Among the many fascinating exhibits are curved daggers *(cembiyes)* carried by 15th-century Ottoman footsoldiers, and the vast imperial tents used by sultans on campaign. The Mehter Band, founded in the 14th century, plays Ottoman military music daily at 3pm *(see p80)*.

### 4 Sakıp Sabancı Museum (Sakıp Sabancı Müzesi)

Known locally as the "Horse Mansion", this lovely museum houses the collection of the late Turkish business tycoon Sakıp Sabancı, encompassing 500 years of Ottoman calligraphy, and Ottoman and Turkish painting of the 19th and 20th centuries. The museum also hosts touring art exhibitions *(see p91)*.

Horse sculpture in the grounds of the Sakıp Sabancı Museum

### 5 Museum of Turkish and Islamic Arts (Türk ve İslam Eserleri Müzesi)

This wonderful collection, in the 16th-century palace of İbrahim Paşa, spans 1,300 years of the finest works of Turkish and Islamic art, including beautiful calligraphy, manuscripts and Turkish miniatures *(see p57)*.

Mehter Band at the Military Museum

### Istanbul Museum of Modern Art (İstanbul Modern Sanat Müzesi)

For centuries, Turkish art has been known for tradition rather than innovation, but contemporary Turkish artists are exploring new avenues. Set in a beautifully converted warehouse on the Bosphorus, the Istanbul Modern is an ideal platform *(see p89)*.

### Rahmi Koç Museum (Rahmi Koç Müzesi)

An Ottoman foundry and nearby shipyard on the Golden Horn are the perfect setting for this world-class collection of all things mechanical, from vintage cars to model planes – and even a submarine *(see p74)*.

### Sadberk Hanım Museum (Sadberk Hanım Müzesi)

Two lovingly restored Bosphorus mansions house an inspiring collection of ancient Anatolian artifacts, Ottoman costumes and ceramics *(see p91)*.

Attic vase, Sadberk Hanım Museum

### Naval Museum (Deniz Müzesi)

For centuries, the Ottoman navy ruled the seas, and its achievements are celebrated in this marvellous museum. Among the highlights are flamboyantly decorated royal barges *(see p89)*.

### Pera Museum (Pera Müzesi)

The Pera is a museum with an intriguing mix of fine art, modern exhibitions and ancient weights and measures *(see p80)*.

## Top 10 Less-Famous Museums

**1 santralistanbul**
See contemporary art in the old Silahtarağa power plant. ⊗ *Eyüp • (0212) 311 78 78*

**2 Mevlevi Monastery**
Whirling dervishes are the main draw in this monastery-turned-museum *(see p82)*.

**3 Yapı Kredi Vedat Nedîm Tör Museum**
The Yapı Kredi bank funds this small private collection of art and artifacts *(see p82)*.

**4 Railway Museum, Sirkeci Station**
The Orient Express silver service is the star among 300 exhibits *(see p58)*.

**5 SAV Automobile Museum**
Inspect the pick of a century of motor transport, from Rolls Royce to Ferrari *(see p92)*.

**6 Aşiyan Museum**
A Bosphorus mansion pays homage to 20th-century poets and thinkers *(see p90)*.

**7 Bilim ve Teknoloji Müzesi**
See displays of historical tools from astronomy and medicine, to war. ⊗ *Has Ahirlar Binası, Gülhane Parkı • (0212) 528 80 65*

**8 Florence Nightingale Museum**
The museum includes the nurse's private quarters and surgery room *(see p96)*.

**9 Aviation Museum (Havacılık Müzesi)**
This collection of old planes and models is near Atatürk International airport.
⊗ *Yeşilköy • (0212) 663 24 90*

**10 Atatürk Museum**
This suburban house is now a memorial museum to the great man. ⊗ *Halaskargazi Cad, Şişli • Map T4 • (0212) 240 63 19*

Left **Haghia Sophia** Centre **Church of St Saviour in Chora** Right **A gate in the Theodosian Walls**

# TOP 10 Byzantine Monuments

### 1 Haghia Sophia (Ayasofya)

Built by Emperor Justinian in the 6th century, Haghia Sophia is one of the world's greatest architectural achievements. Justinian was so proud of his basilica that he proclaimed: "Glory to God who has thought me worthy to finish this work. Solomon, I have outdone you" *(see pp12–13)*.

**Relief carved on base of Egyptian Obelisk, Hippodrome**

### 2 Hippodrome (At Meydanı)

Once a Byzantine race track 450 m (1500 ft) long, the Hippodrome could hold 100,000 people. It was the scene of celebrations and, on occasion, bloodshed; the Nika Riots in 532 ended with 30,000 dead *(see p57)*.

### 3 Cisterns

To ensure good water supply in times both of peace and of siege, the Byzantines built a series of vast underground water cisterns beneath their city. The finest are the Basilica Cistern (Yerebatan Sarnıcı) *(see p58)* and the Cistern of 1,001 Columns (Binbirdirek Sarnıcı) *(see p60)*.

### 4 Church of St Saviour in Chora (Kariye Camii)

The main reason to visit this 11th-century Byzantine church is its glorious collection of mosaics and frescoes, which depict biblical scenes *(see pp22–3)*.

### 5 Theodosian Walls (Teodos II Surları)

Over the course of 1,000 years, the curtain walls built by Emperor Theodosius II in 412–22 proved to be a necessity – they withstood more than 20 attacks by Huns, Arabs, Bulgarians, Turks and Russians, finally succumbing to the Ottomans in 1453 (see p32). The walls have now been partially restored *(see p75)*.

### 6 Mosaics Museum (Mozaik Müzesi)

Only fragments remain of the Great Palace of the Byzantine Emperors. This small museum houses one of them – the mosaic passageway, discovered in the 1930s, that led from the palace to the royal box in the Hippodrome. The beautifully crafted floor depicts wild animals and hunting scenes *(see p60)*.

**Basilica Cistern**

### 7 Bucoleon Palace (Bukoleon Sarayı)

At the bottom of the hill behind Sultanahmet, built into the old sea wall, is the last standing fragment of the Imperial Bucoleon Palace (see p61).

### 8 Aqueduct of Valens (Bozdoğan Kemeri)

This beautifully preserved 4th-century aqueduct, which remained in use until the 19th century, was a key part of the system that carried fresh water into the Byzantine capital from the Belgrade Forest (see p73).

**Haghia Eirene**

### 9 Haghia Eirene (Aya İrini Kilisesi)

One of the oldest churches in the city, Haghia Eirene stands in the outer courtyard of the Topkapı Palace. It was the city's main church until Haghia Sophia was built. The church has excellent acoustics and is only open to the public for concerts (see p61).

### 10 Church of the Pammakaristos (Fethiye Camii)

This large 12th-century Byzantine church served as the worldwide headquarters of the Greek Orthodox faith during the 15th and 16th centuries. It was converted to a mosque by Murat III in 1591. The former side chapel is now a museum housing some magnificent mosaics (see p73).

## Top 10 Notable Byzantine Rulers

### 1 Constantine (306–37)
Constantine moved the capital of the Roman Empire to Constantinople (see p32).

### 2 Theodosius II (408–50)
Theodosius codified the law, founded a university and built the city walls (see p75).

### 3 Justinian I (527–65)
Justinian founded many great buildings including Haghia Sophia (see p12–13), as well as reforming the law.

### 4 Theodora (527–48)
A bear-keeper's daughter turned stripper and prostitute, Theodora ruled alongside her husband Justinian I.

### 5 Justinian II (685–95 and 705–11)
Justinian's enemies deposed him then cut off his nose, because a disfigured man could not be emperor. He later regained the throne wearing, it is said, a prosthetic nose of solid gold.

### 6 Irene of Athens (797–802)
Irene was the first woman to rule the Empire on her own.

### 7 Basil I (867–86)
The homosexual lover of Michael III, Basil was crowned joint emperor in 866, then killed Michael to rule alone.

### 8 Zoë (1028–50)
Zoë wed three times after becoming empress aged 50.

### 9 Romanus IV Diogenes (1067–71)
Romanus was defeated by the Seljuks at Manzikert in 1071 and was exiled as a result.

### 10 Constantine XI Palaeologus (1449–53)
The last of the Byzantines died fighting on the city walls during the conquest of 1453.

eft **Atik Valide Mosque** Centre **Sinan's tomb, Süleymaniye Mosque** Right **Church of St George**

# Places of Worship

### Süleymaniye Mosque (Süleymaniye Camii)

This vast mosque, which dominates the skyline of the Golden Horn, is the crowning achievement of Koca Mimar Sinan, greatest of Imperial architects *(see pp20–21)*. Built in 1550–57 in the grounds of the old palace, Eski Saray, it is a suitably grand memorial to its founder, Süleyman I *(see pp32, 33, 58)*.

**Blue Mosque**

### Blue Mosque (Sultanahmet Camii)

Commissioned by Ahmet I, the Blue Mosque was built by the Imperial architect Mehmet Ağa, a pupil of the great Sinan, in 1609–16. It takes its name from the blue İznik tiles on its inner walls *(see pp14–15)*.

**The light and airy interior of Fatih Mosque**

### Fatih Mosque (Fatih Camii)

The original Fatih Mosque was built by Mehmet II to celebrate his capture of Constantinople in 1453; its name means "the Conqueror's mosque". The present mosque was built in the 18th century, after an earthquake of 1766 destroyed the original *(see p73)*.

### Eyüp Mosque (Eyüp Camii)

Also rebuilt after the 1766 earthquake, this mosque at the top of the Golden Horn is one of the holiest places in Islam. It is built around the tomb of a 7th-century saint, Eyüp el-Ensari, standard-bearer of the Prophet Mohammed *(see p74)*.

### Atik Valide Mosque (Atik Valide Camii)

One of Istanbul's finest mosques and Sinan's last great work, the "Old Mosque of the Sultan's Mother" was completed in 1583 for the formidable Nur Banu, wife of Selim III and mother of Murat III *(see p95)*.

### Church of St George (Aya Yorgi)

The Church of St George stands within the Greek Orthodox Patriarchate complex. Built in 1720, it includes a superb 11th-century mosaic of the Virgin Mary *(see p76)*.

*It is essential to dress modestly when visiting a mosque. It's also a good idea to wear shoes you can slip on and off easily.*

### Neve Shalom Synagogue (Neve Şalom Sinagogu)

Built in 1949–51 for the Sephardic Jewish community, this is the largest of several synagogues in Istanbul. There have been Jews in the city since Roman times, but numbers rose in 1492 when Jews expelled from Spain were welcomed by the Ottomans. ⊗ *Büyük Hendek Cad 67 • Map F2 • (0212) 293 75 66, 292 03 86 • Phone to visit*

### Church of St Mary of the Mongols (Kanlı Kilise)

Princess Maria, illegitimate daughter of Byzantine Emperor Michael VIII Palaeologos, married Khan Abaka of the Mongols. On his death in 1281, she founded a convent and this church – Istanbul's only Greek Orthodox church to have been granted immunity from conversion to a mosque by Mehmet the Conqueror *(see p76)*.

Detail, Church of St Mary of the Mongols

### Church of St Anthony of Padua (Sent Antuan Kilisesi)

Istanbul's largest Roman Catholic church, built in 1906–12, is also home to a small community of Franciscan monks *(see p82)*.

### Christ Church

Consecrated in 1868 as the Crimean Memorial Church, this fine Gothic Revival building was renovated and renamed in the 1990s. It is the largest Protestant church in Istanbul *(see p82)*.

## Top 10 Tips on Islamic Etiquette

**1 Shoes**
Remove your shoes before entering a mosque or a Turkish home.

**2 Men and Women**
A man should not touch a woman (other than family), even to shake hands, unless the woman proffers her hand or cheek first.

**3 Left Hand**
In some Islamic countries one should avoid eating or passing food with the left hand; in Turkey this is not observed.

**4 Pork and Alcohol**
Although many people in Turkey do drink alcohol, you should never offer alcohol or pork to a Muslim – and do not consume yourself if unsure of your companions' views.

**5 Family Rooms**
Some restaurants and cafés have separate family rooms *(aile salonu)* into which women will automatically be conducted. Men may only sit there with their families.

**6 Dress**
Dress modestly – no bare knees, shoulders or midriffs (for either sex).

**7 Covering the Head**
It is considered polite for a woman to cover her head when entering a mosque.

**8 Ramazan**
Avoid eating and drinking in public during daylight hours in the month-long fast of Ramazan.

**9 Sightseeing**
Don't go sightseeing in mosques at prayer times (particularly noon on Fridays).

**10 Joking about Islam**
Don't joke about Islam or criticize anything related to it.

Left **Fresh fish sandwiches** Centre **Cold *meze*, including *tarama* and *haydari*** Right ***İmam bayıldı***

# 箇10 Culinary Highlights

### 1 Meze
Most Turkish meals begin with *meze* – collections of small starters. The range of *meze* is vast, and you can easily eat enough for a whole meal. Cold options range from *haydari* (yoghurt with mint and garlic) to *midye pilakisi* (mussels cooked in olive oil) or *çerkez tavuğu* (cold chicken in walnut and bread sauce). Hot options may include chicken liver kebabs, calamari, grilled cheese, or something more adventurous such as *koç yumurtası* (fried sheep's testicles).

### 2 İmam Bayıldı ("The Imam Fainted")
This strangely named dish of aubergine stuffed with tomatoes and onions is a Turkish classic – the Imam in question supposedly found it so delicious that he passed out in ecstasy. Aubergine is a fundamental ingredient of Turkish cuisine; it is said that Ottoman court chefs could prepare it in 150 ways.

### 3 Çoban Salatası ("Shepherd's Salad")
This salad combines tomato, cucumber, chopped pepper, lettuce, coriander, celery, lemon juice and olive oil in a light, healthy, colourful and refreshing dish. Turkish tomatoes are among the finest in the world.

### 4 Dolma
The word *dolma* means "filled up", and is used to describe any stuffed food, from walnuts to peppers or aubergine. The most common version, eaten cold, is vine leaves stuffed with rice, onion, nuts and herbs.

### 5 Kebabs and Köfte
Turkey's most famous culinary export is the kebab – called *kebap* in Turkish. *Döner kebap* is wafer-thin slices of roast meat (usually lamb) carved from a spit; the *şiş kebap* is cubed lamb or chicken grilled on a skewer. *Köfte* is minced meat cooked as meatballs or flattened onto a skewer and grilled as an *izgara kebap*.

**Kebabs and Köfte**

### 6 Seafood
Istanbul's proximity to the sea means that *taze balık* (fresh fish) is very popular with locals. The catch of the day is often grilled and served with rice or chips and salad. Shellfish and calamari are served as *meze*. A delicious Black Sea dish is *hamsi pilavı* (fresh anchovies and rice).

### 7 Stews (Güveç)
Often served in traditional *lokanta* restaurants *(see p110)* and generally popular in winter, hearty stews are mostly made with lamb, tomatoes and onions.

Döner kebap *translates literally as "rotating meat".*

### Börek

8 These savoury pastries are served either as part of a *meze* or on their own as fast food. They can be flat or rolled, and are filled with cheese and onion, spinach or meat. They make an excellent light snack.

### Pastries

9 Sweet pastries are sold in dedicated shops and by street vendors; tourist restaurants will offer them as dessert. The most famous is *baklava* (flaky pastry drenched in syrup), but there are many variations with honey, syrups, marzipan, almonds and pistachios. All are heaven to eat and calorie hell.

Turkish pastries

### Tea and Coffee

10 The lifeblood of Turkey, both *çay* (tea) and *kahve* (coffee) are drunk black, strong and sweet, in small quantities. Tea is served all day and on all occasions. You can ask for it weaker and without sugar. Coffee is drunk less frequently; it is more expensive than tea, and is served with a glass of water. All instant coffee is known as Nescafé.

## Top 10 Culinary Specialities

### 1 Elastic Ice Cream
*Sahlepli dondurma* uses wild orchid tubers as a thickening agent. The ice cream can stretch into a "rope" 60 cm (2 ft) long!

### 2 İşkembe Çorbası (Tripe Soup)
This local delicacy is said to be good for hangovers.

### 3 Kanlıca Yoghurt
Firm and creamy, the yoghurt from Kanlıca is the country's finest.

### 4 Lokum (Turkish Delight)
Turkish Delight was invented by an Istanbul sweetmaker *(see p32)*. It's now sold everywhere and in many flavours, including mint and lemon. The original shop is still open. ⊙ *Hamidiye Cad 81, Bahçekapı* • *Map Q2* • *(0212) 522 85 43*

### 5 Simit
*Simit* is a round sesame bread like a New York pretzel.

### 6 Gözleme
*Gözleme* are large rolled pancakes with savoury stuffing.

### 7 Mantı
These pasta cushions are stuffed with minced lamb and served in a thin garlic sauce.

### 8 Aşure (Noah's Pudding)
As the story goes, this celebratory pudding was first made by Mrs Noah, from whatever scraps remained on the Ark at the end of the Flood.

### 9 Elma Çayı (Apple Tea)
You may be offered this as an alternative to tea when visiting carpet shops.

### 10 Rakı
A clear spirit, *rakı* can be made of any fruit, but most common is the aniseed-based version similar to Greek *ouzo*.

Aşure *has 40 ingredients, including chickpeas, beans and dried fruit.*

Left **Kanyon, Levent** Centre **Glass lamps in the Grand Bazaar** Right **Browsing in the Book Bazaar**

# 🔟 Shops and Markets

### 1 Grand Bazaar (Kapalı Çarşı)

One of the oldest, biggest and most exciting shopping malls in the world, the Grand Bazaar was set up to trade silk, spices and gold in the 15th century – and still sells all three, alongside jazzy glass lampshades, leather jackets and, of course, carpets *(see pp18–19)*.

**Egyptian Bazaar**

### 2 Egyptian Bazaar (Mısır Çarşısı)

Also known as the Spice Bazaar, this is the best place in town to buy little presents, with a sea of spice stalls, piles of Turkish Delight and plenty of cheap and cheerful souvenirs *(see p69)*.

### 3 Bağdat Caddesi

This 6-km (3.5-mile) long tree-lined thoroughfare on the Asian side of Istanbul is one of the city's best-known shopping streets. It is home to high-end designer shops, such as Burberry and Dolce & Gabbana, as well as high-street chains, including Zara, GAP and French Connection. You will also find department stores and smaller, independent boutiques here, which cater to most fashion tastes. The area is packed with restaurants, cafés and bars, useful for when weary shoppers need to rest their feet. ⓢ *Ferry to Kadıköy and then dolmuş to Bostancı*

### 4 Book Bazaar (Sahaflar Çarşısı)

The Book Bazaar started out selling scraps of parchment with Koranic text, but now offers a wide range of antiquarian and second-hand books (including paperbacks) in a variety of languages *(see p70)*.

### 5 İstiklal Caddesi

The city's main modern shopping street, İstiklal is packed day and night. If you need a break from sessions hunting for bargain designer clothes (in İş Merkezi) or the perfect glass teacups (in Paşabahçe) there are plenty of cafés to choose from.

### 6 Kanyon, Levent

Join the city's most stylish shoppers at Kanyon, Istanbul's biggest and, in some eyes, best shopping mall *(see p83)*.

### 7 Nişantaşı

Nişantaşı and neighbouring Teşvikiye are where local fashionistas spend their money on well-known international brands, including Versace and Dior. It is perhaps less exciting for those who can get the same thing at home *(see p83)*.

➡ *If you're buying a large item, shop around to get a sense of prices. When bargaining, take your time and remain polite.*

### İstinye Park

This architecturally impressive luxury shopping mall, which opened in September 2007, is slightly oustide the city centre in the residential area of İstinye. The light-filled corridors lead to shops, restaurants and leisure facilities. Designer shops include Hugo Boss, Louis Vuitton and Turkish boutique chain Vakko.
◈ İstinye Bayırı Cad, No. 73 Sariyer
• (0212) 345 55 55 • www.istinyepark.com

### Arasta Bazaar (Arasta Çarşısı)

This small, upmarket bazaar offers the best souvenir shopping in Sultanahmet. Situated in converted Ottoman stables, it sells good-quality carpets, jewellery and handicrafts in a relatively calm environment, conveniently close to many major sights and hotels (see pp60, 114).

### Çukurcuma, Galatasaray

Many travellers fall in love with this charming old quarter of Beyoğlu, with its eclectic range of antiques and second-hand dealers, whose wares flow out onto the streets around Turnacıbaşı Sokağı. Great for a morning's browsing (see p83).

Antiques shop, Çukurcuma

## Top 10 Things to Buy

**1 Carpets**
Carpets (see pp44–5) are the true glory of Turkish art – and you can have one on your own hall floor.

**2 Jewellery**
Precious metals are sold by weight, with a mark-up for workmanship. There are plenty of options, including designing your own jewellery.

**3 Leather**
Jackets, bags, wallets and belts are great value and come in all styles, colours and qualities. Again, custom-design if you have enough time.

**4 Clothes**
Shop around and you can find good quality and great design at rock-bottom prices.

**5 Textiles**
Both cottons and silks are made here, and are extremely cheap. Silk scarves are a great-value present.

**6 Spices**
Great heaps of coloured spices are hard to resist. If you buy saffron, check it's the real thing – there's a cheaper alternative (safflower) on sale.

**7 Historic Reproductions**
Reproduction Ottoman miniatures are easy to carry, and look great back home.

**8 Souvenirs**
For fun, buy someone back home pointed slippers or a sparkly belly-dancing outfit.

**9 Blue Beads**
The ubiquitous blue bead is actually a charm to ward off the "evil eye"; believe that or not, they make attractive gifts.

**10 Food**
Turkish Delight, almonds and hazelnuts, honey and all sorts of other comestibles make great presents.

Left **Clear design on reverse side of a silk carpet** Centre **Weaver at work** Right **A** *cicim* **flat-weave**

# 🔟 Facts about Turkish Carpets

### 1 Origins
Turkish rug-weaving skills are of ancient origin and have been passed down the generations. They were developed by Central Asian nomads, who used thickly woven goats' hair to make tents, floor coverings and even cradles. This material was portable, warm and virtually waterproof. People soon began to use these weaves as wall decorations.

### 2 Flat-Weaves
A rug is only considered to be a carpet *(hali)* if it has a knotted pile. In flat-weave rugs the vertical (warp) and horizontal (weft) threads are woven flat. *Kilims* are the most basic form, with the design (weft) threads woven into the warp; in *cicims*, a third thread is woven in to create the design, which looks as if it is embroidered. More intricate still are *sumaks*, in which additional design yarns cover the entire surface.

### 3 The Oldest Carpets
*Kilims* have been made in Turkey for around 8,000 years; fragments of pile carpet survive from about 2,000 years ago. The oldest complete carpets in Turkey are 13th-century Seljuk examples made in Konya and Beyşehir in central Anatolia.

**Hereke carpet**

### 4 Weaving Materials
The basic materials used for making Turkish carpets are wool, mercerized cotton and pure silk. Most finer carpets have a cotton warp (which forms the base), with a wool or silk weft; flat-weaves are generally made entirely from cotton.

### 5 Natural Dyes
Cheaper wool or cotton carpets use chemical dyes, but the finest still use traditional natural colours, such as woad or indigo for blues, madder root for shades from brick-red to orange, pinks and purple and camomile, sage and saffron for yellow.

### 6 Hereke Imperial Carpet Factory
The factory at Hereke, 60 km (38 miles) east of Istanbul, was set up in 1843 to provide carpets for the Ottoman court. Its carpets, made from Bursa silk, were larger and more finely woven than any known before.

### 7 Prayer Rugs
Prayer rugs *(namazlık)* usually contain an image of a *mihrab* (prayer niche). The rug was designed to be carried around and laid down in the direction of Mecca for prayers five times a day.

*Look out for felt textiles too – Turkey is the world centre for felt-making, with a tradition going back several hundred years.*

**Prayer rug**

## Top 10 Tips on Buying a Carpet

**1 Choose Your Location**
Before you travel, decide where you will put your rug, to work out in advance the size and colour you want.

**2 Window-Shop**
Look in a fixed-price store to get an idea of what you like and roughly what it will cost.

**3 Take Your Time**
In the carpet shop, relax – drink tea, and don't feel guilty if the owner gets out every carpet in the shop for you.

**4 Get Knotted**
Check the number of knots – the more, the better.

**5 Beware Chemical Dyes**
Most cheap wool or cotton carpets use chemical dyes, and may be chlorine-bleached to give an aged look. Dab a corner with a damp tissue to see if any dye comes off.

**6 Check the Provenance**
Enquire about the age of the carpet, where it was made, and the traditions in that area.

**7 Haggle**
Start at about half of the original price and work up.

**8 Postage**
Turn down "free" postage. If you carry the rug with you, you can use your duty-free allowance; if it is posted, you will have to pay duty.

**9 Taxes**
An invoice and/or credit-card payment will increase the cost, because the vendor will have to declare the sale for VAT. If you are buying a fully taxed product, get the form to reclaim the tax on departure.

**10 Certification**
All antiquities need a Ministry of Culture certificate for export *(see p109)*.

### 8 Symbolism
Women wove their lives and longings into their carpets. Look for motifs symbolizing good luck (the *elibelinde* or "arms-akimbo" motif), fate (an eight-pointed star), the mother goddess (hands on hips), and heroism (rams' horns).

### 9 Number of Knots
The more knots in a carpet, the denser the weave and the more durable the product – and the clearer the design will appear on the reverse side. A poor quality carpet might have only 9 knots per sq cm (75 per sq inch); a good wool-on-cotton carpet will have 49 knots per sq cm (320 per sq inch); the finest Hereke silk carpet could have an astonishing 400 knots or more per sq cm (2,090 per sq inch) – or 3,240,000 knots per sq m (2,709,030 per sq yd).

### 10 Regional Styles
Carpets used to be made in a profusion of highly distinctive regional styles, but those days are rapidly vanishing as carpet-makers simplify their designs to appeal to the export market.

 *A reliable carpet vendor will be happy to give you whatever documentation you need for tax or export purposes.*

Black Eyed Peas, One Love Festival

# Festivals and Events

### 1 International Istanbul Film Festival

Since its inception in 1982, this fortnight-long festival has screened more than 3,000 films from 76 countries. A highlight of the festival is the Award for Lifetime Achievement, instituted in 1996 – winners include French stars Alain Delon and Jeanne Moreau. Most festival screenings are held in cinemas in the vicinity of İstiklal Caddesi. ◎ *Various venues • (0212) 334 07 00 • Apr • www.iksv.org*

### 2 Cherry Festival

The pretty village of Polonezköy *(see p52)* celebrates its cherry harvest, as well as its Polish heritage, in the annual Cherry Festival. A unique event in Istanbul, it features Polish song, dance and other cultural events. The festival is by far the busiest time of year in this otherwise peaceful village, which is also known for its honey, flowers and traditional culture. ◎ *Jun • www.polonezkoy.com*

### 3 Efes Pilsen One Love Festival

This two-day midsummer extravaganza combines top international acts like Morrissey, Black Eyed Peas and Manu Chao with Turkish rock and dance bands. ◎ *Call to check venue • (0212) 334 01 00 • Jul • www.pozitif.info*

Mozart's *Il Seraglio*, International Istanbul Music and Dance Festival

### 4 International Istanbul Music and Dance Festival

An impressive array of soloists, ensembles and orchestras has graced the stages of this prestigious festival since it was established in 1973. Mozart's opera The Abduction from the Seraglio is staged each year in Topkapı Palace. ◎ *Various venues • (0212) 334 0700 • Jun • www.iksv.org*

### 5 International Asia-to-Europe Swimming, Rowing and Sailing Competitions

Competitors in this trio of events cross the Bosphorus from a variety of starting points: Kanlıca for swimmers, Arnavutköy for rowers, and Kandilli for yachtsmen. All three races end at Kuruçeşme. Other events include water-skiing, jet-skiing and underwater-swimming displays; folk dancing; and military band performances. ◎ *Jul • (0212) 560 0707 • www.bogazici.cc*

Asia-to-Europe Sailing Competition

Dates for Şeker Bayramı: 8–10 Aug inclusive (2013); 28–30 Jul inclusive (2014)

Italian jazz band Funk Off perform on İstiklal Caddesi, International Istanbul Jazz Festival

### 6 International Istanbul Jazz Festival

The Jazz Festival's origins lie in a concert by Chick Corea and Steve Kujala at the 1984 Istanbul Music Festival. It was established as an independent event in 1994. The musical range is broad, and you are as likely to encounter Björk or Elvis Costello as you are Brad Mehldau. The choice of venues is eclectic, with traditional clubs, outdoor stages and even a boat cruising on the Bosphorus. ◈ Various venues • (0212) 334 07 00 • Jul • www.iksv.org

### 7 Istanbul Grand Prix

Istanbul Park, out on the Asian side of the Bosphorus at Tuzla, is a fixture on the Formula 1 Grand Prix calendar. Every August the engines roar to a sell-out crowd of more than 125,000 people, with flights and hotel rooms booking up months in advance. During the rest of the year the park hosts national competitions and minor events, as well as tours of the track for visitors. ◈ Istanbul Park, Tuzla (Asian side) • Aug • Call ahead for tickets (0216) 556 98 00 • www.istanbulparkcircuit.com

### 8 International Istanbul Fine Arts Biennial

Istanbul's Biennial showcases contemporary visual arts from Turkey and around the globe. Each festival is directed by a curator of a different nationality, who chooses a theme and arranges the programme of exhibitions, conferences and workshops. ◈ Various venues • (0212) 334 07 00 • Sep–Nov, every other year (odd numbers) • www.iksv.org

### 9 Sugar Festival (Şeker Bayramı)

The Sugar Festival marks the end of the fasting month of Ramazan (Ramadan). People hand out sweets, visit relatives, and enjoy cultural events – and Istanbul's bars and clubs are busy again. Many take advantage of the holiday period by going away for a few days. ◈ Three days, dates vary

### 10 Feast of Sacrifice (Kurban Bayramı)

Also known as Eid-ul-Adha, the Feast of Sacrifice commemorates the Koranic version of Abraham's sacrifice. It falls two months and ten days after the end of Ramazan. Muslims celebrate by slaughtering a sheep on the morning of the first day of the festival. Friends and family are invited to a lavish meal, but much of the meat goes to charity. Note that this is Turkey's major annual public holiday – nearly everything closes, and the public transport system is seriously stretched. ◈ Four days, dates vary

Dates for Kurban Bayramı: 15–18 Oct inclusive (2013); 4–7 Oct inclusive (2014)

Left **Istanbul Toy Museum** Right **Horse-drawn carriage, Büyükada**

# Activities for Children

### 1 Aqua Club Dolphin
This large water park on the outskirts of the city has plenty of slides and rides. It's ideal for a day cooling off, away from city streets and sightseeing hotspots.
⊗ *Cemal Paşa Cad, Esenkent • (0212) 672 61 61 • Open 9am–6pm daily (to 7pm in summer) • Adm charge • www.aquaclubdolphin.com*

**Süleymaniye Mosque, Miniatürk**

### 2 Miniatürk
Perfect for children and for tourists in a hurry, Miniatürk packs all Turkey's most important buildings into one beautiful park on the edge of the Golden Horn – at 1:25 scale *(see p73)*.

### 3 Princes' Islands (Adalar)
Take the ferry to Büyükada or Heybeliada, then ride by horse-drawn carriage to the beach for a day of rest and fun. Remember to book the return trip or it can be a long walk *(see p52)*.

### 4 Istanbul Toy Museum (İstanbul Oyuncak Müzesi)
This is one of Istanbul's newest museums, with around 4,000 exhibits – from rag dolls made by Turkish children, to planes, tin toys, model trains and a Wild West gallery *(see p97)*.

### 5 Bosphorus Ferries
Ferries zip back and forth across the Bosphorus, often dodging under the bows of vast tankers and weaving their way past yachts or humble fishing boats. With great views and ultra-cheap prices, they provide some of the best-value entertainment in Istanbul *(see pp28–9, 104)*.

### 6 Turkuazoo
Children will love this giant aquarium with its 90-m (295-ft) underwater tunnel offering visitors a panoramic view of the resident sea creatures. ⊗ *Forum Shopping Centre, Bayrampaşa, 5km (3 miles) from Atatürk International Airport • (0212) 640 27 40 • Open 10am–6pm Mon–Fri, 10am–8pm Sat–Sun • Adm*

**Scuba diver and fish at Turkuazoo**

*Children with a mechanical turn of mind will also love the Rahmi Koç Museum See p74*

### Fortress of Europe (Rumeli Hisarı)

This castle, built by Mehmet the Conqueror in four months in 1452, has plenty of space for children to let off steam – three towers, huge courtyards and an amphitheatre (see p90).

Mehter Band, Military Museum

### Mehter Band

For centuries the Mehter Band accompanied the Ottoman army into battle, playing martial music. Today, dressed in their crimson, black and gold uniforms, its members play at the military museum (see p80). It's rousing stuff – loud and entertaining.

### Children's Cooking Courses

Friendly teachers make this a fun half-day activity for children as young as three, accompanied by a parent. ◈ Yıldırım Cad 111, Tahtaminare Mahellesi, Fener • Map L2 • (0212) 534 47 88 • www.istanbul foodworkshop.com

### Horse Racing and Riding

The Veliefendi race track has horse racing several times a week. If the kids want to try for themselves, they can be entertained at the Pony Club, where they can ride on the small horses for free. ◈ İstanbul Veliefendi Hipodromu, Ekrem Kurt Bulvarı, Bakırköy • (0212) 444 08 55 • Race meetings mid-Apr to mid-Nov, 2–3 times per week • Adm charge • www.tjk.org

## Top 10 Green Spaces

**1 Büyük Çamlıca**
Istanbul's highest hill offers wonderful views (see p98).

**2 Maçka Parkı**
Formerly in the grounds of Dolmabahçe Palace. There are a few cafés and, in summer, a small funfair. ◈ Map B5

**3 Golden Horn Parks**
Since its rehabilitation, the western shore of the Golden Horn has become one long parkland, running from Fener to Eyüp. ◈ Map A4–B5

**4 Sultanahmet Square**
The large open space around Haghia Sophia and the Blue Mosque merges, via a formal garden with a fountain, into the Hippodrome (see p60).

**5 Gülhane Parkı**
Once the outer grounds of Topkapı Palace, Gülhane Park is today the largest open area in the old city (see p61).

**6 Beykoz Woods (Asian Side)**
While the waterfront village of Beykoz is famous for its glass and for its fish restaurants, the woods behind are a lovely spot for a shady walk. ◈ Map V3

**7 Belgrade Forest (Belgrat Ormanı)**
This woodland is very popular for picnics (see p52).

**8 Emirgan Parkı**
Emirgan Park hosts the annual Tulip Festival in April (see p92).

**9 Yıldız Parkı**
Yıldız Park was once the grounds of Çırağan Palace (see pp89, 92).

**10 Polonezköy**
This rustic spot, 25 km (16 miles) northeast of Istanbul, is surrounded by a large beech forest, and is popular for walks (see p52).

Left **Leb-i-Derya** Right **Vogue**

# Top 10 Restaurants

### Asitane
**1** The complex flavours of Ottoman court cuisine are resurrected (based on extensive research) at Asitane. Hundreds of years later, almond soup, melon stuffed with minced lamb and goose kebabs are still fit for a sultan *(see p77)*.

### Leb-i-Derya
**2** This is one of the more stylish eateries in the new city, offering cocktails, fabulous food, beautiful people, a stunning view and late-night music. You need to come early to get a seat on the roof terrace *(see p85)*.

### Changa
**3** Food, drink and design come together to create a hip dining experience at this Taksim eatery near the Bosphorus. The fusion menu expertly blends Asian and Mediterranean influences. There's also a great cocktail list with several unusual choices *(see p85)*.

### Seasons Restaurant
**4** The Seasons is the restaurant of the Four Seasons Hotel, which was once an Ottoman prison. Glass rather than thick walls now encloses its pretty courtyard garden. The modern Mediterranean food is imaginative and delicious, and the service is gracious *(see p63)*.

### Feriye Lokantası
**5** Situated in a 19th-century police station on the Bosphorus shore, this fashionable restaurant is taking a fresh look at Turkish cuisine, combining traditional recipes with European flair in one of the most exciting culinary experiences in the city *(see p93)*.

### Vogue
**6** Stick-thin women of extreme beauty sip green apple martinis at this ultra-trendy rooftop restaurant, all white leather and chrome. Chic modernism infuses both the menu and the decor *(see p93)*.

### Mikla
**7** Reserve a terrace table at the Marmara Pera Hotel's stylish rooftop restaurant for the perfect view of the Golden Horn – and of the city, 17 floors below. The Mediterranean cuisine has Turkish and Nordic touches. The decor is elegant – there's even a swimming pool by the bar. A cocktail or two later and you can sink into the soft sofas to recover.
◈ *The Marmara Pera, Meşrutiyet Cad 15, Beyoğlu • Map J5 • (0212) 293 56 56 • $$$$*

**Seasons Restaurant**

*Reservations are advised at all the restaurants listed here.*

### 360

8 Rub shoulders with the swanky young set of Istanbul on 360's superb terrace bar, taking your time to drink in the stunning views of both the Bosphorus and the Golden Horn, then withdraw to the spacious, well-lit interior to sample such eclectic delights as samphire and soya sprouts, Vietnamese beef tartar, polenta-crusted calamari, seafood risotto, lamb loin confit, Margarita sorbet and pistachio *baklava* (see p84).

**View from the terrace, 360**

### Balıkçı Sabahattin

9 A truly traditional Turkish experience, this wonderful fish restaurant (open since 1927) is situated in an old house with antique carpets and copper pots. There's also an outdoor terrace with lively Gypsy violinists. The food is excellent, although there is no menu – you choose from a wide range of *meze* and the catch of the day (see p63).

### Giritli

10 Cretan dishes such as ceviche-style sea bass and cracked brine-cured green olives transport diners to their own little Greek island for the night. The fixed-price menu includes drinks, a selection of mezes and perfectly prepared fish. The restored historic house location and pretty restaurant garden are a bonus (see p63).

## Top 10 Entertainment Venues

### 1 Al Jamal
Offers a luxurious evening of top-notch food and belly-dancing (see p84).

### 2 Orient House
Enjoy whirling dervishes and belly dancing at this venue (see p71).

### 3 Babylon
Babylon entertains with its selection of rock, world music and other acts (see p84).

### 4 Cemal Reşit Rey Concert Hall
Daily concerts include Western and Turkish classical, and world music. ⓝ *Darulbedayi Cad 1, Harbiye • Map B4 • (0212) 231 54 97 • www.crrks.org*

### 5 Aksanat (Akbank) Cultural Centre
This arts centre offers music and theatre. ⓝ *İstiklal Cad 8 • Map L4 • (0212) 252 35 00 • www.akbanksanat.com*

### 6 Kuruçeşme Arena
Big-name bands perform by the Bosphorus at this open-air arena. ⓝ *Muallim Naci Cad 60, Kuruçeşme • Map U4 • (0212) 263 39 83 • www.turkcellkurucesmearena.com*

### 7 City Monuments
Try *son-et-lumière* in Sultanahmet Square, or concerts in Haghia Eirene (see p61).

### 8 Nardis Jazz Club
Live jazz performed in an intimate setting (see p84).

### 9 Salon İKSV
Istanbul's top arts organization hosts great classical and jazz concerts (see p84).

### 10 Süreyya Opera House
This Art-Deco-inspired 1920s theatre hosts opera and ballet. ⓝ *Bahariye Cad 29, Kadıköy • Map U5 • (0216) 346 15 31 • www.sureyyaoperasi.org*

➤ For more restaurant listings **See pp63, 71, 77, 85, 93, 99**

Left **Archaeological Museum, İznik** Right **Koza Park, Bursa**

# 🔟 Excursions from Istanbul

### 1 Princes' Islands (Adalar)

With deserted beaches, pine forests and ancient monasteries, these nine islands in the Sea of Marmara offer a restful break from the city. This is an easy day trip; most ferries from Istanbul (Kabataş) call at the four largest islands – Kınalıada, Burgazada, Heybeliada and Büyükada. On Büyükada and Heybeliada, walking or horse and carriage are the only means of transport – cars are allowed only for essential services. ◈ *12 km (8 miles) southeast of Istanbul*

**Harbour of Burgazada, Princes' Islands**

### 2 Yalova

Ferries also run to Yalova, a spa on the southern shore of the Gulf of İzmit. Turks flock here for the hot springs and pools. ◈ *24 km (16 miles) southeast of Istanbul*

### 3 Belgrade Forest (Belgrat Ormanı)

Belgrade Forest is the largest area of woodland near Istanbul. Its huge park makes a first-rate spot for family picnics. ◈ *20 km (13 miles) north of Istanbul*

### 4 Polonezköy

Polonezköy was established as a Polish enclave in the mid-19th century. Only a few hundred Poles remain today, but the village's history and rural charm live on. Polonezköy is popular with day-trippers for its old wooden houses, the availability of pork (forbidden under Muslim law) and relaxing country walks. ◈ *25 km (16 miles) northeast of Istanbul*

### 5 Black Sea Beaches

Kilyos and Şile, both on the Black Sea, are the nearest beaches to Istanbul – and are wonderful for a day trip, although there's not much space on the sands during summer weekends. At Kilyos there are dangerous sea currents, so use only the marked-out areas for swimming. ◈ *Kilyos is 27 km (17 miles) from Istanbul; Şile (Asian side) 72 km (45 miles)*

### 6 Gallipoli (Gelibolu)

A one-day tour can take in the major World War I battlefields, memorials and cemeteries in the Gallipoli National Historic Park (Gelibolu Yarımadası Tarihi Milli Parkı); visits can be arranged from Istanbul, Eceabat and Çanakkale. At Anzac Cove (Anzak Koyu) – where thousands of Australians, New Zealanders and Turks were killed in 1915 – Antipodeans gather each 25 April for the Anzac Day memorial service. Book a hotel well in advance. ◈ *On the Aegean coast, 350 km (219 miles) west of Istanbul*

*Few İstanbullus refer to Princes' Islands by their full name, Kızıl Adalar (the Red Islands), calling them simply Adalar (the Islands).*

### 7 Edirne

Ottoman capital in the 15th century, Edirne's history includes occupation by Greeks, Bulgarians and Russians. Best known for the Selimiye Mosque, Sinan's 16th-century masterpiece, the town is also noted for its fine Ottoman buildings and the Yağlı Güreş (oil-wrestling) festival, which takes place in summer. ⊗ *230 km (144 miles) northwest of Istanbul*

**Selimiye Mosque, Edirne**

### 8 Bursa

Historic Bursa is home to some of Turkey's greatest Ottoman architecture, including the mosque and *türbe* (tomb) of Murat I. Also of note are its suburb, Çekirge, famous for its spas, and the nearby Uludağ National Park, the country's most fashionable ski resort. ⊗ *90 km (60 miles) south of Istanbul*

### 9 Troy (Truva)

Homer's *Iliad* tells of a ten-year siege of the ancient city of Troy by a Greek army in the 13th century BC. Historians assumed Troy was a mythical place until excavations near the Dardanelles – begun by German archaeologist Heinrich Schliemann in the 19th century – uncovered the remains of no fewer than nine cities dating from 3,000 BC onwards, built one on top of another. Homer's Troy was probably the level called Troy VI (1800–1250 BC) – the most impressive sight is the great wall of Troy VI. ⊗ *380 km (238 miles) from Istanbul on the Aegean coast • (0286) 283 05 36 • 8:30am–5pm daily • Adm charge*

### 10 İznik

At İznik (known in Roman-Christian times as Nicaea), Emperor Constantine convened a council in AD 325 to produce a unified statement of Christian belief: the Creed of Nicaea. The city was renamed İznik by Orhan Gazi when he captured it in 1331. İznik is famous for its ceramic industry, and especially its painted tiles, which adorn many Ottoman mosques. ⊗ *87 km (54 miles) southeast of Istanbul*

It's best to visit Belgrade Forest on a weekday; the park gets very crowded at weekends, especially in summer.

53

# AROUND TOWN

ISTANBUL'S TOP 10

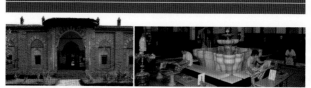

Left **Museum of Turkish and Islamic Arts** Right **Cağaloğlu Baths**

# Sultanahmet and the Old City

MANY OF THE CITY'S GREATEST SIGHTS *are to be found in this historic area, which was in turn the centre of Byzantium, Constantinople and Ottoman Stamboul. Archaeologists have dated settlements in this strategic spot at the entrance to the Golden Horn back to the 6th millennium BC, but recorded history begins around 667 BC, when Greek colonist Byzas founded Byzantion on Seraglio Point (now home to the Topkapı Palace). After his arrival in AD 324, Constantine transformed this port into the dazzling jewel of Constantinople, a new capital for the Roman Empire. By 1453, when the Ottomans seized power, the city was run down and ruinous, and the new rulers stamped their authority – both religious and secular – on its buildings.*

**View of the Blue Mosque**

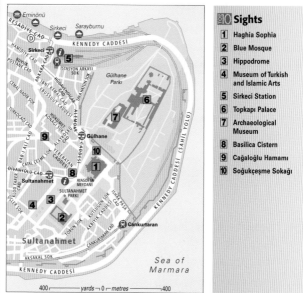

## Sights

1 Haghia Sophia

2 Blue Mosque

3 Hippodrome

4 Museum of Turkish and Islamic Arts

5 Sirkeci Station

6 Topkapı Palace

7 Archaeological Museum

8 Basilica Cistern

9 Cağaloğlu Hamamı

10 Soğukçeşme Sokağı

Preceding pages **View across the Sea of Marmara to Asian Istanbul, with the Egyptian Bazaar and the New Mosque in the foreground**

### 1 Haghia Sophia (Ayasofya)

Consecrated by Justinian in 537, the "Church of Holy Wisdom" is an enduring tribute to the skill of its architects, Anthemius of Tralles and Isidore of Miletus, who created a monument that has withstood wars and earthquakes. The scale of its vast central dome was not surpassed until the construction of St Peter's in Rome, 1,000 years later (see pp12–13).

Haghia Sophia viewed from its gardens

### 2 Blue Mosque (Sultanahmet Camii)

Begun in 1609, Sultan Ahmet I's mosque was built opposite Haghia Sophia and directly on top of Constantine's Great Palace to stress the supremacy of Islam and the Ottoman Empire over Christian Byzantium (see pp14–15).

### 3 Hippodrome (At Meydanı)

Now a peaceful park, the Hippodrome was the Byzantine chariot racetrack – a stadium capable of holding 100,000 people. Laid out in the 3rd century AD by Emperor Septimus Severus, it was enlarged and connected to the adjacent Great Palace by Constantine. There are three great monuments in the Hippodrome: the Egyptian Obelisk (Dikilitaş) of c.1500 BC, which Constantine transported from Luxor; the Serpentine Column (Yılanlı Sütun) from the Temple of Apollo at Delphi in Greece, made in 479 BC; and the Column

Egyptian Obelisk and Serpentine Column, Hippodrome

of Constantine VII Porphryogenitus (Ormetaş), which is of unknown date and was named after the emperor who had it restored in the 10th century. The stadium once held four great bronze horses, but these were looted by the Crusaders in 1204 and now grace St Mark's Cathedral in Venice. ⊗ Map Q5

### 4 Museum of Turkish and Islamic Arts (Türk ve İslam Eserleri Müzesi)

This museum is housed in the magnificent palace built by İbrahim Paşa (c.1493–1536), Grand Vizier and son-in-law to Süleyman the Magnificent. It contains a superb collection of more than 40,000 artifacts dating from the 7th century to the present, with exhibits of fine art, crafts, and Turkish domestic life in its evolution from nomad's tent to modern home.
⊗ At Meydanı 46 • Map Q5 • (0212) 518 18 05 • Open 9am–5pm Tue–Sun • Adm charge • www.tiem.gov.tr

Stamboul is a variant form of İstanbul. Both names pre-date the Conquest of 1453 (see p32).

57

### 5 Sirkeci Station (Sirkeci Garı)

Officially opened in November 1890, the glamorous eastern terminus for the Orient Express service was built by German architect August Jachmund, in an eclectic style drawing together elements of Istanbul's varied architectural traditions. The station also houses a railway museum (see p35) and a superb restaurant (see p63). Currently, Sirkeci is still the last stop for all trains to Istanbul from Europe; a new tunnel is planned that will connect it with Haydarpaşa on the Asian shore. ⓢ İstasyon Cad • Map R2 • (0212) 520 65 75 • Museum open 9am–5pm Tue–Sat • Free

### 6 Topkapı Palace (Topkapı Sarayı)

The great palace of the Ottoman Empire was both the sultan's residence and the centre of government from 1459 to 1853. The whole complex can take a full day to explore; the highlights are undoubtedly the Harem and the Treasury (see pp8–11).

"Fruit Room", Topkapı Palace Harem

### 7 Archaeological Museum (Arkeoloji Müzesi)

This is one of the world's great historical museums. It has three principal sections: the Museum of the Ancient Orient, which contains, among other things, the city gates of Babylon; the Tiled Kiosk, with a superb display of ceramics; and the main museum, where royal sarcophagi found at Sidon in Lebanon are star exhibits (see pp16–17).

Roman statue of Apollo, Archaeological Museum

### 8 Basilica Cistern (Yerebatan Sarnıcı)

This beautiful "Sunken Palace", as the Turkish name has it, had a prosaic purpose: it was built as a vast underground water-storage tank. Begun by Constantine, it was expanded by Justinian in 532 to ensure that Constantinople was always supplied with water; covering an area of 9,800 sq m (11,720 sq yards), it once held 80 million litres (about 18 million gallons). The cistern roof is supported by 336 pillars, 8 m (26 ft) in height. Look for the upside-down Medusa heads, reused from older Greek buildings. Istanbul's most unusual tourist attraction is also popular as a film location and a venue for concerts. ⓢ Yerebatan Cad 13 • Map R4 • (0212) 522 12 59 • Open 9am–6:30pm daily • Adm charge • www.yerebatan.com

---

**Süleyman I**

Known to the West as "the Magnificent", Süleyman I preferred the title Kanuni – "the law-giver". Taking the throne aged 26 in 1520, he ruled for 46 years. During that time he doubled the size of the Ottoman Empire and, as caliph (supreme head of the Islamic faith), consolidated Sunni authority over Shia Islam. He also wrote the Codex Süleymanicus, which built a comprehensive legal system that defined the concept of justice, and guaranteed equal treatment for all. Süleyman was a great patron of the arts, as well as a poet and goldsmith.

---

Sultanahmet is named after Sultan Ahmet I, who commissioned the Blue Mosque (see pp14–15).

### Cağaloğlu Baths (Cağaloğlu Hamamı)

One of the city's best-known and most picturesque bathhouses, Cağaloğlu Hamamı was built in 1741 by Sultan Mahmut I, with the intention of raising funds to support his library in Haghia Sophia. International figures from King Edward VIII to Kaiser Wilhelm, from Franz Lizst to Florence Nightingale, are all reputed to have bathed here. In more recent times it has been used as a location for countless films and fashion shoots. ◈ *Prof Kazım İsmail Gürkan Cad 34 • Map Q3 • (0212) 522 24 24 • Open daily: men, 8am–10pm; women, 8am–8pm • Adm charge • www.cagalogluhamami.com.tr*

### Soğukçeşme Sokağı

This steeply cobbled street, which runs between the outer walls of the Topkapı Palace and Haghia Sophia, is a sequence of pretty Ottoman merchants' homes. The street was restored as part of a 1980s project that was one of the first of its kind in Istanbul. Nine of the houses form the Ayasofya Konakları (see p114), the city's first "special hotel". ◈ *Map R4*

Soğukçeşme Sokağı

## A Day in Sultanahmet

### Morning

Start your day at the dawn call of the *müezzin*, so that you are ready to visit the **Blue Mosque** as soon as it opens. From there, cross the square to **Haghia Sophia**, then pay a visit to the **Basilica Cistern**, the **Hippodrome** and the **Museum of Turkish and Islamic Arts** before having a gentle stroll through the **Arasta Bazaar** *(see p60)* to the **Mosaics Museum** *(see p60)*. This may sound like too much for a single morning, but the distance between each of these attractions is small, and (aside from the first two) most of the sites are fairly simple. You'll need a little time to relax after this, so choose one of the cafés or restaurants on **Divanyolu** *(see p60)* for lunch, and write a few postcards bought from local vendors.

### Afternoon

Now choose one of two options: either walk across to the **Topkapı Palace** and spend the whole afternoon embroiled in Ottoman court intrigue, mayhem and murder; or wander through the side streets to the **Cağaloğlu Baths** for a Turkish bath before rejoining **Soğukçeşme Sokağı** and making your way to the vast **Archaeological Museum**. When you've had your fill, continue down the hill for a peaceful stroll along the seafront at Eminönü; then take the tram back up the hill to Sultanahmet and choose one of the many wonderful rooftop bars or restaurants from which to watch the sun set over the city and the floodlights playing on Haghia Sophia and the Blue Mosque.

Left **Mosaics Museum** Centre **Baths of Roxelana** Right **Calligraphy at the Istanbul Craft Centre**

# 🔟 Sultanahmet: Best of the Rest

### 1 Sultanahmet Square (Sultanahmet Meydanı)

This leafy square, once the hippodrome of Constantinople, lies between the Blue Mosque and Haghia Sophia. ◈ *Map R4*

### 2 The Milion Monument (Milyon Taşi)

The marble pilaster of the Milion can be found in the northern corner of Sultanahmet Square. From the 4th century AD it was used as "point zero" for the measurement of distances to the many cities of the Byzantine Empire. ◈ *Haghia Sophia • Map R4*

### 3 Baths of Roxelana (Hürrem Sultan Hamamı)

These baths were built for Süleyman the Magnificent, and are named after the sultan's apparently scheming wife. ◈ *Ayasofya Meydanı • Map R4 • (0212) 517 35 35 • Open 8am–10pm daily • www.ayasofyahamami.com*

### 4 Arasta Bazaar (Arasta Çarşısı)

The bazaar was originally built as stables in the 17th century. Around 40 shops sell carpets and other souvenirs. ◈ *Map R5 • Open 9am–9pm daily*

### 5 Mosaics Museum (Mozaik Müzesi)

Little remains of Emperor Justinian's vast 6th-century palace but this mosaic floor. ◈ *Arasta Bazaar • Map R6 • (0212) 518 12 05 • Open 9am–4:30pm Tue–Sun • Adm charge*

### 6 Istanbul Craft Centre (Caferağa Medresesi)

Watch craftspeople create art, from ceramics to calligraphy, in this 16th-century Koranic college, then take the product home – or sign up for a course yourself. ◈ *Caferiye Sok, Soğukkuyu Çıkmazı 1 • Map S5 • (0212) 513 36 01 • Open 9am–7pm Mon–Sat • Free*

### 7 Kaiser Wilhelm Fountain

German Emperor Wilhelm II presented this Neo-Byzantine fountain to Sultan Abdül Hamit II in 1901. ◈ *At Meydanı • Map R4*

### 8 Divanyolu Caddesi

Divanyolu was once the *Mese* – the main thoroughfare – of Byzantine Constantinople and Ottoman Stamboul, and continued all the way to the Albanian coast. ◈ *Map Q4*

### 9 Cistern of 1001 Columns (Binbirdirek Sarnıcı)

There are in fact only 224 columns in this elegant 4th-century cistern. It is now home to several cafés and hosts live music and events. ◈ *Binbirdirek, İmran Öktem Cad 4 • Map Q4 • (0212) 518 10 01 • 9am–9pm daily • Adm charge • www.binbirdirek.com*

### 10 Sultanahmet Hamamı

Enjoy the 17th-century architecture while you are scrubbed clean *(see also pp24–5)*. ◈ *Divanyolu Cad, Doktor Emin Paşa Sok No 10 • Map Q4 • (0212) 513 72 04 • www.sultanahmethamami.com*

Around Town – Sultanahmet and the Old City

Left **Sokullu Mehmet Paşa Mosque** Centre **Church of SS Sergius & Bacchus** Right **Church of St John**

# 🔟 Old City: Best of the Rest

### 1 Haghia Eirene (Aya İrini Kilisesi)

Built in the 6th century on the site of an earlier church, Haghia Eirene was the city's cathedral until Haghia Sophia was built. Later an Ottoman arsenal it is now used for concerts. ⬡ *Topkapı Palace (1st courtyard)* • *Map S3* • *Open only for concerts and events*

### 2 Imperial Mint (Darphane)

The Ottoman Imperial Mint was founded in 1496. It moved to Topkapı in 1723; today, this complex houses laboratories for the state conservation department and hosts concerts and exhibitions. ⬡ *Topkapı Palace (1st courtyard)* • *Map S3*

### 3 History of Islamic Science and Technology Museum

This well laid-out museum exhibits fantastic models of scientific inventions. ⬡ *Gülhane Park* • *Map R3* • *(0212) 528 80 65* • *Open 9am–5pm Wed–Mon* • *Adm charge* • *www.ibtav.org*

### 4 Sea Walls

Built in 438 by Cyrus, Prefect of the East, and extended by Theodosius *(see p75)*, the walls are best viewed from the main coastal road. ⬡ *Kennedy Cad* • *Map M–S6*

### 5 Bucoleon Palace

Three vast marble windows stare sightlessly out to sea from this last standing fragment of the Great Palace, built into the sea wall. ⬡ *Kennedy Cad* • *Map Q6*

### 6 Church of SS Sergius and Bacchus (Küçük Ayasofya Camii)

Known as "Little Haghia Sophia", this church was built in 527 and converted into a mosque in 1500. The marble columns and carved frieze with a Greek inscription are original. ⬡ *Küçük Ayasofya Camii Sok* • *Map P6*

### 7 Kumkapı

The old Byzantine harbour is now a huddle of lively fish restaurants *(see p63)*. ⬡ *Map M6*

### 8 Sokollu Mehmet Paşa Mosque

Built by Sinan for Grand Vizier Sokollu Mehmet Paşa, this lovely mosque behind the Hippodrome contains some fine İznik tiles, an elaborately painted ceiling and four tiny black stones from the Kaaba in Mecca. ⬡ *Camii Kebir Sok* • *Map P5* • *9:30am–4:30pm Tue–Sun; may need the keyholder to see inside the mosque*

### 9 Yedikule Castle

This Ottoman fortress is built onto a section of the Theodosian Walls *(see p75)*. ⬡ *Yedikule Meydanı Sok* • *Bus 31, 80, 931* • *Open 9am–4:30pm Thu–Tue* • *Adm charge*

### 10 Church of St John of Studius (İmrahor Camii)

Only the outer walls remain of this once-great monastery, built in 463. It was one of the Byzantine Empire's main centres of scholarship. ⬡ *İmam Aşir Sok* • *Free*

Left **Çorlulu Ali Paşa Medresesi** Centre **Café Meşale** Right **Sultan Pub**

# Bars, Cafés and Casual Eateries

### Çorlulu Ali Paşa Medresesi
Lounge on cushions in one of several atmospheric tea-shops with locals puffing on the *nargile*. No alcohol. ◈ *Divanyolu 36 • Map Q4*

### Doy-doy
This cheap and cheerful place has a good selection of kebabs, pizza, salads and vegetarian options. No alcohol. ◈ *Sifa Hamamı Sok 13 • Map Q6*

### Sultanahmet Köftecisi
A long-lived local institution, this superb source of affordable, delicious Turkish food, right on Sultanahmet Square, has now been surrounded by other cafés with suspiciously similar names. Make sure you find the right one! ◈ *Divanyolu 12 • Map Q4*

### Lale (The Pudding Shop)
Once an essential stop on the "Hippy Trail", with a message board and copious quantities of cheap food, Lale has lost a little atmosphere but is still great for backpackers. The food is good value, the service is friendly, and they offer draught beer and free Wi-Fi. ◈ *Divanyolu Cad 6 • Map Q4*

### Sultan Pub
This is the epitome of modern Istanbul – an excellent rooftop restaurant, a pub with TV blaring sports downstairs, a pavement café (great cappuccinos and cakes), a souvenir shop and a Byzantine cistern as a basement. ◈ *Divanyolu Cad 2 • Map Q4*

### Café Camille
This lovely café, just off the main drag, provides a very welcome respite from sight-seeing with its coffee drinks, fresh juices, salads and other delicious light bites. ◈ *Çatalçeşme Sok 2, off Bab-i Ali Cad 36 • Map Q4*

### Çiğdem Pastanesi
Enjoy traditional Turkish tea or a well-made cappuccino with plenty of creamy froth at this classic patisserie. If you're in the mood for a light snack, the sticky, honey-drenched baklava is a local favourite. ◈ *Divanyolu Cad 62 • Map Q4*

### Café Meşale
A quiet place for a cup of tea and *nargile* during the day, in the evening Café Meşale becomes a restaurant with live music and Whirling Dervish performances. ◈ *Arasta Bazaar • Map Q5*

### Cheers
Space may be at a premium here, but there are large beers – also loud music, low prices and crowds of travellers swapping tall tales. The shady pavement tables are a good place to relax at midday. ◈ *Akbıyık Cad 20 • Map R5*

### Yeşil Ev Beer Garden
Part of the Yeşil Ev Hotel, this delightful garden bar with a glassed conservatory offering coffee, cakes and alcohol is a great place to chill out. ◈ *Kabasakal Cad 5 • Map R5*

**Price Categories**

| For a typical meal of meze and main course for one without alcohol, and including taxes and extra charges. | $ under $7 |
| | $$ $7–13 |
| | $$$ $13–18 |
| | $$$$ $18–28 |
| | $$$$$ over $28 |

Balıkçı Sabahattin

 Restaurants

### Sarnıç
The atmosphere is fabulous in this romantically converted Byzantine cistern serving Turkish/French cuisine. Book ahead. ✪ Soğukçeşme Sok • Map R4 • (0212) 512 42 91 • $$$$

### Orient Express
This cavernous 19th-century Gothic station restaurant (see p58) offers surprisingly good traditional Turkish food. ✪ Platform 2, Sirkeci Station • Map Q2 • (0212) 522 22 80 • $$$

### Giritli
Fine fish and a bountiful array of unusual mezes are the stars at this Cretan-style eatery. ✪ Keresteci Hakkı Sok 8 • Map R6 • (0212) 458 22 70 • $$$$$

### Buhara 93 Restaurant
Turkish kebabs and pizza are a speciality here, and there's a large garden where you can enjoy live music. ✪ Nakil Bent Sok 15/A • Map Q6 • (0212) 518 15 11 • $$$

### Amedros
By day this is a friendly café. In the evening it becomes a bistro serving Turkish and European food, with good vegetarian options. ✪ Hoca Rüstem Sok 7, off Divanyolu • Map Q4 • (0212) 522 83 56 • $$

### Restaurant en la Luna
Go native in this quiet back-street restaurant. The mainly Turkish food is excellent and copious, and the staff are friendly. ✪ Utangaç Sok 23 • Map R5 • (0212) 518 72 67 • $$$

### Balıkçı Sabahattin
One of the city's finest fish restaurants since 1927. Head here for a special night out. ✪ Seyit Hasankuyu Sok 1, off Cankurtaran Cad • Map R5 • (0212) 458 18 24 • $$$$

### Kumkapı
There are many meyhanes (taverns) to choose from in this old fishing neighbourhood, serving fresh fish and meze washed down with rakı. Musicians play traditional fasil to the tables and expect to be tipped. ✪ Map M6 • $$

### Seasons Restaurant
Top-class contemporary European cuisine with a hint of Asian fusion. ✪ Four Seasons Hotel, Tevfikhane Sok 1 • Map R5 • (0212) 402 30 00 • $$$$$

### Rumeli Café
This popular restaurant in an old printing factory serves a Turkish and Mediterranean menu. Good vegetarian options. ✪ Ticarethane Sok 8 • Map Q4 • (0212) 512 00 08 • $$$

Left **Spices in the Egyptian Bazaar** Right **İznik tiles, Rüstem Paşa Mosque**

# Bazaar Quarter and Eminönü

IN 1453, FOLLOWING HIS CONQUEST OF *Constantinople, Sultan Mehmet II* chose this area, close to the Graeco-Roman Forum of the Bulls, as the place to begin construction of a model city based on Islamic principles. The key ingredients were mosques and medreses (religious schools), charitable institutions, accommodation for travellers, and a Grand Bazaar – the latter funding all the others and a great deal more besides. All these were

constructed – and many still remain – in one of the city's most fascinating and vibrant districts, where you can buy, with equal ease, a plastic bucket and an antique silk carpet, an ancient religious text or a kilo of peppercorns.

**Waterfront scene at Eminönü**

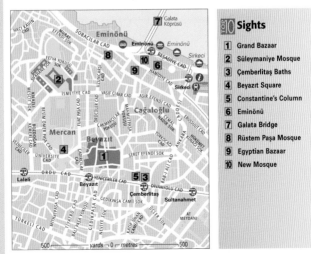

## Sights

1. Grand Bazaar
2. Süleymaniye Mosque
3. Çemberlitaş Baths
4. Beyazıt Square
5. Constantine's Column
6. Eminönü
7. Galata Bridge
8. Rüstem Paşa Mosque
9. Egyptian Bazaar
10. New Mosque

Preceding pages **Interior view of the Süleymaniye Mosque**

### 1 Grand Bazaar (Kapalı Çarşı)

The bazaar was one of the first institutions established by Mehmet the Conqueror after 1453. Its oldest part is the domed İç Bedesten, a lockable warehouse used for trading and storing the most valuable wares. Today, as well as covered streets containing thousands of shops and stalls, there are cafés, restaurants, tea houses, water fountains and even ATM machines – all designed to keep you browsing and buying for as long as possible. There are also several *hans* – originally travellers' inns, now mostly workshops and small factories *(see pp18–19)*.

Shoppers in the Grand Bazaar

### 2 Süleymaniye Mosque (Süleymaniye Camii)

The Süleymaniye Mosque, built for Süleyman I in 1550–57, is the largest and most lavish in the city. Süleyman and his wife Roxelana are both buried here, while the great Mimar Sinan, architect of the mosque, is buried just outside the main complex in a tomb he designed and built himself *(see pp20–21)*.

### 3 Çemberlitaş Baths (Çemberlitaş Hamamı)

Nur Banu, wife of the drunken Selim the Sot (son of Süleyman and Roxelana), commissioned these baths from Sinan in 1584. In those days they were run as a charitable foundation; today they are distinctly more upmarket. Their gracious domed halls make them a popular tourist attraction *(see pp24–5)*.

Süleymaniye Mosque

### 4 Beyazıt Square (Beyazıt Meydanı)

This grand open space has been one of the city's principal meeting places for centuries. Popularly known as Beyazıt Square, its official name is Freedom Square (Hürriyet Meydanı). It stands on the site of the Graeco-Roman *Forum Tauri* (Forum of the Bulls), which was extended by Emperor Theodosius in 393. The forum gained its name from the bronze bull at its centre, a place of sacrifice in the pre-Christian era. Some of its colonnades, carved in the form of peacock feathers, were reused in the building of the Basilica Cistern *(see p58)*, while others lie abandoned along the tram tracks on Ordu Caddesi. Part of the Column of Theodosius is built into the foundations of Beyazıt Hamamı (now shops). The square hosts a daily flea market, and is home to the Beyazıt Mosque, Istanbul University and the Museum of Calligraphy *(see p70)*. ✎ *Map M3*

**Fishing on the Galata Bridge**

### Constantine's Column (Çemberlitaş)

Built of Egyptian porphyry, this column, 35 m (115 ft) tall, once stood in the centre of the Forum of Constantine, topped with a statue of Constantine dressed as the god Apollo. It was erected as part of the inauguration of the Roman Empire's new capital in 330. Constantine buried holy relics – said to have included the axe Noah used to build his ark – around the base. Its Turkish name, Çemberlitaş (Hooped Column), refers to the reinforcing metal hoops added in 416 and renewed in 1701. ⚑ Divanyolu Cad • Map P4

**Constantine's Column**

### Emperor Constantine

The son of a leading army officer, Constantine (c.280–337) became one of a triumvirate of rulers of the Roman Empire. In 312, following a religious vision, he defeated his main rival, Maxentius, while fighting under the sign of the Christian cross. On becoming sole emperor in 324 he declared Christianity the state religion. In 325 he called the Council of Nicaea, which laid down the basic tenets of the faith. In 330 he inaugurated his new capital, Constantinople. On his deathbed, he formally converted to Christianity, and was buried at the city's Church of the Holy Apostles (see p73).

### Eminönü

From the Grand Bazaar, steep alleys crowded with market stalls lead down through Tahtakale to the Eminönü waterfront. It's a great place to roam, with mosques and markets, Byzantine warehouses, street sellers offering everything from pretzels to fake watches, and a bank of piers with ferries to every part of the city, all split by the swirl of traffic along the dual carriageway that leads around the coast. ⚑ Map N1

### Galata Bridge (Galata Köprüsü)

The predecessor of this modern bridge across the Golden Horn was an iron pontoon structure of 1909–12. It was underequipped for modern traffic, and its pontoons, by blocking water flow, trapped pollution in the Golden Horn. It was replaced in 1992 by the current two-level concrete bridge. The city views from the upper level, especially at sunset, are breathtaking; the old bridge, initially used as a footbridge near Hasköy, was later demolished by city authorities. ⚑ Map F3

### Rüstem Paşa Mosque (Rüstem Paşa Camii)

This enchanting mosque was built by Sinan in 1561. It was commissioned by Süleyman the Magnificent's daughter Mihrimah in memory of her husband, Rüstem Paşa, Süleyman's Grand Vizier. The mosque blazes with richly coloured İznik tiles, inside and out, while galleries and windows flood the hall with light. ⚑ Hasırcılar Cad • Map N1 • (0212) 526 73 50 • Open 9am–dusk daily • Free

*Share your travel recommendations on traveldk.com*

### 9 Egyptian Bazaar (Mısır Çarşısı)

This marketplace was built in 1660 as part of the New Mosque complex. Its name derives from the fact that it was originally financed by duties on Egyptian imports, although it is better known in English as the Spice Bazaar because for centuries, spices were the main goods sold here. These days, the bazaar has given itself over entirely to satisfying the tourist trade – it's the best place to buy small presents from *lokum* (Turkish Delight) to phials of saffron, from pistachios and almonds to incense or coffee. Belly-dancing outfits are also available. ⊗ *Eminönü • Map P1 • Open 8am–7pm Mon–Sat*

### 10 New Mosque (Yeni Cami)

This large, rather gloomy mosque was commissioned in 1597 by Valide Sultan Safiye, mother of Sultan Mehmet III. Work was interrupted when the architect was executed for heresy and Safiye was banished after her son's death. It was completed in 1663 by Valide Sultan Turhan Hayice, mother of Sultan Mehmet IV. The interior is richly decorated but has relatively poor-quality İznik tiles. Beside the mosque are the tombs of Valide Sultan Turhan Hatice, Mehmet IV, five other sultans and many princes and princesses. ⊗ *Eminönü • Map P1 • (0212) 527 85 05 • Open 9am–dusk daily • Free*

Interior of the New Mosque

## A Day's Shopping

### Morning

🕐 Start the day clean and refreshed following a visit to the **Çemberlitaş Baths**, then pop into the **Nuruosmaniye Mosque** *(see p70)* before getting down to the real business of the day in the **Grand Bazaar**. Depending on how much time and money you spend here, either have lunch at one of the cafés in the Bazaar or walk on through **Beyazıt Square** and down the hill to the **Süleymaniye Mosque** to pay your respects at the tombs of Süleyman and Roxelana. If you didn't eat earlier, lunch at the Darüzziyafe Restaurant *(see p71)*, or at one of the cafés next to the mosque.

### Afternoon

Leave the mosque along İsmetiye Caddesi, turn left into Uzunçarşı Caddesi and head down the hill through crowded market streets, where metal- and woodworkers still ply their trade, before turning right on Tahtakale Caddesi, a sensory treat with its traditional spice and coffee sellers. Carry on downhill and eventually you will end up in Eminönü, where you can visit the **Rüstem Paşa Mosque** and look at the **New Mosque** before a last round of shopping – if you have the stamina – in the **Egyptian Bazaar**. Between the New Mosque and the Egyptian Bazaar is the market for flowers, plants, seeds and songbirds. Have dinner at Hamdi Et Lokantası *(see p71)* or the Orient Express in Sirkeci Station *(see p63)* – or take the tram back up to Sultanahmet and rooftop views of the sunset.

Left **Kalenderhane Mosque** Centre **Istanbul University** Right **Nuruosmaniye Mosque**

# 🔟 Best of the Rest

### 1 Book Bazaar (Sahaflar Çarşısı)
Manuscripts have been traded in this courtyard since medieval times, although printed books were banned until 1729. Now the market sells antiquarian books and second-hand paperbacks. ◈ *Sahaflar Çarşısı Sok • Map M4*

### 2 Museum of Calligraphy (Türk Vakıf Hat Sanatları Müzesi)
In a culture that forbade the use of the human image, calligraphy was a high art. On display are manuscripts, tools and a tableau of an early workshop. ◈ *Beyazıt Meydanı • Map M4 • (0212) 527 58 51 • Closed for renovation, phone for opening times • Adm charge*

### 3 Beyazıt Tower (Beyazıt Kulesi)
This elegant marble tower, built in 1828 as a fire lookout, stands in the grounds of Istanbul University. ◈ *Ordu Cad • Map M3 • Closed to the public*

### 4 Beyazıt Mosque (Beyazıt Camii)
Built in 1506 by Beyazıt II, this is the oldest surviving imperial mosque in Istanbul. ◈ *Yeni Maharet Cad • Map M4 • (0212) 212 09 22*

### 5 Atik Ali Paşa Mosque (Atik Ali Paşa Camii)
This 15th-century copy of the original Fatih Mosque is named after its builder, Grand Vizier to Beyazıt II. ◈ *Yeniçeriler Cad • Map P4*

### 6 Tulip Mosque (Laleli Cami)
The Tulip Mosque was built by Mustafa III in 1763, with lavish use of coloured marble in the new Ottoman Baroque style. Mustafa is buried here. ◈ *Ordu Cad • Map D5 • Open prayer times only*

### 7 Nuruosmaniye Mosque (Nuruosmaniye Camii)
Completed by Sultan Osman III in 1748, Nuruosmaniye was the first Baroque mosque in the city. ◈ *Vezirhanı Cad • Map P4*

### 8 Kalenderhane Mosque (Kalenderhane Camii)
The original 5th-century bathhouse on this site was converted in the 9th century into the Monastery of Maria Kyriotissa, then into a mosque. Don't miss the superb Byzantine marble in the prayer hall. ◈ *16 Mart Şehitleri Cad • Map E5 • Open prayer times only*

### 9 Bodrum Mosque (Bodrum Camii)
A working mosque since 1500, this was originally a Byzantine monastery, founded by Admiral Romanus Lecapenus. ◈ *Sait Efendi Sok • Map D5 • Open prayer times only*

### 10 Istanbul University
Founded in 1863, the university moved to its present campus in 1866. Security is very tight, but it is usually possible to walk through the grounds during the working week. ◈ *Beyazıt Meydanı • Map M2–3 • (0212) 440 00 00*

*Beyazıt Tower was built on the site of Mehmet the Conqueror's original palace, which burnt to the ground in 1541.*

**Price Categories**

For a typical meal of meze and main course for one without alcohol, and including taxes and extra charges.

| | |
|---|---|
| $ | under $7 |
| $$ | $7–13 |
| $$$ | $13–18 |
| $$$$ | $18–28 |
| $$$$$ | over $28 |

Havuzlu Lokantası

# Cafés and Restaurants

### 1 Pandeli
Occupying a gorgeous, domed, İznik-tiled dining room above the Spice Market, Pandeli has been an Istanbul institution since it opened in 1901. Book in advance. ◈ Mısır Çarşısı 1 • Map P1 • (0212) 527 39 09 • $$$

### 2 Café Ay
Rest your weary feet and enjoy coffee or a sandwich at this café inside the Grand Bazaar. ◈ Takkeciler Sok 41–5, Kapalı Çarşı • Map N3 • (0212) 527 98 53 • $

### 3 Darüzziyafe
Once the soup kitchen of the Süleymaniye Mosque, this atmospheric restaurant serves first-rate Ottoman food. No alcohol. ◈ Şifahane Cad 6 • Map M2 • (0212) 511 84 14 • $$$

### 4 Havuzlu Lokantası
This is the best of the simple restaurants in the covered bazaar, with excellent kebabs and meze served to the traders as well as the shoppers. Arrive early – it can get crowded. ◈ Gani Çelebi Sok 3, Kapalı Çarşı • Map N3 • (0212) 527 33 46 • Open lunch only, closed Sun • $

### 5 Tarihi Kuru Fasulyeci
This restaurant has been serving up simple, hearty Ottoman cuisine for 80 years. Its speciality is rice and beans, slowly cooked. A good lunch stop. ◈ Süleymaniye Cad, Prof Siddik Sami Onar Cad 11 • Map M2 • (0212) 513 62 19 • No credit cards • $

### 6 Asmalı Konak
The testi kebap – chicken or lamb cooked in a sealed clay pot – is delicious. ◈ Bıçkı Yurdu Sok 29/30 • Map Q4 • (0212) 514 45 56 • $$$$

### 7 Hamdi Et Lokantası
Specialities include erikli kebap (minced suckling lamb). ◈ Kalçın Sok 17, Tahmis Cad • Map P1 • (0212) 528 03 90 • $$

### 8 Café Mimar Sinan
A favourite with students, with kilim-covered benches outdoors. ◈ Süleymaniye Cad, Prof Siddik Sami Onar Cad 37/43, Tiryakiler Çarşısı • Map M2 • $$

### 9 Orient House
A cultural evening offers dinner, Turkish music and belly dancing. ◈ Tiyatro Cad 25/A, Beyazıt • Map M5 • (0212) 517 61 63 • $$$$$

### 10 Kofteci Ramiz
Part of a chain, this grill and self-service salad bar serves good quality kofte and other grilled meats, as well as soups and desserts. No alcohol. ◈ Bab-i Ali Cad • Map Q4 • (0212) 527 13 40 • $$

Recommend your favourite café on traveldk.com

Left **Church of Pammakaristos** Centre **Parecclesion dome, Church of St Saviour** Right **Miniatürk**

# The Golden Horn, Fatih and Fener

THE GOLDEN HORN, A FJORD-LIKE RIVER INLET *that divides the old and new cities of European Istanbul, is enjoying a new lease of life. A major clean-up campaign, including the construction of a huge fountain to oxygenate the water, has begun to banish the foul-smelling pollution that for many years drove people from the area. As a result, run-down Fener and Balat are being eyed greedily by developers, the old-city shore has miles of parks and walkways, and the new-city shore is home to attractions such as Miniatürk and the Rahmi Koç Museum. The Turkish Navy's decision to move out of the old Jewish neighbourhood of Hasköy in 2007 left another area ripe for development.*

Pierre Loti Café

## Sights

1. Church of Pammakaristos
2. Miniatürk
3. Aqueduct of Valens
4. Fatih Mosque
5. Prince's Mosque
6. Pierre Loti
7. Eyüp Sultan Mosque
8. Rahmi Koç Museum
9. Church of St Saviour in Chora
10. Theodosian Walls

### 1 Church of Pammakaristos (Fethiye Camii)

Built by Emperor John II Comnenus in the 12th century, this was the headquarters of the Greek Orthodox Patriarchate from 1456 to 1568. The church was later converted into a mosque, and in 1591 renamed *Fethiye* (Victory) to celebrate Murat III's conquest of present-day Georgia and Azerbaijan. The side-chapel is now a museum, containing a wonderful series of Byzantine mosaics – some of the finest in Istanbul. ◈ *Fethiye Kapısı • Map K3 • Open 9am–5pm daily • Adm charge*

### 2 Miniatürk

Here's a chance to take in all of Turkey's finest sights in a single afternoon – this intriguing park on the shore of the Golden Horn contains 1:25 scale models of the country's most impressive structures, from the Bosphorus Bridge to Haghia Sophia. Other attractions include a miniature railway, model cars and boats, a cinema, a maze and a playground. ◈ *İmrahor Cad, Sütlüce • Map T4 • (0212) 222 28 82 • Open 9am–7pm daily (9pm in high season) • Adm charge • www.miniaturk.com.tr*

**Aqueduct of Valens**

### 3 Aqueduct of Valens (Bozdoğan Kemeri)

West of Süleymaniye are the near-perfect remains of the two-storey aqueduct built by Emperor Valens in 368. Repaired many times in the intervening years, the aqueduct remained in use until the 19th century, bringing water from the Belgrade Forest to the centre of the Great Palace complex, near the Hippodrome. ◈ *Atatürk Bulvarı (north side of Saraçhane Parkı) • Map D4*

### 4 Fatih Mosque (Fatih Camii)

This huge Baroque mosque is the third major building to have occupied this site. The first was the Church of the Holy Apostles (burial place of many Byzantine emperors, including Constantine). Mehmet the Conqueror then constructed Istanbul's first great imperial mosque on the church's crumbling remains, but his building was destroyed in an earthquake in 1766. Today's mosque was built mainly in the 18th century by Sultan Mustafa III. It contains the tombs both of Mehmet the Conqueror and of his wife Gülbahar Hatun. Every Wednesday there is a busy street market outside. ◈ *Fevzi Paşa Cad • Map C3–4 • Open 9am–dusk daily • Free*

**Fatih Mosque**

## Built to Last

There are 11 fortified gates and 192 towers in the Theodosian Walls. The outer wall is 2 m (6 ft) thick and 8.5 m (28 ft) tall, separated from the 5-m- (16-ft-)-thick, 12-m- (39-ft-) high inner wall by a 20 m (66 ft) moat. The walls of Byzantium were built to withstand anything, and did so for 1,000 years. When, finally, they were breached in 1453, the last Byzantine Emperor, Constantine IX, vanished into history, last seen fighting on the wall itself.

### Prince's Mosque (Şehzade Camii)

This elegant mosque and complex of *medrese*, courtyard, tombs and *imaret* (soup kitchen) was built by Süleyman the Magnificent in honour of his son Prince Mehmet. It is one of the first imperial designs by the great architect Sinan *(see p21)*. The tomb of Helvacı Baba is a popular pilgrimage destination. ✪ *Şehzade Başı Cad 70, Saraçhane • Map D4 • Open daily (tombs open 9am–5pm Tue–Sun) • Free*

### Pierre Loti

During his time in Istanbul, Pierre Loti – the pseudonym and nom de plume of French sailor, author and Turkophile Julien Viaud – frequented a café in Eyüp, and the surrounding area is now named after him. Arriving in the city in 1876, Viaud fell in love with a local woman whose name he gave to the title of his novel, *Aziyade*, which chronicles their difficult relationship. The area known as Pierre Loti Hill can be painlessly visited via the cable car, from beside Eyüp Mosque. The fantastic views of the Golden Horn are best admired from the hilltop Pierre Loti Café *(see p77)*.

### Eyüp Sultan Mosque (Eyüp Sultan Camii)

Istanbul's holiest mosque was built by Mehmet the Conqueror in 1458, over the *türbe* (burial site) of the Prophet Mohammed's friend and standard-bearer, Eyüp el-Ensari, whose tomb opposite is the third holiest pilgrimage site in Islam (after Mecca and Jerusalem). The mosque courtyard, where the coronations of Ottoman sultans took place, has intricately painted İznik tiles, and is usually filled with worshippers queuing to pay their respects. ✪ *Eyüp Meydanı (off Camii Kebir Cad) • Map A4 • (0212) 564 73 68 • Tomb open 9:30am–4:30pm • Donations*

Eyüp Sultan Mosque

### Rahmi Koç Museum (Rahmi Koç Müzesi)

This eclectic museum is named after its founder, the industrialist Rahmi Koç. The main part of the collection – a magnificent assortment of vintage cars, steam engines, motorbikes, boats, the imperial railway carriage of Sultan Abdül Aziz, and much more besides – is situated in a 19th-century shipyard building. Outside are aircraft, boats, restored shops and a submarine. Across the

Eyüp Sultan Mosque was flattened in the earthquake of 1766 and rebuilt in 1800.

road, in a restored Ottoman anchor foundry with Byzantine foundations, are model engines, trains, cars and more boats. There is also an excellent café (see p77) and the gourmet Halat Restaurant. ⊗ Hasköy Cad 5-27 • Map B5 • (0212) 369 66 00 • Open 10am–5pm Tue-Fri, 10am–7pm Sat, Sun • Adm charge • www.rmk-museum.org.tr

### Church of St Saviour in Chora (Kariye Camii)
First a church, then a mosque, now a museum, the Church of St Saviour in Chora was built in the late 11th century and restored in the early 14th by Theodore Metochites, who also commissioned the superb series of mosaics and frescoes that he hoped would secure him "a glorious memory among posterity till the end of the world" (see p22–3).

### Theodosian Walls (Teodos II Surları)
Built by Emperor Theodosius II in 412–22 and partially restored, the walls enclosing the old city from the Sea of Marmara (Yedikule) to the Golden Horn (Ayvansaray) are startlingly intact. You can walk sections, especially at Yedikule (see p61), although some isolated stretches are not safe to visit alone. The moat has been turned into one long vegetable garden. ⊗ Map A5

**Theodosian Walls**

## A Day along the Golden Horn

### Morning

Start the morning at **Fatih Mosque**; look out for the tombs of Sultan Mehmet and his wife behind the prayer hall. Walk down to Fener to see the **Church of St George** at the **Greek Patriarchate** (see p76), then cut through Fener's backstreets to reach **St Mary of the Mongols** (see p76). Admire the Byzantine mosaics in the museum section of the **Church of Pammakaristos** and then head towards Edirnekapı to see the mosaics and frescoes at the **Church of St Saviour in Chora**. Take a well deserved break and feast on Ottoman culinary delights at **Asitane Restaurant** (see p77), with a strong Turkish coffee to boost your energy levels.

### Afternoon

Have a look at the remarkable **Theodosian Walls** before heading down to explore the streets of **Balat** (see p76) and pay a visit to **Ahrida Synagogue** – Istanbul's oldest. Walk along the seafront to Eyüp and join the queues paying their respects at the tomb of Eyüp Ensari in the **Eyüp Sultan Mosque**. If your legs are starting to tire, jump into the **cable car** to **Pierre Loti**, but better still, walk uphill through **Eyüp Cemetery** (see p76) and have a cup of tea or two – while admiring the views – at the **Pierre Loti Café** (see p77). If you chose to skip lunch – or perhaps even if you didn't – then dine in style at **Aziyade Restaurant** (see p77) for a perfect end to the day.

Left **Church of St Stephen of the Bulgars** Centre **Eyüp Cemetery** Right **Church of the Pantocrator**

# Best of the Rest

## 1 Church of the Pantocrator (Molla Zeyrek Camii)

This fine, sadly decayed Byzantine church, now a mosque, is all that remains of a once-powerful monastery. ◈ İbadethane Sok, Küçükpazar • Map D3 • (0212) 532 50 23 • Bus 28, 61B, 87 • Open 20 mins before and after prayer times • Small tip

## 2 Aynalı Kavak Palace (Aynalı Kavak Kasrı)

This 17th-century Ottoman palace has an exhibition of Turkish musical instruments. ◈ Kasımpaşa Cad, Hasköy • Map D1 • (0212) 250 40 94 • Bus 47, 54 • Open 9:30am–4pm daily except Mon & Thu • Adm charge

## 3 Church of St Stephen of the Bulgars (Bulgar Kilisesi)

The body of this late-19th-century church was entirely prefabricated in Vienna, in cast iron. ◈ Mürsel Paşa Cad 85, Balat • Map L2 • Bus 55T, 99A • Open 9am–5pm daily • Free

## 4 Rose Mosque (Gül Camii)

The Rose Mosque was originally the 9th-century Church of St Theodosia. ◈ Vakıf Mektebi Sok 16, Fatih • Map D2 • (0212) 534 34 58 • Open prayer times • Small tip

## 5 Church of St George (Aya Yorgi)

This church is the centre of the worldwide headquarters of the Greek Orthodox Church. ◈ Sadrazam Ali Paşa Cad 35, Fener • Map L2 • (0212) 525 54 16 • Bus 55T, 99A • Open 9am–5pm daily • Free

## 6 Balat

Balat was once home to the city's Sephardic Jewish and Armenian communities. Don't miss the 15th-century Ahrida Synagogue. ◈ Map K1–2 • Bus 55T, 99A • Synagogue: Gevgili Sok. (0212) 523 74 07. Open by appointment

## 7 Church of St Mary of the Mongols (Kanlı Kilise)

This beautiful church was built by Maria Palaeologina, a Byzantine princess who married a Mongol khan, and later became a nun. ◈ Tekvir Cafer Mektebi Sok, Fener • Map L3 • (0212) 521 71 39 • Bus 55T, 99A • Open by appointment

## 8 Palace of the Porphyrogenitus (Tekfur Sarayı)

Now just a shell, the Tekfur Palace once housed Byzantine emperors. ◈ Şişhane Cad, Edirnekapı • Map J1 • Bus 87, 90, 126 • Groups only, by appointment with Haghia Sophia

## 9 Eyüp Cemetery

A steep uphill walk leads past hundreds of Ottoman-era gravestones. There's a superb view of the Golden Horn. ◈ Camii Kebir Sok • Map A4 • (0212) 564 73 68 • Bus 39, 55T, 99A

## 10 Azap Kapı Mosque (Azap Kapı Camii)

Architect Sinan's 16th-century creation has an elegant marble mihrab. ◈ Tersane Cad, Azapkapı • Map E3 • Bus 46H, 61B • Open prayer times only

Look out for the magnificent marble floor in the Church of the Pantocrator.

Pierre Loti Café

**Price Categories**

For a typical meal of *meze* and main course for one without alcohol, and including taxes and extra charges.

| | |
|---|---|
| $ | under $7 |
| $$ | $7–13 |
| $$$ | $13–18 |
| $$$$ | $18–28 |
| $$$$$ | over $28 |

# TOP 10 Bars, Cafés and Restaurants

### 1 Café du Levant, Sütlüce
Part of the Rahmi Koç museum *(see p74)*, it serves stylish Gallic cuisine. ⊗ *Hasköy Cad 27 • Map A4 • (0212) 369 66 07*

### 2 Pierre Loti Café, Eyüp
The interior of this hilltop café has traditional tiles, tea-making paraphernalia and exhibits relating to the novelist Pierre Loti *(see p74)*. Outside, the shady terrace offers fine views. ⊗ *Gümüşsuyu Karyağdı Sok 5 • Map A4 • (0212) 581 26 96*

### 3 Cibali Kapı Balıkçısı, Fener
This traditional tavern serves fresh fish and wonderful *meze*. ⊗ *Kadir Has Cad 5 • Map E3 • (0212) 533 28 46*

### 4 Barba Giritli Balık Lokantası, Fener
This two-storey restaurant offers excellent fish and *meze* such as *hamsi* (anchovies) and *ezme* (hot pepper dip). ⊗ *Kadir Has Cad 3 • Map E3 • (0212) 533 18 66 • $$$$*

### 5 Köfteci Arnavut, Balat
Serving up *köfte* (meatballs) since 1947, this little eatery is the perfect place for a traditional Turkish lunch. The doors close when the *köfte* run out, usually by mid-afternoon. ⊗ *Mürsel Paşa Cad 139, Köprübaşı • Map L2 • (0212) 531 66 52 • $*

### 6 Ottoman Restaurant, Fener
Ottoman *beğendi* – grilled lamb on aubergine cooked with cream and spices – comes with fine views. ⊗ *Kadir Has Cad 11, Cibali • Map E3 • (0212) 631 75 67 • $$$$*

### 7 Aziyade Restaurant, Pierre Loti
This huge hotel restaurant serves traditional Ottoman dishes. ⊗ *Turkuaz Boutique Hotel, İdris Köşkü Cad, Eyüp • Map A4 • (0212) 497 13 13 • $$$*

### 8 Kömür, Fatih
Locals flock to this simple café for delicious and ultra-cheap self-service dishes of Black Sea food. ⊗ *Fevzipaşa Cad 18 • Map C4 • (0212) 631 40 04*

### 9 Zeyrekhane Restaurant, Fatih
Ottoman food is served on a terrace with fine views. Booking is advised. ⊗ *İbadethane Arkası Sok 10, Zeyrek • Map D3 • (0212) 532 27 78 • Closed Mon • $$$*

### 10 Asitane Restaurant, Edirnekapı
Dishes with delicate Ottoman flavours are served in a classy setting, with a summer courtyard. Reservations are recommended. ⊗ *Kariye Oteli, Kariye Camii Sok 6 • Map C1 • (0212) 635 79 97 • $$$*

*Traditional Ottoman dishes include minced chicken with nuts and spices; and lamb roasted with onions, dried fruit and nuts.*

Left **Church of SS Peter and Paul** Right *The Feast of Trotters* (artist unknown), Pera Museum

# Beyoğlu

SET ON A STEEP HILL NORTH OF THE GOLDEN HORN, *facing the old town of Stamboul, is the "new town" of Beyoğlu, previously known as Pera – simply, "the other side". The area is hardly "new"; there has been a settlement here for 2,000 years. In the early Byzantine era, Pera was populated by Jewish merchants. In the late 13th century, Genoese merchants were given Galata* as a reward for helping the Byzantines recapture the city from the Crusaders. In Ottoman times, European powers established embassies and trading centres, and Istanbul's commercial centre shifted here from the Grand Bazaar area. Today, Beyoğlu is the heart of modern European Istanbul, its streets (such as pedestrianized İstiklal Caddesi) lined with consulates, churches, stylish bars and all the latest shops.

Galata Tower and the waterfront of Beyoğlu

## Sights

1. Galata Tower
2. Pera Palace Hotel
3. İstiklal Caddesi
4. Galatasaray Baths
5. Military Museum
6. Taksim Square
7. Çukurcuma
8. Pera Museum
9. Church of SS Peter and Paul
10. French Street

## 1 Galata Tower (Galata Kulesi)

One of the city's most distinctive sights, the 70-m (230-ft) high tower was built in 1348 by the Genoese, the Byzantine Empire's greatest trading partners, as part of their fortification of Galata. Since then, the tower has survived several earthquakes, and been restored many times. There are 11 floors. A lift climbs to a viewing balcony, nightclub and restaurant on the top floor – the views of the Golden Horn and the city are fabulous. In the evenings, the restaurant hosts a dinner and cabaret with Turkish folk dance and belly dancing (see p84). ◉ Büyük Hendek Sok • Map F2 • (0212) 293 81 80 • Viewing platform open 9am–7pm daily (dinner show from 8pm–1am) • Adm charge

## 2 Pera Palace Hotel (Pera Palas Oteli)

Built in 1892 mainly for travellers on the Orient Express, the Pera Palace is Istanbul's most famous hotel. British thriller writer Agatha Christie stayed here often in the years 1924–33 and is said to have written Murder on the Orient Express in Room 411. Over the years, the hotel has also been frequented by figures such as Mata Hari, Leon Trotsky, Greta Garbo and Atatürk. In 1981, the Atatürk Museum Room was

Pera Palace Hotel, circa 1929

opened in his favourite room in the hotel, number 101. The exhibit displays many of his personal items. ◉ Meşrutiyet Cad 98 • Map J5 • (0212) 222 80 90 • www.perapalace.com

## 3 İstiklal Caddesi

Packed with shoppers by day, Beyoğlu's main street (see p84) is an entertainment hub by night. It is pedestrianized, but you can hop on the tram, which runs the street's entire length. Be aware that the street numbers on İstiklal Caddesi are in the process of being changed. ◉ Map J6–L4

## 4 Galatasaray Baths (Tarihi Galatasaray Hamamı)

Wealthy İstanbullus come here to be sweated, scrubbed and scraped in one of the finest hamams in Istanbul, built by Beyazit II in 1481 and modernized without destroying the charm. The elegant decorations and fountains make it an aesthetic delight. Men and women bathe separately. ◉ Turnacıbaşı Sok 24 (off İstiklal Cad) • Map K5 • (0212) 252 42 42 (men) & (0212) 249 43 42 (women) • Open 7am–10pm (men), 8am–9pm (women) daily • Adm charge

Entrance area, Galatasaray Baths

Taksim Square

## Taksim Square (Taksim Meydanı)

The busy hub of modern Beyoğlu, Taksim Square was the end of the water supply line laid down by Mahmut I in 1732 – his original stone reservoir still stands at the square's southern end. On the western side of the square is the Monument of Independence, a patriotic sculpture of Atatürk and other revolutionary heroes erected in 1928. • Map L4

## Military Museum (Askeri Müze)

Housed in the former military academy where Atatürk was educated, the museum contains thousands of exhibits telling the story of warfare from Ottoman times to World War II. Chain mail, bronze armour, swords and embroidered tents are displayed in separate halls. One room is devoted to Atatürk's career. A highlight is the performance each day by the Mehter Band, recreating the military music of the Janissaries, the elite Ottoman corps. • Vali Konağı Cad, Harbiye • Map B4 • (0212) 233 27 20 • 9am–5pm Wed–Sun (Mehter Band 3pm daily) • Adm charge

Military helmet

## Çukurcuma

The old quarter of Beyoğlu is today a centre for the furnishings and antiques trades. Its mansions and warehouses have been beautifully restored, and this is now a great place to browse for anything from antique cabinets to modern upholstery materials or 1960s comics. • Map K5

## Pera Museum (Pera Müzesi)

The old Bristol Hotel has been revived as the home of this museum and gallery, privately run by the Suna and İnan Kiraç Foundation set up by wealthy Turkish industrialists. The first two floors display the Kiraç family's collections of Kutahya tiles and ceramics and Anatolian weights and measures. The next floor has an intriguing collection, most of it by European artists, detailing life at the Ottoman Imperial court from the 17th century onwards. The top storeys are given over to temporary shows. • Meşrutiyet Cad 141 • Map J5 • (0212) 334 99 00 • Open 10am–7pm Tue–Sat, noon–6pm Sun • Adm charge

### Military Marches

The Mehter music performed daily in the grounds of the Military Museum has been widely influential. Founded in the 14th century during the reign of Osman I, the Ottoman Janissary bands accompanied the army as it marched to war, intimidating the enemy through the sheer volume of their huge drums, cymbals and zurnas (traditional reed instruments). The rousing military style of Mehter music strongly influenced the compositions of Beethoven and Mozart, as well as the da Souza military marches played by today's brass bands.

Share your travel recommendations on traveldk.com

### 9 Church of SS Peter and Paul (Sen Piyer Kilisesi)

When their original church was requisitioned as a mosque in the early 16th century, the Dominican brothers of Galata moved to this site, just below the Galata Tower. The church was built in the style of a basilica with four side altars. It also has a sky-blue cupola studded with gold stars over the choir. Mass is said here in Italian every morning. Ring the bell by the tiny door (accessed through the courtyard) to gain admittance. ◎ *Galata Kulesi Sok 44, Karaköy • Map F3 • (0212) 249 23 85 • Open 10:30am–noon Sun*

### 10 French Street (Fransız Sokağı)

This narrow street (officially called Cezayir Sokağı) was spruced up and now exudes a Gallic charm – hence its name-change. Several charming cafés, an art gallery and even century-old coal-gas street lamps recreate Beyoğlu's late-19th-century French atmosphere. Its restaurants serve fine French cuisine, and roof-top bars offer views aplenty. ◎ *Map K5*

French Street

## A Day in Beyoğlu

### Morning

🕐 Walk over the Galata Bridge and head up to the **Galata Tower**. Take the lift to the top to walk the perimeter balcony and enjoy the breathtaking morning view. Back at the bottom, refresh yourself at a traditional tea garden before taking a leisurely stroll up **Galip Dede Caddesi** to peer into the tiny music shops and have a go on a traditional Turkish instrument if the fancy takes you. Continue on towards **Tünel** and learn about the Whirling Dervishes at the **Mevlevi Monastery** *(see p82)*. For lunch, try a small street café on bohemian **Asmalı Mescit Sokağı**, or go Gallic on **French Street**.

### Afternoon

Walk up **İstiklal Caddesi** browsing the music shops, fashion stores and **Beyoğlu İş Merkezi** *(see p83)*, then visit the **Church of St Mary Draperis** and the **Church of Saint Anthony of Padua** *(see p82)*. Get to the **Military Museum** in time for the 3pm performance by the Mehter Band. Head to **Çukurcuma** via Taksim Square, stopping off for refreshment along the way if you need to catch your breath. After browsing the vast array of antique shops in Çukurcuma, relax at the **Galatasaray Baths**. Refreshed, wander past the **Galatasaray High School** and cut through to boisterous **Nevizade Sokağı** to choose a place to wine and dine. Fish is the speciality here – start with a few *meze* then try the catch of the day, washing it down with a glass of *rakı*.

Around Town – Beyoğlu

Left **Nostalgic tram, İstiklal Caddesi** Right **Çiçek Pasajı**

# İstiklal Caddesi

### Tünel
The 573-m (1,880-ft) Tünel is a funicular that runs up the steep slope from Galata Bridge to Beyoğlu. Built by the French in 1874, it is one of the world's oldest metros. ⊗ *Map J6*

### Christ Church
The centre of the Anglican community in Istanbul, this church was consecrated in 1868 as the Crimean Memorial Church, using English money and Maltese stone. ⊗ *Serdar Ekrem Sok 83 • Map J6 • (0212) 251 56 16 • Free*

### Mevlevi Monastery (Mevlevi Tekkesi)
This late 18th-century monastery belonged to a Sufi sect of Islamic mystics and is now the Whirling Dervish Museum (Mevlevihane Müzesi). Sufi Whirling Dervishes still dance here. ⊗ *Galip Dede Cad 15 • Map J6 • (0212) 245 41 41 • Open 9am–4pm Wed–Mon • Adm charge; book in advance for dancing*

### Royal Swedish Consulate
Built in 1757, this magnificent embassy was reconstructed after a fire in 1870. ⊗ *İstiklal Cad 497 • Map J6 • (0212) 334 06 00 • Open for special events only*

### Yapı Kredi Vedat Nedim Tör Müzesi
This small art gallery was set up by one of Turkey's largest banks. ⊗ *İstiklal Cad 285 • Map J5 • (0212) 252 47 00 • Open 10am–6:45pm Mon–Fri, 10am–5:45pm Sat, 1–5:45pm Sun • Free'*

### Galatasaray High School (Galatasaray Lisesi)
Originally founded by Sultan Beyazıt II in 1481 to train Imperial pages, this is still Turkey's premier school. ⊗ *İstiklal Cad • Map K5 • (0212) 249 11 00 • Closed to the public*

### Balık Pazarı
A fabulous fish, fruit and veg market by day, by night these alleys are filled with cheap and lively restaurants. ⊗ *Map J5*

### Çiçek Pasajı
Housed in the Cité de Pera (1876), one of several ornate Victorian arcades along İstiklal, this former flower market is now an entertaining (if touristy) tavern quarter *(see p85)*. ⊗ *Map K4*

### Church of St Anthony of Padua
This red-brick Neo-Gothic building is the largest working Catholic church in the city. It was built in 1912 by Istanbul-born Italian architect Giulio Mongeri. ⊗ *İstiklal Cad 171 • Map J5 • (0212) 244 09 35 • Open 8am–7:30pm daily (closed 12:30–3pm Sun) • Free*

### Nostalgic Tram
The horse-drawn tram service that rumbled along İstiklal Caddesi in the 19th century was electrified in 1914 (the horses were taken off to war). The service closed in 1961, but was revived in 1990. Its cheery red carriages have become an icon of Beyoğlu. Buy tickets at either end of the line. ⊗ *Map J5–L4*

Left **Music shop on Galip Dede Caddesi** Right **Ali Muhiddin Hacı Bekir**

# 🔟 Shopping

### Aznavur Pasajı
This Italian-style arcade has been on İstiklal Caddesi since 1883. You can buy a range of handmade goods here, including jewellery, clothes and souvenirs, on any of the nine floors. ◈ *İstiklal Cad 108, Galatasaray Meydanı • Map K5*

### Galip Dede Caddesi
Musical instruments, such as the traditional *oud*, handmade violins and second-hand accordions, are sold at a string of specialist music shops in this small street. ◈ *Tünel • Map J6*

### Çukurcuma
These streets between Cihangir and Galatasaray are the best spot for antique-hunting. ◈ *Map K5*

### Avrupa Pasajı
The 22 shops in this quiet, attractive old arcade carry a fine selection of jewellery, ceramics and other traditional Turkish crafts. There are also quirkier souvenirs such as old prints and maps. ◈ *Meşrutiyet Cad 16 • Map J5*

### Beyoğlu İş Merkezi
A haven for bargain-hunters, the three-storey Beyoğlu İş Merkezi is filled with tiny shops selling mainly high-street fashion labels. Many of the products here are slight seconds or surplus, hence the rock-bottom prices. A tailor's shop in the basement can make alterations on the same day. ◈ *İstiklal Cad 187 • Map J5*

### Mavi Jeans
Jeans made from organic cotton and hip T-shirts are among the stylish offerings available from one of Turkey's most popular fashion brands. ◈ *İstiklal Cad 123 • Map K5*

### Koton
You'll find both men's and women's fashions at this reasonably priced Turkish chain store. Designs are updated regularly and include party- and daywear. ◈ *İstiklal Cad 54 in Demirören AVM • Map K4*

### Paşabahçe
The flagship showroom of one of the world's largest glass manufacturers sells affordable modern and traditional glassware, all made in Turkey. ◈ *İstiklal Cad 150 • Map J5*

### Robinson Crusoe
Pick up the latest Elif Safak or Orhan Pamuk novel – or discover a favourite Turkish writer of your own – at this high-ceilinged temple to the written word. Also carries a good selection of English-language magazines. ◈ *İstiklal Cad 195A • Map J5*

### Ali Muhiddin Hacı Bekir
*The* place for *lokum* (Turkish Delight), this is the Beyoğlu branch of the confectioners who invented the stuff in 1777. Other tasty treats include *akide* (colourful boiled sweets), *helva*, *baklava* and marzipan. ◈ *İstiklal Cad 83A • Map K4*

Left **Nardis Jazz Club** Centre **Al Jamal** Right **Riddim**

# 🔟 Nightlife

### Nardis Jazz Club
There's live music every night. Find a table near the stage and choose from the menu of salads and pasta. ⊗ *Kuledibi Sok 14 • Map F3 • (0212) 244 63 27*

### Babylon
Babylon is indisputably the city's best venue for live music of every kind. ⊗ *Şeyhbender Sok 3 • Map J6 • (0212) 292 73 68*

### Al Jamal
Stretch out on the chandelier-lit sofa seating and splash out for quality belly dancing (including male dancers in drag) and fine food. Al Jamal attracts high-rolling Turks rather than the usual tourists, and offers a more authentic experience. ⊗ *Taşkışla Cad 13, Maçka • Map H1 • (0212) 296 09 69*

### Indigo
With a resident DJ and live guest acts, this dimly lit, super-hip club is for serious lovers of electronic music. ⊗ *İstiklal Cad, Akarsu Sok 1–5 • Map J5 • (0212) 244 85 67*

### Süheyla
Süheyla is one of the best places to hear *fasıl* – the music of the *meyhanes (see p110)*, part Turkish classical, part wild Gypsy, always enthusiastically and noisily greeted by the sing-along crowd. The set menu includes unlimited *rakı*. ⊗ *Kalyoncu Kulluk Cad 19 (behind Balık Pazarı) • Map J5 • (0212) 251 83 47*

### Riddim
Resident DJs and occasional live acts serve up a mix of R&B, reggae, hip-hop, Latin and world music in this slick but tourist-friendly club. ⊗ *Sıraselviler Cad 35/1 • Map L4 • (0212) 251 27 23*

### Garajİstanbul
Tucked away on a Beyoğlu backstreet, this club offers an adventurous program of theatre performances, live bands and other cultural events. ⊗ *Kaymakam Reşat Bey Sok 11A, off Yeni Çarşı Cad • Map K5 • (0212) 244 44 99*

### 360
The beautiful people flock to this rooftop terrace. The club offers lounge music with dinner, and a resident DJ for a funkier dance sound after midnight. The 360° views are superb. ⊗ *İstikal Cad 311 • Map J5 • (0212) 251 10 42*

### Peyote
This popular local venue for alternative and world-music bands draws a hip, young crowd with its low prices and up-and-coming acts. ⊗ *Kameriye Sok 4, off Hamalbaşı Cad • Map J4 • (0212) 251 43 98*

### Salon İKSV
An intimate venue for classical, jazz, world music and other concerts, as well as dance performances and theatre. There are also interesting modern adaptations of traditional dramas. ⊗ *Sadi Konuralp Cad 5, off Refik Saydam Cad • Map J6 • (0212) 334 07 00*

**Price Categories**

For a typical meal of meze and main course for one without alcohol, and including taxes and extra charges.

| | |
|---|---|
| $ | under $7 |
| $$ | $7–13 |
| $$$ | $13–18 |
| $$$$ | $18–28 |
| $$$$$ | over $28 |

Leb-i-Derya

# 🔟 Bars, Cafés and Restaurants

**Nevizade Sokak**
Several little fish restaurants on one tiny street serve the catch of the day, washed down with *rakı*. ◈ Map K4 • $$$

**Ara Café**
There's an intellectual, artistic vibe at this café serving fresh, light food (but no alcohol). It is decorated with the work of Turkey's most famous photographer, Ara Güler. ◈ Tosbağa Sok 8, off Yeni Çarşı Cad • Map J5 • (0212) 245 41 05 • $$$

**Refik**
A true *meyhane* with *meze*, free-flowing wine and a bohemian clientele, Refik is stuck in the past and all the better for it. ◈ Sofyali Sok 10–12 • Map J6 • (0212) 243 28 34 • $$

**Galata House**
This is a true original – a restaurant in a converted British jail. It serves delicious Russian-Georgian-Turkish food. ◈ Galata Kulesi Sok 15 • Map F2 • (0212) 245 18 61 • Closed Mon • $$$

**Yakup 2**
The Yakup 2 has a smoky, alcohol-rich atmosphere popular with large groups. The food is excellent, with a wide choice of *meze*, salads and grills. ◈ Asmalımescit Sok 21 • Map J6 • (0212) 249 29 25 • $$

**Hala Mantı**
Hearty Turkish food such as *mantı*, a kind of pasta, are served at this popular eatery. ◈ Büyükparmakkapı, Çukurlu Çeşme Sok 14/A • Map L4 • (0212) 293 75 31 • $

**Leb-i-Derya**
Start with a cocktail, then sample their speciality, the 40-spiced *steak Mahmudiye*. Come early if you want to eat on the tiny roof terrace. Reservations are essential at weekends. ◈ Kumbaracı Yokuşu 57/6 • Map J6 • (0212) 293 49 89 • $$$

**Zencefil**
Light, tasty vegetarian food in European style is on offer at this lovely little café-restaurant with a summer garden. ◈ Kurabiye Sok 8–10 • Map K4 • (0212) 243 82 34 • $

**Pano Şarap Evi**
Beer and wine flow freely at this popular historic backstreet wine house. ◈ Hamalbaşı Cad 12/B • Map J4 • (0212) 292 66 64

**Changa**
This chic modern restaurant in an Art-Nouveau building serves fabulous Pacific-fusion cuisine. An inset glass floor allows guests to watch the chefs below. ◈ Sıraselviler Cad 47 • Map L5 • (0212) 249 13 48 • Closed Sun • $$$$$

Around Town – Beyoğlu

Recommend your favourite bar on traveldk.com

85

Left **Istanbul Museum of Modern Art** Right **View across the Bosphorus to the Asian shore**

# The Bosphorus

THE BOSPHORUS IS ONE OF THE WORLD'S *busiest waterways, part of the only shipping lane from the Black Sea to the Mediterranean. Just 32 km (20 miles) long and varying in width from 3 km (about 2 miles) to 672 m (2,205 ft), it connects the Black Sea to the Sea of Marmara, dividing Europe from Asia. The straits are governed by international maritime law, so Turkey has authority only over vessels flying a Turkish flag. Navigation can be difficult, since the mixture of fresh water from the Black Sea and salt water from the Sea of Marmara creates complex cross-currents. All of this is fascinating, but to most of us, what really counts is the beauty of the waterway and the historic buildings that line its shores.*

Imposing walls and bastions of the Fortress of Europe

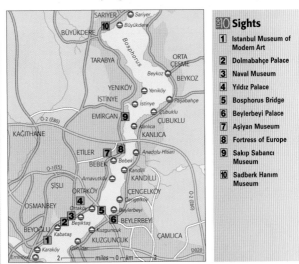

## 🔟 Sights

1. Istanbul Museum of Modern Art
2. Dolmabahçe Palace
3. Naval Museum
4. Yıldız Palace
5. Bosphorus Bridge
6. Beylerbeyi Palace
7. Aşiyan Museum
8. Fortress of Europe
9. Sakıp Sabancı Museum
10. Sadberk Hanım Museum

Preceding pages **İznik tiles on one of the interior walls of the Blue Mosque**

### 1. Istanbul Museum of Modern Art (İstanbul Modern Sanat Müzesi)

This cutting-edge gallery's small permanent collection of modern Turkish painting, sculpture and photography is augmented by touring exhibitions, video and audio installations, and an art-house cinema. ⊗ *Meclis-i Mebusan Cad, Karaköy • Map G2 • (0212) 334 73 00 • www.istanbulmodern.org • Open 10am–6pm Tue–Sun (to 8pm Thu) • Adm charge*

Alabaster bathroom, Dolmabahçe Palace

### 2. Dolmabahçe Palace (Dolmabahçe Sarayı)

In 1853, Sultan Abdül Mecit removed his entire family and government from the Topkapı to this European-style palace at Beşiktaş on the Bosphorus shore (see pp26–7).

### 3. Naval Museum (Deniz Müzesi)

Ottoman Turkey's great maritime history is celebrated in this vividly accessible museum, which consists of two buildings beside the ferry landing in Beşiktaş. In the first block are lavishly adorned Imperial caïques – high-prowed barges that were used for ferrying the royal family along the Bosphorus. The largest, built for Sultan Mehmet IV in 1648, was 40 m (130 ft) long and required 144 *bostancıs* (oarsmen) to row it. The other building holds a selection of figureheads, captured standards, weaponry, paintings and engravings – along with furnishings from Atatürk's private yacht, the *Savarona*.

Rowing boat used by Atatürk, Naval Museum

⊗ *Hayrettin Paşa İskelesi Sok, Beşiktaş • Map C5 • (0212) 327 43 45 • Tram Kabataş then 5-min walk • Open 9am–5pm Wed–Sun • Adm charge*

### 4. Yıldız Palace (Yıldız Sarayı)

Much of this rambling palace was built by Sultan Abdül Hamit II (ruled 1876–1909), a highly skilled carpenter whose former workshop now houses the Yıldız Palace Museum. The park and its pavilions are also open to the public. In the grounds is the Imperial Porcelain Factory, now mass-producing china where once they manufactured fine porcelain. ⊗ *Yıldız Cad, Beşiktaş • Map C4 • (0212) 258 30 81 • Palace open 9:30am–4:30pm Wed–Mon; park open 10am–4pm daily (to 5:30pm in winter) • Adm charge*

Şale Pavilion, Yıldız Palace Park

### 5 Bosphorus Bridge (Boğaziçi Köprüsü)

In 1973, to mark the 50th anniversary of the establishment of the Republic of Turkey, this soaring creation, linking Europe and Asia across the Bosphorus straits, was officially opened. At 1,560 m (5,120 ft) long, it is the world's sixth-longest suspension bridge. Pedestrians are not allowed onto the bridge, so if you want plenty of time to admire the view, cross at rush hour when the heavy traffic routinely becomes gridlocked. ✆ Map C4

Marble fountain in an atrium of Beylerbeyi Palace

### 6 Beylerbeyi Palace (Beylerbeyi Sarayı)

This small, frivolously ornate powder-puff of a palace was built in 1860–65 by Sultan Abdül Aziz as a summer retreat. It was here that Sultan Abdül Hamit II lived out his days in captivity after he was deposed in 1909. You will either be charmed or overwhelmed by the incredible detailing of architect Sarkis Balyan's Oriental Rococo style. Look for the inlaid stairs in the Fountain Room, the hand-decorated doorknobs, the Bohemian crystal chandeliers, the Hereke carpets and the walnut-and-rosewood furniture made by Abdül Hamit himself (see also p89). ✆ Çayırbaşı Cad (next to Bosphorus Bridge) • Map C5 • (0216) 321 93 20 • Bus 15 from Üsküdar • Open 9am–5pm (to 4pm Oct–Apr) Tue, Wed, Fri–Sun (guided tours only) • Adm charge

### 7 Aşiyan Museum (Aşiyan Müzesi)

The poet and utopian philosopher Tevfik Fikret (1867–1915), founder of the Edebiyat-i Cedid (New Literature) movement, built this wooden mansion, now on the campus of Boğaziçi University, in 1906. It recalls the movement with the personal belongings and photos of the members. ✆ Aşiyan Yolu, Bebek • Map U4 • (0212) 263 69 82 • Open 9am–4:30pm Tue, Wed, Fri, Sat

### 8 Fortress of Europe (Rumeli Hisarı)

In 1452, as he prepared for his final attack on Constantinople, Mehmet II built this vast fortress at the narrowest point of the Bosphorus, opposite the earlier Fortress of Asia (Anadolu Hisarı) (see p92), to cut the flow of supplies reaching the city. The

---

#### Princely Paranoia

Terrified both of plots to seize his throne and of seaborne attack by foreign warships on Dolmabahçe Palace, Sultan Abdül Hamit II (ruled 1876–1909) removed himself from the Dolmabahçe to live at the much smaller Yıldız Palace (see p89), the core of which – the State Apartments (Büyük Mabeyn) – dates to the reign of Sultan Selim III (ruled 1789–1807). Abdül Hamit built a sprawling complex of pavilions and villas in the palace grounds, and he supposedly never spent two nights in the same bed. He was overthrown in April 1909.

castle's three main towers are surrounded by a huge curtain wall with 13 bastions. The main tower later became a prison. Following restoration in 1953, the fortress is now a venue for open-air theatre. ◎ *Yahya Kemal Cad* • *Map U4* • *(0212) 263 53 05* • *Open 9am–4:30pm Thu–Tue* • *Adm charge*

### 9 Sakıp Sabancı Museum (Sakıp Sabancı Müzesi)

The summer residence of the Sabancı family of industrialists from 1951 to 1999, the Atlı Köşk (Horse Mansion) is now a museum set in stunning gardens that overlook the Bosphorus. The exhibits include calligraphy of the Ottoman era, and paintings by leading 19th- and 20th-century Turkish artists. The modern extension is a well-designed art gallery housing major touring exhibitions. ◎ *Sakıp Sabancı Cad 22, Emirgan* • *Map U3* • *(0212) 277 22 00* • *Open 10am–6pm Tue–Sun (to 10pm Wed)* • *Adm charge*

### 10 Sadberk Hanım Museum (Sadberk Hanım Müzesi)

A must-see collection includes Turkish embroidery as well as Anatolian figurines, Assyrian cuneiform trade tablets, Hittite coins, and gold jewellery. ◎ *Piyasa Cad 25–9, Büyükdere* • *Map U2* • *(0212) 242 38 13* • *www.sadberkhanimmuzesi. org.tr* • *Open 10am–5pm Thu–Tue* • *Adm charge*

Sadberk Hanım Museum

## A Walk Through Karaköy

### Morning

🕐 Start your day at the fish market off **Karaköy Square**. From here, Haraçcı Ali Sok brings you to the **Jewish Museum** in the 17th-century Zülfaris synagogue. Turn left along **Voyvoda Caddesi**, named for Vlad the Impaler whose decapitated head (it is said) was displayed here. This was the old banking centre and has some fine old buildings. The **Kamondo Steps** lead towards the Galata Tower. Walk back down along Karaköy Caddesi and turn right to visit **Yeraltı Camii**, a 19th-century mansion hiding a mosque and the ruins of a Byzantine Castle.

### Afternoon

Back in Karaköy Square, turn left onto **Rihtim Caddesi**. The **Güllüoğlu** *baklava* shop here is the finest in Turkey, with pastries sold by the kilo; the **Galata Rihtim Köftecisi** nearby offers a healthier option for lunch. Follow the road round between two fine small mosques, the **Nusretiye Mosque** (on the right), built by Kirkor Balyan in the 1820s, and the **Kılıç Ali Paşa Mosque**, built by Sinan in 1580 and named after a famous admiral in Süleyman I's navy. Turn right onto the main road and, just after the Mimar Sinan University building, turn right again. Follow the signs through the old docks area to **Istanbul Modern** *(see p89)* where you can watch the sunset with a cocktail in the chic café-bar over-looking the Bosphorus. Then take the metro to Kabataş and the funicular up the hill to Taksim, for dinner and a view at **Changa** *(see p85)*.

For more on Bosphorus cruises **See pp28–9**

Left **Fortress of Asia** Centre **Çırağan Palace Gateway** Right **Ortaköy**

# Best of the Rest

### 1 Museum of Painting and Sculpture (Resim ve Heykel Müzesi)

Fine art from the 19th and 20th centuries is displayed in the Crown Princes' Suite at Dolmabahçe Palace. ◈ *Hayrettin Paşa Iskelesi Sok, Beşiktaş • Map C5 • (0212) 261 42 98 • Bus 25E, 28, 40, 56 • Open 10am–4:30pm Tue–Sat • Free*

### 2 Çırağan Palace (Çırağan Sarayı)

Sultan Abdül Aziz spent a fortune on this confection of a palace, built in 1874, before pronouncing it damp and moving out. It is now a luxury hotel. ◈ *Çırağan Cad 32, Beşiktaş • Map C5 • (0212) 258 33 77 • www.ciragan-palace.com • Bus 25E, 40*

### 3 Ortaköy

This pretty village beside the Bosphorus Bridge has many waterfront cafés, restaurants and clubs, and a weekend craft market. ◈ *Map C5 • Bus 25E, 40*

### 4 Automobile Museum (SAV Otomobil Müzesi)

Here you will find Turkey's largest collection of antique cars. ◈ *104 Nato Yolu, Bosna Bulvarı, Çengelköy (Asian side) • Map U4 • (0216) 329 50 30 • Open Tue–Sun • Adm charge*

### 5 Arnavutköy

Once noted for its strawberries, the village of Arnavutköy is now better known for the charming *yalıs* (wooden mansions) that line its waterfront. ◈ *Map U4 • Ferry or road*

### 6 Küçüksu Palace (Küçüksu Kasrı)

Beykoz, with two rivers known to the Ottomans as the "Sweet Waters of Asia", was a playground for the Imperial court. This palace was built as a hunting lodge in 1857 for Abdül Mecit. ◈ *Küçüksu Cad, Beykoz (Asian side) • Map V3 • (0216) 332 33 03 • Bus 15 from Üsküdar • Open 9:30am–4pm Tue, Wed, Fri–Sun • Adm charge*

### 7 Fortress of Asia (Anadolu Hisarı)

Built by Beyazit I in 1391, this fortress on the Asian Side is a smaller counterpart to the Fortress of Europe, added by Mehmet II in 1452, directly across the Bosphorus *(see p90)*. ◈ *Map U4 • Boat or road to Kanlıca • Call (0212) 263 53 05 to visit*

### 8 Emirgan Park (Emirgan Parkı)

This attractive park with botanic planting is the venue for the Tulip Festival each April. ◈ *Emirgan Sahil Yolu • Map U3 • (0212) 277 57 82 • Bus 25E, 40 • Open 7am–10:30pm daily*

### 9 Tarabya

First settled by wealthy Greeks in the 18th century, the village of Tarabya has some fine fish restaurants. ◈ *Map U2 • Ferry or road*

### 10 Anadolu Kavağı

This is the last stop for the Bosphorus ferry. Climb the hill to the Genoese Castle, a ruined 14th-century Byzantine fortress. ◈ *Map V2 • Asian side; ferry or road*

Kordon

# 🔟 Bars, Cafés and Restaurants

### Amerikan Pasajı
Choose from among the *nargile* cafés in this alley. Some stay open all night and allow you to bring in food from the stalls nearby. ⊗ *Tophane-Karaköy • Map F3*

### Laledan, Beşiktaş
Part of the luxurious Çırağan Palace Hotel Kempinski, the Laledan serves great brunches in a fairytale setting. ⊗ *Çırağan Cad, Beşiktaş • Map C5 • (0212) 258 33 77 • $$$$$*

### Vogue
Booking is essential at this chic restaurant serving sushi and fusion cuisine, situated on the 13th floor of a tower block. ⊗ *Spor Cad 48, BJK Plaza A, Blok 13, Beşiktaş • Map C5 • (0212) 227 25 45 • $$$$*

### Feriye Lokantası
Picturesquely situated on the Ortaköy waterfront, the Feriye serves delicious Ottoman dishes including charcoal-grilled lamb. Book ahead. ⊗ *Çırağan Cad 40, Ortaköy • Map U4 • (0212) 227 22 16/7 • $$$$*

### The House Café
This café serves unusual pizzas (like pear, roquefort and honey), together with seafood, and brunch staples. Its waterfront decking is a draw in summer, when office workers come for a post-work drink and young people for after-dinner partying. ⊗ *Yıldız Mahallesi, Salhane Sok 1, Ortaköy • Map U4 • (0212) 227 26 99 • Reservations recommended for brunch*

### Angelique
On the first-floor waterfront terrace is the upmarket Da Mario Italian restaurant (summer only), while the second and third floors serve international cuisine and become a nightclub after the dishes are cleared away. ⊗ *Muallim Naci Cad, Salhane Sok 5, Ortaköy • Map U4 • (0212) 327 28 44/5 • $$$$*

### Istanbul Jazz Center
A major venue during the annual jazz festival, this lively place serves food on the terrace and inside. Live music every night except Sunday. ⊗ *Çırağan Caddasi Salhane Sok 10, Ortaköy • Map U4 • (0212) 327 50 50*

### Kordon
This chic seafood restaurant offers stunning views and mouthwatering food. ⊗ *Kuleli Cad 51, Çengelköy (Asian side) • Map U4 • (0216) 321 04 73 • $$$$*

### Reina
Dance to European club sounds at this unashamedly pretentious nightspot. ⊗ *Muallim Naci Cad 44, Ortaköy • Map U4 • (0212) 259 59 19 • Adm charge Fri, Sat; free at other times*

### Abracadabra
Overlooking the Bosphorous, this restaurant has an artistic vibe. Innovative dishes, such as salmon tartar with bulgar, slow-cooked duck and curried banana mousse, are served here. ⊗ *Arnavutköy Cad 50 • Map U4 • (0212) 358 60 87 • $$$$*

Left **Leander's Tower** Right **Doll's house, Istanbul Toy Museum**

# Asian Istanbul

ASIAN ISTANBUL IS PREDOMINANTLY RESIDENTIAL, *but this little-visited part of the city has many hidden treasures.* Around Üsküdar you can see several of Sinan's mosques, take in the jaw-dropping views from the top of Büyük Çamlıca and visit the Florence Nightingale Museum in the Selimiye army barracks. You can wander the markets in Kadıköy and drop into the cafés along Bağdat Caddesi. The pretty harbour at Moda attracts day-trippers, while passengers arrive and depart in droves at castle-like Haydarpaşa Station. Frequent ferries from Eminönü make it an easy hop between continents.

**Tomb of the warrior Karacaahmet**

## 🔟 Sights

1. Leander's Tower
2. Şemsi Paşa Mosque
3. Yeni Valide Mosque
4. İskele Mosque
5. Atik Valide Mosque
6. Karaca Ahmet Cemetery
7. Florence Nightingale Museum
8. Haydarpaşa Station
9. Kadıköy
10. Istanbul Toy Museum

If you are telephoning anyone on the Asian side from the European side, don't forget to add the code: 0216.

### Leander's Tower (Kız Kulesi)

According to Greek myth, Leander drowned while trying to swim the Dardanelles from his home town of Abydos on the Asian side to meet his lover Hero, a priestess in Sestos on the other shore. He is commemorated in the English name for this 18th-century tower on an islet offshore from Üsküdar. Its Turkish name means "Maiden's Tower", in reference to a legendary Byzantine princess who was told that she would die of snakebite and was locked up on the island for her own protection, only for a snake to arrive in a basket of figs. In its time, the tower has served as a quarantine centre and a customs office; nowadays it houses a restaurant. It had a cameo role in the 1999 James Bond film *The World Is Not Enough*. ◈ *Map W3* • *(0216) 342 47 47* • *Tower open 12:30–6:30pm Mon–Fri, 9:15am–6:30pm Sat & Sun; restaurant open to 1am*

### Şemsi Paşa Mosque (Şemsi Paşa Camii)

Legend has it that birds will not land on or dirty this mosque out of respect for its beauty and the reputation of its architect. It is one of Mimar Sinan's last works *(see p21)*, built in 1580 for Şemsi Ahmet Paşa, Grand Vizier to Süleyman I. Made of white stone, it is very modest in size and sits in a picturesque location among the water-front fish restaurants. ◈ *Sahil Yolu* • *Map W2* • *Ferry Üsküdar* • *Open daily* • *Free*

Ablutions fountain, İskele Mosque

### Yeni Valide Mosque (Yeni Valide Camii)

This imposing mosque was built in 1710 by Ahmet III for his mother, Gülnuş Emetullah. ◈ *Hakimiyeti Milliye Cad* • *Map X2* • *Ferry Üsküdar* • *Open daily*

### İskele Mosque (İskele Camii)

This beautiful mosque is also known as the Mihrimah Mosque – it was a present, built in 1547–8, from Süleyman I to his favourite daughter, Mihrimah. Its raised portico offers fine views down to the main square. ◈ *Hakimiyeti Milliye Cad* • *Map X2* • *(0216) 321 93 20* • *Ferry Üsküdar* • *Open daily (closed at prayer times)* • *Free*

### Atik Valide Mosque (Atik Valide Camii)

Set on a hill, the huge complex of the Old Mosque of the Sultan's Mother was completed in 1583 for Nur Banu Valide Sultan, the Venetian-born Jewish wife of Selim II. Sinan's finest work, it retains many glorious details. ◈ *Çinili Cami Sok* • *Map Y3* • *Bus 12C from Üsküdar* • *Open prayer times only*

Şemsi Paşa Mosque, Üsküdar

### 6 Karaca Ahmet Cemetery (Karacaahmet Mezarlığı)

The largest graveyard in Turkey, this Muslim cemetery was founded in the 14th century. It is named after the warrior Karacaahmet, whose highly venerated tomb is here. It is a pleasant place in which to stroll among the old cypresses and ancient, symbolic tombstones. ◈ *Nuh Kuyusu Cad, Selimiye • Map Y5 • Bus 12 • Open 9:30am–5:30pm; tomb open 9:30am–4:30pm daily*

### 7 Florence Nightingale Museum

In the northwest tower of the Selimiye Barracks is a moving tribute to the formidable Englishwoman Florence Nightingale (1820–1910), who in 1854 gathered a group of 38 women and set up a hospital in Istanbul to nurse thousands of Turkish and allied soldiers wounded during the Crimean War – inventing modern nursing practice along the way. The museum contains her photographs and medallions, gifts from Sultan Abdül Mecit, and the lamp from which she got her nickname, "the Lady of the Lamp". The vast, forbidding barracks in which the museum is situated were begun in 1828 by Mahmut II to replace an earlier military building constucted by Selim III. ◈ *Selimiye Kışlası, Çeşme-i-Kebir Cad • Map X5 • (0216) 556 81 66 • Ferry to Harem • Open 9am–5pm Mon–Fri • Free • Visitors should send fax (0216) 310 79 29 requesting permission to visit, at least 2 days in advance, giving names, nationalities, passport details and contact number*

**Bust of Florence Nightingale**

### 8 Haydarpaşa Station

Haydarpaşa Station is the largest station in Turkey and the most westerly train stop in Asia. It was completed in 1908 by German architects Otto Ritter and Helmuth Cuno, a gift from the German government of Kaiser Wilhelm II. These days, the station is the departure point for travellers heading further into Anatolia or across to Syria; trains to Europe depart from Sirkeci Station (see p58). However, a tunnel beneath the Bosphorus is under construction that will link the two continents and two stations. ◈ *Haydarpaşa İstasyon Cad • Map C6 • (0216) 336 04 75 • Ferry to Haydarpaşa or Kadıköy*

---

#### Nursing Pioneers

Florence Nightingale is justly famous for her pioneering wartime work. By contrast, Mary Seacole, born in Jamaica in 1805, is now a largely forgotten heroine. Seacole had nursed family members since her childhood, and at the onset of the Crimean War she decided to offer her services to England. Told that there were no vacancies for nurses, she headed straight for the battlefield, and nursed soldiers injured on the front line. After the war, she was fêted by British high society and published her autobiography, but her contribution has never been properly acknowledged.

---

**Haydarpaşa Station**

Food shopping in the Old Bazaar, Kadıköy

### 9 Kadıköy

Kadıköy, first settled as long ago as the Neolithic era, was the site of the Greek colony of Chalcedon, founded in 676 BC, nine years before the establishment of Byzantion *(see p56)*. However, Chalcedon proved to more be vulnerable to invaders than Byzantion, and it failed to flourish. Today, Kadıköy is a popular and attractive shopping area, but it has maintained its cosy, neighbourhood feel. The lively market area by the docks has fresh fruit and vegetables galore and is a good place to stock up on provisions. Fenerbahçe – one of Turkey's top football clubs – has its grounds, Şükrü Saraçoğlu Stadium, close by, so watch out for traffic jams on match days. A nostalgic tram rumbles through the area down to fashionable Moda *(see p98)*, where you can enjoy a pleasant seafront stroll. ❾ *Map C6 • Frequent ferries from Eminönü*

### 10 Istanbul Toy Museum (İstanbul Oyuncak Müzesi)

Highlights of this collection of toys and miniatures from around the world include a toymaker's shop, a French miniature violin from 1817, and a US doll from the 1820s. ❿ *Ömerpaşa Cad, Dr Zeki Zeren Sok 17, Göztepe • Map U5 • (0216) 359 45 50/1 • Open 9:30am–6pm Tue–Sun • Adm charge • www. istanbuloyuncakmuzesi.com*

## A Day in Asia

### Morning

🕐 Take an early ferry from Eminönü to **Üsküdar** and, from there, sail to the legend-steeped **Leander's Tower.** The top of the tower is a great place to have a mid-morning snack. Back on the Asian shore, explore the mosques of Üsküdar, then make your way south to the majestic **Haydarpaşa Station**, and the **Selimiye Army Barracks** (having faxed ahead as they are still a military headquarters), the site of the Crimean-War-era military hospital and the fascinating **Florence Nightingale Museum**. Afterwards, you may wish to take a contemplative walk among the sombre memorials of the **British Crimean Cemetery** *(see p98)* and the peaceful sea of tombstones in the **Karaca Ahmet Cemetery**, with its estimated one million inhabitants.

### Afternoon

If, after this, you feel like a change of mood, head south into **Kadıköy** with its bustling shops and markets. Stop for lunch in one of the lively bars and cafés of **Kadife Sokak** (Bar Street) *(see p99)*, many of which have live music. Afterwards, catch the tram down to **Moda** *(see p98)* for a stroll along the seafront promenade with an ice cream or, more expensively, take your credit card for a spin through the designer stores along **Bağdat Caddesi** *(see p98)*. Have an early supper at trendy **Zanzibar** *(see p98)* on the quay at Caddebostan before taking a taxi to the ferry terminus at Kadıköy and catching an evening ferry back across to the European side.

➜ If you're planning to have dinner in Kadıköy then return by ferry to the European side, note that the last ferry departs at 11pm.

97

Left **View of the city from Büyük Çamlıca** Right **Waterfront at Moda**

# Best of the Rest

### İskele Meydanı

Üsküdar's lively main square (officially named – but never called – Demokrasi Meydanı) contains the Yeni Valide and İskele mosques and the Baroque, four-sided Fountain of Ahmet III, built in 1728. ◈ *Map X2 • Ferry to Üsküdar*

### Mimar Sinan Bazaar (Mimar Sinan Çarşısı)

This former bathhouse, built by Sinan in 1574–83 *(see p21)* was converted into a bazaar in 1962. ◈ *Hakimiyet-i Milliye Cad, Üsküdar • Map X2 • Ferry to Üsküdar*

### Rumi Mehmet Paşa Mosque (Rumi Mehmet Paşa Camii)

Commissioned by Grand Vizier Rumi Mehmet Paşa and finished in 1471, this is one of Istanbul's oldest surviving mosques. ◈ *Rumi Mehmet Paşa Mah, Eşref Sok, Üsküdar • Map W2 • Ferry to Üsküdar*

### Tiled Mosque (Çinili Cami)

Don't miss the glorious explosion of İznik tiles inside this mosque, built in 1640. ◈ *Çinili Hamam Sok 1, Üsküdar • Map Y3 • Ferry Üsküdar, then 20 mins walk • Open prayer times only*

### British Crimean War Cemetery

Most of the 6,000 Crimean War soldiers in this cemetery died of cholera rather than in battle. The War Memorial was erected in 1857. ◈ *Off Burhan Felek Cad • Map X6 • Ferry Harem then 15 mins walk*

### Büyük Çamlıca

This park is set at Istanbul's highest point, with spectacular city views. ◈ *Map V5 • Dolmuş (minibus) or taxi from Üsküdar*

### Church of the Holy Cross (Surp Haç Kilisesi)

One of several Armenian churches in Üsküdar, the Church of the Holy Cross was built in 1697. Istanbul has an Armenian population of around 60,000 – less than a quarter of what it was during the Ottoman era. ◈ *Selamsız Kozanoğlu Sok 3, Üsküdar • (0216) 333 02 50*

### Moda

One of the most fashionable areas of Asian Istanbul, Moda is a favourite haunt of locals on Sunday afternoons, when crowds flock to its cafés, restaurants, boutiques and ice cream shops. ◈ *Map C6 • Ferry to Kadıköy, then tram*

### Bağdat Caddesi

A window-shopper's dream, it boasts a host of top fashion stores, including Louis Vuitton, French Connection and Tommy Hilfiger – as well as Turkish chains such as Koton. ◈ *Map U6 • Ferry to Kadıköy then taxi or dolmuş*

### Kuzguncuk

Wander through the streets of wooden houses in Istanbul's old Jewish quarter and stop in to see the painted ceiling at Beth Yaakov Synagogue – one of several synagogues on the main street, İcadiye Caddesi. ◈ *Map C5*

Around Town – Asian Istanbul

**Price Categories**

For a typical meal of
meze and main course
for one without alcohol,
and including taxes and
extra charges.

$ under $7
$$ $7–13
$$$ $13–18
$$$$ $18–28
$$$$$ over $28

Interior of Çiya

# 🔟 Bars, Cafés and Restaurants

## 1 Kanaat, Üskudar

This traditional *lokanta* is as popular today as when it opened in 1933. It offers inexpensive but excellent Turkish food and very tempting puddings. ✪ *Selmanipak Cad 9 • Map X2 • (0216) 553 37 91 • $$*

## 2 Çiya, Kadıköy

The kebabs in this informal restaurant are wonderful – the salads and *meze* are worth a look, too. There are tables on the street and the roof terrace. ✪ *Caferağa Mah, Guneşlibahçe Sok 32 • Map U5 • (0216) 418 51 15 • $*

## 3 Otantik, Kadıköy

Otantik offers no-frills, hearty Anatolian cuisine with *gözleme* (stuffed crêpes), fresh chicken, lamb casseroles and stuffed cabbage leaves. ✪ *Muvakkithane Cad 62–4 • Map U5 • (0216) 330 71 44 • $$*

## 4 Kadife Sokak, Kadıköy

Known to locals simply as Barlar Sokak ("Bar Street"), this is bursting with bars, cafés, restaurants and clubs catering mainly to the young. Listen to avant-garde jazz or electronica in Karga, taste fine wines in the garden at Isis, or simply sit back and chill in Arka Oda. ✪ *Map U5*

## 5 Buddha Rock Bar, Kadıköy

This is a popular student bar, offering a range of cheap drinks, an energetic crowd, and live rock and blues alternating with a DJ. ✪ *Caferağa Mah, Kadife Sok 14 • Map U5 • (0216) 345 87 98 • $$*

## 6 Sayla Mantı, Kadıköy

This low-key restaurant serves excellent Turkish ravioli. ✪ *Bahariye Cad, Nailbey Sok 32 • Map U5 • (0216) 449 08 42 • $*

## 7 Deniz Yıldızı, Kadıköy

Allow yourself time to sit and watch the boats from this old restaurant-bar on the seafront. Open all day, the Denizati serves sandwiches and salads, beer and coffee – plus a full restaurant menu. ✪ *İskele Cad, Eski Kadıköy İskelesi • Map U5 • (0216) 414 76 43 • $$$*

## 8 Tarihi Moda İskelesi, Moda

In an ornate little building on the old quayside, this café serves decent food and is a perfect spot for breakfast. ✪ *At the far end of the pier, off Moda İskele Cad • Map U6 • $$$*

## 9 Hatay Meyhane, Bostancı

A hugely atmospheric tavern, its walls covered in fading photos, the Hatay serves a menu with no fewer than 40 kinds of *meze* from the Antakya region near Turkey's border with Syria. You'll need to book a table at weekends. ✪ *Bağdat Cad 526 • (0216) 361 33 57 • $$$*

## 10 Zanzibar, Caddebostan

From Waldorf salad to pizza, the offerings at this trendy restaurant set in a 19th-century seafront mansion are decidedly Westernized. The desserts are scrumptious, as are the views. ✪ *Cemil Topuzlu Cad 102/A • (0216) 385 64 30 • $$$*

# STREETSMART

ISTANBUL'S TOP 10

Left **Customs sign** Centre **Tourists waiting outside a mosque** Right **September in Istanbul**

# ⁂10 Planning Your Visit

### 1 Tourist Offices Abroad
Turkey has tourist offices in many cities around the globe, including London, Paris, Rome, Madrid, Los Angeles and New York.

### 2 Turkish Embassies and Consulates
Several countries have Turkish embassies and consulates. The embassy staff will direct you to the consulate if it isn't in the same building.

### 3 Visas and Passports
To enter Turkey you need a full passport valid for at least six months. Citizens of the following countries require visas, paid for in hard currency at the point of entry into Turkey: UK (£10), Canada (US$60), Australia (US$20), USA (US$20) and Ireland (€10). Photos are not required. You receive a multiple-entry tourist visa valid for three months. South Africans or people with British National Overseas passports must apply for a visa at a consulate before travelling. New Zealand nationals receive a free tourist visa on arrival, valid for up to three months.

### 4 Duty-Free Allowances
Visitors may bring 50 cigars, 200 cigarettes, 200 g pipe tobacco, 5 litres wine or spirits, 5 x 100 ml bottles of perfume, 1 kg sweets and 1 kg chocolate, 500 g tea, 1.5 kg coffee and 1.5 kg instant coffee into Turkey. You may also buy 400 cigarettes, 100 cigars and 500 g pipe tobacco from the Turkish duty-free shops on arrival. Penalties for possessing narcotics are very harsh.

### 5 Travel Insurance
You are strongly advised to take out travel insurance with full medical cover, including repatriation by air. If buying a Europe-only policy, check that it will also cover you on the Asian side of Istanbul.

### 6 Inoculations
Before travelling to Istanbul make sure your basic inoculations are up-to-date, and check with your doctor about hepatitis A and hepatitis B vaccinations.

### 7 Climate
Summers are sunny and dry, with the odd thunderstorm. It can reach 40° C (104° F), but 31–3° C (88–91° F) is normal at noon in August, dropping to around 23° C (74° F) at night. Winter can be cool and damp, with a little snow and likely January temperatures of around 8° C (46° F) at midday and 2° C (36° F) overnight.

### 8 When to Go
In May, June and September the weather is pleasant and there are fewer tourists than usual. In November or February, prices are slashed.

### 9 What to Pack
In summer, pack light clothes for the midday heat with a jacket for the evenings, plus a hat and sunblock. In winter, take a coat and umbrella. To visit mosques, wear long trousers or a skirt that covers the knees, and a shirt that covers the shoulders. Women should also bring a scarf with which to cover the head. Don't forget to bring mosquito repellent and an adaptor plug.

### 10 Choosing an Area
Sultanahmet has charming hotels, great restaurants and easy access to key sights. If you are a night owl, stay in Beyoğlu, where you'll find most of the best restaurants and clubs. For peace and quiet, stay in the Bosphorus villages.

**Turkish Embassies Abroad**

**Australia**
*(06) 295 02 27/8*

**Canada**
*(613) 789 4044/3440*

**Ireland**
*(0353) 1668 5240*

**New Zealand**
*(04) 472 1290/2*

**South Africa**
*(012) 342 60 53/4/5*

**UK**
*(020) 7393 0202*

**USA**
*(212) 949 0159*

Preceding pages **Carpet-seller in the Grand Bazaar**

Streetsmart

Left **Train at Sirkeci Station** Centre **Inter-city coach from Esenler** Right **Ferries at Karaköy**

# 🔟 Getting to Istanbul

### 1 International Flights

The national carrier, Turkish Airlines, flies to and from more than 100 airports worldwide. Other major airlines and low-cost carriers also fly to Istanbul. Flights are 3.5 hours from London and 9 hours from New York. ✈ *Turkish Airlines: (0212) 444 08 49 (central reservations)* • *www.thy.com*

### 2 Domestic Flights

Turkish Airlines competes with domestic operators including Onur Air, Atlas Jet and Fly Air.

### 3 Airports

Istanbul has two main airports, Atatürk International and Sabiha Gökçen. Most major airlines fly into Atatürk International, 24 km (15 miles) west of the city centre, on the European shore. Sabiha Gökçen, on the Asian side, is 50 km (30 miles) from Taksim. A few smaller carriers such as Japan Air Lines (JAL) and Air France fly here, as does the UK budget airline easyJet.

### 4 Airport–City Links

Atatürk International has good transport links. Taxis and hotel buses are fixed-price (taxis around US$15–20). Havaş buses run at 30-minute intervals to Akmerkez (Etiler, 45 minutes) and Taksim (about 40 minutes). An airport bus also meets the boat at Bakırköy and

the metro connects the airport with Sultanahmet and (via the funicular) with Taksim. From Sabiha Gökçen buses link with ferries to/from Bostancı, 14 km (9 miles) from the airport. A costly taxi ride is the only other option, which could wipe out the benefit of a budget flight.

### 5 Trains

You can travel to Istanbul by train – from Western Europe or from Moscow – but it is a two- or three-day trip. Inter-rail, Eurodomino and Balkan Flexipass tickets are valid in Turkey, but Eurail passes are not. ✈ *Rail Europe: 0870 837 13 71 (in UK); 1-877 257 28 87 (in US)* • *www.raileurope.co.uk (UK); www.raileurope.com (US)*

### 6 Train Stations

International trains and those from European Turkey use Sirkeci Station, Eminönü; trains from Anatolia come into Haydarpaşa Station on the Asian shore. ✈ *Train information: (0212) 527 00 50 (European lines); (0216) 336 20 63 (Asian lines)* • *www.tcdd.gov.tr*

### 7 Coaches

Coaches travel to Istanbul from all over Europe. In the UK, contact Eurolines. Coaches within Turkey are comfortable and popular but ticket prices are complicated. ✈ *Eurolines: (0870) 580 80 80* • *www.eurolines.co.uk*

### 8 Coach Stations

Istanbul's main coach station is at Esenler, about 10 km (6 miles) northwest of the city centre. There is a second station at Harem, just behind Haydarpaşa Station on the Asian shore. ✈ *(0212) 658 05 05 (Esenler); (0216) 553 37 63 (Harem)*

### 9 Ferries

Ferries run to Turkey from Italy, Greece and Northern Cyprus. The UKR Ferry Shipping Company runs a regular ferry across the Black Sea from Odessa. ✈ *www.ukrferry.com (UKR); www.ido.com.tr (Istanbul Fast Ferries)*

### 10 Cruises

Istanbul is not on the Mediterranean schedule of all the major cruise companies, but most of them come into the city a few times a year, including P&O, Swan Hellenic, Costa Cruises and MSC Cruises. ✈ *www.pocruises.com; www.swanhellenic.com; www.costacruises.com; www.msccruises.com*

### Istanbul Airports

**Atatürk International**
*Havalimani Baş Müdürlüğü* • *(0212) 463 30 00* • *www.ataturkairport.com*

**Istanbul Sabiha Gökçen International**
*Pendik (Asian Side)* • *(0216) 585 50 00* • *www.sgairport.com*

Left **Licensed yellow *taksi*** Centre **Ferry** Right **Modern tram, Sultanahmet**

# Getting Around Istanbul

### Taxis
A licensed taxi *(taksi)* is yellow and shows a light on top when available for hire. Before you set off, always check that the meter is switched on. Better still, fix the fare before you get in. Ask a local what the fare should be and haggle hard *(see p111)*. There should be no change in taxi prices from day to night. If you cross the Bosphorus, the bridge toll will be added to your fare.

### Dolmuş
These cheap, shared minibus taxis run along set routes, and will only depart when they are full (really full – dolmuş means "stuffed") but will pick up or set down where you want along the route. Ranks have a blue sign with a black D on a white background. They don't operate in the city centre.

### Metro
There are two metro sections: one runs from Levent to Taksim, the other from Aksaray via Kocatepe to the airport. The metro is being extended under the Golden Horn to connect with Yenikapı.

### Tram
The tram is a small but splendid affair that runs from the airport through the old city, across the Galata Bridge and along the Bosphorus to Dolmabahçe Palace, linking to Taksim via the funicular. It is cheap, frequent, air-conditioned and it beats the traffic. It operates 6am–midnight daily. The Nostalgic Tram *(see p82)* runs along İstiklal Caddesi between Taksim and Tünel, and along Bahariye cad between Kadıköy and Moda.

### Funiculars
The Tünel, connecting Galata to Beyoğlu, is one of the world's oldest undergrounds *(see p82)*. A second funicular runs from the Bosphorus shore (at Kabataş) to Taksim.

### Tickets
Buy tokens from kiosks near stations and stops. If you are around for more than a couple of days, get an Istanbul Card that can be used on all buses (except double-deckers), trams, the metro and ferries. Just lower your card to the reader as you enter whichever form of public transport you are taking, and recharge it when necessary. The deposit for the card is 6 TL and you can load money from kiosks, stations or vending machines.
§ *Transport information: www.iett.gov.tr*

### Ferries
The main ferry docks are at Eminönü. There are others at Karaköy and Kabataş. A useful route runs along the Marmara coast to Bakırköy, from where there is a shuttle bus to the airport *(see p103)*. There are regular sailings from Eminönü to Kadıköy and Üsküdar on the Asian side, but the most scenic way to cross is on the Bosphorus ferry *(see pp28–9)*. Called *vapur*, these boats are run by the Istanbul Seabus Company (İDO).
§ *(0212) 444 44 36*
• *www.ido.com.tr*

### By Car
Driving in the city centre is a nightmare. If you have come to Istanbul by car, use the ring roads that skirt the city centre and park as soon as possible. The larger business hotels have parking, but those in the old city do not. To take in sights spread out around the city walls, Golden Horn or along the Bosphorus, hire a car and driver – most hotels can arrange this for you.

### On Foot
You will miss many of the best aspects of the city, such as the small alleys and markets, if you don't walk. Wear shoes that you can slip on and off easily for mosques. Traffic will only stop at light-controlled crossings.

### Tours
There are plenty of tours on offer, by bus, car or on foot *(see p105)*. Look out, too, for short breaks to sights such as Gallipoli and Troy, Edirne or Bursa *(see pp52–3)*.

*There are few radio-controlled taxi networks, but staff in hotels, restaurants and shops are always happy to find a cab for you.*

Left **Galeri Kayseri bookshop** Centre *The Guide* Right **Tourist office, Sultanahmet**

# TOP 10 Sources of Information

### 1 Tourist Offices in Istanbul
There are several official tourist offices and kiosks around the city. Most staff speak English.

### 2 Websites
For travel advice, visit www.mfa.gov.tr (Turkish Foreign Ministry); for the latest travel health advice, go to www.mdtravel health.com. For tourist information, see www. tourismturkey.org (the Ministry of Tourism), www.gototurkey.co.uk (the Turkish Tourist Office in London), www. istanbul.com (the official Istanbul Tourist Office), www.kultur.gov.tr (the Turkish Ministry of Culture and Tourism) and www.nisanyan.net (a listing of small hotels). The definitive US-run Turkey tour site is www. turkeytravelplanner.com.

### 3 Magazines
*The Guide* (bi-monthly) and *Time Out* (monthly) have entertainment and dining listings. *Istanbul Forever* is a bi-monthly magazine available free in hotels. *Cornucopia* covers the arts, history and general culture of Turkey.
🖰 www.theguideturkey. com; www.cornucopia.net

### 4 Newspapers
The bestsellers are *Sabah* and *Hürriyet*. The English-language paper, *Turkish Daily News*, prints entertainment listings. You can get day-old international papers at major hotels and kiosks in tourist areas. 🖰 www. turkishdailynews.com

### 5 Foreign-Language Bookshops
There are several shops offering books in English and other languages, but centrally located Galeri Kayseri is the main English-language retailer. For second-hand books, look in the Book Bazaar in Beyazıt *(see p70)*.
🖰 www.galerikayseri.com

### 6 Maps
The free city map available from tourist offices and most hotels is all that most people need. For more detail, look for the Freytag & Berndt Istanbul City Map (scale 1:10,000).

### 7 Private Guides
Most travel agents and tour operators in Turkey will be happy to provide a private guide in one of half a dozen major languages. The guide should be accredited by the Ministry of Tourism.

### 8 Guided Tours
There are tours by bus, boat, on foot or a mix of them, with full-and half-day options. Plan Tours do an open-topped double-decker bus tour of the city that can be a good way to get your bearings. There are also tours by night and trips to cultural evenings – including belly dancing.

### 9 Government Advice
The UK Foreign Office and US State Department websites give detailed, up-to-date advice on the risks of travel. 🖰 www. fco.gov.uk (UK); www. travel.state.gov (US)

### 10 Finding Your Way Around
Getting around is not always easy – make sure you have full directions and a map before you set off. Write your destination down and show it to the driver or a passerby – chances are they won't understand your accent. Give/get directions by district first, nearest major landmark next, then the street. Once you are in the vicinity, ask and keep on asking.

---

**Tourist Offices**

**Sultanahmet**
*At Meydanı* • (0212) 518 18 02/87 54

**Beyazıt**
*Beyazıt Meydanı*
• (0212) 522 49 02

**Guided Tour Operators**

**Plan Tours, Elmadağ**
*Cumhuriyet Caddesi 131/1*
• (0212) 234 77 77
• www.plantours.com

**Viking Turizm, Taksim**
*Mete Caddesi 18*
• (0212) 334 26 00
• www.vikingturizm. com.tr

---

*Other travel health websites include www.thehtd.org/content/ travel.asp and www.masta-travel-health.com*

Left **Public phone kiosks** Centre **PTT logo** Right **Blue Mosque lit for Ramazan celebrations**

# Practicalities

### 1 Time
Turkey is 3 hours ahead of Greenwich Mean Time in summer (March–October) and 2 hours ahead for the rest of the year.

### 2 Electricity
The current is 220V, and plugs have two round pins. You'll need a transformer to use 110V appliances from the US.

### 3 Opening Hours
Banks open 8:30am–noon and 1:30–5pm Monday to Friday; a few larger branches also open on Saturday mornings. All have 24-hour cash dispensers. Post offices open 9am–5pm Monday to Saturday. Shops are open 10am–6pm Monday to Saturday, with some local stores, malls and large shops open longer. Museums are usually open 9am–5pm (closed Monday or Tuesday).

### 4 Public Holidays
In addition to the five state holidays, there are two principal religious festivals: Şeker Bayramı, which follows the holy month of Ramazan (Ramadan in other countries), and Kurban Bayramı *(see pp46–7)*. During Ramazan, no water or food is allowed to touch the lips during daylight hours. Nothing actually shuts down, but daily life is disrupted (although the parties at night can be spectacular).

The dates of Ramazan, Şeker Bayramı and Kurban Bayramı move backwards by 11 days each year. Christmas Day is not a Muslim festival, but is still celebrated by a large number of Turks.

### 5 Post and Couriers
Post offices and boxes can be recognized by a yellow and blue PTT logo. Stamps can only be bought at post offices and PTT kiosks. The post can be slow, so if you want to send purchases home, use a courier firm for speed – all the main courier companies have offices in Istanbul.

### 6 Internet
Most tourist hotels, of any standard, have a computer with free Internet access in the lobby. Many also offer free Wi-Fi, as do some cafés.

### 7 Telephone
Turkey's mobile phone system is compatible with UK phones, but US cellphones may not work. To save on charges, buy a local pay-as-you-go SIM card or an international card such as sim4travel. Public phones accept credit cards or a phone card bought from a post office. Hotel phones are usually expensive.
🔗 www.sim4travel.co.uk

### 8 Dialling Codes
The international dialling code for Turkey is 90. Istanbul has two area

codes: 0212 for the European side, 0216 for the Asian side.

### 9 Language
In tourist areas there will always be someone who speaks some English. Written Turkish uses the Western alphabet, but there are some differences in pronunciation. C is pronounced *"j"* as in *"jam"*; ç is *"ch"* as in *"church"*. S is as in snake; ş is *"sh"* as in *"shut"*. I is used as in igloo; the dotless *"i"* (ı) is more like *"uh"*. The ğ is silent, but is used to draw out the preceding vowel. So Cağaloğlu is actually pronounced *jar-low-loo*.

### 10 Photography
You are allowed to take photos inside most major monuments and museums, but flash is usually banned and in a few places they also bar tripods. There may be a photographic charge on top of the entry fee.

### State Holidays

**1 January**
*New Year's Day*

**23 April**
*National Sovereignty & Children's Day*

**19 May**
*Youth & Sports Day*

**30 August**
*Victory Day*

**29 October**
*Republic Day*

*Power sockets are often in short supply in hotel rooms, so if you have a laptop, phone and camera to charge, bring a multi-plug.*

Left **50-Turkish-lira note** Centre **ATM** Right **Tipping is customary in restaurants**

# Money

### 1 Currency
The Turkish lira comes in 5, 10, 20, 50, 100 and 200 TL notes and 1 TL coins. One TL is split into 100 kuruş, which come in 5, 10, 25 and 50 kuruş coins. New notes and coins were issued in 2009 when the New Turkish Lira (YTL) became obsolete. You are allowed to bring unlimited foreign currency and up to US$5,000-worth of TL into Turkey, but you'll probably get a better exchange rate if you wait until you are in Turkey to exchange your money.

### 2 Small Change
Make sure that you have plenty of small-denomination notes and coins with you at all times, as few traders seem to have any and many will assume that you don't actually want any change from a larger note. Cab drivers may compound this by sleight of hand *(see p111)*.

### 3 Using Foreign Currency
Most souvenir shops are happy to accept lira, US dollars, euros or pounds sterling. Your change will come in lira.

### 4 ATMs and Banks
There are plenty of banks, but changing money can be slow. The many 24-hour cash dispensers (ATMs) accept all Maestro and Cirrus bank cards with a PIN number, and will also give a cash advance on credit cards. Most are programmed with several languages, but pay out only in Turkish lira.

### 5 Exchange Offices
If you have cash to exchange, the best place to go is an exchange office *(döviz)*. These kiosks are found in all the main tourist areas. They are faster and usually offer a better rate of exchange than the banks. They rarely accept traveller's cheques.

### 6 Credit Cards
Most outlets dealing with tourists will accept major credit cards such as Visa and MasterCard. American Express cards are less popular because commission is higher. You may be asked to pay a premium to cover the cost of the commission.

### 7 Traveller's Cheques
You can cash traveller's cheques at foreign exchange desks at banks and post offices and at American Express and Thomas Cook offices, but few outlets, including hotels, will accept them.

### 8 Haggling
Turkey is extremely good value for visitors. The only exception is fuel, which is very expensive. However, haggling for a bargain is part of daily life, and in places like the Grand Bazaar and the old city it's a necessity. Take your time, shop around and don't feel pressurized. When you are ready, offer half the price and take it from there. Don't be afraid to haggle for a fixed-price taxi ride, either, but don't expect to bargain for goods in upmarket shops.

### 9 VAT and VAT Refunds
VAT (KDV in Turkish) is included in fixed-price goods. There are various rates, but the most common is 18 per cent. Prices may rise if you ask for a VAT invoice – a trader who writes an invoice will have to pay tax. To reclaim tax on departure, shop at places displaying a tax-free sign and get a Global Refund Cheque to reclaim the tax (in cash) at the airport. You may be asked to produce the goods, so keep them with you.

### 10 Tipping
A service charge may be included *(servis dahil)* at a restaurant. If it is not, leave 10 per cent. There are no set rates for hotel staff, but at least 5 TL for porters and room cleaners (daily) is acceptable. Hamam attendants will generally expect up to 10 per cent of the price. Don't tip taxi drivers.

 *Where possible, get your hotel rate quoted in Turkish lira not dollars – you'll save money.*

Streetsmart

Left **Bottled water** Centre **Pharmacy sign** Right **Police car**

# 🔟 Security and Health

### 1 Water and Food Hygiene
While Istanbul tap water is considered safe, it is advisable to drink bottled water. The standard of hygiene in most cafés and restaurants is good.

### 2 Avoiding Bugs
If you are vulnerable to stomach upsets, foods to avoid include salad, seafood from street stalls and unpackaged ice cream. If you do get a bug, don't eat for 24 hours, then try 24 hours on black tea, water, yoghurt and dry bread. If you still feel ill, seek medical assistance.

### 3 Medical Assistance
A pharmacy (eczane) can treat minor ailments and many drugs are available over the counter, without prescription. In every district one pharmacist will be open around the clock for emergencies, with the rota (nöbetçi) posted in all pharmacists' windows. All hotels will call a doctor for you. There are also good free public clinics (poliklinik) for minor problems.

### 4 Hospitals
Istanbul has public and private hospitals – the latter tend to offer a higher standard of medical care and cleanliness.

### 5 ID
It is illegal to be out in public without photo ID. If all you have is your passport and you don't wish to risk carrying it around, take a photocopy of the relevant page.

### 6 Crime
Istanbul has very low crime levels compared to most major cities. Take normal precautions. If you feel threatened, raise your voice and ask locals for help (see also p111).

### 7 Terrorist Threat
Turkey has suffered bombing campaigns by PKK Kurdish nationalists and al-Qaeda. PKK bombs have targeted suburban districts and coastal resorts. Al-Qaeda bombs have been more central, hitting synagogues, the British Consulate and the HSBC bank in Istanbul.

### 8 Emergency Phone Numbers
Emergency service operators may not speak English. Ask a Turk to call for you or contact the Tourist Police.

### 9 Police
The Turkish police are trying hard to improve their image and, as long as you don't break the law, they will be polite and helpful. In tourist areas, report losses, theft or other problems at the Tourist Police office.
🌐 Tourism Police, Yerebatan Caddesi 6, Sultanahmet • (0212) 527 45 03 • Open 24hrs daily (translators present 8:30am–5pm Mon–Fri) • www.iem.gov.tr

### 10 Consulates
While embassies are situated in the Turkish capital of Ankara, most countries still maintain consulates in Istanbul. These should be your first stop in case of trouble – they will assist with missing documents, arrange repatriation, or help you to find legal representation if needed.

## Emergency Numbers

**Police**
*155*

**Ambulance**
*112*

**Fire**
*110*

**General Emergency**
*115*

*Hospitals*

**Amerikan Hastanesi**

*Güzelbahçe Sokak 20, Nişantaşı Map C4*
• *(0212) 444 37 77*

**Florence Nightingale Hastanesi**
*Abide-i Hürriyet Caddesi 164, Çağlayan, Şişli • Map T4 • (0212) 224 49 50*

**International Hospital**
*İstanbul Caddesi 82, Yeşilköy • (0212) 663 3000 or (0212) 468 44 44*

**Acıbadem Hastanesi**
*Tekin Sokak 8, Kadıköy, (Asian side) • (0216) 544 44 44*

*Turkey has no medical agreements with other countries. You'll have to pay for treatment and claim it back on your insurance.*

Left **Turkish women wearing head scarves** Right **"No Smoking" sign**

# ⁑ Special Concerns

### Children
Children are welcome almost everywhere, but give very blond children a hat or they will attract uncomfortable levels of attention. Some large hotels arrange activities for children, and most will provide babysitting on request.

### Babies
Be sure to pack plenty of supplies. You can get everything you need in Istanbul, from nappies to baby food, but it isn't always easy to find them in tourist areas since supermarkets tend to be in the suburbs.

### Women
Some Turkish women wear strappy tops and short skirts, but a growing number are returning to wearing scarves. A few – often Arab tourists – wear full burkas. Western women are seen as free and easy – Turkish men will flirt and younger women will be hassled, but you can usually stop it with a polite but firm response. Wear clothes that cover the shoulders and knees, walk purposefully and avoid quiet streets at night if alone.

### Gay Travellers
Homosexuality is not illegal in Turkey, but it is frowned upon by Islam. There is a thriving gay scene in Istanbul, but locals are not always far out of the closet and there is significant homophobia. Don't be too demonstrative in public and be careful where you go on nights out; some local gay bars are decidedly seedy. But there are many safe venues in Beyoğlu and several useful websites including www.trgi.info.

### Disabled Travellers
On the whole, the city is difficult to navigate in a wheelchair. Older, historic buildings tend to be totally or partially inaccessible and many mosques refuse access to wheelchairs. But the biggest problem is Istanbul itself – with its seven, often steep, hills and cobbled roads and pavements. The Turkish Tourist Office in London publishes a helpful guide to facilities for disabled travellers.

### Older Travellers
You are guaranteed courteous service and assistance – Turkish people revere seniors. At monuments and museums, look out for over-65 discounts.

### Student and Youth Travellers
There are three hostels accredited by Hostelling International. A 50 per cent reduction on entry to museums and monuments is possible with an ISIC (International Student Identity Card). This will also give you intercity train discounts. Discounts may also be possible with a WYSE (World Youth Student and Educational) Travel Confederation card (formerly the FIYTO).
- www.hihostels.com
- www.aboutwysetc.org
- www.isic.org

### Religion
Ninety-nine per cent of Turks are Muslim, but the degree to which they practise their religion varies greatly. There are some fundamentalists, but the vast majority believe utterly in a secular state and are completely tolerant of other religions.

### Smoking
The Turks smoke a lot of pungent black Turkish tobacco. However, smoking is prohibited in most enclosed public areas, including taxis, ferries, trains and also shopping centres. The ban also applies to cafés, bars and restaurants.

### Export Regulations
Any object over 100 years old needs a certificate of permission to be exported. Museums usually issue these on behalf of the Ministry of Culture; a reputable dealer should arrange the paperwork for you. If you attempt to smuggle out antiquities you will find yourself facing large fine or even a jail sentence.

Left **Saray** *muhallebici* Centre **Typical** *lokanta* **fare** Right **A nargile café**

# Eating and Accommodation Tips

## Types of Restaurant

*Lokantas* are day-to-day eateries. They range from self-service cafeterias to full-service brasserie-style places. Prices are affordable, but few serve alcohol. A cheap self-service café may also be known as a *bufé*. The *restoran* is upmarket; if the word *balık* is included, the place specializes in fish and seafood.

## Fast Food

The *kebapçı* serves kebabs and *lahmacun*, a sort of thin pancake with a savoury topping; the *dönerci*, döner kebabs and other roast meat. The *pideci* is the Turkish equivalent of a pizzeria.

## Meyhanes, Nargile and Other Cafés

If you fancy a drink and live music with a meal, try a *meyhane*. If you want to chill out in a haze of smoke, head for a *nargile* café, where you'll be plied with sweet tea while you suck on a hubble-bubble waterpipe. The simple *kahvehane* (tea room) is generally a male preserve, where men, spend their time playing games of backgammon. Some cafés have a separate section for women and families (*aile salonu*) at the back, as do some restaurants. Local bars in central Istanbul are often rather grim. If you want to go for a drink, the best choice is a tourist hotel.

## Vegetarian Food

Few restaurants in Istanbul cater specifically to vegetarians, but while vegetarian *(veciteryan)* main courses are rare, staff are generally helpful and most places serve a selection of vegetable *meze* which can make a delicious main meal.

## Muhallebicis and Pastanes

A *muhallebici* sells milk puddings; *pastanes* sell pastries, such as *baklava*, to take away.

## Choosing Your Meal

In central Istanbul, many restaurants have menus in several languages, but off the beaten track ordering a meal is more difficult. Try the "show and point" method – the waiter brings a tray of *meze* and you indicate the ones you want. For the main course try using a phrase book (*see pp126–7*), or ask your hotel concierge to write down some recommended dishes for you.

## Choosing a Hotel

On the whole, the standard of hotels is high. The government-run star system is based on facilities, not on a hotel's atmosphere or efficiency – so don't rely on stars alone. There are online booking services, many with discounts. The US site www.tripadvisor.com offers honest reviews by other travellers.

## Guesthouses and B&Bs

The dividing line between guesthouse, pension and small hotel is blurred in Turkey. There are family-run guesthouses but – with literally one or two exceptions owned and run by foreigners – there is no equivalent of the British bed & breakfast (B&B), or the French *chambre d'hôte*, where you lodge and dine with a local family. Self-catering apartments are only just starting to take off.

## Out of Season

Istanbul stays open year round, but prices drop dramatically out of season (Nov–Mar, excluding Christmas). Hotels are available for between one-third and one-half of their rack rate. Even shopping prices come down.

## Special Hotels

The charming places categorized as "special hotels" are usually in Istanbul's many restored buildings. They are generally small and often the nicest places to stay. However, rooms may also be small, there might not be a lift, and there may be a shower rather than a bathtub. Service is usually excellent and the desk staff, at least, normally speak good English. Special hotels are also being joined now by a sprinkling of stylish boutique hotels.

*Vegetarians should note that even "vegetarian" dishes may contain some meat – ask if they are "etsiz" (meat-free).*

Left **Fake brand-name perfumes** Centre **Bust of Atatürk** Right **Covering up outside a mosque**

# 🔟 Things to Avoid

### 1 Drugs
Turkey is used as a staging post by traffickers from Afghanistan and Iran, and street drugs, though not a major part of the local culture, are available to those who want them. Penalties for trafficking or possession are extremely harsh. Never agree to carry things home for other people – Turks or fellow travellers.

### 2 Fakes
There is a thriving industry creating fakes, from carpets and Roman coins to Rolex watches and Gucci bags. If you are happy to have a fake and it is sold as such, that's fine. But if you are spending serious money, be sure to do so at a reputable outlet and that your purchase comes with full provenance.

### 3 Unscrupulous Cab Drivers
Most cab drivers are fine, but some, particularly in the old city, charge three times the going rate and try to cheat on payment, pretending, for instance, that the 50 TL note you just gave them was only 5 TL. Inspect every note and say what it is out loud as you hand it over – also keep small notes at all times, as the drivers will rarely have change.

### 4 Prostitutes
Most nightclubs in Turkey are sleazy places. There is a thriving trade in women from former Soviet states (called "natashas" by locals). Chances are that the woman sidling up to you will prove a ruinous proposition, not only in inflated drink prices (over $1,000 for the evening, quoted by some) but also in hospital visits later on.

### 5 Marriage Proposals
Turkish men have a taste for soulful romance delivered with a twinkle in the eye. Enjoy, but keep it light. All too many women fall for the banter only to discover a couple of years down the line that the real draw was their EU or US passport. If you think you have found true romance, take it slowly and make sure.

### 6 Earthquakes
Istanbul is on an earthquake belt and it rumbles regularly: the last major quake was in 1999 when, tragically, more than 23,000 people died in Greater Istanbul. But large quakes are few and far between. If one does occur while you are there, keep calm, make sure you have shelter and drinkable water, and try to make contact with your consulate.

### 7 Pickpockets
Pickpockets and muggers operate in the market streets around the Grand Bazaar. Take the precautions normal for a crowded city – carry a handbag with a zip and a cross-shoulder strap, put your wallet in the front pocket of your jeans, and stay aware.

### 8 Criticizing Turkey
The Turks have great national pride and no sense of humour when it comes to their country. Criticizing Turkey in any way is a huge social faux pas. It is actually illegal to show disrespect to Atatürk, the Turkish government, flag or the security services.

### 9 Offending Islamic Sensibilities
As Islamic societies go, Turkey is very laid back but, while it is not necessary to dress from head to toe in basic black, you should respect the culture and beliefs (see p39). Avoid public displays of affection between couples and, above all, do not make jokes about Islam.

### 10 Traditional-Style Public Conveniences
The number and cleanliness of modern public conveniences (bay for men, bayan for women) has improved hugely in recent years, but there are still some traditional "squat" toilets around. However, most sights, cafés and restaurants have excellent facilities. Tip an attendant 50 kuruş. Carry tissues as there may not always be paper.

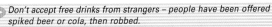

*Don't accept free drinks from strangers – people have been offered spiked beer or cola, then robbed.*

Left **Çırağan Palace Kempinski** Centre **Four Seasons** Right **Conrad Istanbul**

# Luxury Hotels

### 1 Çırağan Palace Kempinski, Beşiktaş

Its terrace lapped by the Bosphorus, this Ottoman palace has a spa, health club and two of the city's best restaurants. Most of the 313 rooms are in the modern extensions, but for a real treat take one of the 11 suites in the original palace. ✆ *Çırağan Cad 32 • Map C4 • (0212) 326 46 46 • www.kempinski.com/ istanbul • $$$$$*

### 2 Four Seasons Hotel, Sultanahmet

The sheer opulence of the Four Seasons belies its past as an Ottoman prison. The 65 rooms are exquisitely furnished with antiques and *kilims*, there is a health club for the virtuous and sybaritic alike, a magnificent glass-roofed restaurant and superb views over the Sea of Marmara. ✆ *Tevkifhane Sok 1 • Map R5 • (0212) 638 82 00 • www. fourseasons.com • $$$$$*

### 3 Eresin Crown, Sultanahmet

Standing on the site of the great Byzantine Palace, this truly luxurious hotel even has its own museum. All 60 rooms and suites have parquet floors and Jacuzzi baths. There are two restaurants, a bar and a terrace with fine sea views. ✆ *Küçük Ayasofya Cad 40 • Map R4 • (0212) 638 44 28 • www.eresin crown.com.tr • $$$$$*

### 4 Ceylan Intercontinental, Taksim

This hilltop tower offers some of the finest views in a city where peerless views are commonplace. It has 382 rooms and suites, bar, restaurants, terrace, health club and 24-hour business centre. Join Istanbul high society for tea with live music in the botanic garden or tea lounge. ✆ *Asker Ocağı Cad 1 • Map B5 • (0212) 368 44 44 • www.inter conti.com.tr • $$$$$*

### 5 Hyatt Regency, Taksim

A resort hotel with 360 rooms and suites, the Hyatt has a health club, pool, tennis courts and business facilities, as well as elegant decor and great views. ✆ *Taşkışla Cad • Map B5 • (0212) 368 12 34 • www.istanbul.hyatt. com • $$$$$*

### 6 Conrad Istanbul, Beşiktaş

Each of the 590 rooms in this huge, S-shaped hotel has a view. The facilities are second-to-none, and the furnishings chic. Its bars and restaurants offer Italian and Turkish cuisine. ✆ *Yıldız Cad, • Map C5 • 0212 227 30 00 • www. conradistanbul.com • $$$$$*

### 7 Marmara Pera Tepebaşı

In the heart of Beyoğlu, with a signature café-restaurant and rooftop pool, this chic hotel has fabulous floor-to-ceiling windows in every room. ✆ *Meşrutiyet Caddesi • Map J5 • (0212) 251 46 46 • www.themarmara hotels.com • $$$$$*

### 8 Bosphorus Palace, Beylerbeyi (Asian Side)

This confection of gilt and crystal on the banks of the Bosphorus is the restored *yalı* (mansion) of a 19th-century Grand Vizier. With only 14 rooms, it is intimate as well as glamorous – perfect for a romantic dinner. A private boat commutes to the city centre. ✆ *Yalıboyu Cad 64 • Map U4 • (0216) 422 00 03 • www.bosphorus palace.com • $$$$$*

### 9 Ritz-Carlton, Şişli

"Ritz" is a byword for luxury, and the Istanbul hotel's 244 rooms and suites more than live up to expectation. There are spas for the women, and a whisky and cigar bar for the men. ✆ *Süzer Plaza, Elmadağ • Map U4 • (0212) 334 44 44 • www. ritzcarlton.com • $$$$$*

### 10 Central Palace, Taksim

This boutique hotel has 49 spacious rooms, with workstations, Jacuzzis and even steam baths. No alcohol is served or sold, but you can bring your own to your room. ✆ *Lamartin Cad 18 • Map B5 • (0212) 313 40 40 • www.thecentralpalace. com • $$$$$*

*Unless otherwise stated, all hotels accept credit cards, and have en-suite bathrooms, air conditioning and Internet access.*

Radisson SAS Bosphorus, Ortaköy

**Price Categories**

For a standard, double room per night (with breakfast if included), taxes and extra charges.

| | |
|---|---|
| **$** | under $45 |
| **$$** | $45–80 |
| **$$$** | $80–180 |
| **$$$$** | $180–300 |
| **$$$$$** | over $300 |

# 🔟 Large Upmarket Hotels

### 1 Germir Palas
It is easy to miss the entrance to this mid-town gem on Üsküdar's main street. The lobby and bars are plush, and the rooms are well decorated with interesting textiles. The terrace restaurant is great in summer, with fine views over the Bosphorous. The street-level Vanilla Café is very stylish. 🛇 Cumhuriyet Cad 7, Taksim • Map Y2 • (0212) 361 11 10 • www.germir palas.com • $$$$

### 2 Taxim Suites, Taksim
These 20 fully serviced suites are good high-end value for those who need a bit more space, giving you a one-bed apartment for less than the cost of a five-star hotel room. With Taksim Square on the doorstep, there are plenty of places to eat nearby. 🛇 Cumhuriyet Cad 31 • Map B5 • (0212) 254 77 77 • www.taxim suites.com • $$$$

### 3 Mövenpick Hotel Istanbul, Levent
This hilltop hotel with 249 rooms and suites offers great views, slick service, good bars and restaurants, and a health club. The top selling-point, however, is the lobby café, with sumptuous chocolates, cakes and Mövenpick ice cream. 🛇 Büyükdere Cad 4 Levent • Map U3 • (0212) 319 29 29 • www.moven pickhotels.com • $$$$

### 4 Radisson SAS Bosphorus Hotel, Ortaköy
The location is the real gem – the peaceful village of Ortaköy, beside the Bosphorus. This hotel has a patio restaurant overlooking the water, and 120 rooms with contemporary decor. Allow plenty of time for taxis into town during rush hour. 🛇 Çırağan Cad 46 • Map U4 • (0212) 310 15 00 • www.radissonsas. com • $$$$

### 5 Polat Renaissance, Yeşilyurt
Near the airport and World Trade Centre, this 416-room hotel has a luxury pool and health club, fine restaurants, bars and cafés, and good business facilities. 🛇 Sahilyolu Cad • (0212) 414 18 00 • www.polat renaissance.com • $$$$$

### 6 The Marmara Istanbul, Taksim
This large, modern hotel on Taksim Square has 376 comfortable rooms with city views, as well as a fully equipped gym, outdoor pool, hamam and several top-class restaurants. 🛇 Taksim Meydanı • Map L4 • (0212) 251 46 96 • www.themarmara hotels.com • $$$$$

### 7 Best Western Eresin Taxim Hotel, Taksim
You can even get hypo-allergenic pillows at this four-star hotel. The 70 rooms and suites include some triples. The lounge bar has live piano music in the evenings. 🛇 Topçu Cad 34 • Map B5 • 0212 256 08 03 • www.eresin taxim.com.tr • $$$

### 8 Swissôtel The Bosphorus, Maçka
Perched on the hilltop, with fabulous Bosphorus views, this is one of the giants, with 585 rooms and suites, wellness centre, shopping arcade, restaurants and rooftop bars. 🛇 Bayıldım Cad 34 • Map C5 • (0212) 326 1100 • www.istanbul. swissotel.com • $$$$$

### 9 Ataköy Marina Hotel
Situated on the shores of the Sea of Marmara in the Bakirköy district, the Ataköy Marina Hotel is only 8 km (5 miles) from Ataturk Airport. Facilities include tennis courts, swimming pool and meeting rooms. There is a shuttle bus to Sultan-ahmet 10 km (6 miles) away. 🛇 Sahilyolu • (0212) 560 41 10 • www.ataköy marinahotel.com.tr • $$$$$

### 10 Hilton Hotel, Harbiye
Conveniently located for Taksim and the business districts, this grand hotel has 498 rooms, fitness centre, tennis courts, two pools, hamam, conference facilities and much more. 🛇 Cumhuriyet Cad • Map B5 • (0212) 315 60 00 • www.hilton.com • $$$$$

Note that all hotel price indications in this guide are given in US dollars, based on an exchange rate of 1TL (Turkish Lira): US $0.67

113

Left **Hotel Empress Zöe** Centre **Blue House Hotel** Right **Yeşil Ev**

# TOP 10 Characterful Hotels, Sultanahmet

**1 Yeşil Ev**
The 19 rooms in this restored mansion vary in size, but they all contain antiques and most face the garden. ⊗ *Kabasakal Cad 5 • Map R5 • (0212) 517 67 86 • www.yesilev. com • $$$$*

**2 Ayasofya Konakları**
The first of the "special hotels" in Sultanahmet, this stretches along nine restored houses and has 64 rooms. The café or restaurant make a good rest point between Topkapı Palace and the Archaeological Museum. ⊗ *Soğukçeşme Sok • Map R4 • (0212) 513 36 60 • www.ayasofyakonaklari. com • $$$*

**3 Hotel Dersaadet**
Its name means "place of felicity and beauty" – perfect for this Ottoman house at the foot of the hill behind Sultanahmet Square (the Hippodrome). There are superb views of the old city or the sea from all 17 rooms. ⊗ *Küçük Ayasofya Cad, Kapıağası Sok 5 • Map Q6 • (0212) 458 07 60/1 • www.hoteldersaadet. com • $$$*

**4 Hotel Empress Zöe**
Old houses surround a lush garden and ruins of a 15th-century bath house at this delightful hotel, supposedly once the home of the Empress Zöe *(see p37)*. Its 25 rooms and suites are decorated in Turkish style. There is an informal bar service in the evenings. ⊗ *Akbıyık Cad, Adliye Sok 10 • Map R5 • (0212) 518 43 60/25 04 • www.emzoe. com • $$$*

**5 Blue House Hotel**
This Wedgewood-blue hotel is in a quiet street behind the Arasta Bazaar, its relative calm broken only by the muezzin, and dervishes whirling in the restaurant opposite. All 27 rooms have superb views – the Blue Mosque (Sultan Ahmet Camii) seems close enough to touch. ⊗ *Dalbastı Sok 14 • Map R5 • (0212) 638 90 10 • www.bluehouse.com. tr • $$$$*

**6 Best Western Acropol Hotel**
The 28 rooms in this restored Ottoman house have wooden floors and painted ceilings – but also wireless Internet and double glazing. The fifth-floor restaurant has fine views. Free airport transfers are offered. ⊗ *Akbıyık Cad 25 • Map R5 • (0212) 638 90 21 • www. acropolhotel.com • $$$*

**7 Hotel Kybele**
Intimate, family-run and friendly, and a couple of steps from Divanyolu, this Aladdin's Cave of a hotel is a treasure trove of Turkish history, with hundreds of lamps and other Ottoman antiques decorating the public rooms, 16 bedrooms and garden. ⊗ *Yerebatan Cad 35 • Map R4 • (0212) 511 77 66/7 • www.kybelehotel. com • $$$*

**8 Arena Hotel**
In an alley behind Sultanahmet Square, this was once the owner's home and is decorated with mementos. Most of the 27 rooms, including four suites, are spacious, with a sea view – and baths (unusual in many special hotels). ⊗ *Küçük- kayasofya Mah, Şehit Mehmet Paşa Yokuşu, Üçler Hamam Sok 13–15 • Map P6 • (0212) 458 03 64 • www. arenahotel.com • $$$*

**9 Sarı Konak Oteli**
The owners of this 19-room hotel pride themselves on providing a "home from home". The café has 360° views, and breakfast is served in a Byzantine courtyard. A 10 per cent discount is given for cash payments. ⊗ *Mimar Mehmet Ağa Cad 42–6 • Map R5 • (0212) 638 62 58 • www.sari konak.com • $$$*

**10 Sarnıç Hotel**
This 21-room hotel behind the Blue Mosque has a lovely rooftop terrace restaurant. Guests can inspect the magnifi- cent 5th-century Byzantine cistern *(sarnıç)* under the hotel. Turkish cookery classes are available. ⊗ *Küçük Ayasofya Cad 26 • Map Q6 • (0212) 518 23 23 • www.sarnichotel.com • $$*

Left column margin: **Streetsmart**

*Unless otherwise stated, all hotels accept credit cards, and have en-suite bathrooms, air conditioning and Internet access.*

## Price Categories

For a standard, double room per night (with breakfast if included), taxes and extra charges.

| | |
|---|---|
| **$** | under $45 |
| **$$** | $45–80 |
| **$$$** | $80–180 |
| **$$$$** | $180–300 |
| **$$$$$** | over $300 |

Hotel Kariye, Edirnekapı

# 🔟 Characterful Hotels Further Afield

### 1 Anemon Galata, Beyoğlu

This 27-room hotel in a restored Art Nouveau mansion is just a short walk from Beyoğlu's shopping and nightlife. ✎ Büyük Hendek Cad 5, Kuledibi • Map F2 • (0212) 293 23 43 • www.anemon hotels.com • $$$$

### 2 Antik Hotel

This comfortable hotel built around a 1,500-year-old water cistern has fine views over the Sea of Marmara and makes visitors feel very welcome. The cistern itself has been converted into a subterranean nightclub and is a popular party spot. ✎ Ordu Cad, Darphane Sok 10 • Map M4 • (0212) 638 58 58 • www.antik-hotel.com • $$$

### 3 Hotel Kariye, Edirnekapı

This late-19th-century wooden mansion has 27 rooms and suites (with modern amenities) and a garden overlooking the Golden Horn. ✎ Kariye Camii Sok 6 • Map J3 • (0212) 534 84 14 • www. kariyeotel.com • $$$

### 4 Barceló Saray, Beyazıt

A comfortable and stylish 96-room boutique hotel just a stone's throw from the Grand Bazaar, this is an ideal place for avid shoppers or for those wanting a change of pace while still being in the heart of the action. ✎ Yeni-çeriler Cad 85 • Map N4 • (0212) 458 98 00 • www. barcelosaray.com • $$$

### 5 Vardar Palace Hotel, Taksim

The public rooms of this former palace (built in 1901 and converted to a hotel in 1989) retain some Seljuk-style decoration. There are 40 spacious bedrooms, fine views from the roof terrace, and a pleasant restaurant downstairs. ✎ Sıraselviler Cad 16 • Map L4 • (0212) 252 2888 • www.vardarhotel.com • $$

### 6 Eklektik Guesthouse, Galata

A funky guesthouse in a restored Ottoman house, this has seven rooms decorated in styles from 60s retro to colonial. ✎ Kadribey Cikmazı 4, Serdari Ekrem Cad • Map F2 • (0212) 243 74 46 • www. eklektikgalata.com • $$

### 7 Hotel Villa Zurich, Cihangir

A short walk from Taksim Square, the 42-room Villa Zurich has a breakfast terrace with Bosphorus views. ✎ Akarsu Yokusu Cad 44/46 • Map G2 • (0212) 293 06 04 • www. hotelvillazurich.com • $$

### 8 Sumahan Hotel, Çengelköy (Asian Side)

Magnificently converted from an old rakı distillery by its architect owners, the 18-room Sumahan on the Asian shore of the Bosphorus is fast getting a reputation as one of Istanbul's best small hotels. Perhaps not the best sightseeing base (transport can be difficult, although the hotel runs shuttle boats), it is ideal for a romantic break. ✎ Kuleli Cad 51 • Map U4 • (0216) 422 80 00 • www. sumahan.com • $$$$$

### 9 Turquhouse Boutique Hotel, Pierre Loti

The Turquhouse covers the whole hill behind the Pierre Loti Café, with superb views across the Golden Horn. It has 67 rooms (some triples and family rooms), in restored Ottoman houses. Most guests are Turkish. ✎ Merkez Mahallesi İdris Köşkü Cad Eyüp, Pierre Loti Tepesi Tesisleri • Map A4 • (0212) 497 13 13 • www. turquhouse.com • $$$

### 10 Bebek Hotel, Bosphorus

Long since one of the favourite drinking haunts of Istanbul high society, where they sipped their gin while admiring their floating palaces, this 21-room hotel has been updated. For a little chic luxury, this could well be ideal. The only drawback is heavy traffic heading back to the centre. ✎ Cevdetpaşa Cad 34, Bebek • Map U4 • (0212) 358 20 00 • www. bebekhotel.com.tr • $$$$

*Note that all hotel price indications in this guide are given in US dollars, based on an exchange rate of 1TL (Turkish Lira): US $0.67*

Left **Side Hotel & Pension** Centre **Apricot Hotel** Right **Büyük Londra**

# Budget and Self-Catering

### 1 Naz Wooden House Inn, Sultanahmet

This wooden bed and breakfast is right in the heart of the old city. The seven imaginatively decorated rooms are very good value, while the roof terrace has views worth ten times the price. ✪ Akbıyık Değirmeni Sok 7 • Map R6 • (0212) 516 71 30 • www.naz woodenhouseinn.com • $

### 2 Apricot Hotel, Sultanahmet

A restored Ottoman mansion with hardwood floors (and ceilings) and traditional furnishings, the Apricot Hotel has 24 rooms, six with either a Jacuzzi or a Turkish bath. Barbecues are held on the terrace in summer. ✪ Amiral Tafdil Sok 18 • Map R5 • (0212) 638 16 58 • www.apricothotel.com • $

### 3 Side Hotel & Pension, Sultanahmet

You can choose between a full-service hotel (half with air conditioning, half with fans), two self-catering apartments and a more basic pension (without air conditioning) – all side by side, and under the same management. You couldn't get closer to Haghia Sophia (Ayasofya), and the views from the roof are simply superb. ✪ Utangaç Sok 20 • Map R5 • (0212) 517 22 82 • www.sidehotel. com • $$

### 4 Büyük (Grand) Londra, Beyoğlu

Faded decadence at its most alluring, the Londra has been an atmospheric and economic place to stay ever since the early 1900s, attracting Ernest Hemingway and other not-so-famous writers since (and featuring in the Turkish hit film Head On). Some of the eccentrically decorated rooms overlook the Golden Horn; many have been renovated over the years. ✪ Meşrutiyet Cad 53 • Map J5 • (0212) 245 06 70 • www.londrahotel. net • $$

### 5 Galata Residence Hotel, Karaköy

The 15 apartments in this vast 19th-century mansion (formerly owned by the Camondo family) have their own kitchens, bathrooms, air conditioning and TV, and are cleaned daily. There's a bar in the basement and superb views from the rooftop restaurant. ✪ Bankalar Cad, Felek Sok • Map F3 • (0212) 292 48 41 • www. galataresidence.com • $

### 6 Hotel Sultanahmet, Sultanahmet

A popular budget choice on the main drag, the Sultanahmet does the basics well, with clean neat rooms and friendly staff. ✪ Divanyolu Cad 20 • Map Q4 • (0212) 527 02 39 • www.hotelsultan ahmet.com • $

### 7 Istanbul Holiday Apartments

Each of these seven restored buildings – two near the Galata Tower, one in Cihangir, Sultan-ahmet, Taksim, Kabataş and one near Beşiktaş – offers several apartments sleeping 1 to 6 people. ✪ Map F3, Map G2, Map C5 • (0212) 251 85 30 • www.istanbulholiday apartments.com • $$

### 8 Hotel Bulvar Palace, Saraçhane

This is a great deal – a four-star hotel at budget prices. The location near the Grand Bazaar is good, and the 70 rooms and 10 suites are comfortable and well equipped. Free airport transfers thrown in on request. ✪ Atatürk Bulvari 152 • Map D5 • (0212) 528 58 81 • www. hotelbulvarpalas.com • $$

### 9 Şebnem Hotel, Sultanahmet

The Şebnem is a small, welcoming guesthouse, with 15 simply decorated rooms (including one triple and one family room). ✪ Adliye Sok 1 • Map S5 • (0212) 517 66 23 • www. sebnemhotel.net • $

### 10 Hotel the Pera Hill, Beyoğlu

The rooms are decent-sized, clean and basic. The location, just a few steps from Beyoğlu, is fabulous. ✪ Meşrutiyet Cad 39 • Map J5 • (0212) 245 66 06 • www.hotel theperahill.com • $

*Unless otherwise stated, all hotels accept credit cards, and have en-suite bathrooms, air conditioning and Internet access.*

## Price Categories

For a standard,
double room per
night (with breakfast
if included), taxes
and extra charges.

| | |
|---|---|
| $ | under $45 |
| $$ | $45–80 |
| $$$ | $80–180 |
| $$$$ | $180–300 |
| $$$$$ | over $300 |

Splendid Palace, Büyükada (Princes' Islands)

# 🔟 Staying Out of Town

### 1 Splendid Palace Hotel, Büyükada (Princes' Islands)

There are touches of Art Nouveau elegance in this very grand *belle époque* hotel, built in 1908 around a central courtyard. The 70 rooms and four suites all have balconies and wonderful views. ◈ *23 Nisan Cad 53 • (0216) 382 69 50 • www. splendidhotel.net • $$*

### 2 Merit Halki Palace, Heybeliada (Princes' Islands)

A beautifully restored old wooden house, the hotel offers lovely views across Heybeliada and the Sea of Marmara from the terrace restaurant, pool and balcony. ◈ *Refah Şehitleri Cad 94 • (0216) 351 00 25 • www.halki palacehotel.com • $$$*

### 3 Anzac Hotel, Çanakkale

Travellers rave about the superb service at this small hotel, well placed for Troy and Gallipoli. There are 25 rooms, a restaurant and rooftop bar (in summer). ◈ *Saat Kulesi Meydanı 8 • (0286) 217 77 77 • www.anzac hotel.com • $$*

### 4 Hotel Akol, Çanakkale

This modern high-rise hotel overlooking the waterfront in the town centre makes up in friendly efficiency what it lacks in atmosphere. It has a restaurant with good food but appalling decor, a rooftop bar, pool, and comfortable rooms with balconies and great views. ◈ *Kordon Boyu Cad • (0286) 217 94 56 • www. hotelakol.com • $$$*

### 5 Otantik Club Hotel, Bursa

A restored Ottoman merchant's house, this offers fresh air and greenery – a refuge from Bursa's crowded streets. The 29 spacious rooms have Ottoman-style decor. ◈ *Botanik Parkı, Soğanli • (0224) 211 32 80 • www.otantikclubhotel. com • $$$*

### 6 Safran Hotel, Bursa

This saffron-yellow converted Ottoman mansion with ten rooms has a somewhat functional, modern interior but could not be more conveniently located, right in the heart of the old city. It has a good restaurant with live music on some evenings. ◈ *Ortapazar Cad, Arka Sok 4, Tophane • (0224) 224 72 16/7 • www. safranotel.com • $*

### 7 Polka Country Hotel, Polonezköy

Paying homage to the village's central European roots, this is like a Polish hunting lodge, all heavy beams, polished wood, comfy armchairs and wall trophies. The facilities include 15 rooms, a café-bar, restaurant and sauna. This is a great place for a weekend escape to greenery and fresh air. ◈ *Cumhuriyet Yolu 20 • (0216) 423 32 20/1 • www.polkahotel.com • $$*

### 8 Iznik Foundation Guesthouse, Iznik

Owned by the people who have revived Iznik's distinguished tradition of ceramics, this basic but comfortable lakefront guesthouse, with only ten rooms, is friendly and convenient for exploring the town and the beach. ◈ *Sahil Yolu Vakıf Sok 13 • (0224) 757 60 25 • www. iznik.com • $$*

### 9 Rüstem Paşa Kervansaray, Edirne

This 16th-century inn was originally built by Sinan (see p21) for Rüstem Paşa, Grand Vizier to Suleyman I. It is still atmospheric, but don't expect luxury – it's fairly spartan. Thick stone walls make it cool in summer, cold in winter. The camel courtyard is a great spot to relax in. ◈ *Iki Kapılı Han Cad 57 • (0284) 212 61 19 • www.edirnekervansaray hotel.com • $$*

### 10 Fener Motel, Şile, Black Sea

This attractive modern low-rise resort hotel, near the beach, has 27 simply furnished stone-built rooms with verandas, and a campsite. ◈ *Balibey Mah, Aglayan Kaya Cad 18, Şile • (0216) 711 28 24 • www.fenermotel.com • $*

---

*Note that all hotel price indications in this guide are given in US dollars, based on an exchange rate of 1TL (Turkish Lira): US $0.67.*

# General Index

Page numbers in **bold** type refer to main entries.

# Acknowledgments

## The Author

Melissa Shales is an award-winning travel writer. As author, contributor or editor, she has worked on more than 100 guide-books. She has written travel articles for many magazines, and was editor of *Traveller* magazine. During 2004–06 she was Chairman of the British Guild of Travel Writers.

The author would like to thank the following for their generosity, hard work and patience during the research of this book: the Turkish Tourist Office, particularly Joanna Marsh in London and İlginay Altuntaş in Istanbul; Emma Levine; and Victoria Gooch.

**Produced by** Coppermill Books, 55 Salop Road, London E17 7HS
**Editorial Director** Chris Barstow
**Designer** Ian Midson
**Copy Editor** Charles Phillips
**Editorial Consultant** Fay Franklin
**Proofreader** Antony Mason
**Fact-checker** Arzu Bölükbaşı
**Indexer** Hilary Bird
**Main Photographer** Antony Souter
**Additional Photography** Philip Entickna, Izzet Keribar, Linda Whitwam, Francesca Yorke
**Illustrator** Chapel Design & Marketing
**Maps** Simonetta Giori, Dominic Beddow (Draughtsman Ltd).

FOR DORLING KINDERSLEY
**Publisher** Douglas Amrine
**Publishing Manager** Christine Stroyan
**Senior Art Editor** Maite Lantaron
**Senior Cartographic Editor** Casper Morris
**DTP Designer** Natasha Lu
**Production Controller** Elizabeth Warman
**Revisions Team** Namrata Adhwaryu, Emma Anacootee, Şebnem Atılgan, Jennifer Barnes Eliot, Nadia Bonomally, Imogen Corke, Nicola Erdpresser, Anna Freiberger, Claire Jones, Batur Kızıltuğ, Shikha Kulkarni, Maite Lantaron, Hayley Maher, Helen Partington, Ellen Root, Preeti Singh, Sadie Smith, Conrad Van Dyk, Ajay Verma.

## Picture Credits

Key: a-above; b-below/bottom; c-centre; f-far; l-left; r-right; t-top.

The publishers would like to thank the following individuals, companies and picture libraries for their kind permission to reproduce their photographs.

ALAMY IMAGES: Roger Cracknell 08/Greece 28crb; ATLANTIDE PHOTO TRAVEL: Massimo Borchi 30–31; AXIOM PHOTOGRAPHIC AGENCY: 54–5.

BRIDGEMAN ART LIBRARY: 32 bl, 33br. CAPAMARKA ENTERTAINMENT GROUP: 84tc; MAHMUT CEYLAN: 47t; 4CORNERS IMAGES: 64–5.

GALERI KAYSERI: 105TL; GETTY IMAGES/HULTON ARCHIVE: 32tr, 33cl; GÖKHAN KALİ: 46t.

ISTANBUL DOORS GROUP: 50tr. İZZET KERİBAR: 100–101. ESBER METİN: 46br. AYLİN ÖZMETE: 46c; pera palace: 79tr.

SHUTTERSTOCK: Vitaly Titov and Maria Sidelnikova 104tc; SONIA HALLIDAY PHOTOGRAPHS: Topkapı Palace 11 bl; STAR GAZETE: MURAT DUZYOL 109TL.

TURKUAZOO: 48br.

All other images are © Dorling Kindersley. For further information see *www.dkimages.com*

# Phrase Book

## Pronunciation

Turkish uses a Roman alphabet of 29 letters: 8 vowels and 21 consonants. Letters that differ from the English alphabet are: c, pronounced "j" as in "jolly"; ç, pronounced "ch" as in "church"; ğ, which lengthens the preceding vowel and is not pronounced; ı, pronounced "uh"; ö, pronounced "ur" (as in "further"); ş, pronounced "sh" as in "ship"; and ü, pronounced "ew" as in "few".

## In an Emergency

| | | |
|---|---|---|
| Help! | **İmdat!** | eem-**dat** |
| Call a doctor! | **Bir doktor çağrın!** | beer dok-**tor** **chah**-ruhn |
| Call an ambulance! | **Bir ambulans çağrın!** | beer am-boo-**lans** **chah**-ruhn |
| Call the police! | **Polis çağrın!** | po-**lees chah**-ruhn |
| Fire! | **Yangın!** | yan-**guhn** |
| Where is the nearest telephone/hospital? | **En yakın telefon/hastane nerede?** | en ya-**kuhn** teh-leh-**fon**/has-ta-**neh** **neh**-reh-deh |

## Communication Essentials

| | | |
|---|---|---|
| Yes | **Evet** | eh-**vet** |
| No | **Hayır** | h-'**eye**'-uhr |
| Thank you | **Teşekkür ederim** | teh-shek-**kewr** **eh**-deh-reem |
| Please | **Lütfen** | **lewt**-fen |
| Excuse me | **Affedersiniz** | **af**-feh-der-see-neez |
| Hello | **Merhaba** | **mer**-ha-ba |
| Goodbye | **Hoşça kalın** | hosh-**cha ka**-luhn |
| Morning | **Sabah** | sa-**bah** |
| Afternoon | **Öğleden sonra** | ur-leh-den **son**-ra |
| Evening | **Akşam** | ak-**sham** |
| Yesterday | **Dün** | dewn |
| Today | **Bugün** | **boo**-gewn |
| Tomorrow | **Yarın** | **ya**-ruhn |
| Here | **Burada** | **boo**-ra-da |
| There | **Şurada** | **shoo**-ra-da |
| What? | **Ne?** | neh |
| When? | **Ne zaman?** | **neh za**-man |
| Where? | **Nerede** | **neh**-reh-deh |

## Useful Phrases

| | | |
|---|---|---|
| Pleased to meet you | **Memnun oldum** | mem-**noon** **ol**-doom |
| Where is/are? | **nerede?** | **neh**-reh-deh |
| How far is it to? | **ne kadar uzakta?** | **neh ka**-dar oo-zak-ta |
| Do you speak English? | **İngilizce biliyor musunuz?** | een-gee-**leez**-jeh bee-**lee**-yor moo-soo-nooz? |
| I don't understand | **Anlamıyorum** | an-**la**-muh-yo-room |
| Can you help me? | **Bana yardım edebilir misiniz?** | ba-**na** yar-**duhm** eh-deh-bee-**leer** mee-see-neez? |
| I don't want | **istemiyorum** | ees-**teh**-mee-yo-room |

## Useful Words

| | | |
|---|---|---|
| big | **büyük** | bew-**yewk** |
| small | **küçük** | kew-**chewk** |
| hot | **sıcak** | suh-**jak** |
| cold | **soğuk** | soh-**ook** |
| good/well | **iyi** | ee-**yee** |
| bad | **kötü** | kur-**tew** |
| open | **acık** | a-**chuhk** |
| closed | **kapalı** | ka-pa-**luh** |
| left | **sol** | sol |
| right | **sağ** | saa |
| near | **yakın** | ya-**kuhn** |
| far | **uzak** | oo-**zak** |
| up | **yukarı** | yoo-ka-**ruh** |
| down | **aşağı** | a-shah-**uh** |
| early | **erken** | er-**ken** |
| late | **geç** | gech |
| toilets | **tuvaletler** | too-va-let-**ler** |

## Shopping

| | | |
|---|---|---|
| How much is this? | **Bu kaç lira?** | boo **kach** lee-ra |
| I would like | **istiyorum** | ees-**tee**-yo-room |
| Do you have? | **var mı?** | var muh? |
| Do you take credit cards? | **Kredi kartı kabul ediyor musunuz?** | **kreh**-dee **kar**-tuh ka-**bool** eh-**dee**-yor moo-soo-nooz? |
| What time do you open/close? | **Saat kaçta açılıyor/ kapanıyor?** | Sa-**at** kach-**ta** a-chuh-**luh**-yor/ ka-pa-**nuh**-yor |
| this one | **bunu** | boo-**noo** |
| that one | **şunu** | shoo-**noo** |
| expensive | **pahalı** | pa-ha-**luh** |
| cheap | **ucuz** | oo-**jooz** |
| size (clothes) | **beden** | beh-**den** |
| size (shoes) | **numara** | noo-ma-**ra** |
| white | **beyaz** | bay-**yaz** |
| black | **siyah** | see-**yah** |
| red | **kırmızı** | kuhr-muh-**zuh** |
| yellow | **sarı** | sa-**ruh** |
| green | **yeşil** | yeh-**sheel** |
| blue | **mavi** | ma-**vee** |
| brown | **kahverengi** | kah-**veh**-ren-gee |
| shop | **dükkan** | dewk-**kan** |
| That's my last offer | **Daha fazla veremem** | da-**ha faz**-la veh-**reh**-mem |

## Types of Shop

| | | |
|---|---|---|
| antiques shop | **antikacı** | an-**tee**-ka-juh |
| bakery | **fırın** | fuh-**ruhn** |
| bank | **banka** | **ban**-ka |
| book shop | **kitapçı** | kee-tap-**chuh** |
| cake shop | **pastane** | pas-ta-**neh** |
| chemist's/pharmacy | **eczane** | ej-za-**neh** |
| greengrocer's | **manav** | ma-**nav** |
| leather shop | **derici** | deh-ree-**jee** |
| market/bazaar | **çarşı/pazar** | char-**shuh**/pa-**zar** |
| newsstand | **gazeteci** | ga-**zeh**-teh-jee |
| post office | **postane** | pos-ta-**neh** |
| shoe shop | **ayakkabıcı** | 'eye'-**yak**-ka-buh-juh |
| supermarket | **süpermarket** | sew-per-mar-**ket** |
| tailor | **terzi** | ter-**zee** |
| travel agency | **seyahat acentesi** | say-ya-**hat** a-jen-teh-**see** |

## Sightseeing

| | | |
|---|---|---|
| castle | **hisar** | hee-**sar** |
| church | **kilise** | kee-**lee**-seh |
| mosque | **cami** | **ja**-mee |
| museum | **müze** | **mew**-zeh |
| palace | **saray** | sar-'**eye**' |
| park | **park** | park |
| square | **meydan** | may-**dan** |
| information office | **danışma bürosu** | da-nuhsh-**mah** **bew**-ro-soo |
| Turkish bath | **hamam** | ha-**mam** |

## Transport

| | | |
|---|---|---|
| airport | **havalimanı** | ha-**va**-lee-ma-nuh |
| bus/coach | **otobüs** | o-to-**bewss** |
| bus stop | **otobüs durağı** | o-to-**bewss** doo-**ra**-uh |
| coach station | **otogar** | o-to-**gar** |
| dolmuş | **dolmuş** | dol-**moosh** |
| fare | **ücret** | ewj-**ret** |
| ferry | **vapur** | va-**poor** |

| sea bus | deniz | deh-**neez** |
| | otobüsü | o-to-**bew**-sew |
| station | istasyon | ees-tas-**yon** |
| taxi | taksi | **tak**-see |
| ticket | bilet | bee-**let** |
| ticket office | bilet | bee-**let** |
| | gişesi | gee-sheh-**see** |
| timetable | tarife | ta-ree-**feh** |

## Staying in a Hotel

| Do you have a | Boş odanız | bosh o-da-**nuhz** |
| vacant room? | var mı? | var muh? |
| double room | iki | ee-**kee** |
| | kişilik | kee-shee-**leek** |
| | bir oda | beer o-**da** |
| twin room | çift yataklı | cheeft ya-**tak**-luh |
| | bir oda | beer o-**da** |
| for one person | tek kişilik | tek kee-shee-**leek** |
| room with | banyolu | **ban**-yo-loo |
| a bath | bir oda | beer o-**da** |
| shower | duş | doosh |
| porter | komi | ko-**mee** |
| key | anahtar | a-nah-**tar** |
| room service | oda servisi | o-da ser-vee-**see** |
| I have a | Rezervasyonum | reh-zer-vas- |
| reservation | var | yo-**noom** var |

## Eating Out

| I want to | Bir masa | beer **ma**-sa |
| reserve | ayırtmak | 'eye'-uhrt-**mak** |
| a table | istiyorum | ees-**tee**-yo-room |
| The bill please | Hesap lütfen | heh-**sap** lewt-fen |
| I am a | Et yemiyorum | et **yeh**-mee-yo- |
| vegetarian | | room |
| restaurant | lokanta | lo-**kan**-ta |
| waiter | garson | gar-**son** |
| menu | yemek | ye-**mek** |
| | listesi | lees-teh-see |
| wine list | şarap | sha-**rap** |
| | listesi | lees-teh-see |
| breakfast | kahvaltı | kah-val-**tuh** |
| lunch | öğle | ur-**leh** |
| | yemeği | yeh-meh-**ee** |
| dinner | akşam yemeği | ak-**sham** |
| | | yeh-meh-**ee** |
| starter | meze | **meh**-zeh |
| main course | ana yemek | a-**na** yeh-**mek** |
| dessert | tatlı | tat-**luh** |
| rare | az pişmiş | **az** peesh-meesh |
| well done | iyi | ee-**yee** |
| | pişmiş | peesh-meesh |
| glass | bardak | bar-**dak** |
| bottle | şişe | shee-**sheh** |
| knife | bıçak | buh-**chak** |
| fork | çatal | cha-**tal** |
| spoon | kaşık | ka-**shuhk** |

## Menu Decoder

| balık | ba-**luhk** | fish |
| bira | **bee**-ra | beer |
| bonfile | **bon**-fee-leh | fillet steak |
| buz | booz | ice |
| çay | ch-'eye' | tea |
| çorba | chor-**ba** | soup |
| dana eti | da-**na** eh-**tee** | veal |
| dondurma | don-door-**ma** | ice cream |
| ekmek | ek-**mek** | bread |
| et | et | meat |
| fırında | fuh-ruhn-**da** | roast |
| fıstık | fuhs-**tuhk** | pistachio nuts |
| gazoz | ga-**zoz** | fizzy drink |
| hurma | hoor-**ma** | dates |
| içki | eech-**kee** | alcohol |
| incir | een-**jeer** | figs |
| ızgara | uhz-**ga**-ra | charcoal grilled |
| kahve | kah-**veh** | coffee |
| kara biber | ka-**ra** bee-**ber** | black pepper |
| karışık | ka-ruh-**shuhk** | mixed |

| kaymak | k-'eye'-**mak** | cream |
| kıyma | kuhy-**ma** | minced meat |
| köfte | kurf-**teh** | meatballs |
| kuzu eti | koo-**zoo** eh-**tee** | lamb |
| lokum | lo-**koom** | Turkish delight |
| maden suyu | ma-**den** soo-**yoo** | mineral water (fizzy) |
| meyve suyu | may-**veh** soo-**yoo** | fruit juice |
| midye | **meed**-yeh | mussels |
| patlıcan | pat-luh-**jan** | aubergine |
| peynir | pay-**neer** | cheese |
| pilav | pee-**lav** | rice |
| piliç | pee-**leech** | roast chicken |
| şarap | sha-**rap** | wine |
| şeker | sheh-**ker** | sugar |
| su | soo | water |
| süt | sewt | milk |
| tavuk | ta-**vook** | chicken |
| tereyağı | teh-**reh**-yah-uh | butter |
| tuz | tooz | salt |
| yoğurt | yoh-**urt** | yoghurt |
| yumurta | yoo-moor-**ta** | egg |
| zeytinyağı | zay-**teen**-yah-uh | olive oil |

## Numbers

| 0 | sıfır | **suh**-fuhr |
| 1 | bir | beer |
| 2 | iki | ee-**kee** |
| 3 | üç | ewch |
| 4 | dört | durt |
| 5 | beş | besh |
| 6 | altı | al-**tuh** |
| 7 | yedi | yeh-**dee** |
| 8 | sekiz | seh-**keez** |
| 9 | dokuz | doh-**kooz** |
| 10 | on | on |
| 11 | on bir | on beer |
| 12 | on iki | on ee-kee |
| 13 | on üç | on ewch |
| 14 | on dört | on durt |
| 15 | on beş | on besh |
| 16 | on altı | on al-tuh |
| 17 | on yedi | on yeh-dee |
| 18 | on sekiz | on seh-keez |
| 19 | on dokuz | on doh-kooz |
| 20 | yirmi | yeer-**mee** |
| 21 | yirmi bir | yeer-mee **beer** |
| 30 | otuz | o-**tooz** |
| 40 | kırk | kuhrk |
| 50 | elli | eh-**lee** |
| 60 | altmış | alt-**muhsh** |
| 70 | yetmiş | yet-**meesh** |
| 80 | seksen | sek-**sen** |
| 90 | doksan | dok-**san** |
| 100 | yüz | yewz |
| 200 | iki yüz | ee-**kee** yewz |
| 1,000 | bin | been |
| 100,000 | yüz bin | **yewz** been |
| 1,000,000 | bir milyon | **beer** meel-**yon** |

## Time

| one minute | bir dakika | beer da-**kee**-ka |
| one hour | bir saat | beer sa-at |
| half an hour | yarım saat | ya-**ruhm sa**-at |
| day | gün | gewn |
| week | hafta | haf-**ta** |
| month | ay | 'eye' |
| year | yıl | yuhl |
| Sunday | pazar | pa-**zar** |
| Monday | pazartesi | pa-**zar**-teh-see |
| Tuesday | salı | sa-**luh** |
| Wednesday | çarşamba | char-sham-**ba** |
| Thursday | perşembe | per-shem-**beh** |
| Friday | cuma | joo-**ma** |
| Saturday | cumartesi | joo-**mar**-teh-see |

# Selected Street Index

# Mennonite in a
# Little Black Dress

*A Memoir of Going Home*

கூஒை

Rhoda Janzen

Atlantic Books
LONDON

First published the United States of America in 2009
by Henry Holt and Company, LLC.

First published in Great Britain in paperback and export and
airside trade paperback in 2011 by Atlantic Books, an imprint of
Atlantic Books Ltd.

1 3 5 7 9 10 8 6 4 2

A CIP catalogue record for this book is available from the British Library.

Paperback ISBN: 978 0 85789 031 3
Export and airside ISBN: 978 0 85789 040 5

Printed in Great Britain

Atlantic Books
An imprint of Atlantic Books Ltd
Ormond House
26–27 Boswell Street
London WC1N 3JZ

www.atlantic-books.co.uk

∞

*For Mary Loewen Janzen*

# CONTENTS

# Mennonite in a Little Black Dress

∞

# ONE

∞

# The Bridegroom Cousin

The year I turned forty-three was the year I realized I should have never taken my Mennonite genes for granted. I'd long assumed that I had been genetically scripted to robust physical health, like my mother, who never even catches a head cold. All of my relatives on her side, the Loewens, enjoy preternaturally good health, unless you count breast cancer and polio. The polio is pretty much a done deal, thanks to Jonas Salk and his talent for globally useful vaccinations. Yet in the days before Jonas Salk, when my mother was a girl, polio crippled her younger brother Abe and also withered the arm of her closest sister Gertrude. Trude bravely went on to raise two kids one-armed, and to name her withered arm Stinky.

> _____ Yes, I think "Stinky" is a cute name for a withered arm!
>
> _____ No, I'd prefer to name my withered arm something with a little more dignity, such as Reynaldo.

Although breast cancer also runs in my family, it hasn't played a significant role. It comes to us late in life, shriveling a tit or two, and then often subsiding under the composite resistance of chemo and buttermilk. That is, it would shrivel our tits if we had tits. Which we don't.

As adolescents, my sister Hannah and I were naturally anxious to see if we would turn out more like our mother or our father. There was a lot at stake. Having endured a painfully uncool childhood, we realized that our genetic heritage positioned us on a precarious cusp. Dad was handsome but grouchy; Mom was plain but cheerful. Would we be able to pass muster in normal society, or would our Mennonite history forever doom us to outsider status?

My father, once the head of the North American Mennonite Conference for Canada and the United States, is the Mennonite equivalent of the pope, but in plaid shorts and black dress socks pulled up snugly along the calf. In the complex moral universe that is Mennonite adulthood, a Mennonite can be good-looking and still have no sartorial taste whatsoever. My father may actually be unaware that he is good-looking. He is a theologian who believes in a loving God, a servant heart, and a senior discount. Would God be pleased if we spent an unnecessary thirty-one cents at McDonald's? I think not.

At six foot five and classically handsome, Dad has an imposing stature that codes charismatic elocution and a sobering, insightful air of authority. I've considered the possibility that his wisdom and general seriousness make him seem handsomer than he actually is, but whatever the reason, Dad is one of those people to whom everybody listens. No matter who you are, you do not snooze through this man's sermons. Even if you are an atheist, you find yourself nodding and thinking, *Preach it, mister!*

Well, not nodding. Maybe you *imagine* you're nodding. But in this scenario you are in a Mennonite church, which means you sit very still and worship Jesus with all your heart, mind, and soul, only as if a snake had bitten you, and you are now in the last stages of paralysis.

I may be the first person to mention my father's good looks in print. Good looks are considered a superfluous feature in a Mennonite world leader, because Mennonites are all about service. Theoretically, we do not even know what we look like, since a focus on our personal appearance is vainglorious. Our antipathy to vainglory explains the decision of many of us to wear those frumpy skirts and the little doilies on our heads, a decision we must have arrived at only by collectively determining not to notice what we had put on that morning.

My mother, unlike my father, is not classically handsome. But she does enjoy good health. She is as buoyant as a lark on a summer's morn. Nothing gets this woman down. She is the kind of mother who, when we were growing up, came singing into our bedrooms at 6:00 a.m., tunefully urging us to rise and shine and give God the glory, glory. And this was on Saturday, Saturday. Upbeat she is. Glamorous she is not. Once she bought Hannah a black T-shirt that said in glittery magenta cursive, NASTY!! She didn't know what it meant. When we told her, she said sunnily, "Oh well, then you can wear it to work in the garden!"

Besides being born Mennonite, which is usually its own beauty strike, my mother has no neck. When we were growing up, our mother's head, sprouting directly from her shoulders like a friendly lettuce, became something of a family focus. We'd take every opportunity to thrust hats and baseball caps upon her, which made us all shriek with unconscionable laughter. Mom would laugh good-naturedly, but if we got too out of hand, she'd predict that our Loewen genes would eventually assert themselves.

And they did. Although I personally have and appreciate a neck, I was, by my early forties, the very picture of blooming Loewen health: peasant-cheeked, impervious to germs, hearty as an ox. I rarely got sick. And the year before the main action of this memoir occurs, I had sustained a physical debilitation—I won't say *illness*—so severe that I thought I was statistically safe for years to come.

I was only forty-two at the time, but my doctor advised a radical salpingo-oopherectomy. For the premenopausal set, that translates to "Your uterus has got to go." A hushed seriousness hung in the air when the doctor first broached the subject of the hysterectomy.

I said, "You mean dump my whole uterus? Ovaries and everything?"

"Yes, I'm afraid so."

I considered a moment. I knew I should be feeling a kind of feminist outrage, but it wasn't happening. "Okay."

Dr. Mayler spoke some solemn words about a support group. From his tone I gathered that I also ought to be feeling a profound sense of loss, and a cosmic unfairness that this was happening to me at age forty-two, instead of at age—what?—fifty-six? I dutifully wrote down the contact information for the support group, thinking that maybe I was in denial again. Maybe the seriousness and the pathos of the salpingo-oopherectomy would register later. By age forty-two I had learned that denial was my special modus operandi. Big life lessons always kicked in tardily for me. I've always been a bit of a late bloomer, a slow learner. The postman has to ring twice, if you get my drift.

My husband, who got a vasectomy two weeks after we married,

was all for the hysterectomy. "Do it," he urged. "Why do you need that thing? You don't use it, do you?"

In general, Nick's policy was, if you haven't used it in a year, throw it out. We lived in homes with spare, ultramodern decor. Once he convinced me to furnish a coach house with nothing but a midcentury dining table and three perfect floor cushions. You know the junk drawer next to the phone? Ours contained a single museum pen and a pad of artisan paper on a Herman Miller tray.

Nick therefore supported the hysterectomy, but only on the grounds of elegant understatement. To him the removal of unnecessary anatomical parts was like donating superfluous crap to Goodwill. Had the previous owners left a beer raft in the garage, as a thoughtful gift to you? No thanks! We weren't the type of people who would store a beer raft in our garage—not because we opposed beer rafts per se, but because we did not want to clutter an uncompromising vista of empty space. Nick led the charge to edit our belongings, but I willingly followed. Had you secretly been wearing the same bra since 1989? Begone, old friend! Were you clinging to a sentimental old wedding dress? Heave ho! Nick's enthusiasm for the hysterectomy made me a little nervous. I kept taking my internal temperature, checking for melancholy. The medical literature I was reading told me I should be feeling really, really sad.

But in the weeks before the surgery my depression mechanism continued to fail me. I remained in a state of suspicious good cheer, like my mother, who had also sustained the trial of early menopause. I called her up. "Hey, Mom," I said. "How did you feel about having to lose your uterus when you were my age?"

"Fabulous," she said. "Why?"

"Did it make you sad?"

"No, I got to take the day off."

"But did you mourn the passing of your youth?" I pressed.

She laughed. "No, I was too busy celebrating the fact that I wouldn't have to have my period anymore. Why, sometimes I used to have to change my pad once an hour! The flow was so thick—"

"Okay, gotcha!" I interrupted. My mother was a nurse, and she had a soft spot in her heart for lost clots, used pads, yellowed bandages, and collapsed veins. If I didn't cut her off, she'd make a quick transition to yeast infections and all would be lost.

After I had talked to my mother, a friend told me gently that I needed to prepare myself for the upcoming shock of not having a uterus. My fifty-four-year-old friend was troubled, she said, by my cavalier attitude to this major rite of passage. I thanked her. Ah, in my heart I had known that my mother's cheery zeitgeist was not the norm! I got good and nervous. I called the doctor's office. "Does a salpingo-oopherectomy come with any weird side effects?" I asked. "For instance, a rash?"

"No rash," said the physician's assistant. "You'll be sore for a couple of weeks, though. No sex for two months."

"Will it decrease my libido?"

"No."

"Will it make me fat?"

"Not unless you stop taking care of yourself."

"Then why do I need a support group?" I asked.

"Many women appreciate a community to support them during this transition," she said earnestly. "Many women find that it is hard to adjust to a new phase in which their childbearing years are over."

I decided to compromise between a posture of pleasant indifference, which was what I actually felt, and a posture of gentle, sensitive loss, which was what I tried to feel over a journal and several pots of soothing elderberry tea. Because I was sensitively writing in a journal, trying honestly to face and feel my emotions, I figured I could give myself permission to dispense with the support group. I'd never been much attached to my uterus to begin with, since I had elected not to bear children. So boo to the support group. What I mean is, God grant those supportive gals abundant sisterly blessings!

But God knew that the journal was a fake, and he ended up punishing my callous insensitivity. (Have I mentioned that the Mennonite God is a guy? Could anyone have doubted it?) During the surgery, Dr. Mayler, who is in most cases quite competent, accidentally punched a hole in two of my organs. He didn't notice. Oops. When I came to, I was piddling like a startled puppy.

So I who had always been the picture of vigorous health was returned to my husband two weeks later in a wheelchair, thin as a spider and clutching a pee bag that connected to my body via a long transparent tube. The first couple of days I was too ill to care, but then my mother's disposition began to assert itself. The truth started to sink in: Pee bag. Tube. I kept watching bubbles drift down the tube, thinking: *I am peeing. Right now. At this very moment.* Or: *I am eating and peeing <u>at the same time.</u>* I am woman, hear me pee! That is, hear me empty the pee bag into a plastic basin that is too heavy for me to lift!

I lay there doing nothing, unless you count peeing, which was an ongoing activity. But instead of mourning my lost uterus, I took naps and read the *New York Times*, which in my regular life I never have enough time to finish. Reading the paper at my leisure smack in the middle of the day was not unlike being on vacation—*deluxe!* said my Loewen genes. The new doctors had told me there was a chance that I would be permanently incontinent, a possibility that would seriously mess with my love life, not to mention my gym schedule. But like my mother, I immediately began telling myself that permanent incontinence wasn't the end of the world. It was better, for instance, than quadriplegia. I had great friends, a husband, and a cat. Large-sized diaper products, although hazardous to the environment and destined for decades in the landfill, were cheap. Why, just the other day, I had seen a coupon for Depends.

Because of Nick's rough childhood, we were both worried about how he would handle a much more difficult convalescence than either of us had bargained for. Nick's mother, who had a long history of mental illness, had subjected her children to what nineteenth-century doctors called "a tyranny of vapors"—meaning that she used her many aches and complaints to control folks. No matter what was going on in the lives of her children, it was all about Regina. As an adult, Nick had distanced himself from her, loathing the trope of the Invalid Woman, and he had often told me that he wouldn't be with me if I were one of those clinging, hysterical types.

During our infrequent visits with Regina, I tried to distract her by getting her to talk about her extreme beauty. This wasn't a stretch. Even at eighty-one, Regina had that vavavoom Italian wow factor. She really was physically beautiful—Nick had to get it from somewhere—and she looked twenty-five years younger than she was. She usually wore a tremendous glam wig and stretch pants. I didn't mind asking pressing questions about how many men had asked to marry her. All in a day's work.

I have a story that sums up the essential Regina. Twelve years ago, Nick and I were poor grad students when we got the call that his father had had a severe stroke and was dying in a West Virginia hospital. We couldn't afford to fly, so we hopped in the car and drove nonstop from Chicago to Fairfax, about a twelve-hour drive. We drank gallons of coffee, driving as fast as we dared, willing

Nick's father to stay alive until we got there. When we finally pulled up to the hospital, we didn't even stop for the restroom; we ran upstairs as fast as we could, chuffing down the critical-care corridor. There they were, Nick's dad at death's door but still in the game, and Regina, looking every bit the lovely and distraught wife. She jumped up and stretched out her arms to me. "Dear!" she exclaimed intensely. *"What do you think of my hair!"*

Having Regina for a mother would have freaked anybody out. Would Nick be so repelled by the sight of a feeble female that he would be unable to take care of me?

The lion's share of the gross-out work would fall on him—changing dressings, cathing me, emptying my pee bag into a basin, disposing of my urine like a good old-fashioned chambermaid. "I'll do my best," he said gamely. "But that pee bag's fucked up."

Then Nick surprised us both. He turned out to be a natural in the sickroom. Crisp, competent, almost jovial, he sailed into my sickroom opening windows, fluffing pillows, and lubricating tubes. He appeared with cups of coffee and odd sandwiches. I'd wake to a tray of peanuts, a new maroon nail polish, and a literary journal. "Here," he'd say briskly, handing me a midmorning gin-and-tonic. "Time to take your pills!"

My best friend, Lola, happened to be in the States that summer, and she flew in to hang out with me. Lola was kind of like a support group, and her timing was perfect. I didn't want Nick to have to bathe and toilet me too; it was bad enough that he had to swish my pee. We were the type of married couple who prefers not just separate bathrooms but bathrooms separated by two thousand square feet. I had been intermittently sharing bathrooms with Lola, however, for upwards of thirty-five years, so during her visit, she helped me into and out of the shower. I had gotten so weak that I couldn't even wash my own hair. But Lola and I hardly ever got to spend time together now that she had married an Italian, so, pee bag notwithstanding, what we really wanted to do was maximize our two weeks together. We were on fire to go shopping.

In Italy, most expat Americans find the shopping scene challenging. One, things are hugely overpriced. Two, Italy has a sale only twice a year. Three, Italy does not offer clothing sizes for women with generous opera-singer bottoms. So Lola has to wait to go shopping until she comes stateside, and that summer, in spite of my postsurgery frailty, we were itching to go to Nordstrom Rack. We were trying to find a way to make an afternoon at Nordstrom Rack a reality. "Let's just tuck your pee bag into a colorful tote, and then you can carry it like a purse," said Lola.

"But you'll be able to see the cord coming out of the bottom of my skirt," I objected. "And what about the fact that I can't walk yet?"

"You can lean on a shopping cart," Lola said. "It will be like one of those walkers with a built-in basket. And I don't think anybody will really notice your pee tube, since it's transparent."

"Yes, but bubbles of urine are passing through it all the time," I said, worried. "Look, here's one now, this very second." As it drifted by, my cat Roscoe tried to attack it. "Hey, dumbass," I said to him, "that's not a toy. That's URINE. I don't know, Lola. Am I ready to pee in public?"

"You know what?" said Lola. "Just put it out there. Like a disability you've come to accept. Love me, love my pee tube. People diddle around in public with their gross psoriasis, scratching and brushing. Or think of that guy at the diner who showed up for breakfast with an open wound on his head. Waffles and pork links and a big tender scab with the blood barely clotted. Or think of new mothers who whip out their nipple and breast-feed in public, in front of God and everybody!"

"That's true," I said, much struck. "None of the local diners appreciated the head wound, but *everybody* thinks it's just fine to breast-feed in public! If women can whip out a big milky nipple, maybe I can flaunt my pee tube."

"If you got it, flaunt it!" Lola urged.

And so it was that I sallied forth into public carrying my pee bag in an aqua patent tote, shopping with urinous enthusiasm. The excursion was extremely successful, too, except for the part when I accidentally stepped on the pee bag's clamp and flooded the passenger side of my car with my own urine. Lola stoically hosed out the VW, reasoning that urine duty was a small price to pay for all of the excellent deals we had found. And less than a week later my doctors upgraded me to the kind of pee bag you strap on with Velcro around your leg, under your skirt, like a nasty secret. I taught for half the semester like that. And dang, I'm here to tell you that when it's ninety degrees outside, nothing reminds you of your own mortality like a steaming hot bag of urine hugging your thigh.

I'm happy to report that I made a full recovery from the netherworld of tube and clamp. Six months after the fix-it surgery I was back at the gym, pounding the treadmill with a new sense of gratitude for my interior plumbing. Whereas before I had taken for granted my miraculous ability to run without wetting my leg, I now silently praised my bladder. "Good show! You're holding up great in there, honey! Four more miles! You can do it!" I'd sneeze and think, *Brava! You have achieved true excellence, my friendly little sphincter!* It took about a year before I stopped intoning St. Francis of Assisi's prayer every time I sat down on a toilet.

Which is all to say that given the surprising events of the Year of the Pee Bag, I assumed I was safe from ill health and trauma for decades. But no.

Nick and I had recently moved to a small rural community about forty-five minutes from where I worked. Although the move dramatically increased my commute, Nick had a new job running the psych ward at the local hospital, and he needed to be close enough to troubleshoot at any hour. With his job had come a big promotion. We therefore bought a charming lake house that I wouldn't have been able to afford on my own. This was the first time in our fifteen-year marriage when I was dependent on Nick's financial contribution. Until we moved to the lake house, we had been living in a midcentury rancho close to my college. The rancho had been a fixer, but I had been able to afford the entire mortgage and all our living expenses on my modest academic salary. Nick, an artist by preference and calling, had never held a job long, and when he was employed, he prioritized his art. Painting in oils is expensive.

Two months after the move to the expensive lakefront property, Nick left me for a guy he'd met on Gay.com.

I don't know why it made it worse that the man's name was Bob, but it did. Bob the Guy. From Gay.com. It's funny how when your husband leaves you for a guy named Bob, you begin to revisit memories from the summer before, when hindsight sheds new light on your husband's role during the highs and lows of your convalescence. What you once thought of as evidence of your husband's tenderness you begin to imagine as guilt for dating guys with big wangs. What you once thought of as "Giving You Space to Hang Out with Your Girlfriend from Italy" strikes your imagination as "Threesomes with Ryan and Daren from the Gym." The truth hurts, especially when you're slow to see it.

And also: will somebody please tell me why husbands never seem to ditch their wives until the wives develop a varicose vein the size of a Roman aqueduct? It's like they're *waiting* for the vein. If our husbands must leave us for guys named Bob, why can't they do it pre-vein, while we are young and gorgeous? Why can't they do it pre–pee bag? Look, I know I'm not the ambassador of all women who have worn a pee bag while their husbands commence illicit relationships with guys named Bob, and so I wouldn't dream of speaking for all of us. But I do know that I would have much preferred to have been ditched *before* the pee bag. That whole pee bag summer I cherished Nick's brisk yet dear postoperative care. I adored how he'd come into the room chatting about a book, a friend, current events, whatever, and how he'd go down on one knee to empty the pee bag into a basin, talking the whole time of things unrelated to urine, as if squirting his wife's urine were no big deal—too insignificant to mention!

Well, here the Loewen genes must do the cosmic shrug. Life does not allow us the luxury of filling out our own questionnaires.

_____ Yes, I want my husband to leave me pre–pee bag.

_____ No, I'd rather he left me post–pee bag.

Okay, so. The *same week* that my husband left me, I was driving home on a two-lane road from a board meeting to the house I could no longer afford. It was the first snow of the season, around nine o'clock at night. Although it had been snowing for a mere twenty minutes, almost everybody had slowed way down, giving the first snow of the season the respect that it deserves. Suddenly a partially inebriated youth lost control of his vehicle, skidded into my lane, and smacked my little VW Beetle head-on. As his headlights bore down on me, I had time to exclaim aloud, "Oh my god, I'm gonna die."

I heard the crunch, and I remember thinking it sounded hissier and more protracted than the big bangs of the movies. The whole collision was slower than it ought to have been. Gradually I became aware that the windshield was in my mouth. I began spitting, and I sat there for what seemed a long time, tonguing chunks of glass.

Somebody was saying, "Don't move, ma'am. Don't move."

Snow was drifting in. "Ma'am, you've been in an accident!"

I meant to say, with crisp acerbity, "Duh!" What I actually said came out in a feeble whisper. "Nick."

"Who's Nick?" They were strapping me to something.

"My husband." Snow was melting in my eyes. Melted snow was running down my cheeks in rivulets.

"Ma'am, we'll get Nick for you just as soon as we get you to the hospital."

Ah, that was one service the paramedics could not perform.

The nineteen-year-old who had hit me was being strapped into an ambulance. The good fellow confessed to the paramedics that the accident had been his fault. He even looked at me and said, "Sorry, Lady," before he passed out—heartbreaking, poor thing! He was covered in blood and his shirt was gone.

The accident left me with assorted broken bones and Frankenbruises the size of my head. I spat compulsively for two days. When the doctors let me go home, my body looked just as it felt: hips, thighs, and breasts mottled the same steely blue of the lake. I'd cracked my patella, but I couldn't use crutches because I had two broken ribs and a fractured clavicle, so I wheeled myself around the house on my office chair, pushing off with my left arm.

In the days that followed I had plenty of time to wonder if I had somehow been complicit in my own accident. Curtis, the young man who had hit me, was still in Urgent Care; I couldn't talk to him about what had happened. And I couldn't trust my own memory, since I had sustained a granddaddy of a concussion. The doctors told me I had passed out on impact. This information directly contradicted my vague memory of consciousness throughout the experience. Had I had time to swerve and failed? Had my misery pulled Curtis's Jeep Cherokee down on me? Was I a magnet of self-pity? I rolled pensively around the house in my office chair, smelling the candles, lotions, and bouquets my girlfriends had promptly lobbed at me. "Do something for YOU, sweetie!" the cards urged in Oprah-like tones. And I was obedient. Never in all my years had I been so pedicured/exfoliated/fragrant/ditched for a guy named Bob.

Nick was gone. My marriage was over. Under circumstances like these, what was a forty-three-year-old gal to do?

I'll tell you what I did. I went home to the Mennonites. Oh, I had been back to California for the occasional holiday, and I had flown in for my father's enormous retirement bash five years earlier. But in twenty-five years I had not spent any real time in the Mennonite community in which I'd been raised. When Nick absconded with Bob, I could no longer afford the six-month sabbatical I had planned. To study away from home for six months, I would have had to rent an apartment and pay for living expenses, in addition to paying the mortgage and utilities at home. I was broke and broken. Clocked in the chops by a lead glove, I was out cold. What the hell—it was so bad it couldn't get any worse. *Bring on the Borscht*, I thought. So after mending in Michigan for two months, I went home for the holidays.

In the style of Mennonite autocrats, my father likes to exercise his right to bellow for my mother to drop whatever she's doing and come and see something in the study.

My mother was up to her elbows in flour, bunning out Zwiebach in the kitchen. "Mary!" came the stern shout. "Come see this!" My mom obediently scooted, holding her forearms upright in front of her, doctor-style. I knew what would be next, and I refused to set down the manuscript I was editing until I had to. A few minutes later my father's voice, full of preacherly gravitas, called once more: "Rhoda! Come see this!"

Dad was at his most dadlike when I was trying to work, and I needed to concentrate. I needed money. Fast. The waterfront house was now on the market, and my realtor had tranquilly assured me that it would sell when the time was right, but I was nervous. It was a beautiful house, but it had its drawbacks. I wondered what would happen if we all wrote truthful ads for our real estate.

> Gorgeous lakefront property, just an icy commute away on deadly highway! This special house is so big you'll close all the vents and pray for a mild winter! Unimpaired views for peeping toms! Possums visit the deck! Finished walkout with carpet you wouldn't have picked! In fact, this carpet is downright unattractive! Current resident selfishly intends to take Bosch dishwasher and Lord of Refrigerators. Two sex offenders just blocks away! Schedule an appointment today!

Because of the house situation, I had agreed to ghost-edit a scholarly monograph on sacred dramatic literature of the late fifteenth century. I was working on the second chapter, which was about Feo Belcari's mechanical innovations in the staging of the *sacre rappresenatzione*. If you are one of the folks who have never heard of Feo Belcari, I can fix that right up for you. You know those Christmas Eve church plays in which your white-blonde niece gets to play the angel Gabriel year after year because she has a startling strange paleness that looks, and I mean this in a good way, a little like an albino? And remember the moment when she appears in a white sheet in the baptistery, maybe singing "It Came Upon a Midnight Clear" in a threadlike soprano? Feo Belcari was the guy in the late 1400s who figured out a way to have your niece/Gabriel come down on metal wires at the front of the church. That about sums it up, but the chapter I was editing was fifty pages or so.

What I was doing was unusual—unusual, I mean, beyond the fact that there are maybe 16.2 people in the entire world who would like to know more about the sacred dramatic literature of the fifteenth century. (Okay, I admit it: I'm one of them.) Sometimes academics manage to wheedle their best friends into reading their manuscripts and making critical comments. It is not unreasonable that English professors are often targeted for this favor. If you also happen to be a grammarian who creepily knows how to diagram every sentence in the English language, there is an even more urgent demand for your services. I'm the sicko who can explain why a gerundive phrase must attach to a possessive adjective pronoun rather than an object pronoun. True, you wouldn't want me at a party, but if the survival of the human race depended upon the successful parsing of the Constitution, you'd be knockin' on my door, baby.

This time, though, I was doing more than tidying up the grammar as a favor to a colleague. I was being paid to read for logic, clarity, concision, and development. It was a tough gig for three reasons. One, the author was a better researcher than writer. Two, fifteenth-century Italy was four centuries and one continent away from my own area of academic training. Three, my Italian was a little rusty, and all those citations and footnotes were slowing me down a tad.

I wasn't working for glory. I was working for cash. Usually scholars take a less fixed, more interpretive approach to deadlines, preferring to think of them as suggestions, not firm commitments. But with this project I couldn't do that. I had a hard calendar deadline. Luckily my parents had assured me that if I came out to visit them, they would see to it that I had all the time and privacy in the world.

So I was curious to see what oddity or newsy Internet tidbit could justify my father's imperious summons, especially when the man knew I was working—nay, especially when my very presence in his home expressly rested on parental promises to leave me alone and let me work. When I entered my father's study, he was leaning back in his chair, looking highly pleased with himself. "Check this out!" he commanded.

On the computer screen was an e-card, a holiday greeting, themed on the Twelve Days of Christmas. The audio was playing the carol. Twelve drummers marched slowly across the screen. "How about THAT?" demanded my father.

"Hey," I said. "Wow."

"See that?" he said. "That would be your nine lords a-leaping!"

Now came the maids a-milking, along with frisky animated cows.

"Isn't that CUTE?" my mother asked. "They have udders."

"Here come the four birds a-calling. Watch this!" advised my dad.

"Twoooooo French Hens," sang my mother, making a motion that I should join in. She was still holding her arms cocked at the elbow, her hands covered with floury bits of dough. Since she couldn't make the hula motion dear to her heart, she swayed from the waist in happy 2-4 time.

"Good one," Dad said, apparently much satisfied, when the partridge and its fellows had finally scrolled offscreen.

This paternal summons had been occurring every twenty minutes or so. Every time the command sounded, I set aside my pen to go see pictures of raindrops or a snapshot of a baby squirrel nursing among a litter of puppies. And I can't forget Various Birds & Sayings. Would not the Western world get more work done if it took a break for Various Birds & Sayings? For instance, let's say you have a close-up of a mourning dove. The dove is doing nothing urgent, just sitting there on a branch. The photographer has captured the dove in all its splendid nullity. He has framed it in a font calculated to promote introspection: **YOUR LIFE BEGINS WITH THIS MOMENT**. Pure magic!

The next morning was the kicker, the *piqûre*, if you will. My very Mennonite mother and I were standing in line at Circuit City to return a pair of cell phones that were theoretically supposed to propel my parents into the twenty-first century. (My parents had grown up without cultural advantages such as electricity, toilets, coffee, fabric—I could go on here, but you get the gist. Me, aghast: "Do you mean to tell me that even your *underwear* was made out of flour sacks?" Mom: "Oh, some of the flour sacks had a very pretty floral print! Little bluets and pansies! I liked them!")

Unfortunately, my father had selected the cheapest of the

cheap cell phones, a choice that had resulted in insurmountable programming difficulties. I'd taken a crack at setting up the phones myself, and even with a pencil eraser, a magnifying glass, and the directions of a chipper phone company employee named Monique, I had to admit defeat. For my mother, it looked as if the promise of long-distance chats with grandchildren was not going to materialize. But she had made her peace with this.

"That's okay," she told me. "Plus if I called Si on a cell phone, he wouldn't pick up anyway." She says these things as if they are perfectly reasonable.

"Would he just ignore a phone ringing in his pants?"

"Well, he doesn't really believe in cell phones," she apologized. For my father, belief in cell phones was somehow optional. It was a deeply subjective matter, like reincarnation. Inviting cell phones into your heart like Jesus was clearly something he was unprepared to do.

So there my mom and I were, in line four days before Christmas. Around us weary consumers clutched their disappointments, but my mother was in her usual cheerful spirits. The presence of strangers less than eight inches away notwithstanding, my mother suddenly said, "If there aren't any single men to date where you are, I know someone for you."

"Who?"

"Your cousin Waldemar. Waldemar is a professor in Nova Scotia," she said earnestly. "And he has a beach house."

I took a measured breath. "Wally is my *first cousin*," I said. "That's both incestuous and illegal."

My mother considered this thoughtfully. "Well," she said, "I think it should be fine since you can't have kids anyway. Maybe you can adopt."

The thought of my cousin Wally and me, two midlife scholars, sitting hand in hand and anxiously waiting to hear the news in an adoption office, was a little overwhelming.

"Waldemar would make a terrific father," pressed my mother. "You should see him with his nieces and nephews."

This was all so rich I had no idea how to reply. Should I go with the fact that as a postmenopausal forty-something, I had long acknowledged my deficiency in not wanting to become a mother? Or how about stressing my mother's charming distance from the law of the land that forbids first cousins to marry? Or how about demanding to know why my mother had zeroed in on Cousin Wally, an accounting professor, when there are so many cousins with whom I actually do have something in common? Or how about the fact that, all things considered, I preferred to find my own dates, thank you very much?

I decided to go with the latter. Now was as good a time as any to mention that although my husband had quite recently ditched me for Bob the Guy from Gay.com, I had already been out on a couple dates. I knew the new guy wasn't going to be the love of my life, but he was sweet.

One of my friends, Carla, who said I could use her real name in this memoir as long as I described her as a svelte redhead, offered to run my love life for five bucks. "What are you looking for in a guy?" she asked, whipping out a little notepad.

"Hmm," I said thoughtfully. "He has to be kind. And culturally literate. And on the path to consciousness . . . reflective, open. No cynics or angry atheists. He has to have a sense of humor. That's important. And he should be tall. And employed at work he loves. And—"

"Whoa, there, Nellie," Carla interrupted. "I'm gonna give you some free advice. You ready for this? How about we *lower the bar*? How about we look for someone who's straight, for starters?"

This guy I had been seeing occasionally might not have been Mr. Right, but he was Mr. Straight.

Mom was disappointed when I told her I had been on a couple of dates with someone, but she took it in stoic stride. "What's your fellow like?"

I was too emotionally battered to utter polite fibs. "Sort of a slacker, really. A relaxed pothead. He wears his pajamas to the grocery store."

"Oh," said my Mennonite mother. Then she nodded supportively. "A relaxed pothead sounds nice."

It made sense, I suppose, that a woman who would promote endogamous marriage would not blink at a pothead. I thought I would try to elicit more information along these lines.

"Maybe my cousin Wally smokes a little weed," I said speculatively (although I would bet my few remaining financial assets that he does not).

"Noooooooooo," said Mom. "Your cousin Waldemar would NEVER do weed! He drives a tractor! In his spare time!"

"How does driving a tractor prevent you from smoking weed?"

By now several people near us in line were obviously eavesdropping. The man standing in front of us was trying not to smile.

"If you drive a tractor in your spare time," my mother said firmly, "it means that you have a strong work ethic, which is probably why Waldemar has had the gumption to earn himself a nice beach house."

"Surely he doesn't drive his tractor on the beach?"

"No! He drives it at Orrin and Maria's, of course! He gives the nieces and nephews rides on the tractor."

"Oh! I thought you meant that he was *working* on the tractor, not entertaining!"

"Waldemar works very hard," Mom said proudly. "You know perfectly well that a tractor can be hard work and fun too. Like marriage."

One of the best things about my mother is that she will follow you anywhere, conversationally speaking. She will answer any question at all, the stranger the better. Naturally, I cannot resist asking her things that no normal person would accept. "Mom," I said, serious as a pulpit, "would you rather marry a pleasant pot-head or your first cousin on a tractor? Both are associate professors," I hastened to add.

"You marry your pothead if you like," she said generously, "as long as you wait a while. Let's say two years. But as for me and my house, we will serve the Lord."

"Hey!" I said, indignant. "How do you know the pothead *doesn't* serve the Lord? As a matter of fact, this pothead does serve the Lord! He's more religious than I am!" (I felt safe in asserting this because I had once heard the pothead softly singing "Amazing Grace.")

"I think that the Lord appreciates a man on a tractor more than a man smoking marijuana in his pajamas," Mom said earnestly. "I know I do."

"Okay, okay," I said, as we neared the counter. "I give up. I will marry Cousin Wally. Just as soon as he asks me. You'll be our first houseguest at our beach house in Nova Scotia. But I'm warning you now, there's gonna be a little weed on your pillow. Instead of a mint."

She chuckled comfortably. "That's okay. I don't like mints."

# TWO

# Touch My Tooth

I hope it's clear by now that the Mennonites wouldn't want me. The only reason they're nice to me is that my dad is famous, my mom makes great pie, and I babysat their kids when I was twelve. Once in the course of babysitting I got Jamie Isaac, who wore diapers until he was five and who now is a computer analyst with three kids, to eat wet cat food.

Connie Isaac, Jamie's mother, was a Mennonite folksinger who released an album with the winning title *Sing Alleluia!* The Isaacs lived four houses down from us—Mennonites tend to live in clumps—and we were on intimate terms with the lyrics of *Sing Alleluia!* Our parents had naturally forbidden us to listen to the radio or to anything that smelled secular, such as rock and roll, but Connie Isaac's *Sing Alleluia!* passed muster. There was one song that we sang relentlessly. It told the story of a Mennonite farm child, Little Anna Barkman, who couldn't come out and play because she was learning proper Mennonite work habits, counting over grains of red turkey wheat. Connie Isaac had invited her daughter Christie, Jamie's older sister, to sing the role of Little Anna Barkman on the album. In a voice high and clear as an alpine tinkle, young Christie tunefully lisped the chorus.

Red color,
good shape,
heavyweight,
one by one!
Each grain,
my tiny friend!
When two jars are full
my work is done!

Well, I'm here to tell you that in the Janzen household we could not get enough of Christie Isaac singing about her tiny friends, especially after Connie Isaac made her first payment to me for babysitting services rendered.

Connie Isaac paid me in fresh brown *potatoes*.

I think we can all agree that the lives of most twelve-year-olds improve significantly with an incoming flow of brown potatoes. You may not be able to buy that bootleg lip gloss your heart yearns for, but you can prepare tasty potato dishes for the whole family. And cooking is one thing a Mennonite girl knows how to do.

I have been happily and busily cooking since age five, when I served up my first kettle of Borscht, made with boiled lettuce instead of cabbage. (Say what you will, but it is easy to get confused in the face of such look-alike vegetables.) The women in our family are the kinds of cooks whom you can't kerfuffle. You need a dinner for ten an hour from now? No problem. We'll rustle up homemade bread, noodles, gravy, sausage, whatever. Mennonite food has its delicious moments—more on that later—but our true gift lies in the *ease* with which we cook. Some cooks struggle with timing, with menu planning, with missing ingredients. Not us. Our seven side dishes always come up at exactly the same time, and if we have run out of something, which we rarely do, we have improvised a delicious substitution. We're idiot savants when it comes to food preparation. You've heard of those developmentally delayed folks who can shout out what day of the week it was on May 16, 1804? That's us, only we're shouting, "Dinner's ready!"

So I wasn't surprised when Mom stuck her head unceremoniously into the guest bedroom. As I needed a desk tall enough for me to wedge my legs under, I was working at one I had improvised from a narrow side table and two drawers propped under the legs. "Will you make some soup?" asked my mother brightly.

"Right now?"

"Whenever you get a chance. We've decided to celebrate Christmas Eve early this year, since we're leaving on Christmas morning for Hannah's. We're going to open presents at Aaron and Deena's. Caleb had the idea of us all bringing a different kind of soup, so we'll have that and Zwiebach."

I nodded. Soup, okay. It was a good idea, actually. Zwiebach are double-decker buns, tasty and soft. You get a small but select thrill when you pull them apart, as with Oreos. Zwiebach, however, are not filled with anything. You slather them with unsalted butter and homemade rhubarb jam for Vaspa, the Sunday evening meal. Or you serve them with everyday Mennonite soups. The chief pleasure of eating Zwiebach is that the top part of the bun, about the size of a golf ball, sits there like a tempting knob. It says, *Oh, you know you wanna!* It's very tactile.

I have my grandmother's recipe for Zwiebach. I mean I have the actual fifty-year-old piece of paper, written on the back of a *Kalendarblatt*, a leaf from a calendar. As far as I know, this is the one time my mother's mother—whom I call Oma—ever wrote a recipe down. In 1960, when my mother was first married, she wrote from the tiny parsonage in North Dakota to ask her mother in Canada for the recipe. Oma sent the page from the calendar covered in barely legible *Spitzbubben*, the old-style Russian–Mennonite German script from the nineteenth century. Nobody except scholars can read this style of penmanship anymore. Even I couldn't do it without Mom's help. In the recipe Oma's voice comes through, practical and vague, advising her daughter to use whatever she has handy in the larder—butter, or margarine, or even chicken fat. Oma assumed that ingredients would vary according to season and budget. She also assumed that knowledge of the correct quantities would miraculously come to my mother in the night. "Take some milk or some water and warm it and then add it to some flour," she advised helpfully. On the calendar side Oma added a brief personal note: "I don't think Heinrich will be coming home before Christmas."

"I'm going to be making a nice chicken dish for Joel and Erlene Neufeld," my mother told me. "Joel and Erlene just adopted three siblings, and the oldest is five. Poor little things. Their mother abandoned them in a motel. The oldest managed to squeeze through the window to go out and look for food. So Joel and Erlene really have their hands full. You make the soup, and I'll make the chicken dish for Joel and Erlene."

"You want a Menno soup or a worldly soup?"

"Oh, make something we haven't tried!"

In the spirit of filial accommodation, I saved my document to a flash drive and trailed after her to the kitchen.

Together we stood at the sink, washing our hands. She was running her tongue over a tooth she had chipped the week before. "I wasn't even eating nuts," she said. "It just dropped off. Maybe because I grind my teeth in my sleep. Here, feel it."

I obediently reached over to touch my mother's jagged tooth.

My mother unwrapped a Kleenex that she had taken from her pocket. The Kleenex contained half a grayish incisor.

"Please explain to me why you are carrying that around in a Kleenex," I said.

She looked at me, surprised. "It's a bone," she said sunnily. "They can glue it back on."

"Gluing a tooth back on is like trying to reattach a broken fingernail. Just let it go, man."

She was the nurse in the family, the Solomon of all medical disputes. "This tooth still has a lot of use in it. Did I ever tell you about Hilde's tooth?"

"Did it drop out?"

"No. Hilde had a big gap between her two front teeth when we were growing up. She just hated it. She used to cover her mouth when she laughed because she was so ashamed of the space between her teeth."

"I like a smile like that," I said. "Aaron's got a gap-toothed smile, and it looks great on him."

"Hilde's space was much bigger than Aaron's. One day after she got a job she went to the dentist and had a little tooth made, and she put it there. It looked funny."

"You mean she got a bridge, to hide the gap?"

"No, a whole separate little tooth, wedged right in the middle of the other two. But this little tooth was narrower and smaller than a regular tooth."

I savored the idea of a compact go-to fairy tooth tucked between its fellows, just the snug essence of tooth. In Low German there's a funny word for the frosty heart of a watermelon: the *Abromtje*, the Little Abraham. I had always loved that word. It called up the image of a homunculus curled inside the melon, like an exceptionally stern miniature dad in there. My aunt's wee tooth reminded me of the *Abromtje*; it would sit small and spare as a haiku, no more than strictly necessary, packing its little wallop of power. How satisfying if we could all fit our cattywampus spaces with tiny dream teeth! And how satisfying to look in the mirror as my Aunt Hilde must have done sixty years ago, congratulating herself on this fake tooth the size of a Chiclet. She must have thought, *From now on, when people look at me, they won't see my absence, my loss, my lack. They won't see the thing I never had. They'll see space filled with bone. They'll see the story of my teeth. They'll see absence as presence, the hole made whole.*

I was well into chopping my squash. Beside me Mom was cutting up the chicken for the folks who had adopted the three kids from the motel. Suddenly she said, as if musing aloud, "Here's the ulna and the radius."

I suppose the high road here would be to attribute my mother's inappropriate conversational overtures to her career as a nurse. It is a well-known truism that nurses like to talk about pus while offering their children a second helping of mashed potatoes. Once my mother edified us with a lunch story about bathing a morbidly obese patient. Under the patient's tremendous awning of stomach fat, my mother had discovered a half-eaten sandwich, much decomposed. I was eating tuna on rye at the precise moment of narration. The truth is, though, that my mother was like this long before she went back to school. She may have even become a nurse because she had a secret hankering to discuss putrefaction even as she served *Rollkuchen* to distant cousins from Bielefeld.

"Don't say that," I said automatically.

"Why not? This chicken has an ulna."

"Yes, but it's gross to say *ulna* and *radius* when you're cooking."

She considered this before rejecting it altogether: "No it isn't. This chicken has an ulna!"

"That doesn't mean you need to talk about it. Let's institute a don't-ask-don't-tell policy."

"On just the ulna, or the radius too?"

"No Latinate names on any chicken bones. I propose that when you really feel compelled to discuss chicken bones, you say, *Chicken bones*."

"All right," Mom said tractably, "but I'm still going to think of it as the ulna."

"If you insist. I suppose that is your right as a Mennonite and a matriarch."

"Learning bone names is like riding a bike," she said. "Once you know the bones, you can't not know them. But saying *ulna* isn't nearly as bad as eating a side dish of chicken intestines."

This was the kind of semantic leap I had learned to expect. On the subject of chickens in particular, there could be no surprises. This was a woman who had once departed for Hawaii with a frozen fryer in her suitcase, on the theory that the chicken would be thawed by the time her flight landed in Honolulu. If your mother takes frozen uncooked chicken in her suitcase to Hawaii, all bets are off. You just go with the flow. "I suppose that eating a side dish of intestines is preferable to eating them as an entrée," I said cordially, starting on an onion.

"When my friend Chue Lee invited me to her family's Hmong banquet, they served a little side dish of chicken intestines beside every plate. I went over early to help them butcher. Did you know that the Hmong use everything—the feet, the head, the beak, the intestines, everything? They carefully rinse out the intestines to get the fecal matter out—"

I made a noise of protest.

"Sorry. But you wouldn't want to eat chicken intestines that contained feces!"

"We're moving in the wrong direction here," I said, peeling a Granny Smith for my soup.

"The Hmong hide the texture and the taste by adding a bunch of hot chile-pepper spices."

"Did Dad eat his portion of chicken intestines?"

She guffawed. "No. Him? No! I ate his."

"Are you trying to tell me that you *liked* the spicy rinsed intestines?"

"No, but I didn't want Chue Lee to think we weren't enjoying them."

"Would you rather rinse the intestines or eat them?"

She considered. "Rinse them. Although when I was rinsing them, the smell reminded me of our old chicken coop."

She began singing a merry little ditty she had taught us in our youth. The Teutonic charm of this song is that the rhyme scheme creates a momentary anticipation of an off-color word—off-color by 1930s standards, that is. You're supposed to drag out the musical line as long as possible, really flirt with the whole pottymouth thing, and then at the last possible second you substitute the G-rated lyric:

Oh Mistress Bliss
went out to pi—      [pick]
some pretty flowers.
And in the grass
she wet her a—      [ankle]
way up high!
And in the cart

she let a far—        [farmer]
pass her by,
and in the coop
she let a poo—       [poor]
old chicken die!

My mother always reduced me to a kind of reluctant speech-lessness.

Then without further transition she suggested that since I had my apron on, maybe I wouldn't mind making two more loaves of cranberry-nut bread. I asked if the loaf I had made the day before was already gone. She nodded. "Your father likes it."

The night before, Dad had insisted on interpreting the cranberry bread as a pudding. He had cubed tremendous chunks of it into a cereal bowl and then drenched the chunks with half-and-half. Now he came wandering into the kitchen. "Are you going to make more of that pudding? Good flavor," he said.

"Actually, Dad, it's cranberry *bread*, not pudding."

He disputed this in his big preacher's voice. "I feel it has more in common with a pudding," he said with a note of authority. "What kind of soup are we bringing to Aaron and Deena's?"

"Curried butternut squash. Caleb and Staci said—"

"Staci has lost about seventy-five pounds," said my father approvingly. "She's a go-getter, that gal. She's been taking some classes at the seminary. Growing and stretching."

"And her hair looks very elegant now," said my mother. With the chicken in the oven, she was sitting at the kitchen table, working on the newspaper jumble. "Unscramble the following six letters: V-I-Y-T-L-E."

"Good for Staci," I said. "She must feel terrific."

"Their little Joon. She's a live wire, that one."

"Does she still have a shine for gymnastics?"

"She hops on one foot. A very athletic little girl," he said. "And smart. She sure likes being read to."

Later that evening we pulled up to my brother's house, which demonstrated its sincere commitment to the Christmas season with a tornado of twinkle lights and a crèche on the lawn. Who wouldn't appreciate a Baby Jesus whose manger had been garlanded with self-wired ribbon and clusters of silk roses featuring, it looked like, baby's breath? Even the cow figurine was wearing a handsome floral lei. If I were a cow figurine, I too might don a respectful boutonniere to herald the Messiah.

It's not that I'm opposed to the idea of a crèche. My mother has a very old, very beautiful paper crèche that was given to her parents just after they made it out of the Old Country in the troubled years following the Russian Revolution. Theirs was a hard story, as with so many of the émigrés. My own grandparents had almost starved to death; they had lost everything; their first children had died. When they finally received their clearance to board the train in Dolinsk, my grandparents had between them only the following: two babies spotted with measles, their precious Bible, and a tiny heirloom rose brooch. They had to wait a long time in England until the babies could pass the health inspections; the rickets from starvation were so bad that little Netha couldn't even lift her own head until she was four. They thought they'd have to throw Netha's body overboard on the voyage; but she, and they, stubbornly survived, frail but fierce. My great-aunt Helena Boldt, who had emigrated to Saskatoon five years earlier, presented the crèche to my grandparents in 1925. It was their first gift in Canada.

I used to stare dreamily at the crèche every Christmas when I was growing up. I still love the lacy cutwork, the gorgeous colors, the Moroccan princes kneeling with their urns and bejeweled boxes. Atop the cardboard haymow are two plump curly angels, holding a banner that says in old German script PRAISE TO GOD IN THE HIGHEST. Inside the diorama a haloed Mary sits with a tiny iconic adult Jesus on her lap. He's raising one prophetic finger, as if about to speak. I imagined Oma nodding at that crèche, believing that the Infant King was commending her personally for having risked everything to start over in a new and barren land. "And well done on that heirloom rose brooch," Jesus would say. "Splendid work pinning it inside your drawers!"

Three generations do their work, however. Gone are the days when a crèche was a family treasure to be cherished by lamplight in the parlor. In the span of less than a century, what was once a private celebration of faith has become a public assertion. Who am I to say that's all bad? True, I would no more construct a shrine on my front lawn than proselytize, but, hey, faith witnesses many forms.

Deena's parents were semiretired Mennonite florists, and thus Aaron and Deena's decor revealed unlimited and enthusiastic access to Thiessens' Nora Flora. Deena could make decor magic out of anything, especially semitransparent fabric with metallic threads, wire bows, silk flowers, and shiny balls. She was also resourceful with toy trains, cookie jars, wallpaper borders, and shadowboxes. I prefer my flowers in water, my trains in Europe, and my wallpaper in the trash. Call me old-fashioned, but whenever I see those wire-fortified ribbons, I have a secret stab of nostalgia for old-timey ribbon, the kind whose ends flop like spaniel ears. I'm suspicious of unnaturally perky ribbon.

Above the main Christmas tree in the great room was a display ledge on which Deena had arranged four lesser trees, festooned and frantically blinking. But the thing that really commanded attention, high up there on that ledge, was an oversize mechanical fur bear. It was raising a perpetual fake candle to its lips, as if to blow it out. What this bear and its need for darkness had to do with the spirit of Christmas I do not know. But over the audio stylings of ambient Mannheim Steamroller, I could hear the bear's motor. It emitted a tiny agonized silence-of-the-lambs bleat, not unlike the miniature scream of auto-flush toilets at the airport.

"What a beyoooootiful winter wonderland!" exclaimed my mother.

"Festive!" interjected my father.

My other sister-in-law, Staci, made a beeline for me.

Staci and I live three thousand miles apart, and we interact only on the occasional holiday when I am in town. Staci is one of those brisk, efficient, gets-it-done gals who raise children, sell Pampered Chef products, head up the PTA, and plan fund-raisers for victims of house fires. Staci is a no-bullshit person; she tells it like it is. One of the things I like about her is that she doesn't bother pretending we're close when we obviously aren't. I am sometimes away for years at a time, and during the interim Staci does not phone, does not send birthday cards depicting realistic kittens, does not ask me to proofread her annual Christmas newsletter. Between holidays we have no relationship whatsoever.

Yet when circumstances throw us together, she rolls up her sleeves and goes for it. If family holidays involved a relay, she'd be the one up front to grab the baton. Staci, who attended a Mennonite college but who is not an ethnic Mennonite, has always assumed an easy intimacy that came as a surprise to our household. Aside from my mother, Mennonites do not usually discuss their bodies, especially at dinner. They do not confide secrets, or talk about controversial topics, or provide updates on the state of their libido. Staci, however, might make an eloquent argument against her church's Easter pageant, in which she is playing the guide to Jesus's donkey. Or she might disclose that she has been dying her hair since age twenty-three. She might share highs and lows from her recent weight loss of seventy-five pounds. This relaxed bonhomie declared itself the very evening my brother brought her home to dinner some twenty years ago. On that occasion Staci confided in front of us all, somewhere between the *Pluma Moos* and *Pereshki*, that she had a painful rash, and would my mother mind taking a look at it? My mother did not mind in the least, and tripped off down the hall to inspect her future daughter-in-law's private itchy region.

"Staci," I said now, returning her hug, "what a gorgeous new look for you!"

"Can I just ask what you do about bread?" Staci asked, as if continuing a conversation we had started moments earlier. We hadn't spoken in five years. "Because I've gained back six pounds in the last two weeks. Bread is so my downfall."

The last time I had seen her, we had all been playing a Password-type game in which I was trying to get Staci to guess the word *Dracula*. Deploying the hushed intensity of a game-show contestant, I offered what I thought was a reasonable clue:

"Bram Stoker's—"

"Lean Cuisine!" she shouted.

Through my head flashed the sassy headline VAMPIRE COUNTS CARBS! Truly, Bram Stoker's Lean Cuisine was a splendid marketing idea. *New taste sensation from Bram Stoker! All of the protein, none of the fat!* Maybe we could expand the line with a lo-cal Mummy Wrap.

Now Staci went on, "Also potatoes. I just can't do potatoes. They go straight to my"—she patted her heinie significantly. "How do you do it? Do you cook for yourself now that Nick has left you? Is it hard to cook just for one? Or do you eat out of a can in front of the kitchen sink?"

In the dining room we all gathered to pay homage to Deena's imaginative decor, where no surface had escaped yuletide festivity. Its attractions included a wreath made of prodigious shiny balls, and a preponderance of more free-rolling balls the size of grape tomatoes that Deena had scattered, carelessly, among the plates and goblets. She had also affixed a tiny silver ball to the stem of every wineglass—not that we would be drinking wine. Mennonites tend toward militant sobriety. But there was always sparkling apple juice for holiday celebrations.

"Wine?" asked Staci, reaching behind her to the sideboard. Bless her, she had brought some in gentle defiance of Mennonite tradition. Alas, it was a sweet rosé, served ice-cold, like beer. Ah well. I nodded, pushing my goblet toward her as she said, "I don't think there's anything wrong with drinking the occasional glass of wine now and then, as long as you don't get drunk. 'Be ye not drunk with wine'"—she quoted the Bible, throwing this challenge at my father. His expression at the head of the table did not change. He looked like a peaceful Buddha. "If Christ drank wine, that's good enough for me!" she added defiantly.

"Me too," I said.

"A toast," said my brother Aaron, "to family celebrations!"

My siblings and I raised our rosé; my parents saluted with sparkling apple cider.

"Because," Staci continued unfazed, "the real test of wisdom comes when you can show non-Christians that you're *responsible*. It's more impressive to non-Christians if they see us partaking *responsibly* than if they see us just condemning alcohol willy-nilly. I don't think there's anything wrong with keeping a pack of Heineken in the fridge. Sometimes Caleb comes home from a long day at work and he has two beers." Her expression dared someone, anyone, to protest.

Caleb apologized, "It takes the edge off."

"Why not?" asked Staci fiercely. "I mean, why *not*? You're not hurting anyone. And it certainly isn't as if you're drinking and driving!"

Alas, my father was still not in the mood to bite. He was in the mood to eat soup. So Staci returned to her former line of questioning. If she couldn't rouse my father to defend the Mennonite position on teetotaling, she would revert to asking me intensely personal questions during Christmas Eve dinner.

I knew it was just a matter of time before Staci would bring up the subject of HIV testing, since my husband had left me for a man named Bob. At some point she would want to follow the AIDS thread. I believe that she would have preferred to inquire after my genital health there on the spot, in front of my brothers. Given her willingness to discuss genitals, I suspect that the only reason she did not broach this subject during Christmas Eve dinner was that my parents were present.

Therefore Staci moved on to another compelling dinner topic: Plan B, Personal Finance and Failed Marriage. "So, Rhoda. Can I ask what your house payment is? What on earth are you going to do with that house? Can you even afford it on your salary?"

"I like this bean soup," said Caleb.

"I haven't made any decisions yet," I told Staci.

"Does everybody at the college know that your husband left you for a man? Do you think they're judging you? Are you worried that they're gossiping about you and Nick and his gay lover?"

"Maybe she doesn't want to talk about it," Caleb said. "Great curry squash, by the way."

"I taste curry in this soup," my father said.

"That's because it's a curry squash soup," I said. "Don't you like curry?"

"I like it," he affirmed, "as long as it doesn't make the house smell like curry." He sniffed, suspicious.

"Oh, Si," said my mother. "She made it at *our* house. Not here. It's *our* house that smells like curry." She took a sip of sparkling apple cider before adding, "I liked curry much more before we went to Calcutta. In Calcutta they prepared meals down in the courtyard. They sat on the ground and cut up meat right there with the flies and chickens. In Calcutta, when you blew your nose, the mucus was so thick and black—"

"Mom!" This appalled protest was shouted by everyone present, except my father. My siblings and I may have our differences, but we were united in our determination not to visualize the black mucus of Christmas past.

From the kids' table in the other room came the sound of one of my many nephews whining. There was a slap and an impatient reprimand from the oldest granddaughter, Phoebe, who was now old enough for Uggs and eye-rolling.

Her cousin Jacob nonetheless shouted, "Mommy, Zach called me a goob again! He doesn't like this soup! He says it tastes"— stifled giggles all around—"like a *dirty Pop-Tart*!"

"Dirty *in your diaper*!" shouted Danny.

Staci looked exasperated. "That's curry!" she called over her shoulder. "It's a flavor. It's supposed to taste like that!"

"Boys," said Caleb in a stern voice that sounded exactly like my own father's thirty-five years earlier. "Do you want me to come over there?"

Little Joon suddenly materialized, tugging her daddy's arm. "Knock knock," she whispered shyly.

"Who's there?" said Caleb tenderly, bending way down to her ear.

"Boo."

"Boo hoo?"

"Baby stop crying," she mouthed ecstatically, and ducked her head into Caleb's armpit.

"What do you think of the broccoli cheese?" Staci asked me. "Because I didn't even taste it. I can't eat my own cooking. I don't eat cheese. It bloats me like you wouldn't believe. How did you manage to not gain weight when you were recuperating from your accident? Because you can't be back at the gym yet, can you?"

"Not yet," I said.

"She can't even reach around to do up her own zipper," said my mother. To my father she added, "Try some of this bacon-potato."

He did so with preacherly gravitas. "I can taste some kind of pepper in it," he said. "It has a kick."

"That's *cayenne* pepper," my mother affirmed joyously.

"Rhoda," said Staci, "I hear you've been dating again. Do you mind if I ask if it's serious? Because maybe you should think about waiting a while before you start dating again."

"I've tried all four soups!" my father said.

"When you have a broken tooth," said my mother, "soup is exactly the right thing to eat. There's a space in your mouth that your tongue keeps feeling for, and it's so tender that the best thing for it is soup."

"Cures what ails you," agreed Caleb.

"Well, I hope nobody at this table is ailing," said Staci, looking at me pointedly. "I hope nobody has anything *contagious*."

"It's the cold and flu season," said Aaron. "At school they were dropping like flies. There was a Group A streptococci going around."

"Your immune system is probably really vulnerable right now," Staci told me, "because of the amount of stress you're under. Are you feeling the stress? Because you look kind of stressed and run-down. Going through a divorce is supposed to be one of the biggest stressors, and it's probably worse when you find out that your husband has been cheating on you with a guy. I like your hair color, though. Are those highlights?"

"And while all four kinds of soup are tasty," continued my father, as if no one else had been speaking, "the best part is this Zwiebach. Mary, send the Zwiebach around again."

For one golden moment no one spoke. We were all too busy helping ourselves to Zwiebach, breaking bread together.

# THREE

# Fear of Mosquitoes

My parents and I had been on the road since 7:40 a.m., having spent the night in a two-bed, one-room Travelodge accommodation. The room had been distinctly inferior. Thirteen years prior my husband had been hospitalized in a crisis unit on a 5150—"Detention of Mentally Disordered Persons for Danger to Self and Others"—while I suffered the helplessness that comes from loving a man who takes a fistful of pills. Even if his doctors managed to turn him around with medication, who would make him take antidepressants one at a time once he was out of the hospital? And how was I going to manage the medical bills on my tiny grad student's stipend? "That's terrible," my mother had said on the phone. There was an infinitesimal pause while I waited for the bounce-back. It came right on cue: "You are hurting. But at least with Nick in the hospital you'll have some peace and quiet to work on your dissertation!" I therefore recognized her signature style when she observed, on entering the shabby motel room, "It's not elegant. But at least there are towels!"

Whenever my parents used a coupon to procure something, they felt 100 percent committed to liking it.

We three were en route to Bend, Oregon, to visit my sister. The car trip was a little over a thousand miles, half of which we drove on Christmas Day. I had spent the morning drifting in and out of uncomfortable sleep. The night before, my father's snoring had kept me up—that and the fact that I had packed my prescription sleeping pills in a suitcase that was wedged in the trunk of the car. Because the backseat of the Camry was overflowing with beribboned presents for my niece, I didn't have much room to negotiate my legs. I lay with my head on my father's shaving kit, legs crossed Indian-style, but with the crossed legs up in the air against the window.

Around noon my father asked us if we would prefer Burger King or McDonald's. It had been at least a decade since I had visited either of these establishments, so I was unable to offer much input. Mom elected McDonald's, on the grounds of better coffee. "You could use your senior discount to order Rhoda a cup of decaf," she suggested.

My father liked this idea. He did not drink coffee himself, but he had no objection to my drinking it, especially if he could save forty cents.

"See there, Mary," said my father, pointing to a sign in the McDonald's window. "It says here that you can get a McChicken Sandwich for a dollar."

"Okay!" My mother accepted this hint.

Fast food is always a hurdle for cooks, and I admit I blanched at the thought of a sucrotic chicken patty injected with flavorlike chemicals and breaded into the dimensions of a crunchy McSanddollar. I therefore announced that I would have a burger instead. The burger was a full three dollars, so I offered to get the lunch tab, which for the three of us, after the senior discount, came to $6.20.

"No, no!" My father waved my wallet away. "I've got it, I've got it."

Then, as we sat down, he added, "You could have had three *chicken* sandwiches for the price of that one burger."

"Yes, but I like this better."

"You like that burger?"

"I wouldn't exactly say that I *like* it," I said. "But I like it better than the chicken sandwich."

My mother set down her sandwich and busily applied ketchup from a squeeze pouch. "It's a little bland," she admitted, "but some ketchup will perk this right up!" She tested a bite. "Much better!"

"This chicken sandwich, which cost one dollar, is preferable to the Wendy's chicken sandwich I had yesterday, which cost $2.34," said my father. "You want to try it?"

"I'm not really a chicken-patty kinda gal," I said.

"When we get back to the car, we can have the last of that cranberry bread," said my mother. "And there's still some coffee in the thermos from yesterday."

This remark was problematic on a variety of levels.

"Mom," I said, pointing to the cup of decaf that was at that moment steaming in her hand, "why wouldn't you drink *this* coffee with the cranberry bread?"

"This coffee might be gone by then, because I'm drinking it with my McSandwich."

"Then why don't you just get a refill on your way out?"

"They charge for refills!" interrupted my father, sensing an opening. "Even on the senior discount!"

"But . . . since you made the coffee in the thermos yesterday morning, won't it be completely cold by now?"

"Oh, well, room temperature. And it's wet! We could drink it if we were desperate. We could drink it if we had car trouble and had to wait by the side of the road."

"How true," I said helplessly.

We can all agree that a snort of day-old coffee will go a long way toward improving our mood in the case of automotive duress.

"See there?" my father said, nodding at the McDonald's menu. "Says there that you could have had a Ranch Snack Wrap for $1.29!"


How different road trips were with my father than with my mother! Both were refreshing in their way, but the trip with my father as driver unfolded in mile after mile of soothing silence. Dad didn't converse, didn't listen to the radio, didn't enjoy the music that my mother urged him to play every so often. Mom always fortified the Camry with a spiritually edifying variety of CDs, including one by my parents' neighbor Chet Wiens and his Mustard Seed Praise Quartet. There was also a new release by my cousin's daughter Starla, who had carved out for herself a career in opera, but who had recently begun rendering perfervid coloratura show tunes à la Ethel Merman. And there were some instrumental CDs too, particularly one that featured some worshipful stylings upon the pan flute.

But it was one thing at a time for Si Janzen. He wasn't what you'd call a multitasker. He liked to concentrate on driving. Sustained conversation, the kind that involved the exchange of abstract ideas, occurred only during brief rest stops and visits to fast-food establishments, and even then it was sort of frowned on. During the actual drive he might utter relevant, specific commentary on the passing landscape. These comments emerged as part of a topically appropriate metanarrative. "I see some sheep," he'd announce. Or, "There's a big jobber of a Winnebago." Personally, I have always found these remarks rather challenging to respond to, as they seem both to invite dialogue yet simultaneously forbid elaboration. However, over the course of a forty-five-year marriage, my mother had mastered the art of replying to my father's cryptic overtures. She always gave him her full attention, even if he had interrupted her crossword puzzle or Sudoku. To "I see some sheep," she might look up and answer brightly, "Sheep dip!" To "There's a big jobber of a Winnebago," she might reply, "Big gas guzzler!"

Dad always declined our offers to pitch in with the driving. Other drivers made him nervous, especially my mother.

He had a point there. When it was just my mother and I in the car alone together, I preferred to drive, and god knows I'm not a great driver. But I'm better than she is. Fortunately she never asserts an intention to take the wheel. A couple of weeks prior to our trip up to Bend, the two of us had made a three-day trip to Arizona, to visit some of her Bible-college friends who were going to be in Flagstaff to spend time with their daughter Frieda. Because these were Mennonite friends, I knew them too, of course. In fact I had known Frieda long ago, when I had dated her older brother, back when I was in Bible school. (Sidebar: Reinhold and I dated for a whole year without figuring out how to kiss with tongue. It's not that we were bad at French-kissing; it's that we didn't do it at all. We didn't *know about it*, see.)

When I heard that Frieda, Reinhold's likable baby sister, now lived in the desert on the outskirts of Flagstaff, I expressed surprise. "Is there a big Mennonite community down there?" I asked.

"No," said my father. He liked conversations about the whereabouts of Mennonites. "Frieda has had health issues, and her health requires her to live in a warm dry climate."

My mother chimed in, "Allergies, Si. And chronic fatigue syndrome."

"Ohhhh," I said knowingly. I assumed that chronic fatigue syndrome was code for serious depression, and I wondered if Frieda hadn't just needed to ditch the Mennonites for a while. Been there.

"No, she's really ill," Mom said. "She almost died."

"Well, in that case, it's great that a change of climate has helped," I said. "It has helped, hasn't it?"

"It has," my father amended soberly. "Frieda lives in a small condo about thirty minutes away from the city."

"All alone?"

"There is a fellow, a friend, who visits her from time to time," said my father in his best preacher's voice. He added, "And they relate to one another, there in the desert."

On the drive to Arizona, Mom and I exchanged many reminiscences about the family car trips we had taken in my youth. I can't speak for my brothers, but Hannah and I dreaded these trips, due to our father's inflexibility and the suspension of creature comforts. It's hard for me to believe that my father willingly agreed to camping vacations, given how miserable they made him. They were leisurely but urgent; aimless yet planned. My father forced us to hit the road every day by 6:00 a.m., not to arrive at a specific destination, but to experience the bucolic pleasures of driving in the cool of the day.

Perhaps the big draw of camping was that it saved money. To this day I am unclear about whether we couldn't afford real vacations, or whether the cheaper car trip was simply a matter of principle. Whatever the cause, the result was the same: a family of six, two Coleman ice chests, an ancient pump stove, and a tin garbage pail that featured an educational map of the United States—so that we could practice capital cities along the way—all stuffed into a white Volkswagen van.

A typical morning involved rising in the thin light of predawn, stumbling out of our crowded tent to a distant biffy, and drinking lukewarm instant cocoa out of a Styrofoam cup. Because the cocoa was lukewarm, the powder wouldn't wholly dissolve; it rose in lumps to the surface. These were discrete, aggressive lumps, not to be mistaken for the miniature marshmallows, which offered their own chunky texture in the sediment at the bottom.

Hannah and I shivered in the damp while my father yelled at my brothers, whose duty it was to help him disassemble the tent, because they were boys. My brothers worked silently, using the claw end of a hammer to pry up the tent stakes while my father struggled with the collapse of the tent poles. In all my growing-up years I never heard either of my parents take the Lord's name in vain, or utter a single foul four-letter word. However, during tenting season I flinched at such fierce imprecations as "GolDARN it!" and "DagNABBIT!" During the tent dismantle, I often took Hannah by the hand and led her some distance away. My father's simmering impatience made her cry.

Since we'd hit the road after the cocoa but before the breakfast, Mom would wait until the sun was up to unfurl the Pandora's icebox of odors. In the space of the cramped van, those odors assumed a pungency that was the inevitable prelude to carsickness. For breakfast there'd be stale *Schnetke*, bruised bananas, and tepid milk in oft-used Styrofoam cups, rinsed out by me and Hannah as the tent came down. Mom stretched the milk by mixing it with nonfat milk powder and water. This made us gag, but we each were required to down a full cup. Nor were we allowed to pick out the raisins in the *Schnetke*, on the grounds that Jesus did not sufficiently appreciate finicky children. We would jolly well eat what we were served. We would approach the throne of God with a clear conscience and a heart of gratitude. Starving children on the Chaco wanted those raisins!

I was terrified that God would call me to become a missionary to the Chaco. The Chaco was an arid stretch of high-altitude land in South America that defied profitable farming. The Mennonites of my youth had reached enthusiastic consensus concerning the Chaco, with its many indigenous non-Christian peoples: it was ripe for mission work. I'm still not sure of what goes on on the Chaco, but as a child I suspected that it involved proliferating weevils and manioc root. From many Sunday-night-church slide presentations, I learned that a missionary organization called Word Made Flesh often summoned Mennonite missionaries to plant churches on the Chaco. When I saw the slides, I privately concluded that what the Chaco needed was not church planting, but a better selection of fruits and vegetables. Forget church planting; just get busy with watermelons. A juicy sweet watermelon could kick the ass of any manioc root. Probably!

When Word Made Flesh kids appeared in Sunday school, on leave from their vital church-planting work on the Chaco, these missionary children were humorless, pious, and pale. The girls wore their aprons to church. And their conversation was full of references to demons, which didn't surprise me a bit. Where else would you expect demons to hang out but on the Chaco, shriveling the manioc crop?

If any of us kids expressed a lack of gratitude for anything that came out of the icebox, Mom was quick on the draw with the Chaco, pulling it out fast, like a gunslinger in the Old West. Starving children on the Chaco would fight for the pleasure of sipping powdery blue milk out of a Styrofoam cup! I inferred that Styrofoam cups were rare on the Chaco, whereupon that place of blight and godlessness rose a little higher in my estimation.

But even a picture of demons at work among manioc roots could not arrest the nausea. Caleb, chewing banana with his mouth not entirely closed, hollered, "Mom! Rhoda's gonna barf again!" He prodded my arm with his banana.

"I'll say a state capital for every raisin," said Aaron smugly. "Concord. Tallahassee. Boise. Juneau."

"She's holding her mouth!" Then, confidentially to me: "Lookee here." Caleb held up one of the long strings that sometimes attach between the banana peel and the flesh. "Lookit, it's coming out of my eye. Lookit, it's the white thing in your eye when you wake up."

"You're the white thing in your eye, moron!" replied Aaron. "Bet you don't know the capital of Vermont. This raisin is the capital of Vermont. Watch this," Aaron said, shoving Montpelier into one nostril.

Not to be outdone, Caleb shoved the moist banana string into *his* nostril. "Lookit, lookit, lookit."

"That's lame," said Aaron scornfully. "That's just a thing on a banana. *This* is Montpelier!" He retrieved Montpelier with one sticky finger and wiped it on Caleb.

"B.T.!" shouted Caleb joyfully, flicking Montpelier back at Aaron. He missed. Montpelier got stuck in Hannah's white-blonde hair. "Booger territory! Hannah-fofannah, you got a *booger* in your hair!" She began to cry.

"We don't use those words in this family, young man!" barked my father over his shoulder. "Mary, what's going on back there?"

She turned and looked inquiringly at Aaron, the oldest.

"Caleb's saying bad words, Hannah's crying 'cause there's a raisin in her hair, and Rhoda needs to puke."

My mother unexpectedly focused on the raisin. "How did that raisin get in her hair?"

"Caleb put it there."

Mom got stern. "Caleb, you eat that raisin right now. We don't waste raisins in *this* family."

"But—"

"Not a peep, young man. You. Eat. That. Raisin."

Caleb sulkily ate the raisin that had been in his brother's nose, but he made powerful retching noises that helped me along.

"Si, pull over. Rhoda needs to throw up."

The van wasn't air-conditioned, yet it did offer a surprise amenity. Mom had outfitted a plywood bed with a homemade red canvas mattress patterned with white stars. It had matching pillows, and the four of us squeezed on that bed in a damp nest, reading, across the long hot miles of dry chaparral through Nevada and Utah. Sometimes Mom let me and Hannah sleep in the van all by ourselves at night, instead of in the farty tent, which smelled of mold and breath in addition to brothers who cut the cheese. This tent offered no guarantee against mosquitoes. (Creatures of the night freely came and went via the many holes in the tent's screen "windows.")

One night we were slapping and scratching through a particularly buggy bout in one of the more humid states. Outsize mosquitoes hung in the air like smoke from an unseen fire, and we had already done our best with hats, long sleeves, insect repellent, and a campfire. But still they came, still they swarmed, like something out of Hitchcock. Mom finally broke down and walked over to the campground's convenience store for a yard bomb, in spite of my father's protest that yard bombs cost good money. When she came back, she doused the area good and proper, and for a while we played Authors in peace.

That night Hannah and I begged to sleep in the van. It was not until we were tucked in for the night that we heard it: the high, tight frenzy of a legion of mosquitoes inside the van with us. I turned on the flashlight to initiate the smackdown.

"Girls!" warned my dad from the tent. "Go to sleep!"

We'd already found and swatted several big lacy mosquitoes before Dad's second shout, so I knew I had to do something drastic. Wrapping the tent bag turbanwise around my forehead, I sprinted out of the vehicle, scooped up the yard bomb, and slammed myself back inside of ten seconds.

"Girls! Don't make me come over there!"

"We're going to sleep!" I shouted.

But before we did, I unleashed the remains of that yard bomb inside the van. With closed windows. Hannah coughed and sputtered, inhaling the damp droplets of poison. "I can't breathe," she whispered.

"Me neither," I whispered back, "but we'll get used to it. No mosquito would dare attack us after *that*!"

In the morning when Mom came to wake us, she drew back coughing and waving her arms. The toxic cloud of fumes lifted as the outside air rushed in, sweet and fresh. We gulped it gratefully. "Oh Rhoda! What did you *do*?"

"Yard bomb," I gasped.

"You could have killed yourselves! Why, why, did you do this?!" She was practically sobbing. Hannah had gotten up dizzily and was sitting down again, head between her legs.

"There were lots of mosquitoes in the van," I said. "I didn't want to chance it."

When my mother reminded me of this story on our own car trip thirty years later, I chuckled at my early determination to avoid predation at all costs. But the story seemed a pretty good analogue for Hannah's and my Childhood of Fear. Why we were always so afraid I cannot say; we weren't abused, attacked, or violated in any way. On the contrary: as Mennonites, we lived remarkably sheltered lives. No radio, no eight-track tapes, no unsupervised TV, no toys that smelled of worldly values. A yo-yo, okay. A crate that your neighbor's refrigerator came in, knock yourself out. A Slinky, sure. Badminton, by all means. But a big fat no to the following: Barbie's House of Dreams (too adult? too containing-a-bed-onwhich-Barbie-might-seduce-the-other-Barbie?); Lite-Brite (too electric and therefore too vainglorious?); Edible Creepy-Crawlers made from a kit (too satanic?). Even our friends were prescreened for bad influences.

Did the degree to which we were sheltered occasion the fear that Hannah and I both felt with the onset of adolescence? Ah, those were the days when we saw a predator in every man who approached us! Somewhere, somehow, the Mennonite culture had taught us that all non-Mennonite men were would-be rapists. Thus whenever we stepped outside the protective shield of our Mennonite community, we moved in a terrifyingly unfamiliar world. Scared of school events, horrified by what would happen if I let my guard down to have a beer, terrified whenever a boy asked me out, I was as skittery as one of those squirrels that freeze as your vehicle approaches. Even when your gay husband rolls down the window and shouts, "Make your move, junior!" these squirrels seem profoundly indecisive. I always felt bad for those squirrels. I too had faced doom. And, like the squirrels, I had closed my eyes and hoped the doom would just go away.

Hannah and I inferred that non-Mennonites were capable of anything. The world seemed especially hospitable to serial killers in unmarked white vans. For instance, when Hannah and I walked to the Thrifty Drug Store for contraband Bonnie Bell Lip Smackers, we'd always rehearse a Plan A and a Plan B for what we'd do if a serial killer offered us a ride or attempted to thrust us into his unmarked white van. I am happy to report that this never happened to us. However, because our adolescence coincided with the last years before political correctness, we did hear some graphic things about our anatomy. I, who still thought that you could get pregnant from kissing, spent many an evening puzzling over the possible meaning of *titfuck*.

This fear lingered into my adult years. Once in grad school I returned to my apartment to find a note taped to the front door. In scary printed capital letters it read

> FOR ALL THE DONUTS YOU CAN SCARF
> COME TO MY PLACE FRI 7:00 PM,
> I WANT TO GET TO KNOW YOU RODA.
>                                              JIMMY

Jimmy was a sad guy I had met once while doing laundry, and as a dating overture, this gesture strikes me as funny after a distance of twenty-three years. But back then I experienced a complex response whose crescendos came rolling like Elisabeth Kübler-Ross's stages of grief and dying. First there was revulsion: Scarf? *Scarf ?!?* Next, confusion: What kind of a person eats donuts on a Friday night? Then fear: Why does this Jimmy know where I live?

And, finally, panic: Do I *look* like a scarfer of donuts? Ohmygod, does this outfit make me look like Agnes Ollenburger, the biggie Mennonite of our youth who had liposuction on her upper arms and then asked the church for forgiveness?

Jimmy was clearly a serial killer or a pervert. That Friday night I went to the library as usual, but I propped the note in a promi-nent position on my coffee table for police use, in case my body showed up dismembered in a dumpster.

Now at forty-three, on the long drive up to Bend with both my parents, I sat quietly contorted in the crowded backseat, remembering the car trips of my youth, remembering fear like a high-pitched cloud of mosquitoes. And I couldn't think of any-thing that explained why Hannah and I had always been so afraid. Sure, Mennonite culture mistrusted public images of sex; that was a given. On the few occasions when we kids were allowed to watch TV, a parent had to be present. My father monitored the proceedings like a stern prison guard. If any character on any tele-vision show, married or single, made a move toward an on-screen kiss, there was Dad, wielding the remote like a Taser. Quick to change the channel, he'd sometimes mutter in dark disapproval, "Smut!" Sex, it was clear, was a sinful scourge.

But my folks themselves were unafraid. They moved confi-dently through the world, taking risks, opening their home to strangers, traveling like fearless cosmopolites. My father's leader-ship position in the global Mennonite church required a lot of traveling, and my mother happily trailed along. When my father retired, the travel habit stuck—flourished, even, as they began to sign up for monthlong tours with other Mennonite couples.

Geography was important in our family, as demonstrated by the persistence of the tin garbage pail with the state capitals. Yet it wasn't just geographic knowledge that my parents wanted us to have; it was knowledge of the international scene. In an ironic twist, two of the most conservative Mennonite parents took a sharp stand against monologism. An Americentric worldview, they believed, was incompatible with Christian values on the grounds that God loved all nations equally. My folks insisted that we study and travel abroad. They have done extensive globetrotting on every continent except Antarctica, which is probably on their list. They even know and love the Chaco. Considering that both my grandmothers had a third-grade education and never left the village until they emigrated to rural Ontario, it's funny to get postcards from Kinshasa, or Istanbul, or Hyderabad, from a mom like mine: "We saw a spider big as a teapot! Dad doesn't like yoghurt. There are unattended cows walking down the street. Love, Mom." From Calcutta: "They cremate their dead here by burning old rubber tires. I guess they are out of wood. It stinks to high heaven. Love, Mom."

I thought of my parents' fearlessness as we pulled into the parking lot of a Denny's. After a five-hundred-mile day, we had two more hours to drive to Bend. It felt good to stretch our legs under the restaurant table. And I must say that it felt good to be checked out by a couple of guys sitting right across from us. They were maybe half my age, but they were cute.

The server, who had already deposited my father's patty melt and my mother's breaded chicken cutlet, approached with my salad just as my father began to pray—out loud, in a clear audible voice, thanking God for the patty melt, the cutlet, the salad. Then he prayed for his pastor, for the state governor, for the president. He prayed for the couple who had just adopted three siblings, and for the people of Iraq. He prayed for traveling mercies. In his sober voice he noted that we would embrace whatever circumstances God saw fit to bestow, and he petitioned God for the grace and the wisdom to learn the lessons that our journey had to teach.

I prayed to Pharaoh until I was six. Having learned in Sunday school that the Egyptians worshipped their kings as gods, I wanted to hedge my bets. But I always respectfully addressed the sovereign Yahweh before I spoke to Pharaoh—I thought there was one Pharaoh, mighty and eternal—because the Ten Commandments specified, "Thou shalt have no other gods before me." The Mennonite God thus received my A-list requests, such as intercession from wolves, disembodied red eyes, vampires, and volcanoes. Pharaoh received my secondary and tertiary requests, like my earnest plea to be spared raisins and the Chaco.

It had been at least thirty years since I'd believed in the power of prayer as anything other than a way to practice gratitude and ameliorate self-pity. Curiously, although I married an atheist, and although I had spent sixteen years pursuing the very secular path of higher education, I had not rejected the idea of God. But during that time my faith had changed dramatically as I had learned more about context of the church and more about religious belief outside Christianity. A little knowledge goes a long way!

The Mennonites have a prickly history with the idea of education. There's an old Low German proverb that I have always savored, in part because everything is funnier somehow in Low German, in part because it seems personally directed at me: *Ji jileada, ji vikjeada* (the more educated a person is, the more warped). That knowledge would compromise faith is one of those delightfully old-fashioned beliefs that makes us chuckle today, as when we learn that the uterus was once thought to drift about the body, occasionally lodging in neck or elbow. Mennonites often connect their mistrust of education to the passage in the gospel of Mark in which Jesus observes that it is hard for those who trust in riches to enter into the Kingdom of God. The Mennonite idea is that people who privilege money and knowledge will think they have all the answers, and if they think they have all the answers, they won't be interested in seeking God. I can't speak for rich people, but in my experience higher education does not produce people who think they have all the answers, unless you count my brother Aaron. Higher education does just the opposite; it teaches us that we *don't* have all the answers. Socrates summed it up very well: "I know only that I know nothing at all." So unfortunately the Mennonites have it back-assward on this one. Which is something they'd no doubt have figured out if they'd gone to college like normal folks.

A hundred years ago, while still in Ukraine, the Mennonites proudly pointed to their communal literacy, contrasting their disciplined public school system with the illiterate squalor in which their Russian neighbors lived. But the Mennonites made sure not to be *too* literate. They had firm ideas about when to pull out: Boys typically completed high school; girls stopped at grade three. It was enough to be able to figure numbers and read the Bible. Any more education and you might start asking questions that could weaken your faith and take you away from God.

My grandparents' generation of Mennonites was united in its hostility to higher education. Once when I was traveling in Ukraine with a group of older Mennonites, I made friends with a fellow traveler, a stoop-shouldered slip of a widow who had escaped Stalinist Russia by "attaching herself" to a German officer during the occupation. Even at age eighty-four, with decades of prosperity and a happy marriage behind her, Marta refused to discuss the sexual relationship that had saved her life. When I asked her about her German benefactor, all she said was that the attachment had resulted in emigration papers for herself and her four sisters.

Marta was a tiny thing—the top of her silvery head came up to my waist—but she was filled with the spirit to see her old stomping ground, and I found it delightful to adjust my steps to her slower pace. For most of the trip we talked about Marta: her past, her losses, her understanding of the political events in the years after the Russian Revolution. As a girl she had actually seen the infamous anarchist Nestor Makhno. I felt blessed that I had found a traveling companion who remembered the events of the Maknovshchina firsthand. Easy friendships often spring up among travelers, and soon Marta was confiding more than the facts of her story to me. Our intimacy was helped along by difficult physical circumstances, since she had to rely on me for assistance over uneven steps and open trenches and such. She was light as a leaf, and I often picked her up and lifted her over rough patches. Rural Ukraine, with its rank privies, is challenging even for sturdy travelers, let alone for frail octogenarians who lack the lower-body strength to pee standing up. No wonder we became close so quickly.

Toward the end of our time together, Marta and I were on deck aboard the *Glushkov*, sailing toward Yalta and the Sea of Azov. Leaving behind Sevastopol and the Mennonite settlements of her youth, we stood watching the sun set on the Black Sea. It must have suddenly occurred to Marta that she knew very little about the woman who had been at her elbow for the last three weeks. Until that moment Marta hadn't asked me much about my own situation; she knew only that I was Mennonite and that I was Si Janzen's daughter. That had been good enough for her. "My dear," she said, her small hands holding the ship rail, "how is it that a young woman like you comes to be traveling with us old folks to the old places?"

"I wanted to know more about my history," I said.

"How do you fill your days when you aren't traveling?" she asked. "What is it you do, if you don't have a family of your own?"

Ah, sweet woman, I didn't want to disappoint her! If she found out I was a scholar, would she shake her head in sorrow and say *Ji jileada, ji vikjeada*? Would she cease telling me her stories and dismiss me as worldly? For many Mennonites of her generation, getting a Ph.D. was practically sinning against God. But now she had asked point-blank, and I had to 'fess up to the book-learnin'.

I said soberly, "I'm a teacher, Marta. I teach in a college." She turned to face the Sea of Azov, and in the gathering twilight I thought I could see disappointment settling her lips into a frown. She looked out at the water without saying anything. Finally she turned to me, reached up, and patted my shoulder. "That's okay," she reassured me in German. "You're a good person anyway."

Obviously my own parents did not share Marta's bias against higher education. Both my mother and my father have graduate degrees. But they prayerfully chose to study in areas that would not take them afield of their faith. Nursing seems quite consonant with Jesus's biblical ministry to heal the sick, and theology bases its entire raison d'être on the supposition that God exists and cares about what happens to his creation. My parents must have been concerned when I picked an academic field that invited, even demanded, philosophical questioning.

Among my many rebellious behaviors is my refusal to ask God for stuff, especially before meals, especially out loud. Requests for divine intervention usually strike me as jejune and quixotic. Why should God grant one request when another supplicant is asking for the opposite? Why should one believer have the hubris to think her needs deserve special attention in the global schema? I do like the idea of prayer as a way to foreground one's blessings. It unselfs the self, as the theologian Eugene Peterson would say. It's when people start expecting divine intervention that I get nervous, because that's when they start hearing the voice of God telling them, for instance, to go kill a bunch of people in Iraq.

But there was my father seated in front of me at a booth in Denny's, big hands folded, handsome head bowed. Not only did he pray as if God was listening; he prayed as if God might be standing right there, waiting with a salad, like the server. When you're with your parents, old habits die hard. In spite of my embarrassment that the server was trying to contain her amusement, and in spite of the fact that the cute guys who'd been checking me out were now clearly horrified, I bowed my head and shut my eyes. Fearless.

# FOUR

# Wounding Words

"Aunt Rhoda," said Allie, "do you want to come play Super Scrabble with us?"

"You bet," I said.

My sister and I had not yet had a moment to ourselves. We were very close, however, and it was easy to communicate in indirect glances and oblique smiles. We were each other's port-in-the-holiday-storm. I had been on the West Coast for several weeks now, and Hannah would demand a detailed account of what it was like to be plunged back into the Mennonite mainstream. She and I were both waiting for a time when we could grab a cocktail and debrief. Right before my parents and I had arrived, she and her husband, Phil, had been hosting Phil's sister Yvonne, and I was anxious to hear the news on that front.

Hannah's husband was fabulous. Among Phil's many excellent qualities was the expression of zero interest in leaving his wife for a guy he had met on Gay.com. Yet he did have a fatal flaw. Phil's special bugaboo, his personal kryptonite, was his sister Yvonne. Specifically, he had a problem with Yvonne's hair. This criticism we understood to include an implied catalog of behaviors, incursions, and habits that offended him. He returned again and again to the fact that Yvonne's hair looked not unlike a glossy, nest-shaped wig, and that she, his own flesh and blood, ought to know better. He did have a bird's-eye view of the Nest, as he was fully six foot six, a vantage point from which the Nest would have been nigh impossible to ignore. It sat smartly on her head, like the tall black hats worn by beefeaters at Buckingham Palace. Sometimes after Yvonne's visit, Phil found himself humming the changing-of-the-guard song from the *The Wizard of Oz.*

Even from a lateral view the Nest could make you forget what you were saying. Once in grad school, an angry feminist who called herself Lilith but whose real name was Barb attended a swim party in an itsy-bitsy swimsuit. There was a general sense that she had done this on purpose, to make everyone else uncomfortable. From the bikini bottom exploded an epic, wiry bush. This was pubic hair on a Richter scale, hair gone wild, hair raised by wolves. It was hair that had taken over her entire southern region, like kudzu. At that swim party every person present had spent a pained evening with eyes cemented at least five feet above the ground, so as to avoid the magnetic vista of Barb's, I mean Lilith's, frenzied pubes. Trying not to stare at Yvonne's hair was a lot like that.

The Nest, I hasten to add, was premakeover, predivorce. In all fairness to Yvonne, Hannah noted, she did look a lot better now that she was not using as much product. Hannah was always urging Phil to cut Yvonne some slack. Any woman would have found it challenging to keep abreast of bicoastal hair trends, living there in a small Wisconsin mobile home park with a whimsical sidewalk sign that said, WELCOME TO ALL GOD'S CRITTERS!

Many years earlier Yvonne had rejected college in favor of a career with Mary Kay Cosmetics. As a dynamic Independent Sales Director, she proudly drove a pale pink Cadillac that said in modest pink cursive on the rear window, MARY KAY. She was always bringing Hannah and me free samples. "Missy," she'd say in her shoot-from-the-hip voice, "I tell it like it is, and you got some Martha Stewart circles under your eyes, like you just spent four months in jail. Let's cover that mess up! Here's a good concealer. Take it like you own it!"

Yvonne had divorced Stan, her husband of twenty-one years, two years earlier. Whether or not it was true, Hannah and I had always thought—ah, the tragic irony!—that Stan was gay, in a beer-for-breakfast kind of way. Stan had a tiny long-legged Chihuahua named Ms. Ginger that he took everywhere with him. The first time I met Stan, he and Yvonne were arriving at my sister's place in Bend after a long car trip from Wisconsin. Stan and Yvonne sprang energetically from the cab of Stan's truck. They hugged it out with their hosts, shook my hand, and then turned to the task uppermost on their minds: peeing Ms. Ginger after the long trip. Stan was a heavyset fellow in a plaid flannel shirt, belly slung low over his belt. He scooted the trembling Chihuahua onto my sister's lawn. Then his voice lifted a full octave as he admonished Ms. Ginger to do her miniature business on the lawn: "Who's gonna pee-pee! Who's gonna pee-pee! Time to make pee-pees! Make me some pee-pees!"

It must have been hard to be married to a gay-seeming fellow who pluralized urine in a falsetto, Hannah and I agreed, so we nobly tried not to discuss Yvonne's hair. Hannah had seen to it that I had plenty of opportunities to observe Yvonne in action. I had often been invited along on Phil's family outings, had tagged along on Phil's family holidays, and had met all four of Yvonne's boyfriends since the divorce. Nick had always opted out of these visits. He had no desire to while away the evening hours with Yvonne, who, he maintained, never said a single thing that hadn't already appeared as a phrase on *Wheel of Fortune*. Although Yvonne's company was less than stimulating, I figured I needed to show my sister some loyalty and moral support. As soon as Hannah would tell me that Yvonne was going to be present, I would see it as my sisterly duty to scout for a cheap airline ticket. "You've got to come," Hannah pleaded. "The new boyfriend sells cold cuts!"

These were the best cold cuts. Todd, the boyfriend, was very proud of the cold cuts' quality. His cold cuts were sold at the finest grocery establishments. During the three-day weekend that I was privileged to eat these cold cuts every day, I exerted myself to get Todd to use the possessive form of *cold cuts*: he'd add an extra *tz* sound, like the German *z*. "My cold cutzes freshness is unrivaled," he'd say. "I mean, this is some fresh meat. Try the pimento loaf."

During the weekend of the cold cutzes reign up at Phil and Hannah's cabin at Tahoe, Yvonne revealed her follicle situation to me. Phil and Todd were off enjoying the cold cutzes flavor on the lake below. Yvonne and Hannah and I were sitting on the deck with magazines and iced tea; it was about noon. No alcohol was involved. We were all wearing shorts, dressed for a hike we planned on taking later that afternoon. Yvonne was wearing a T-shirt that said, ASK ME HOW TO COVER YOUR BLEMISH! Mine said, I AM THE GRAMMARIAN ABOUT WHOM YOUR MOTHER WARNED YOU. Hannah was wearing a nice periwinkle blouse, very ladylike.

Five minutes earlier Yvonne had suggested that Hannah and I try her full-coverage foundation to even out our color—"Ladies, you gals got the full-blown German complexion, let me tell it to you straight! When I was a kid, I had a pet rat that had eyes just the color of your skin! No offense!"—but since that comment, the three of us had lapsed into pleasant silence, paging through our magazines. To my astonishment Yvonne suddenly stood up, unzipped her shorts, hooked a thumb in her panties, and revealed a patch so hirsute it could have kept a family of five warm through a long Arctic winter. "I just want you to see what I'm dealing with here," she said. "Have you ever seen a thang like that?"

Phil nodded when I later reported on the unexpected appearance of the Thang. I felt like someone who had documented a fabled entity, such as the Sasquatch.

Hannah said, "I'd heard about it, but that was the first time I saw it in full bush. Was it just me, or could you detect the shape of the Virgin Mary?"

I nodded. "If Our Lady of Mercy can appear in a water stain on an underpass, she can surely appear in your sister-in-law's underpants."

"That's nothing," Phil said. "The Thang is old news. We've been hearing about the Thang for years. How about *this*? She told us Todd gave her a dildo for Christmas."

"I'd rather receive a dildo than cold cuts," I said, "especially if the cold cutzes additives involve the taste of liquid smoke."

"Okay, maybe so," Phil conceded. "But which gift would you rather discuss, in detail, with your older *brother*?"

"Which gift would you rather announce *in front of your nine-year-old niece* not ten minutes after having gotten off the plane at the airport?" said Hannah, clearly on board with her husband on this one.

"Cold cuts, like dildos, bring a welcome element of surprise to any family gathering," I asserted.

"Of course Allie was all ears. 'Momma,' she goes, 'what's a dildo?'"

"What'd you say?"

"Yvonne cut in and fielded that one," said Phil. "She said it was a kind of Christmas candy."

"Now that is some spectacular shit," I told my sister. "Oops, I didn't mean to say that in front of you, Al."

"That's okay," my niece said. "My friend Ruby says *shit* all the time."

"I suppose *shit* could itself be a Wounding Word, depending on the context. But in this case, it was not intended to wound. If I wounded you," I told Allie magnanimously, "then I'm sorry."

"I'm not wounded," Al reported. "But I wish Momma would take her turn. This game is kind of slooooooooooooooow."

"Would you accept the word *retard*?" said Hannah. "It's not much, but at least I get my *D* on a triple."

"I accept *retard*," said my mother. "It's a common word. It's much better than *lionhairs*."

"*Lionhairs* was a great word. I would have gotten 118 points!" said Hannah.

"Not to split lionhairs," I said, "but you are a cheater, pure and simple. Under what circumstances would you even use the word *lionhairs*?"

"At our African camp we often have a problem with lionhairs on the chaise lounge," said Hannah defensively.

"Lions are lounging on your lawn furniture, and the only things you're worried about are the lionhairs? Me, I'd be thinking about the lionteeth and the lionhunger."

"Perhaps I am a *retard*," said Hannah, trying to sneak her newest word onto the board.

"*Retard* is not in the dictionary. Also it's a Wounding Word."

"You let Mom get away with *stomalotion*. And *boner*," Hannah protested.

"What's wrong with *boner*?" my mother asked. "That's a perfectly good word. Somebody made a boner."

"Indeed somebody did make a boner," said my sister, frowning at me.

My mother appeared to be using *boner* as a synonym for *goof-up*. I made a mental note to check the etymology. Was there a time when a boner had been a mere boo-boo? If so, when had it become a stiffy? I had plenty of time to consider the lexical shift because my mother was agonizing over her word.

"Mom," I said finally. "Why don't you make *ahoy*? You get your *H* on a quadruple, plus a triple-word score."

The suggestion summoned to my mother's mind a felicitous recollection of bygone sing-alongs. She burst into one of the songs of yesteryear.

> I was drifting along on life's pitiless sea
> When the angry waves threatened my ruin to be.
> When away at my side
> There I dimly descried
> A stately old vessel and loudly I cried,
> SHIP AHOY! SHIP AHOY!
> (and loudly I cried SHIP AHOY!)

When her robust soprano paused for breath, I asked, "Is there a religious surprise in this song?"

She nodded eagerly, continuing:

> 'Twas the *old ship of Zion* thus moving along;
> All aboard her seemed happy; I heard their glad song—

"Go on," I said. Any hymn figuring salvation as a mysterious pirate vessel deserved to be heard. No matter that the hymn had declined in popularity since its heyday in 1938.

"I can't remember the rest of it," she admitted. To make up for the memory lapse, she sang the first part again, only a little louder.

"I want to switch games," said Allie. "Let's play Made for Trade."

My sister and I studiously did not look at each other. Made for Trade was possibly the worst board game of all time, and it had only recently appeared in my sister's household, a Christmas gift from Oma and Opa. It featured a boring historical premise and colonial cardboard figurines significantly too large for the tiny squares.

But of course we busted the game out. There isn't a lot we wouldn't do for Al.

"You can tax any player the object of your choice," Al told me, when I passed an orange spot with tiny illegible font. I put on my reading glasses and frowned at it. "Aunt Rhoda, you have to pick an Event Card," Al said helpfully.

"Okay. You're going down, Oma," I said to my mother, who shrieked dramatically. "Ebenezer Brown hereby taxes you your spinning wheel for five shillings." Then I dutifully drew an Event Card and read aloud:

Is the severe summer drought the result of personal and communal sin? A fast day has been declared. Go directly to the Meeting House, listen to a sermon on sinfulness, and pray for God's mercy in the form of rain. Do not pay the usual tithe.

"Huh?" I said. "Is it just me, or is this Event Card advising us to retaliate against God?"

"No," said my mother. "The blame falls on the *congregation*, not on God."

"But it sounds as if we're going to withhold our tithe because God has inflicted a drought on us."

"We deserved the drought," said my mother.

"Because we were sinful," Al piped in.

"No, we were not sinful. That is, maybe we did some bad things," said my sister emphatically, frowning at Allie, "but we were just doing the best we could according to our nature. God is a loving God. He does not punish his people with drought."

"At school he does," said Allie. Phil and Hannah were sending Allie to a private Catholic school because the local public school was so crappy. "At school God punishes *everybody*."

"In this house God punishes *nobody*," said Hannah. "The world has seen enough Christian guilt, wrath, and vengeance to last a lifetime."

" 'Vengeance is mine, saith the Lord,' " quoted my mother.

"Momma," said Al, "is it okay to pray for mercy in the form of rain?"

"I guess," Hannah conceded. She and Phil were ideologically opposed to all religious institutions, and they knew they were skating a fine line with the whole private-Catholic-school thing. Hannah had often declared that a background in Bible lore had been useful in her own education and cultural training. Still, it was a tough call. In the private Catholic school, the value of the Bible lore would be compromised by Catholic guilt and shame about the body. The public school, on the other hand, would inflict bad math, obsolescent history books, and Mean Girls. Al's enrollment at St. Veronica's had not been a shoe-in, but Phil and Hannah had decided that Christian guilt was better than bad math.

"Well then," Allie went on, reasonably, "could I pray for God's mercy in the form of chocolate?"

"There's chocolate in the pantry, Al. You don't need to ask God for it. Just ask me," said Hannah.

My mother felt this was an excellent opportunity to advance

Allie's theological training. "Sometimes God works through other people and things, such as pantries."

I raised my eyebrows, but she went on, "God provides blessings, such as chocolate, *through* your mama and her pantry. But it's still God who's doing the providing."

"Your turn, Allie," I said. When she frowned meditatively over her Event Card, I briskly tapped my right hand on my left palm, like an old-fashioned schoolmarm with a ruler. "Chop-chop!"

"Aunt Rhoda, you're a big dork."

"Wounding Word," I said.

Playing the colonial game with its posset cups and spinning wheels naturally invited a discussion of how our lives would have been different three hundred years earlier. Hannah pointed out that because of our Mennonite training, we'd have a much easier time of it than most American women. "For Mom it would be completely familiar, really. That's how she grew up, as if it were three hundred years ago."

"Three hundred years!" my mother exclaimed. "No, it wasn't as bad as that! We had an orchard!"

We chose to ignore this.

"In school we're talking about Albuquerque," said Allie. "It was settled by the Spanish, but it didn't become a town until 1706. That was exactly three hundred years ago. The governor got permission from Spain to call it a town by saying it already had a church and some buildings, but it didn't. It was more like a little village in the middle of the desert. People needed medicine there, Oma. Sometimes they died of cholera, so you could be a nurse in Albuquerque and teach everybody how not to get sick."

"The four of us could handle colonial Albuquerque, no problem," agreed Hannah. "We can butcher, make soap, candles, quilts, bread, you name it. I took Spanish in college."

"I can count to twenty," said Allie. "But I can't butcher. Gross. You have to do the butchering, Momma."

"You'll get used to it," Hannah returned. "It's no grosser, really, than trimming the fat off a roast."

"Also gross." So far the Mennonite love of cookery had not manifested in Allie, who consented to help in the kitchen only when bribed.

"Seriously," said Hannah, "would you go back in time if you could?"

"Can I change the course of history?" I asked. "Can I teach girls to read and tell people about germs?"

"No," Hannah decided. "You can go back in time, but you have to go knowing what you know now, and you have to keep it to yourself and just live your colonial life." We had a split vote. Hannah and Al declined not to go back in time, while my mother and I agreed that it would be pleasurable, amusing, and instructive, as long as we could come back.

I couldn't help wondering then if I would go back fifteen years. Would I, to save myself a marriage shadowed by suicide, grief, and despair? Fifteen years earlier, one Saturday afternoon had sealed my fate. I ran into Nick on the top floor of the university library, a space unofficially designated for intellectuals with odd sideburns and thrift store sweaters. The peculiar odor of that top floor motivated my studies like nothing else. It stank deliciously of nineteenth-century bindings and old periodicals. Slumped into the carrels were the überdorks who barricaded themselves behind stacks of books like children with cereal boxes. Occasionally you'd see a loner coming or going in retro polyester duds, arms full of laptop and books stacked right up to the chin. I liked the churchy silence up there, and all the bookish smells. And I liked the way that the intellectuals left you alone behind your own towers. It made me feel like one of those ancient monks in silent but busy fellowship, feather quills scratching the vellum of a sacramentary.

Recognizing Nick from an undergraduate Italian class I was auditing, I suddenly understood that if he was here among the hard-core scholars, he could not possibly be the undergraduate I had mistaken him for. Because of his long hair and boyish charm, I had assumed he was in his early twenties. I now saw that he wasn't when he stopped by my carrel; there was a confidence and a history in the way he nodded at me.

The polo-player logo on his otherwise impeccable Ralph Lauren shirt had been carefully mutilated. Little threads stuck out every which way. "What happened to that?" I asked, pointing at the logo.

"I picked it apart. I'll be goddamned if I'm going to be a free billboard for Ralph Lifshitz and his fantasies about a Waspy Nantucket."

"Then why buy the shirt?"

"Well, look at it." He grinned. "It's a great shirt."

"Shhhhhhh!" came the testy reprimand from a nearby carrel. A man in a floral print dress and Doc Martens was glaring.

"Take a study break," Nick ordered. "Let's go get some lunch. We can practice the *congiuntivo* for the midterm."

That was it for me. I was in, all the way in, even before I noticed that Nick was reading Nietzsche, even before he suggested we go see the Noam Chomsky documentary playing that night in Santa Monica. If I had known then what I know now, I could have just smiled and said, "No, I've gotta finish this. Catch up with you later." How much hurt that would have saved me, how many Wounding Words!

In those first years of marriage, we practically lived at the West Hollywood YMCA. That facility provided the perfect antidote to our rigorous academic work. Having spent my youth being picked last for teams, and having extracted two years' worth of PE excuses from a single tonsillectomy, I came tardily to the sports arena. It wasn't until I was in my late teens, when my brother Caleb patiently taught me to play racquetball, that I realized I was coordinated enough to participate in athletic endeavors. But I tried to make up for it by becoming a competitive asshole. Nick, also a competitive asshole, used to smoke me at the sport. You know how some athletically gifted men enjoy playing with their wives and express pride when the wives manage to scrape up eight points or so? Nick wasn't like that. He played with deadly fury, hitting the ball so hard it sometimes stung the racquet clean out of my grip.

But I loved it. I loved the suspension of idea-driven dialogue. We said as little as possible to each other on the court: "Hindrance." "Cheater." "Game point." There were pros who played the Y, and whenever they'd roll through, we'd sign up for lessons. One of our local members, a woman named Lila Korndahl, was even better than the pro women who offered the occasional seminar. Lila Korndahl was an unprepossessing fifty-three-year-old housewife with frizzy problem hair and thick ankles, but she was universally revered at the West Hollywood Y. Sometimes a hapless visitor would fall for Lila's husband's oh-so-casual offer: "Hey, buddy, waddaya say we bring in our wives, play doubles for, say, fifty bucks?"

Lila Korndahl taught me a skill set that infuriated Nick. Lila was the master of placement, the queen of the drop shot. With a flick of her wrist, she could tap a screaming ball into the corner, where it would yawn and fall asleep, straight down, gentle as a Milk Dud. These drop shots were so widely associated with Lila Korndahl that to be defeated by a slow drop was to be korned.

Sometimes you'd hear rueful shouts from a neighboring court: "Oh! Serve me up summa that steamin' creamed korn!" "Ohhhh! Korn on the cob!"

On the few occasions when I did win against Nick, my triumphs invariably turned on successful drop shots that seemed to freeze in midair, or to brush the wall four inches above the floor before piddling to a full stop below. These shots drove Nick insane. He loved goading me into the strongest, fastest rallies that I was capable of. I am taller and stronger than most women, and I could really hammer that ball. But my control, unlike Nick's, was poor, and my serve uneven. My racquetball philosophy was simple: to kill the ball or die trying. All I wanted was to beat my cocky husband. Amused at my determination, Nick would offer to spot me five points. This affront made me fight even harder. He'd bait me with a back wall rally, the ball coming so fast you couldn't really see it; you'd have to hit blindly, instinctively, in a kind of white heat. Then, just when I'd be lost in the pace, he'd suddenly change it up with a lob or a trick shot. If I ever managed to korn the man, he took it personally. Cookin' with korn was *his* territory.

In fifteen years of marriage I never managed to skunk him 15–1. When I did win, it was always close, and it came down to a breathless grunting fight for the final points. Nick must have missed the day the PE teacher taught good sportsmanship when he was growing up. He'd stalk off the court, enraged, or, worse, he'd destroy his racquet by beating it on the wall. He'd break into a long rich string of obscenities: "Damn queen-of-korn fuckbag korncunt kernels of douchecob, cocksucking shower of golden korn from my ASS!" Sometimes we got asked to leave.

One day he pitched a hissy on the court, shouting and swearing, ending on a typical note: "You play like a korncob CUNT!"

As he shouted this final imprecation, he threw his racquet across the court with all his might and stalked off to the men's locker room. I had been telling myself that this behavior, while childish, was funny, especially since I knew that he would tender an endearing apology within the hour. He'd be sorry and chuckling by the time we hit the coed Jacuzzi. *Lighten up*, I'd tell myself; his strings of insults, all twisted like strands of DNA, were *amusing* in their spicy furor. But that day, gathering up Nick's abandoned things and my own equipment from the bench outside the court, I ran into my friend Cameron, who was waiting with her partner for the court. By the way she looked at me, wide-eyed and full of sympathy, I could tell that she had heard everything. And I could tell that it wasn't funny.

"Cam!" I said breezily. "What's up?"

"Oh, Rhoda," she exclaimed. "Are you okay?"

Now, playing silly games in my sister's kitchen, I thought of how often over the years I had shrugged off Wounding Words. April Silty had a point. Curiously, though, I didn't get any pleasure out of imagining what it would have been like to refuse Nick's invitation to lunch that day in the library fifteen years ago.

I think maybe I'd still nod and smile and have lunch with him. I think maybe I'd still go to the Noam Chomsky documentary later that evening. And maybe I'd even marry him a couple of weeks later. Is it ever really a waste of time to love someone, truly and deeply, with everything you have?

# FIVE

# A Lingering Finish

Hannah was no stranger to romance gone awry. For the first part of Nick's and my marriage, she was still with her first fiancé, Josh. I could go on at length about that guy, but instead I will sum him up with one sentence that sketches his character with an almost Zen-like simplicity: Josh asked Hannah to put him through law school, and then on the very day he graduated, he dumped her. Everyone in my family had tried and failed to like Josh. He was the kind of guy who had what Henry James called a "moist moral surface." When he subjected my sister to so much grief and pain, I gritted my already gritty teeth.

Hannah—cautious, coolheaded Hannah—had surprised us all by doing something much more like me than like her: she turned around and married her boss, Phil, immediately, less than three months after Josh had left her. She became, briefly, a Tasmanian devil of love. (When I tasmaniated on the first date with Nick and married him six weeks later, my family was predictably disapproving. Yet they were not surprised. Getting engaged on the first date was *exactly* the kind of birdwitted, addlepated thing I would do. But not Hannah. And to her boss! The inappropriateness of it took our breath away.)

Everyone privately thought that Hannah's new marriage to her boss would bring nothing but more heartache. For starters, there was the obvious charge of the rebound relationship. Then there was the eighteen-year age difference. Hannah was twenty-six at the time and—have I mentioned this?—scary beautiful. Let's face it: there is nothing odd when a little girl has eyes the lustral blue of the Aegean, or when the same little girl has a silky curtain of white-blonde hair that recalls angels and innocence and unicorns; but when a woman retains these natural attributes at thirty-eight, you begin to suspect a pact with the devil.

Yet Hannah never really seemed to value her good looks; it was I who was desperate to be pretty. In those severe Mennonite skirts, I fixed with longing on the crotch-skimming pastels of my classmates, who according to instinct and custom gave a wide berth to all Children of the Corn. My mother braided my hair so tightly that my eyebrows buckled. This conferred on me a look of wholesome mental illness, like Joan Crawford in *Mommie Dearest*.

Also, because I grew tall so fast, my mother resourcefully sewed strips of contrasting fabric to the bottom of my pants. Hippies were doing this, and many a groovy ribbon enlivened 1960s jeans. However, the Mennonite God circa 1970 had not yet made up his mind about jeans. Jeans belonged in the barn, and moreover on boys. I wasn't allowed to wear them. The pants that came to me from the Seminary Clothes Closet for Sacrificial Missionary Families Who Served the Lord with Joy and Gladness were 100 percent polyester, with a humiliating elastic waist, and a crease stitched down the front of the leg, as if I were in early training to drive a Winnebago back and forth across America's heartland. It was to these pants that my mother attached contrasting strips of polyester, lopping off four or five inches of the pant leg, and then *inserting* the Strip of Shame. When I'd grow another two inches in as many months, she'd insert another strip of contrasting fabric into the *same* pants. No wonder I was desperate to be pretty as a child! I still maintain that under those circumstances it would have been surprising had I *not* initiated elaborate blood pacts with God, offering my firstborn, like the miller's daughter in "Rumpelstiltskin," if only God would make me beautiful when I grew up.

Hannah was born with a mature sobriety that I have never achieved. Somehow she ingested the Serenity Prayer of St. Francis with her mother's milk. This is why she seems the elder of us two, even though she is five years younger. Except for my hasty, tumultuous marriage to Nick, every one of my major life decisions has been prescreened by Hannah. I'd be a dummy not to notice how much wiser she is than I. Torn between grad programs at Yale, UCLA, and Berkeley? Ask Hannah. What appetizer to serve with Indian-glazed salmon? Ask Hannah. How to allocate my TIAA-CREF investment? Ask Hannah. At first you think that her special gift is her beauty, but then you realize, no, it's something older and more dignified, something about pure math and practical balance. She's like one of those alpine pools you discover when hiking the Blüemlisalp in Switzerland—clear, profound, refreshing, exactly what you had in mind. Hannah just seems to make sense of things.

Not that she's arrogant or aggressive. Indeed, the opposite is true. She was so shy as a child that once at the family dinner table she leaned over to whisper in my mother's ear, "Pass the salt." From childhood shyness to adult serenity the transition seemed swift and inevitable. Lest you think that I'm exaggerating out of writerly hyperbole, I'm not the only one who confers on her this oracular status. My whole family turns to her in a crisis. She's the legally appointed power-of-attorney, the executrix of wills, the designated caretaker in case of parental deaths, the one who can be counted on to coordinate a family trip to Alaska. When she was fifteen, she spent a year in Germany, attending a German high school and living with a host family. My mother shook her head with amazement when she came back with most of the spending money she had departed with. Freak.

And Hannah is placid as a snail. Once I asked my mother if she could remember a time when Hannah and I had fought or argued. "Why, no!" said my mother, much struck. "You girls were always together, thick as thieves. It was the boys who fought. Once Caleb whacked Aaron in the head with a stick."

So. At twenty-six, five foot nine, and slender, Hannah was the kind of woman who stopped traffic. Protectively outraged, we thought that her middle-aged boss was trying to hustle a trophy wife, taking advantage of Hannah's emotional state of mind.

That is, we thought so until we met him, which wasn't until both Hannah and Phil had quit their jobs and drifted around Europe for a couple of months. With my usual extravagance, I decided within ten minutes that this man really cherished her, and that he would have loved her even if toads jumped out of her mouth, like the witch-sister in the Grimms' fairy tale. And you know what? My hunch was spot-on. Phil and Hannah have been married for eleven years, and they have an amazing thing going.

Sometimes you can just feel a person's decency, in the same way that sometimes you can intuit a lack of it. Phil had the air of a man who is fully, attentively engaged; Josh, Hannah's first fiancé, had the air of a man trying not to look at his watch. Phil consistently interested himself in the lives of others; Josh talked about himself. Phil looked at my sister with tenderness and humor; Josh looked at her as if she were an especially persistent gnat.

Shortly after Phil and Hannah married, Hannah made one of the most generous gestures I've ever seen. She sent Phil to rescue me when I was at an all-time low, the lowest I've ever been—lower even than I was at that moment, standing on her stair in middle-aged catastrophe. Now, at forty-three, losing a husband to a guy named Bob, with all the other concomitant losses, was, all things considered, livable. But back in 1996, I had hit rock-bottom, with nowhere to go.

I had taken a year's leave from my doctoral program because Nick had been accepted into a grad program in political theory at the University of Chicago. We moved from Los Angeles to Chicago, where I got a part-time job teaching at a music conservatory, and a full-time job as a receptionist at the starchy law firm Skadden, Arps, Slate, Meagher, & Flom.

Nick, who has a master's degree in clinical psychology, was going through a phase in which he categorically refused to take meds for his bipolar disorder. "There's nothing wrong with me," he'd say scornfully. "Bipolarity is a natural condition, not a disease. Why should I take medication for a condition that makes me smarter, more creative, and more aware? If my moods make you uncomfortable, you take the medication."

"But so is cancer a natural condition," I'd object, "and people have no trouble at all taking medication for *that*."

"They would if there were a negative stigma attached to it. They would if taking medication compromised their status as sane, functional citizens. Tell you what. I'll start taking medication for my bipolarity when the rest of the world starts taking medication for its stupidity," he said. And that was *that*.

Stupid, Nick wasn't. I have to admit that Nick is among the smartest men I've ever known. When I was a young adult, *smart* was more important to me than *nice*. Go figure. Any intellectual tap-dance would impress the bejeezus out of me. I was especially starstruck with academic achievement, pathetically overinvested in the uphill trail to building an identity as a scholar. There was a time in my life—sadly, not so long ago—when quickness of mind seemed more important than kindness.

For those first months in Chicago, Nick wrote brilliant elliptical papers that I would furbish up so that they read coherently. Sometimes, though, Nick's writing was so impenetrable that I'd have to ask him to explain what he meant, and he'd be off on one of his furious discursive tirades, angrily citing Durkheim, Nietzsche, Foucault, Gramsci, Hegel. As a humanities grad student, of course I'd read many of the big names in the Western canon, but Nick had read theory and philosophy I'd come across only in footnotes. You'd think that a man tortured by a relentless onslaught of ideas would seek refuge in academia, which has historically functioned as a safe haven for freethinking mavericks. Strangely, Nick voiced nothing but contempt for the ivory tower, perhaps because he himself had never struggled to connect with people, as so many academics have. He thought that in general scholars were mediocre thinkers with limited social skills and a profound need for external validation. (I know I am!)

At that point we had been married five years. Nick's mood instabilities had been difficult but manageable, with no lasting consequences. But this shift was different. Cycling into a manic period, Nick began to sidestep his seminars, despite exceptional feedback on his academic work. He didn't go to school. He went shopping.

Chicago, dear reader, is a luscious place if you have a distinct sense of style (just as Los Angeles is the perfect place if you want to copy someone else's style). Nick, distinct to his toes, encountered no obstacles whatsoever between his style and my credit cards. I had been raised on the notion that when a man cleaves unto a wife, he shall become one with her credit. It had never occurred to me to construct a marriage any other way.

One day Nick came home with a pair of Yohji Yamamoto gloves that had cost $385. This was in 1996, mind you. Granted, these gloves were wondrously conceived: over an interior pebbled leather glove, a leather mitt unzipped and folded back into a gauntlet of sorts. It was just the kind of witty sartorial gesture that a dandified socialite might affect, very Oscar Wilde, if Oscar Wilde would have ditched the lily and firmed up the tummy and got full-sleeve tatts designed by the famed Los Angeles artist Bob Roberts. Nick wasn't a dandified socialite, though. He was a grad student. We were supposed to be living on the ten bucks an hour I was making as a receptionist at the law firm.

"They're great gloves," I remember saying slowly. "But Nick, they cost *three hundred eighty-five dollars*. That's more than half a month's rent."

"You don't get it, babe," said Nick. "I will be wearing these gloves for the rest of my life. They are a *bargain* at three hundred eighty-five dollars!"

That was just the beginning. Soon I longed for the days when he had merely been spending $385 on a pair of gloves. As Nick's mood spiraled down into the blackest depression, he began drinking heavily, destroying furniture, fouling our compatibility with cruelties he couldn't take back. Like many women, I can take a hearty string of expletives, but Nick really knew how to go for the jugular. He had a knack for it. I didn't mind the broken fans, the amputated chairs, the shattered glass, the holes in the wall. I minded the hurtful things he said to me.

Perhaps because I am a writer, or perhaps because I mean what I say, I attributed the same intentionality of expression to Nick. I thought that at some level he must have meant the terrible things he said. He reserved the right to retract or dismiss things he had said previously, and that was hard for me. He thought I was a small-minded literalist to put so much weight on the spoken word—typical of a German background, he teased. Whenever I was coldly logical, verbally precise, or mindlessly conformist, he'd do his impression of a Nazi, squaring his shoulders, extending his right hand in stiff salute.

I have no way of knowing if I am an oversensitive princess. Maybe I am. Maybe I should have had the wisdom and the self-esteem to shrug and say, "Sticks and stones, mister!" But since I'm now revealing deeply personal things, I might as well confess the kinds of comments that hurt me the most. Here are five that rankled:

1. There was no intellectual insight behind my good memory.
2. There was no creative spark beyond my scholarly vocabulary.
3. There was no original taste beneath my aesthetic copycatting.
4. I was fat; I didn't know how to dress myself.
5. My parents had created a toxic environment of religious judg-ment, which I had been stupid enough to believe was love.

Over the first five years I gradually convinced myself that remarks like these were a reflection of the bipolarity. Nasty insults would shoot up like geysers, but underneath, I told myself, Nick loved me. He was with me, wasn't he? That meant he loved me, didn't it?

As Nick's depression escalated that winter, my gently irrelevant solution to this problem was to stay out of his way. I began volun-teering to work twelve-hour shifts at the law firm, which offered the twin rewards of overtime and cab fare if I worked past 10:00 p.m. I loved this job and its big stiff silence. It was the only job I've ever had in which nothing whatsoever was expected of me. Doing nothing, attracting no attention, achieving a kind of gracious invisibility, were the principal conditions of employment. "The previous receptionist," said Lavinia, my interviewer, "sometimes *lacquered her nails* at this desk"—she thwapped the gorgeous mahogany desk at which I was to sit—"Ms. Janzen, I trust that you can resist the temptation to lacquer your nails at this desk?"

"I can."

"Ms. Janzen, yours will be the first face that clients see. Do you think you can consistently cultivate an image appropriate to this firm?"

"I do."

"We will contact you within forty-eight to seventy-two hours."

Within forty-eight to seventy-two hours, I began my sojourn at Skadden, Arps, Slate, Meagher and Flom. I smiled a half smile, I murmured a low-pitched hello, I wore pearls, I pinned my hair back in a discreet chignon. For twelve hours I sat at my handsome desk in a skyscraper on Wacker Drive, in a reception area positively austere in its formality. Even the potted plants stood up straight, groomed and smooth. The carpet was thick as a biscuit, and I barely heard the muffled steps of attorneys and their clients, coming and going with due discretion. Twenty-one stories below, the river lay like a dropped ribbon of ice. From the window I could see only gray skies and the tops of other skyscrapers. Sometimes I thought my headset was the only thing keeping me tethered to the world, that without it I'd drift off and up into all that gray.

As a low-level employee, I probably never would have attracted my boss's notice again, but Lavinia learned that I was a grammarian in a doctoral program, and that I could reliably settle the usage disputes that sometimes flared up in the proofers' room. Later she became even more charitable toward me when she realized that I had a background in European languages and could assist international callers. One day she asked me if there was anything she could do to make my work easier. Easier! I asked for a typing tutorial on my computer. The next day it was in place, and in a few weeks I could really spank those keys. Denial tip: when you are trying very hard not to think about your life, consider the select pleasure of typing the same sentence three hundred times in a row, with gathering, clattering speed.

As Nick fell apart, I fell into what felt like a deep-freeze. When I wasn't in the coldly elegant law office, I wanted to be. I thought about it on the train; I thought about it when I was teaching; I thought about it when I paused on the front step of Nick's and my coach house. I'd always stop on that step to take a deep breath, dreading what I would find behind the door. The law office was my safe zone, my precious nullity. Slowly my wardrobe darkened. I wore navy with navy. The chignon tightened. I began to wear hairspray, to like the bite and scrape of bobby pins. Arriving at dawn and departing long past rush hour, I shadowed in and out of my skyscraper, tied but floating, a spectral semblance of what had once existed, like the ghost of Christmas past.

Once I looked up from a soft trance of nothingness to see Lavinia watching me. Her hair was as severely pulled back as mine, and her dark skirt suit invited no approach. She looked positively presidential. Yet she seemed to hesitate a moment before crossing the deep-pile carpet on silent heels. Leaning in slightly over my desk, she asked in a low voice, "Are you okay?"

Ah, I had heard this before. I had already worried that my unhappiness was starting to show on my face, which seemed to be getting bigger and harsher, like a man's portmanteau. "Is my work slipping?"

"No. It's just that—I wondered if—are you sure you're okay—at home?"

My eyes swam with sudden tears, which I promptly blinked back. I told Lavinia that I was fine, and she nodded approvingly and disappeared down the long hall whose doors I had never opened.

At this juncture it would not be unreasonable for you to ask, "Why didn't you just leave, you chowderhead?" This is the logical question of well-adjusted folks everywhere as they contemplate stories about women in abusive relationships. *Why didn't she just leave? It takes two to tango, my friend! One guy to dish it out and one dumb bunny to take it!* I don't know how other survivors of abusive relationships have answered that question, but answer it they must, if only to themselves. My own answer turns on a profound naïveté, one that reveals a pathetic level of simplicity and underexposure. I didn't leave then because it never occurred to me to leave.

The only marriage I had ever seen up close and personal was my parents'. They didn't argue or fight—or, if they did, they certainly didn't do it in front of us kids. I know now that there were a couple of times when my mother almost left my father, but when I was growing up, the idea of divorce seemed as other-worldly as rock and roll, or eating in restaurants. It was something *other* people did.

It wasn't long after Lavinia's discreet query that I broke down and called my sister. Nick had been drinking and offering to kill me and then himself. He always seemed vaguely surprised that I would express no interest in such a proposal. At that time he had never laid a violent hand on me, and I had never been scared that he would. Once, years later in L.A., he did pull over and shove me forcibly out of a car, and once I had to call the cops on him, but not because I was frightened he would hurt me. Still, I'd been pretty shaken by the reckless driving and the cyclone of broken furniture in our tiny rented coach house. He wasn't just breaking one thing anymore, such as a window or a fan; he was taking down whole rooms, complete sets of dishes.

The evening before I called Hannah, my car had broken down in an iffy part of town. The breakdown came after I had worked all morning at my teaching job and all afternoon at the law firm. I'd stopped to pick up some groceries, my car wouldn't turn over, and some guys with bottles in paper bags were hey-babying me. I didn't have towing insurance, and cell phones, given our budget, had not even been an option. When I finally managed to find a pay phone in the parking lot of a seedy convenience store, Nick flatly refused to come get me.

"Deal with it," he said curtly.

"But there are some gross guys drinking out of a paper bag—"

"I'm sure one of them would be delighted to help you."

"For heaven's sake, Nick. We both know you're going to come get me."

"Hear what I'm saying," he said slowly, as if speaking to an imbecile. "I. Don't. Care. What. Happens. To. You. Anymore."

He eventually did come to get me, but his last assertion took hold. It took hold because it was true.

The next day I deliberately drank cup after cup of caffeinated coffee to steel myself while I waited for the clock to hit 11:00 a.m., which was 9:00 a.m. in Sacramento, where Hannah and Phil then lived. It seems curious to me now that in the midst of all that marital drama I never once thought of calling my sister before 9:00 a.m. It was as if I had internalized the protocols that so rigidly govern a law office.

Hannah asked me a series of matter-of-fact questions. She expressed no surprise whatsoever at my husband's indifference or misbehavior, though this was the first time she was hearing about it as anything other than an amusing anecdote.

"Well," she said practically, "we need to get you out of there. That's the first thing. Do you have enough money to fly here?"

"My cat," I said vaguely. "My computer, my books, my clothes."

"Right. Okay. I'm going to send Phil to come get you. He'll fly out the day after tomorrow; that'll give you a chance to close your bank accounts and pack. He'll be there on Friday. Tomorrow you give your notice at the law firm and the conservatory."

"Two weeks' notice," I said helplessly.

"That doesn't matter, honey." Hannah said, all brisk tenderness. "You just tell them you've had a family emergency. Put yourself on autopilot like a big German robot, and go."

And so it was that I drove numbly across the country with my sister's new husband, a man I barely knew, a man who was willing to do this hard thing for a wife he adored. Through snow and ice Phil drove me, a few domestic items strapped in tarps to the roof of my Camry, backseat full of my cat and a pungent litterbox. Poor Phil! He is not fond of cats. What a trooper he was to keep up a steady stream of chatter as this cat, who was not blessed with traveling skills, crapped nervously in the backseat.

God bless that man, and my sister for sending him to me. Phil knew perfectly well how frozen and unhappy I was, but he asked me no probing questions. Instead he told me long exhaustive stories, stories with no finish in sight. One story, about a guy who had sustained a serious hiking injury somewhere beyond the pale of civilization, went on and on, prolix, a story that unwound its details and characters as we drove through Kansas, Colorado, Utah. I think I was still hearing about that guy by the time we got snowed in in Nevada. I've never been so grateful for anything in my life as Phil's extremely detailed account of that man's broken bones and his changed life thereafter.

All that was more than a decade ago. My marriage, too, had a lingering finish. Since the Chicago debacle, Nick and I had gotten back together, split up, gotten back together, split up, reunited, divorced, and remarried. (I'm not saying I'm not an idiot. In fact—let me be clear—I *am* saying I'm an idiot. But you kinda had to be there. Have I mentioned how charming Nick can be? How persuasive, how penitent?) Our finish was so lingering that when Nick finally left, I was almost relieved at the emphatic turbulence of it, at the finality of Bob and his cock and Gay.com.

Subsequent marital turbulence notwithstanding, the week that I spent at the side of my new brother had its own lingering effect. I have forever after invested Phil with a funny dear heroism. What more incontrovertible evidence of love could a woman ask for than to suggest that her man drop whatever he's doing, fly to the Midwest in a February ice storm, and rescue her sad-sack sister from an imbroglio of bad judgment and denial? Even now I marvel at that bedrock of love and loyalty between my sister and Phil.

My own friends often cited Nick's and my relationship as evidence of a marriage that worked, even though he made no secret of his depression, temper, or colorful language. What my friends saw was a cleverly designed wall like the trapeze structure I was expecting to find in Hannah and Phil's vacation photos—fierce yet fun, real but fake. They saw what Nick was always careful to show in public: our camaraderie, our simpatico mind-set, our adroit badinage. We talked alike; we walked fast; we dressed well; we had the same urban gloss. We knew what each other was thinking. This kind of intimacy is tasty in academic circles.

Moreover, so many of my friends would note Nick's effortless style and then complain that *their* guy wore Humpty-Dumpty pants and/or had been hanging on to the same droopy briefs since 1976. Another thing my friends didn't know was that my own chic wardrobe was a cinematic production directed by my husband. Nick dictated every detail, down to earrings and color/quantity of eyeliner. It's not that I didn't have opinions and tastes of my own. It's just that Nick cared so much more about what I looked like than I did. I had thought I cared a *lot*. But he cared even more. It was easier in the end to accommodate his preferences.

(I'll have my readers know that I have typed the bulk of this manuscript in a hideous red fur robe. Red fur! And I picked it! Sort of. What I mean is, my mother made it, and I'm wearing it. Why, I can't say. But, dammit, it's a tardy assertion of my individuation!)

In spite of Nick's depression, or because of it, he and I managed to achieve a working intimacy. Yet the friends who admired our marriage rarely saw Nick at home, Nick suicidal, Nick raging at the world, Nick slurring from too much vodka. They never saw him pulling apart the petals of an electric fan with his bare hands. (He loves me . . . he loves me not . . .)

The thing is, with Phil and Hannah, *everything* is real.

Nothing says *real*, see, like five days with a cryogenically twisted sister and a crapping cat.

On the other hand, nothing said "I'm pushing reality a bit too far" like the framed montage of Phil on the trapeze at Club Med, proudly displayed in Phil and Hannah's stairwell. I had always associated Phil with the dark dignity of suit and briefcase. His political position as councilman somehow rendered his hijinx on the trapeze all the more improbable. When Hannah had described his latest achievement, I had expected something more along the lines of those rocklike indoor climbing structures you see in malls. In the photos Phil was doing things that made me queasy. I had to give it up for any man who would

- consider the flying trapeze an inviting possibility for recreative memory-making;
- rise at 6:00 a.m. to practice death-defying jumps, while regular vacationers were starting their day the usual way, with margaritas at 10:00 a.m.;
- commit himself to permanent visual record in nothing but skintight cobalt spandex pants.

I was smiling at the pictures when Hannah came looking for me.

"Are those the tops of palm trees?" I asked incredulously.

She nodded.

I pointed to a man whose forearms Phil was clasping as he dangled upside-down by his knees. "Who's that guy?"

"That's the trapeze instructor. Raptor."

"Raptor? Boo," I said. "I don't think so. Raptor made that up."

Let me make it clear that while I respect the right of all individuals to reinvent their identities according to the tacit promise of the American Dream, I have nonetheless always found it pretentious when people abandon their birth names, as when a low-level art gallery employee named Maureen gradually begins calling herself Char, or when your sister's college roommate announces that we are no longer to call her by her given name (Sarah Hostetler); instead we are to call her Lettuce. On this topic, I also want to mention that I had a boyfriend in college whose room-mate legally changed his name from plain old Billy Smigs to Alis-tair John William Smythe III. Really. Alistair John William Smythe III, as if the name came with a tweed jacket and a pipe. Of course this effort to procure dignity immediately backfired. Poor Smegma (as his many detractors then called him) was mocked for the rest of his college career. On the other hand, the tightly knit group of feminists surrounding Sarah Hostetler did obligingly agree to call her Lettuce.

"Funny story," Hannah said. "We had breakfast with Raptor on our last day there, and Phil asked him how he had come to get such a plum job at Club Med. Raptor said that about five hun-dred trapeze artists had shown up for the interview, so he knew that he'd have to come up with something that would make him truly memorable."

"Can you imagine if you were on that hiring committee?" I asked. "You'd have to keep those margaritas coming to get me to sit through five hundred trapeze acts."

"Well, but no. That's not what they did. Raptor walked into a room that had ten or twelve Club Med executives sitting at one long table. They told him that he had two minutes to impress them—'Okay, go,' just like that."

"So what did he do?"

"He imitated a raptor."

"A *veloci*raptor?"

Hannah made like a vulture and/or a lizard, cawing and dip-ping her neck, a passable imitation of one of our American icons, the predacious carnivore from *Jurassic Park*. "He said that ever since then, they'd called him Raptor."

I was willing to admit I'd made a mistake. "Impressive. Bravo for the man recently known as Raptor."

The Club Med's style of interviewing was striking, and I wondered if there were some possibilities here for academia. For every assistant professorship, there are often five hundred qualified applicants. Currently the protocol is to cull the top vitaes, and to solicit dissertation chapters with their accompanying letters of recommendation. We eliminate the obvious duds at the annual Modern Language Association meetings, whose interviews constitute round one. Round two consists of an invitation to three of the most promising scholars for a grueling campus visit in which candidates must strut their stuff in a three-step, two-day interview designed to bring tears to the eyes of the cockiest applicant. First, candidates must present their scholarly research at a question-and-answer forum. They are also required to lecture to a roomful of strange students, engaging them in a dynamic conversation about a literary text they may never have taught before, demonstrating their sophisticated pedagogy in discussion management, all while the hiring committee scribbles notes in the back. Finally, and here's the kicker, candidates attend at least two lunches and two dinners with potential colleagues. At these festive events the members of the hiring department frequently attempt sly yet legal strategies to fish for information about the candidates' marital status and sexual orientation. (Sidebar: Hey! It might be amusing to hand this job to my sister-in-law Staci!)

It seemed to me, though, that Club Med was onto something. Perhaps we needed to rethink those agonizing campus visits. Maybe what we needed instead was to sit back and invite those Ph.D.s to a two-minute demonstration of a memorable skill or behavior. If I personally ever went back on the job market, I could dazzle the hiring committee by draping my own leg around my neck. Revolting, true. Off-topic, sure. But memorable, given the fact that I am forty-three.

I had another question for my sister. "What was Raptor's real name?"

"Stuart."

"He doesn't look like a Stuart."

"Some people don't," said Hannah keenly.

"Phil looks like a Phil," I pointed out.

"I would think twice about dating a guy named Stuart," Hannah admitted.

This seemed reasonable, as the only Stuart I knew liked to wear a long-sleeved aubergine T-shirt that said in pink cursive THIS IS WHAT A FEMINIST LOOKS LIKE. "What other names would you have a hard time dating?"

"Dennis," she said decisively.

"Good one."

Our cousin Dennis collected salt and pepper shakers in the shape of sporty-fresh woodland creatures. Also he displayed them prominently in a custom-built cabinet in his dining room. He had a pair of pert whimsical ceramic skunks that had often figured in our musings on the extended Loewen family.

"You?"

"The obvious answer is Bob," I said. Hannah waved her hand in priestly absolution. "Naturally. Bob would be problematic. As would Nick."

By now we were standing in Hannah's spacious closet. She and I were drinking tea, doing a little holiday cleaning. My motto, like Nick's, was IF YOU HAVEN'T WORN IT IN A YEAR, THROW IT OUT! Hannah interpreted this motto as "If you haven't worn it in a year, put it back in the closet and save it for your nine-year-old daughter's adult years, a mere decade away!"

Considering whether or not we would date nonexistent suitors took us straight through the long wall of jackets and tops. By the

time we hit the skirts, we had rejected all of the following hypo-
thetical romantic partners.

- Men named Dwayne or Bruce
- Men who have the high strange laugh of a distant loon
- Men who expect us to put them through grad school and then who as soon as they graduate with their law and/or medical degree dump you and/or embark on a madcap romp through the gay personals
- Men who are so nervous that on the first date they have writ-ten down on three-by-five-inch index cards conversational over-tures such as "Do you like your classes?" after which these men tuck said cards into the glove compartment, presumably to serve a function of social lubricity later in the date; but because your legs are so long, they accidentally knock open the glove compart-ment, scattering the index cards over the car mat, where you can't help but read them, appalled
- Men who are easily fifty-five years old when you are *eighteen*, which is just plain creepy, especially coupled with the fact that these fifty-five-year-old men are in attendance four out of five nights at the restaurant where you are hostessing
- Men who hang out in bars and/or lounges called the Pepper-mill, Beethoven's, Nibblers, Parrots, and Crackers; and although your sister informs you that the place you misremembered as Parrots was really named Crackers, Parrots is a bad title nonethe-less, and if this restaurant exists somewhere in America's heart-land, as it surely must, then you categorically refuse to date any man who darkens its doubtless faux teak doors
- Men with a certain dance move involving a single knee, repeat-edly raised, and a sidebar finger-snap, not unlike the character of

Betty or Veronica in the high heyday of Archie cartoons, with said dance move not appearing to be retro but rather serious there on the dance floor at Crackers, with the Schmitter also shakin' his thang, but a little less goofily, trying to impress your sister who has flown in from Florida for Thanksgiving, and both guys obviously congratulating themselves that they have scored a date with blonde sisters.

"Our dating history would make my friend Carla cry," I said. "She thinks I'm too choosy when it comes to men. I'll tell you what takes the cake, though," I said. "This happened to Lola before she moved to Italy. She was living in San Francisco after her divorce, and she met this guy she was on the fence about, but he kept talking about his cooking. He said he wanted to make her a gourmet meal."

"So? What's wrong with that?" Like me, Hannah perks up when a man can cook. "What's wrong with this skirt?" Hannah peered at her rear reflection over her shoulder. "Does it make my ass look like a party tray?"

"A little," I said. "Lola was house-sitting a friend's condo, and this guy shows up with a grocery bag full of cool ranch chips, a jar of Prego, and a thing of prefab dried spaghetti. Correct me if I'm wrong," I said, folding the rejected skirt, "but if a man is teetering on the brink, a bag of cool ranch chips is gonna seal his doom forever."

"What is cool ranch—I've seen those flavors on Allie's field trips."

The previous night we had imbibed a fair amount of wine under the auspices of learning how to talk like wine snobs. Now I couldn't resist showing off my new skills. "Some kind of corn chip with artificial flavoring. I believe it shows with a Velveeta topnote and a bracing character of radish, which then gives way to a pow-dery suggestion of sour-cream-'n'-chive, ultimately yielding a powerfully robust beer-belch finish."

"Sicko," said Hannah, standing in her underwear with her hands on her hips.

"Hey, *I'm* not the one who brought the cool ranch appetizer. So Lola said that during dinner it became painfully clear that there was no chemistry whatsoever. This guy excuses himself after dinner, and she thinks that he's just gone to the bathroom."

"And who wouldn't have to go to the bathroom after a bag of chips? Poor guy, he was probably gassy for days. Zip this up."

"Well," I said, obediently zipping, "the guy remains gone for a curiously long time. Finally she gets worried, so she goes to tap on the bathroom door. But the bathroom door is open. He's not in the bathroom."

"This story is starting to creep me out," said Hannah.

"Lola goes into the only place she hasn't checked, the bedroom. And there's the guy, stretched out on the bed, completely naked—"

"Ew!!"

"And he has posed himself like some kind of centerfold gone horribly wrong—"

"Unbelievable!"

"And here's the punch line: he has an indescribably tiny erec-tion. That he's proud of!"

"A peenie!"

"A teeny weenie peenie," I affirmed. "Lola said it was the smallest thing she'd ever seen, like a fuzzy caterpillar."

"What'd she do?"

"She just stood there, amazed and horrified in the doorway of the room. But suddenly a flock of ducks flew up from the water feature in the gated community outside the bedroom's sliding glass door. The ducks began quacking up a storm as if in response to the guy's wee genital salute. Poor Lola couldn't help bursting into laughter. And she burst into laughter all over again when she told me the story, twenty years later," I added, "so it must have been pretty damn funny."

"Funny, yes, but tragic too. A man's not to be blamed for his genital deficiency. However, he has *complete* control over the appetizer. Amazing that Lola had the chutzpah to laugh to his face. I wouldn't have, no matter how much he deserved it."

"Me neither. Remember Mr. Epp?"

"Who? Does this dress look timeless or church-lady?"

"Church-lady. *Easter* church-lady. That neckline is just beggin' for a choir robe." I hummed a few bars of an Easter cantata that the Butler Mennonite Brethren Church had often presented on Palm Sunday.

Hannah looked confused for a second until she placed the tune: "Paid in Full." Then she ignored my advice and put the church-lady dress back on the hanger. "I'll wear this to look in on Phil's mother. You were saying?"

"Mr. Epp was a guy I dated."

"Mister? Why are you calling him Mister?"

"I can't remember his first name."

"That's a little weird." Hannah frowned. "So what about this Mr. Epp?"

"Maybe I never mentioned him to you. I agreed to go out with him on the strength of a single pick-up line. This was in Kansas years and years ago, when Dad was teaching for a semester at the Mennonite college in Hillsboro. You were away at college, and I had flown in for a visit. I got direction-turned coming out of the college gym. So I'm standing there on the step for a second, trying to get my bearings. A guy pauses and says, 'Can I help you?' And

I say, 'Yes, can you tell me where I am?' And he smiles a slow simmering smile and says, 'You're in Kansas, Dorothy.' I thought that was cute enough to go out with him."

"That's pretty cute," Hannah admitted. "It ain't no bag of cool ranch chips. But I take it that your Mr. Epp was not consistently cute?"

"No. It turned out that the Kansas line was the high point. It was all downhill from there. He was one of those guys who get maudlin after two beers. Mr. Epp was driving me home through some rural wheat fields. It felt very rural. And guess what he starts waxing sentimental about?"

"His peenie?"

"Close. *Losing his virginity.*"

"But why?" Hannah asked blankly. "Why would any man talk about such a thing on a first date?"

I shrugged. "Why are there cool ranch chips in the world? It's a question for the philosophers, like the ongoing presence of evil. All I know is that Mr. Epp made a big wet confession of it, in a voice all sloppy with emotion: '*It was in a field like this, under a moon like this, that that little thing called Virginity was lost . . .*'"

"Faugh," said Hannah, grimacing. "Did you kiss him goodnight?"

"I most certainly did not," I said, indignant. "I have *some* standards. I gave him my hand to shake."

"Did he shake it?"

"No." I grinned, knowing how this would gross her out: "He kissed it."

She made inelegant gagging noises.

"Some women like that kind of faux medieval gallantry," I observed.

"Some women like a cool ranch flavor too, but that doesn't make it right. Pour me more tea," she ordered, queenly.

"Gladly." Continuing to show off my witty wine-tasting know-how, I declared, "This tea shows with a devil-may-care dash of cinnamon and a lusty topnote of Darjeeling, with a protracted but bold finish, as if eager to post pictures of its cock on Gay.com, using its wife's computer."

More women should have two comfy chairs and a tea table in their closet. We settled down for a break in the arduous process of making pronouncements on the currency, fit, and fabric of the many items in Hannah's wardrobe.

"Well," said Hannah late in the afternoon, folding the last of the garments for Goodwill, "I'm going to have a whole lot more room in my closet."

I nodded. "You got that right. It's all about being able to let go of the past."

# SIX

# What the Soldier Made

Although the thermos was invented in 1892 by Sir James Dewar and fully operational forty-five years before my mother's childhood, in 1942 her schoolmates never brought anything to drink. To my mother's one-room Mennonite schoolhouse, the idea of a perpetually hot beverage would have seemed futuristic and otherworldly, even if the Mennonites could have kept abreast of important cultural innovations such as the thermos. When Mennonite children were thirsty, they drank out of a bucket of water, from a long-handled *Schleif*. The bucket was drawn up on a rope from a well in the schoolhouse yard.

"Once there was a dead rat in the well," my mother told me conversationally over breakfast. I had been in the act of raising a spoonful of homemade granola to my lips. "My brother Franz brought the dead rat up in the water bucket."

I set my granola down. "What'd he do with it?"

"Some of the boys buried it in the woods. It stank something awful—that sickish-sweet smell of decaying flesh, ugh. And, oh, did it ever make the water rank! We had to drink with our noses pinched shut, like this."

"Lemme get this straight," I said. "You drank the rat water anyway?"

"We were thirsty," she explained. "But we never got the plague!"

Until that moment my father, who was gravely buttering toast, had not participated in the conversation. Now he made a contribution: "In my school, we did not drink from a communal *Schleif.* I brought milk in a jar."

"Gross," I said. "Warm milk in a jar?"

"It was cool milk. The milk stayed cool."

"How could the milk have stayed cool? I thought you didn't have a refrigerator."

"We did not have an icebox. If we wanted to cool something off, we'd pour it into a jar, screw the lid on tight, tie twine around the jar, and lower it down into the well forty or fifty feet. It stayed cool down there."

"Were you embarrassed to bring a jar of milk in your lunch?"

"Nothing embarrassing in that! Why should I have been embarrassed about milk in my lunch? "

"What kinds of lunches did your mothers pack for you?" I asked.

"Lard sandwiches," said my mother. "I didn't like it when the lard looked pink. But it tasted okay with salt. Salt brings out the flavor of lard."

"Peanut butter sandwiches," said my father. "Every day, two peanut butter sandwiches. Occasionally, for a treat, there was a sardine sandwich."

"And you're telling me that a sardine sandwich was not embarrassing?"

"Lard was embarrassing," said my mother.

"That's a given," I agreed. "But sardines?"

"No, I was proud of the sardines. They were delicious," Dad answered reminiscently. "Why don't we ever have sardines?" he asked my mother. "I even gave my friends a taste of my sardine sandwiches. There was a young fellow, name of Fritz Vanderkamp, and we used to tease him about his strange lunches. His mother would send along an unusual sandwich. It was bread on top"—he began chuckling at the memory—"and a pancake on the bottom. He would eat it like this." Dad cupped his hands furtively around an imaginary half-pancake sandwich, hiding it from prying eyes.

Mom and I laughed heartily, as much at my father's merriment as at the partial pancake sandwich. Ah, does it ever change, the Sturm und Drang of embarrassing lunches? My heart went out to poor humiliated Fritz Vanderkamp, who may or may not still be alive. If he is, I hope that he can now contemplate a pancake without shame.

Hannah and I have often thought that it would be pleasurable to revisit the very Mennonite foods that used to shame us as we tried to conceal them in the cafeterias of our youth. After considerable reflection, we came up with a list of Shame-Based Foods, which I urge the reader to imagine tucked into Shame-Based Lunchpails, dooming the transporter whereof to social ostracism at Easterby Elementary School. Well, but wait. That is not quite true. Hannah says that by the time she reached her third or fourth lunchpail, our mother had *accidentally* purchased for her a nonembarrassing Holly Hobbie lunchbox. Knowing that this serendipitous outcome would, like Halley's comet, occur once every seventy-six years, Hannah clung to her Holly Hobbie lunchbox well into junior high.

I had blazed the trail with long-suffering complaints about my own lunchpail. Most children at Easterby Elementary School carried brightly patterned tin boxes, Aquaman and Underdog and so on. The lunchbox that would have set *my* metaphoric pants on fire was Josie and the Pussycats. It is extremely unlikely that a Josie and the Pussycats lunchbox could have rescued me from the pit of uncoolness into which I had already sunk, but at age eight I begged to differ. I figured that Josie and the Pussycats would magically make up for the knee-length homemade skirts or the blonde tails braided with neurotic precision, like Heidi on crack.

However, Mennonite circumstances beyond my control required me to carry a mature navy vinyl bag on a long strap. It was obviously designed for adults, and I have since wondered if it wasn't a diaper bag. (There was a family precedent: for picnics and the rare Disneyland outing, my mother loaded up a plump gray diaper bag with moist tuna sandwiches.) The memory of my mature navy diaper bag goes a long way toward explaining my interest in Prada today.

Our mother wrapped most luncheon foodstuffs in gently used—nay, preowned—wax paper. She eschewed the plastic sandwich bag on grounds of cost. When we complained that the other kids made fun of us, the cheerful parental rejoinder was "When the seventeen of us were your age, my mother packed our sandwiches into two tin Roger's Golden Syrup buckets! At least you have wax paper!"

So here, in order of least to most embarrassing, are the top five Shame-Based Foods for Mennonite youth lunches:

### 5. *Warmer Kartoffelsalat* (Hot Potato Salad)

This tangy potato salad, although delicious, had two significant strikes against it. The first strike was that it had cooled and congealed by the time we opened our Shame-Based Margarine

Containers to eat it. The second strike, and this was somehow more critical, was that we were unable to consume *Warmer Kartoffelsalat* without thinking of our mother's merry little ditty:

Auf den Hügel
da steht ein Soldat.
Er macht in den Hosen
Kartoffelsalat!

(On the hillside
stood a soldier.
In his pants he made
potato salad!)

The reader might well inquire why a pacifist Mennonite family was singing songs about soldiers. Further, and perhaps this is more pressing, the reader might justly inquire why this soldier was making potato salad in his pants. Hannah and I certainly discussed it at length as we compiled our list of Shame-Based Foods. Hannah thought she remembered other verses that suggested that perhaps the soldier had seen a bear; maybe the poor fellow was a-feared, thus soiling himself. So I called my mother from Bend, Oregon, to ask why the soldier had lost control of his bowels. Was he ill? Was he traumatized? Did he have regrets? My mother disclaimed all causal knowledge. "It's just a little soldier standing on a hill making potato salad in his pants," she explained. "Does there have to be more?"

"Sometimes a cigar is just a cigar," I said.

"You're not going to put the *Kartoffelsalat* into your book, are you?"

"It is my opinion that the *Kartoffelsalat* deserves a wider audience. Hide it under a bush, oh no! I'm gonna let it shine! Maybe I'll use it for my epigraph."

"Okay," she said, resigned. "But I want to make it clear that I didn't *write* it. I just *quoted* it."

"Duly noted," I said.

That night as I prepared for bed, I intoned "Auf den Hügel da steht ein Soldat" like a mantra. It was oddly soothing. I found that when uttered out loud, at night, as I brushed my teeth at the sink, the soldier poem assumed the clarity of a haiku, a lucid distillation of the world's mystery. After I had said it five or six times, it began to gather the heft of an orphic utterance, like the prophecies of Nostradamus at his brass bowl in 1555. This soldier may be someone we know *right now*, and he may have already begun the hillside ascent. He shall rise. He shall stand. And his bowels shall move. It's just a matter of time. Who knows why the soldier stands and craps his pants? Not I. Not you. Certainly not he. What can we say but that we like this soldier's attitude? This is one enlightened soldier. See him shrug with gentlemanly insouciance there on the hilltop, as if to say, Eh! My pants may be full, but my heart is warm!

## 4. Damp Persimmon Cookies with a Raisin-Walnut Motif

In recent decades our mother has often understandably boasted that she never gave any of us the grail-like supermarket snacks that glowed in the unattainable lunches of our peers: Ho-Hos, Twinkies, Ding Dongs, Little Debbie pudding-filled pies, crackers and Cheez Whiz in cunning sealed packages. There was one snack that looked deliciously intriguing, but I never did get the opportunity to try it, and now I feel the thrill window has closed. The treat in question was a stiff plastic finger containing four orangey-cheesy crackers and a square dab of hydrogenated sugary peanut butter. Cheese-'n'-peanut butter—what's not to love? I used to long to trade for one of those packets. But trading wasn't an option. I had nothing the other kids wanted.

Everything that went into our mouths was homemade and chemical-free. However, the Shame-Based Lunches' putative nutritional strength was a distant consideration from our mother's number one criterion in preparing school lunches. This was cost. My mother thriftily made persimmon cookies from the bruised culls sold half-off at the Japanese fruit stand. The cookies, spicy and moist and possibly succulent to adults, were the ultimate anti-cookie to us children, we who pined for store-bought treats.

### 3. *Platz*

*Platz* consists of a kneaded egg dough topped with sweetened fruit, in this case the stunted, picked-at-by-birds cherry-plums from the backyard. Hannah and I executed a triple responsibility with regard to the cherry-plums: we had to pick them, pit them, and then prepare the *Platz* topping—three labor-intensive steps to produce a result of which we wanted no part. We did not like *Platz* for the same reasons that we objected to the moist persimmon cookies, but adding to our general disfavor was the fact that when unwrapped from preowned wax paper, *Platz* emitted an embarrassing yeasty odor that made the other kids glance at us headlong and scoot away. This yeast smell was the product of the *Platz*'s final layer, a sandy-crumbed streusel, sticky as well as odorous.

## 2. The *Cotletten*-and-Ketchup Sandwich

As the penultimately embarrassing Shame-Based Food, *Cotletten* were bad enough served hot in a cream gravy besprinkled with minced onion. *Cotletten* are Mennonite meatballs. What makes them Mennonite is the addition of many, many saltine crackers, bagged in a preowned plastic bread wrapper and decimated with a rolling pin. If you add an entire carton of saltines to two pounds of fatty ground beef, throw in an egg or two and some condensed milk to moisten the whole, you will have enough meatballs for a week's worth of appetizing cold lunches. Cold *Cotletten* are hard to describe. Each pungent saltball assumes a jellied viscosity, heavy as a puck. The addition of ketchup is an intriguing choice. It gives homemade bread a moist pink pliancy, not unlike damp Kleenex.

## 1. Borscht

There was really no contest here. Honors for Most Embarrassing Shame-Based Food went hands-down to Borscht, which is the hearty winter soup of the Russian steppes. Our people borrowed it from the Russians during the long Mennonite occupation of Ukraine. Borscht has a distinctive ruby color, a stain to anything it touches. This distinctive color comes from beets. The soup also has a distinctive smell, a noxious blast of savage fart. This fart smell comes from cabbage. As if that isn't appetizing enough, Borscht is served with vinegar and a dollop of sour cream. The vinegar curdles the cream so that the whole thing looks and smells like milk gone bad. Yet there is more. The bottom note, the lingering afterwhiff, presents with an intensity reminiscent of our friend the soldier's lumpy *Hosen*.

Borscht is the Mennonite catnip. It makes our eyes roll back in our head a little. If you meet someone who has a Mennonite name, let's say the new research librarian at your college, the encounter might go like this:

YOU. So you're a Wiebe! May I ask if you're Mennonite?

MR. WIEBE. Yes, on my father's side. We're the Wiebes in Manitoba. I knew some Mennonite Janzens when I went to school in Minnesota. Are those your folks?

YOU. No, mine come from Ukraine via Ontario. I'll have to have you and your wife over for some Borscht sometime.

MR. WIEBE, *trembling.* Borscht? Really?

YOU, *modestly.* Oh, I can get the ole kettle boiling!

MR. WIEBE, *salivating now, with a wild look in his eye.* Do you make the kind with beets in it?

It's important to note that at some point in the last century, Mennonite hausfraus began to substitute Campbell's Tomato Soup for beets. But we purists still prefer the beets. It's the difference between Cracker Barrel and a nice Vermont cheddar. What I'm saying is, there's a place in Mennonite hearts for unlovable foods: beets, braised cabbage, lard. We even do a whimsical little thing with headcheese.

In every company there's always someone who blasts the copy room with microwave lunches. I'm not talking about Jenny Craig. I'm talking about the stygian stink of something that makes your gorge rise, for instance, a leftover seafood *chermoula.* The smell perfuses the copy room, which is where, as we all know, companies like to keep the microwave. Lord knows nobody wants to be the guy whose lunches make people pinch their nostrils shut. But there's a guy like that in every crowd. You may recognize him. He's the passenger who unleashes an early morning saucy wet burrito as soon as your aircraft takes off from Newark, and who, just as you think it can't get any worse, bites the head off a pungent pouch of hot-sauce. Olé!

I turned out to be a variation of that guy. I don't know how it happened, but I grew up to be the gross professor who brownbags a leftover container of cabbage soup, which I heat up at 11:00 a.m., just before other people are ready to smell hot food. My colleagues, mature midlife scholars, are too tactful to make outright gagging noises, but they sure don't come knockin' when that Borscht starts a-rockin'.

Don't get me wrong; it's good soup. As an adult I have even sometimes served it to guests as a kind of novelty, though I naturally don't mention the vinegar thing. People do like Borscht. They regularly have seconds. (On a side note, Borscht is mighty useful as a weight-loss staple, given its low-carb cabbage goodness. I encourage my readers to communicate this information to the diet guru Suzanne Somers. Borscht is my gift to her. I give it freely.)

But Borscht is not what you want to tuck into your child's lunch. Trust me. Complications attach to cold Borscht. Back when I was a child, with what was no doubt our limited technology, the chief function of the thermos was to transport liquid, not to retain heat. The Borscht thermos therefore became a time bomb of toxic stink, an odor so scurrilous it could clear a room. I am also willing to consider the possibility that it was only our thermoses, Aaron's and Caleb's and Hannah's and mine, that did not retain heat. My own thermos never matched my diaper bag, so who knows where my mother found it?

∞

As midlife foodies, Hannah and I formed a plan to make Mennonite foods less embarrassing, more appetizing. We even toyed with the idea of writing our own cookbook. The challenge would be both gustatory and aesthetic. For instance, what could you do to make a boiled hoop-cheese dumpling more fashion-forward, particularly when the white dumpling wears the telltale Mennonite vest of cream gravy? This slightly sour dumpling, called *Verenike* by our people, is unsurpassed in deliciousness, but I am ready to admit that it would not cut it with the ladies who lunch. It has an albescent quality similar to the Mennonite ladies who prepare it. As a people, we are pale as pork chops, flavored by centuries of inbreeding and shame.

Alas, Mennonite cuisine is not what I would call imaginative. At the local farmers' market in my little town, I sometimes see a booth run by Old Order Mennonites, whose women wear head coverings and long modest dresses. The last time I saw the Mennonites I asked them if they had any tiny new red potatoes. The two young women tending the booth looked at each other and tried not to smile. They obviously found my request inexplicable. There were regular-sized potatoes aplenty, right there in front of me. Why on earth would I want tiny runtling potatoes when I could have the big boys? I could see over the young women's shoulders to a basket on the back counter, and in that basket I spied what I was after: marble-sized potatoes, fresh as spring. "How about those?" I asked, pointing.

"Those? You want *those*?" The young woman could hardly contain her amazement. "Those are the culls. We're throwing them away."

"Can I buy them?"

"Okay. Fifty cents."

The young women giggled as I walked away.

But I should have given the Mennonites—and my frugal mother—more credit. Long ago when I was studying in France, I signed up to take a cooking class. This wasn't a course at Gastronomicom or L'École Internationale de Pâtisserie; it was just a course offered by a three-star chef. I was surprised, almost miffed, by the fact that there weren't terribly many surprises, beyond the secrets of cooking with wine. Why, we were learning things I already knew how to do! I felt sheepish, like Dorothy when she realizes that she's been wearing the ruby slippers *all along*. I already knew, for instance, how to make velvety sauces, how to cook a nice cut of meat to any degree of doneness, how to set a tart perfectly and plumply in its pan. *It can't be that easy,* I thought in dismay; *there has to be a special kind of cosmopolite knowledge that, once learned, will change me forever.*

When I came back to the United States, I gave my first sit-down dinner party for ten, planning a decisively L.A. menu of scallops with three-tomato relish and tomatillo vinaigrette. My guests were industry hipsters, non-Mennonites all, people to whom current culinary trends meant something. It was a debut of sorts, and I was nervous. Would my guests taste my turnip potato gratiné and know me for a poseur and a fraud? Would they intuit that I had trained on brown gravy and homemade applesauce?

The dinner went off without a hitch. I even received two requests for the recipe for my lemon tart with raspberry coulis. That night as I cleaned up after the party, I experienced one of those serene Browning moments: "God's in his heaven, all's right with the world!" Finally, the weight of my Mennonite past no longer seemed an insupportable handicap. In fact, with respect to cooking, I was downright glad I had been given the secret Menno starter kit. Without it I could have never been so confident as I simultaneously freshened the appetizers, served the meal, and enjoyed the company of my dinner guests.

Yet it never struck me that I might come out of the Mennonite Closet of Shame foodwise until five or six years ago. I'd spent the last twenty years cooking more or less seriously, learning from Hannah, avidly reading and experimenting with piquant elegancies. Every April my department colleagues throw a banquet for our graduating English majors. Each professor brings a dish. The event lies somewhere between a potluck and an upscale dining experience, as several of my colleagues are excellent cooks. On this occasion I had signed up for an entrée, but a busy schedule had gotten the best of me, and suddenly it was Saturday. Nick said, "Who cares what you bring? Just take something out of the freezer. They're college kids. They'll eat cardboard."

True enough. As a professor, I see firsthand the horrifying things that undergraduates cheerfully consume, from Pop-Tarts to pork rinds. But I thought that our majors deserved something special, something elegant, for this dinner to celebrate their milestone achievement. Alas, there wasn't time for something elegant. So I took out a big pan of frozen *Hollapse* (pronounced *HollapSAY*).

*Hollapse* represents one of the many Mennonite destinations for cabbage. The cabbage is subjected to a Mennonite trifecta of boiling, browning, and baking. Each cabbage leaf is pulled steaming from the head, and it rests like a hammock in the hand. The leaf is then filled with a seasoned meat-and-rice mixture, rounded and shaped, braised and simmered. Each little bundle is secured with a toothpick and put to bed in a tomatoey sauce. The toothpick is hard to detect and might surprise the eater. So might the first whiff of the savage cabbage smell. But *Hollapse* is what I had on hand, and *Hollapse* is what I brought to the department function.

I know that I cannot take it as a compliment that the seniors polished off an enormous kettle of *Hollapse* in record time, because it is true that they would have eaten anything with gusto. But something changed when my student Ricky sat down beside me. He had excused himself to go back for seconds, and now he brought back a plate with three more *Hollapse* stacked up like an Egyptian pyramid. He had ladled a veritable Nile of sauce over the whole. "Dude," he said, "I don't know what these fuckers are, but they're amazing!"

Since then I have increasingly drawn Mennonite recipes into my cooking. I no longer see Mennonite cookery as the madwoman in the attic, the embarrassing relative who must be kept away from the party at all costs. My Mennonite dishes have been getting bolder, sneaking down to elegant tables, quietly presenting themselves before senators and producers and architects. So what if I mix the food of shame with the fruit of knowledge? In the Genesis account of Adam and Eve in the Garden, shame comes inevitably with knowledge. Knowledge actually *causes* shame. Remember when Adam and Eve taste the fatal fruit, only to realize their nakedness? And they reach for fig leaves to cover their naughty bits, thereby beginning a long trajectory of genital embarrassment? That story would end differently if it were up to me. I'd have Eve taste the fruit all right, and also give it to Adam, because who doesn't enjoy feeding the man she loves? Maybe the fig leaf could stay too, since cooks do need aprons after all. But in my version, Eve wouldn't run away and hide. She'd invite God to sit down and take a load off. "I've made a flavorful little *Apfelstrudel*," she'd say. "Try some."

# SEVEN

# The Big Job

Hannah and Phil and I went to a karaoke party that had been offered up for bid at an auction. The hosts had purchased it for six thousand dollars, a sum that included all the bells and whistles of the lounge karaoke: lights, mikes, backups, optional air guitar, mariachi shakers. After the host had broken the ice with an upbeat but mediocre rendition of "New York, New York," the guests, mostly midlife affluent professionals, applauded his bravery. Yet they evinced no willingness to sing show tunes in front of their business acquaintances and peers.

Then a very tiny white-haired woman drifted to the front of the room. Her name was Olive, and she was eighty-five. Olive was Phil's colleague's wife's mother. Olive's progress toward the mike was slow and peripatetic, but she finally got there. She serenely waited for a young man to lower the mike for her, and then she commenced, in a quavery old-lady voice, the familiar tune of "You Are My Sunshine." Every banker, socialite, decorator, and developer at that party surged into the room, martinis sloshing. Olive's voice wobbled delicately under the loud accompaniment, but we could hear her. Then a strange thing happened.

On the chorus everybody joined in, as if by prearrangement. And they sang with gusto. People were waving their lighters. The folks standing in the back clasped their arms about each other's waists and swayed, as in old-time movies. I had never seen anything like it. Powerful was the applause for Olive, who was the undisputed star of the evening. Hannah later managed a short conversation with Olive, who told her that her one regret was that the karaoke machine hadn't offered her the selection she would have preferred to sing: "Brighten the Corner Where You Are."

Olive's revelation naturally led us to speculate about what our mother might have sung had she been in attendance. We imagined our mother getting up there with perfect aplomb to sing one of the songs she had taught us years ago in Pioneer Girls.

> Mein hand on myself
> Und vas ist das hier?
> Das ist mein Tinkerboxer,
> mein Mama dear!

(pointing to various body parts)

> Tinkerboxer! Hornblower! Meatgrinder!
> Rubbernecker! Breadbasket! Hitchhiker!
> Sitter-downer! Seat-kicker! Ja ja ja ja—
> Dat's vat I learned in der Schul, ja, ja!

Part of the charm of this piece was that you had to sing it in a hearty German accent, which I'm here to tell you a roomful of helpless little girls will indeed do when they have no other choice.

I called my mother in California to make sure that Hannah

and I were accurately remembering the various body parts in the Hornblower song. Mom was only too glad to sing all the verses over the phone. Then she giggled over how Hans, Deena and Aaron's five-year-old, had asked her for a second piece of chocolate dump cake. "That's how he says *bundt*," she told me artlessly.

"I foresee that we'll never refer to your bundt cake again by its proper name."

"Guess what I did today?"

"What?"

"I toilet-trained Hans!"

"Isn't Hans a little old to be working on that?" I asked.

"Oh, he can urinate just fine!" exclaimed my mother, always upbeat. "But the silly guy has had the idea that he needs to do his Big Job in a diaper at night."

You can tell a lot about a person's family of origin by examining the elimination vocabulary of the parents. When we were growing up, our mother favored the term *Big Job* (the capital letters are a thing of mine own) to refer to any and all bowel movements. The only exceptions she made were for nonhuman entities, as when a bird dumped on the patio directly in front of where she and I were playing Scrabble, and she would exclaim, "Oh, look at that! That bird did an oompa!" *Oompa* was for the birds. *Big Job* was for the home. Indeed the latter sobriquet accurately reflected our household's premium on hard work, where even natural functions were framed in terms of practical industry and achievement. Come to think about it, *Big Job* captured the very essence of what it means to be Mennonite. Until that very moment I had forgotten the term *Big Job*.

I said suspiciously into the phone, "Are you eating something right at this very moment? While you're telling me about Hans's Big Job?"

"It's a piece of cherry-plum *Platz*," she confessed. "Deena was just letting Hans do his Big Job in the diaper at night! I thought it was high time he moved past that! He's five years old!"

I thought it was high time he moved past it, too. But there was more. I waited patiently while my mother chewed and swallowed the rest of her *Platz*.

"Guess what Deena has been doing to try and get him to go on the toilet."

"You've got me stumped," I said. "What?"

"She's been cutting a hole in his diaper! She's been telling him to sit on the toilet and do his Big Job through the hole in his diaper!"

"Nice visual, Mom. I take it you somehow showed Hans the error of his ways?"

"I did," she said joyfully. "Now Hans is doing his Big Job like a grown-up!"

"Congratulations on this important toilet intervention," I said. "I hope Deena appreciates what a fine job you've done. What a fine Big Job. May I suggest offering her a piece of chocolate dump cake as you tell her the news?"

Fortunately, neither Hannah nor I could recall the pleasure of having been toilet-trained with Mom at the helm. My report on Hans's toilet-training lesson reminded Hannah of the time Mom had taught her to brush her teeth, and Hannah had somehow understood that dental hygiene was a goal she should pursue exclusively on Sundays. "In kindergarten they told us to brush our teeth every day," Hannah explained, "but when Mom said that the body was God's temple, I figured that since we went to church only on Sundays, that's when we should brush our teeth. I was really worried about the mixed signals I was getting."

"Why didn't you just ask Mom? Were you that shy?"

"It wasn't so much an issue of being shy as not wanting to challenge authority," she said.

"Thank you!" I exclaimed. "What is it about being Mennonite that teaches little girls not to challenge authority? We all grow up so obedient, we'll do anything rather than rock the boat."

I told my sister about the first time I became conscious that an adult could make a bad decision. Before my year in Mrs. Eplett's sixth-grade class, I had assumed that teachers, like all authority figures, were equally competent to teach me whatever it was I needed to learn. So did my friend Lola, who was also in the same class thirty-four years ago. She remembers the event much as I do.

We both remember Mrs. Eplett's fierce red wig, which often slipped forward a little, like Paul Revere's as he rode his horse *ventre à terre* in our history book. Mrs. Eplett, a spanker, favored a position over the lap, like a baby. We were terrified of her. Now she was sitting cozily on top of a desk at the front of the room, and she leaned forward as if confiding a secret. "Let's all pledge to keep this discussion strictly confidential," she urged. We nodded, solemn. She waited a beat for effect, and it was so quiet you could hear the portentous click of the clock's second hand. "It is at all times important to face facts," she said. "And here is a fact. Are you ready to face this fact?"

We were ready.

"We have something to discuss about Milla. We need to do this now, while she is absent. Sometimes Milla offends." Mrs. Eplett made a fanning motion at armpit level.

We nodded again. How true. This was serious.

"People don't know when they smell bad. It's often *not their fault*. And Milla's parents weren't born in America, so they have Different Customs. Do you remember when Milla brought that box of garlic snails for us to try?"

We remembered, shuddering.

"Well, Milla's mother cooks with *garlic*. I might not like it. You might not like it. But class: some people like it. And garlic has a heavy odor that gets into your perspiration. That's what we're smelling when we think that Milla has BO!"

We nodded our understanding. Garlicky BO, okay.

Mrs. Eplett exhorted, warming to her subject, "Class, if I had BO, I would want you to tell me. Would you tell me?"

"Sure!" offered Mike Helm.

"Thank you, Mike. I appreciate your attitude. Class, it is our duty to tell Milla that she has BO. We need to make a plan."

The grade six class at Easterby Elementary sat stunned in early-onset schadenfreude. This was rich.

"Is there anyone who is friends with Milla?" asked Mrs. Eplett.

Slowly Lola and I raised our hands. We had been over to Milla's house once or twice, and we knew that Milla, the queen of high-water pants, didn't have many friends. Lola and I were Mennonite, but Milla was fat. Fat was worse than Mennonite. In the playground economy, the only thing as bad as being fat was being gay. Yet gay you could deny. Fat you could not. Milla could not hide her size. In fact, it was as if she went out of her way to accent it, given her pants.

"Rhoda, Lola, good." Mrs. Eplett acknowledged our reluctant hands. "Will you be willing to help us?"

Lola and I nodded hesitantly.

"Excellent," Mrs. Eplett said. "Now here's the plan."

The plan was that Lola and I would lure Milla into the sixth graders' hall at recess. At a prearranged time Milt Perko, the class goofball, would approach us. Milt Perko would be the bearer of the bad news. He was to ask Milla in a plain manly way, on behalf of us all, to wear deodorant. Milt Perko, desktop farter, snapper of bras, purveyor of dirty jokes! Everybody loved Milty, and thus it was Milty who was called to step up in our time of need. Mrs. Eplett nominated him, Mike Helm seconded, and twenty-four hands rose in democratic support.

On the day in question I was in exquisite agony, panicking for poor Milla. I had just read *A Tale of Two Cities*, and as Lola and I led Milla into the sixth graders' hall, I imagined that we were three aristocrats in the tumbrel, heads shaved, modest and pure, awaiting the guillotine. *It is a far, far greater thing that I do now than I have ever done.*

Milty rounded the corner, right on time to the minute. Would the goofball be able to keep a straight face? He approached, hands in pockets, serious as church. He had never looked more unfunny; he looked Mature. Now he walked straight up to us, looked Milla manfully in the eye, and said without preamble, "Milla, the whole class would appreciate it if you would wear some deodorant once in a while. Mrs. Eplett asked me to tell you. And the class voted and everything."

Milla looked suddenly skyward. A fake little doll's smile pinched her lips.

Milty wasn't going to leave until he had an answer. "Okay, Milla? Deodorant, okay? Ban or Sure? You can spray it in your armpit, okay?"

"Okay," she whispered. Then, from out of nowhere, she summoned a queenly spirit: "Now if you don't mind, Milty, we were having a private conversation."

Milty nodded. Mission accomplished. He strode off heroically, whistling.

Milla turned to me and Lola, blinking back tears. She reached for my hand. We three sat on the hall rail all recess, holding hands, talking about Milla's sister Hava as if nothing had gone wrong. As if we weren't holding hands at all.

The pain and panic I felt attending this incident were strangely excruciating. I had nightmares about it for years afterward, and I still sometimes dream of Milty Perko turning the corner of some mental corridor, striding toward me, agent of doom, a grim Ezekiel. Lola and I knew we had betrayed Milla, but it never occurred to us that we had had a choice in the matter. I can't speak for Lola, but in the sixth grade I had absolutely no apparatus with which to resist authority. I couldn't even conceive of articulating opposition to an adult's judgment. And I was light-years away from the confidence it would take to stand on top of my desk and fart *out loud and on purpose*, as Milty Perko occasionally did, to our collective admiration and applause.

"Good god," exclaimed Hannah when I had finished telling the story. "What on earth could Mrs. Eplett have been thinking? What kind of pedagogy results in a public shaming?"

Some years after I had become a professor, my father sent me a newspaper clipping. Its subject was my now-ancient sixth-grade teacher, Mrs. Eplett. I was astonished to learn that she was still alive, but there she was in a photograph that confirmed it, bewigged and chipper. The photograph had been taken at a function celebrating her long contribution to the teaching field. The newspaper article quoted several generations of ex-students whose comments were all effusive in their praise for Ann C. Eplett. "Mrs. Eplett used to whupp our bottoms when we were naughty!" "She was the best teacher of all time! She checked to see if we brushed our teeth before school!" "Mrs. Eplett sent me home because I had headlice!" As I scanned the column of appreciative memories, I experienced a wave of gratitude myself. Although

Mrs. Eplett had been my worst teacher, not my best, I nodded at the eloquent testament to the long-ranging effects our teachers and mentors exert on us.

I said as much to my sister. Hannah answered, "Mentor, schmentor. That was criminal, what Mrs. Eplett did to poor sweet Milla, even if she did always smell like crotch. I wonder whatever happened to her?"

"Lola heard that she became a pediatrician. She has a thriving practice in Orlando."

"Still."

"I know. It probably scarred her for life. It scarred *me* for life!"

"That whole not-questioning-authority thing helps explain why you stayed with Nick so long after you should have left," she said.

"I know," I agreed morosely. "Damn. And the weird thing is, I'm a scholar. Challenging authority is what I *do*. For a living. You give me any argument, and I'll tell you what's wrong with it."

"And that's a charming feature in a sister!" she said. "The weird thing is, you and I can challenge authority in our professional lives. I was the same way when I was working at the bank. But you show me a Mennonite woman, and I'll show you a woman who sucks at asserting herself in her personal life."

It wasn't as though I never challenged Nick. He made it easy to see the ways in which he was dysfunctional, since he pointed them out himself. It's just that he was so tortured, so depressed, so funny and fabulous, that I didn't have the heart to put up the boundaries that I know I should have.

"I wasn't ready to stick my landing the first few times I left him," I said sadly.

"So what? You were ready this time. You don't have to look

back with regret," she said. "In fact, you don't have to look back at all."

"Thing is, I loved him."

"You still love him."

"Damn," I said again. "Middle age is all about learning to live with ambiguity."

"No it isn't," Hannah said thoughtfully. "You've been living successfully with ambiguity since you started questioning the whole Mennonite *Ursprach*. And you've always known that loving Nick didn't mean you should necessarily live with Nick. He's so unhappy that he'd make anybody miserable."

"He didn't make me miserable. Toward the end, maybe."

"He *should* have made you miserable. I don't think middle age is about learning to live with ambiguity; it's just the opposite. It's about finally developing the resolve to reject ambiguity and embrace simplicity. What could be simpler than saying, 'No matter how I feel about him, I will not expose myself to his damage'? I'm not saying it isn't painful. But it is simple."

I shook my head. "You make it sound as if I was the one who left. But I was the coward who never would have left. Who never *wanted* to leave. It was he who left me."

"It's you who are doing the leaving now. Finally! Do you know, of all the times when you guys broke up, this is the only time you've ever seemed at peace?"


That night Hannah and I stayed up late watching Japanese *Iron Chef* on the food network. I didn't have cable, a fact that I liked to pretend was due to my recent financial cutbacks/marital fiasco, but which was really due to my being an academic dork. Tragically, we professors are more likely to pick up a windy biography on Feo Belcari than turn on the TV. Hannah was appalled that this was the very first time I had ever heard of the whole Iron Chef concept—"How can you call yourself a cook and not know what's going on in the food world?"

"Can't I be a decent cook without knowing what other people are cooking?"

"No."

I tried again. "What is the sound of one hand clapping?"

"Get current, or get out of the kitchen," she said.

"Well," I said, reaching, "at least I'm not wearing a fleece vest."

Watching this show was like the helpless feeling you get when you feel cosmically compelled to take a big swig of buttermilk. The smell makes you shudder, but you keep coming back. On the show, a food critic, presented with a dish of Israeli couscous in a rich ruby beet juice, offered some detailed feedback in Japanese, none of which we understood. But the food critic spoke for a long time. He developed his theme, gesticulating elaborately, chasing nuanced implications. Finally he concluded with an oratorical flourish of serious expostulation. Just as he was wrapping it up, there came the calm voice-over of a professional translator. This is how she translated the food critic's long eloquent commentary:

"I'm feeling good." (Pause)

"All over." (Pause)

"Right now."

That night, humming "Brighten the Corner Where You Are," I went to bed conducting a mental review of the day. Hornblower, check. Big Job, check. Couscous, check. Simplicity, check. My heart was broken, my legs were scarred, and I might well lose my house. But, go figure, I was feeling pretty good. All over. Right now.

# EIGHT

# Rippling Water

As a child, I wanted so badly to dance that once I told my Sunday-school class I was going to be on television that very night, tap-dancing on the *Ted Mack Amateur Hour*. The *Ted Mack Amateur Hour* was the *American Idol* of its generation, a variety show that featured early versions of stage parents and their vocally enhanced tots. Quavering with vibrato, befringed in cowboy outfits, children belted out their show tunes and lurched in manic circles, like toys run amok.

Several church moms called my mother, asking in amazed disapproval what channel I was going to be on. The next Sunday part of my punishment was to ask the entire Sunday-school class for forgiveness, just as Mrs. Ollenburger—she of the fleshy upper arms—had begged the church body for forgiveness when she'd had the vainglorious liposuction.

With a pattern of dodgy behavior already established, I was a shoe-in for further scrutiny. Ancient Mrs. Lorenz, my Sunday-school teacher, took it upon herself to ask my mother if it was true that I was allergic to raisins. When faced with a tray of Mrs. Lorenz's brittle oatmeal cookies, we kids would have rather eaten the phone book. Plus these particular cookies were not just stale;

they were crawling with raisins. Mrs. Lorenz handed me a big sandy cookie into which raisins had burrowed like ants in a farm. I took one pro forma nibble and then shook my head at Mrs. Lorenz: I was allergic, so tragically allergic, to raisins. One raisin and my throat would swell up and I could die. The dance drama of the previous Sunday alerted Mrs. Lorenz, who discovered just as soon as Sunday school was over that no, I did not have a deadly raisin allergy. Confessing my sin was bad enough, but the worst part was getting up once more in front of a sizable group to do it.

The attending punishments didn't derail my longing to dance, however. The passion continued unabated into my adult years, until I finally reached the age of independence and had the means to take lessons. Only once did the Mennonite attitude toward dancing actually save me embarrassment. This was in grade eight, when I was enrolled in a hideous earth science course.

Mr. Handwerker taught to the Talented Tenth. The smarty-pants turbodorks (including my brother Aaron) loved him. They clustered in his homeroom with their redolent bologna sandwiches. Aaron was a lordly little spud whose proclivity to name all animals by scientific genus was not socially problematic until he got his height some years later, in high school. In junior high he was teacher's pet. He was in training to take over the surly condescension of Mr. Handwerker. Mr. Handwerker's impatient arrogance made it impossible to admit that I couldn't tell an igneous rock from a sedimentary. Even in the eighth grade I suspected a home truth that life would later confirm: namely, that the separation of igneous from sedimentary rocks *might not even be necessary*. Personally, I began to wonder why we couldn't just mix-'n'-match our rocks. Why labor to categorize them? Were we rehearsing an unspecified but inevitable event in the hereafter, as when the Lord Jesus would separate the sheep from the goats?

Like the biblical fool who builds his house on the sand, Mr. Handwerker had built his reputation on whisking his earth science class to the Grand Canyon for a week of canteens that teemed with tadpoles. Mr. Handwerker was under the impression that this excursion would shape our lives forever. In order to raise funds for the pricey field trip, my eighth-grade earth science class was forced to sell See's suckers, magazine subscriptions, World's Finest chocolate, and lightbulbs. Yet our collective efforts were not enough, as they had been in years past. So for the first time Mr. Handwerker commanded his eighth-grade class to stage a talent show.

Unfortunately my class was not blessed with talent. Moreover, we were exhausted from selling See's suckers, magazine subscriptions, World's Finest chocolate, and lightbulbs. We didn't want to backpack down the steep Hermit Trail; we didn't want to marvel at arrowheads and sedimentary rocks. But like all children whose elders get a bee in their bonnet, we were forced to suck it up and obey. Since my older brother was teacher's pet, and since Mr. Handwerker knew that Mennonite girls could sew, I was the designated mistress of costumes. I sewed my heart out for that nightmarish event. For one number I designed and sewed four pink floral antebellum dresses out of sheets I'd found on clearance at Gottschalks, using wire hangers and taffeta to approximate hoopskirts.

The talent show finale was an all-class hoedown that involved bucolic kerchiefs and square-dancing. The theory was that it would make the audience shout, "Yeehaw!" I still remember the lyrics to the chorus, penned by our own redoubtable teacher.

Werkie forbids us singin'
songs around here
Werkie forbids us dancin'

moves around here
But we don't care what Werkie forbids;
cause we're the singin', dancin' SCIENCE KIDS!

As executive choreographer, Mr. Handwerker thought it would be hilarious to have me, the tallest person in the class, whisk a cartoonishly horrified Glenn Arbus, a tiny twig of a boy, into the center spotlight for a hurly-burly romp. This tall-short dance would provide comic relief, said Mr. Handwerker.

At the rehearsal when Mr. Handwerker first broached this plan, he called me and Glenn front and center, in front of everybody.

"You, Knucklehead," he said to me, pointing, "will grab Twig by the arm and drag him into the spotlight here. And you," he said to Twig, "will act horrified and reluctant. You will dig in your heels while she drags you. You got that?"

Twig stoically shrugged and agreed. Poor chap, it must have been at least as humiliating for him as it was for me. When I recall this moment, I always cling to a rumor that I heard many years ago, that Twig grew up to become a brilliant genetic researcher.

As appalled as I was, I would have done whatever Mr. Handwerker had asked. I didn't know how to resist. I wasn't even aware that resistance existed as an option. Mennonite girls weren't raised that way. However, it did rightly occur to me that the authority of the church would trump the authority of a teacher whose chief interest was the categorization of rocks. I therefore hung my head and mumbled that I didn't think my mother would let me do the dance.

"What's that?" Mr. Handwerker said sharply. "Speak up, Numbskull!" He thought this style of address was a form of wit.

"I have to ask my mom. About the dancing," I said, trying to make this recourse sound like a logical step any eighth grader might take.

"Jesus H. Christ," said Mr. Handwerker. "Okay. You do that."

I did do that. The answer was an emphatic, crisply worded letter that explained why Mary Janzen's daughter would NEVER participate in a public spectacle involving dance, even if there were thousands of rocks in the Grand Canyon that needed categorizing. Mennonites did not dance. Period. Dancing was deeply, passionately verboten on two grounds. The first reason was that dancing led to sex . . . and this, dear readers, had been *documented*. In the Mennonite movement called the *Fröhliche Richtung* (the Joyful Direction), circa 1860, a band of renegade charismatic Mennonites started expressing the joy of the Holy Spirit via dance. During these joyful church-service dances, the aisle that divided the men's side from the women's was crossed. Boys began dancing all too joyfully with girls. Parts were felt! Accounts were written! Diaries were discovered! Adolescents were punished!

The second reason dancing was taboo in the Ukrainian Mennonite church was more a matter of tacit custom than a stated position. There was something about the lighthearted frivolity of dance that suggested a fatal weakness in priorities. Mennonites were supposed to work with dignity, and when the work was done, there would be something to show for it. That was the great beauty of work: there was always a measurable outcome. On the other hand, you could dance until the cows came home, but you'd never have anything to show for your dancing. In fact, it was precisely this lazy, shiftless revelry that was the problem with the native Russian peasants. If idleness was the devil's workshop, then dance was the beanbag on which the devil was enjoying himself a little too freely.

In junior high, I could not know that twenty years later a belated idea would occur to some of the younger Mennonites. Like all ideas that occurred to Mennonites, this one was not fresh. But it was new to them. It struck some of the younger set that *dancing might not be so bad.* However, the only way that Mennonites could endorse a new activity was to make the careful case that God was okay with it. Thus "liturgical movement" made its debut in some Mennonite churches. Always in quotations, "liturgical movement" consisted of three Sunday-school teachers dressed in bad white skirts moving in synchronized patterns. Together these brave ladies would step to the left, then lunge to the right, then lift one arm like an elephant trunk, gesturing toward the heavens. I'm sad to say that "liturgical movement" gave the older Mennonites bilious indigestion. It never really caught on.

If you had told me in the eighth grade that someday three ladies in white prairie skirts would be dancing in front of the pulpit, I would have offered you the baked good of your choice, provided that it did not contain raisins. By the eighth grade I was drawn to the idea of dance so much that I tried to teach myself the Hustle. This effort was doomed because I had access neither to steps nor to music. At school, in the halls between classes, I'd hear snatches from radios: FREAKAZOIDS, REPORT TO THE DANCE FLOOR! How I wanted to! But I didn't know how. What I did know was that if I performed the Twig Dance as a laughingstock, my passion for dance could be ruined forever. And in the end I was saved by the very thing that oppressed me. When my mother forbade me to dance in that talent show, I was actually grateful to be a Mennonite. This is sort of like falling in love with your kidnapper.

Mr. Handwerker, undaunted, forced my friend Bettina Hurrey to do the Twig Dance instead. Bettina and I were both unusually tall for our age. The visual humor of my Twig Dance would have turned on my extreme galloping thinness. I would have looked like Ichabod Crane trying to swat a bee. The humor of Bettina's Twig Dance turned on the fact that Bettina was shaped like a tremendous bratwurst. I understood that Mr. Handwerker was mocking her and Twig, and all big-boned people, and all tiny people, and all tall spidery people, and all people in general. Mr. Handwerker was the meanest teacher alive. During the song and dance I stood toward the back of the stage, clapping and stomping and singing and crying for Bettina, and for petite Glenn Arbus too, even though he had once put a june bug down my shirt.

The gap between Aaron and me was marked by so much more than a divide between left and right brains, between science and the humanities. In fact, I don't have much in common with either of my brothers. In college they remained content with their opportunities in Mennonite circles. Aaron sang close harmonies in a madrigal group, his rich-timbered baritone blending like butter. Caleb played in state volleyball competitions with a Christian organization. They both went to Bible studies. They dated sincere gals who hairsprayed their bangs and went on mission trips. Big and easy in their exuberance, Aaron and Caleb coached, studied, prayed. But by then we had nothing in common.

I felt my tiny Mennonite college was holding me back from a serious literary education. And it *was* holding me back, in a manner of speaking. I found this out to my cost when in grad school I discovered the jaw-dropping level of my underexposure. At twenty all I wanted to do was read philosophy, feminism, and fashion. I was blind to all of the better lessons my solid little Mennonite college could have taught me, lessons about the value of community, of service, of wisdom rather than knowledge.

As they grew older, both my brothers chose to stay rooted firmly in the Mennonite lifestyle. They married young and had big families, and they are active in the church. Our paths have been so different that our infrequent reunions are marked with awkwardness; my brothers don't follow events in the belletristic world, and I don't know what's going on with the soccer-mom, homeschooling set. My brothers never ask me about my life or work, a silence I interpret as disapproval. Whenever I ask them about ideas or politics or beliefs, they change the subject. Instead they share breaking news about their children, or, in the case of Aaron, bulletins about the nomenclature and classification of his herbaria. And the breaking news feels strained, as if the information is a preemptive strike against the possibility of genuine communication.

On my last visit five years ago, Caleb and his friend Gabe Warkentin dropped by as I was making *Quarkkuchen* in my mother's kitchen. Gabe, like us, is the son of a Mennonite pastor. I overhead Gabe say that a mutual old friend, Fran Thiessen, had just gotten married. The groom was a Mennonite named Rob Franz.

"Bummer," said Caleb. "She'll have a bad name: Frau Fran Franz."

They chuckled. From the kitchen I asked, "Why on earth would Franny have taken Rob's name? She was starting to make a name for herself in her career, wasn't she?"

There was a sudden heavy silence. I looked up from my batter, surprised: my brother and Gabe were bristling with palpable disapproval.

"You think a woman should keep her own name when the Bible clearly tells us that the man is to be the head of the house?" asked Gabe gravely.

"Ohhhh," I said. "Gotcha." Until that moment I had had no idea that he was so parochial.

"What's that supposed to mean?" Gabe demanded, angry. Caleb just sat there and frowned at his coffee.

"Nothing," I said, trying to be nice. "In academia women don't take their husbands' names very often anymore, that's all."

"Why not?"

"It's a little old-fashioned. The idea is that the woman's heritage and background are just as important as the man's. Many women see taking a man's name as a gesture of symbolic oppression. It's like saying to the woman, 'Who you are as a person isn't as important as who I am.'"

"Gabe. Maybe we should go," said Caleb, not looking at me.

"Did *you* take your husband's name?" Gabe was upset. He was taking this personally.

"I didn't," I admitted.

"How did he feel about that?"

"The issue never even came up. Nick always assumed I would keep my name."

"I suppose you think the *Word of God* is a little old-fashioned too?" Gabe shot back.

"You know what, Gabe? Don't even go there. She does think so. Let's get outa here," said Caleb.

After they were gone, I asked my mother, "Don't you think it's weird that the boys are so much more conservative than you and Dad?"

"Oh, they'll mellow over time," said Mom. "When you're young, faith is often a matter of rules. What you should do and shouldn't do, that kind of thing. But as you get older, you realize that faith is really a matter of relationship—with God, with the people around you, with the members of your community."

"Do you have a problem with the fact that I never took Nick's name?"

She chuckled. "You're old enough to make your own decisions."

"Would you have taken Rob Franz's name if you had been Franny?"

"I wouldn't have married Rob Franz at all," she said decisively. "That one is a shiftless underachiever. You watch. He'll quit his job and expect Franny to support him. Poor little Franny. She was so cute as a girl. She played the clarinet."

Aaron is a year older than I. We should have been fratty, since we went to the same school, had the same teachers, read the same books. I should have had crushes on his friends, but his friends were severe science types, like him. His crowd hung out in Mr. Handwerker's homeroom, where there was a darkroom for printing black-and-white artistic images of garden slugs—pardon me, of *Arion distincti*—that might win a prize at the Fresno Fair! Aaron and his friends wore their T-shirts tucked into their pants, and wherever one met these boys, they smelled of chemical developer, stop bath, or formaldehyde.

Among Aaron's friends there was one boy who wasn't as bad as the others. Wyatt Reed had floppy brown hair and a quiet smile, and he ate lunch not in Mr. Handwerker's homeroom, but on the lawn in front of the library, like a normal person. One summer he invited me and Aaron to Vacation Bible School at his church. Wyatt was not Mennonite; thus my mother thoroughly checked out Wyatt, his Presbyterian church, and his family, before giving us the thumbs-up. VBS didn't interest me in the slightest, but I was enjoying the way Wyatt's soft stutter became more pronounced when he spoke to me.

Theretofore I had conveniently managed flulike symptoms whenever Vacation Bible School rolled around at our own church, so this was my first venture. Vacation Bible School is like a religious-themed camp, but it takes place at your local church rather than at a piney lodge. Your parents drop you off for two hours, not two weeks. VBS shares some of the camp features: artificially induced rivalries, rowdy Christian songs about Father Abraham, and tearful altar calls. But VBS lacks somewhat in the areas of canoes, campfires, and sleeping bags.

At this VBS the Christian youths were divided into two competitive groups. Wyatt's and my group was called the Clouds. Aaron's group was called the Tornadoes. Why we were represented by inclement weather remains a mystery to this day. But if the Lord had portentously whispered, "Red sky at morning, sailors take warning!" I would have heeded the message, because Wyatt Reed was really almost cute when he stuttered. It was probably his mother who made him tuck his T-shirt into his pants.

The adult leaders, two Athletes for Christ from Virginia, fluffed the rivalry between the Clouds and the Tornadoes by every means possible. We were urged to run relays, chant slogans, and devise secret passwords. In crisp formation we performed a secret salute. Although at the time I was unfamiliar with the mannered architecture of the Third Reich, this VBS had a Riefenstahl quality that was kind of creepy. Clearly these Athletes for Christ had an aesthetic vision for their youth. And they exhorted us to make posters.

I spent a pleasurable afternoon working on mine. It was akin to pop art, very groovy, with bluish clouds scattered like grazing sheep. I edged each of the clouds with metallic silver paint. In block letters the caption read A SILVER LINING IN EVERY CLOUD. "I like the s-s-s-s-silver lining," Wyatt said.

That night when the Clouds' Athlete for Christ got up to lead the salute and display the posters, I experienced an abrupt shift in my worldview. Some bottom dropped out in my core filiation. When the Athlete for Christ placed my poster up on the easel there in front of the church social hall, I suddenly saw my poster in a new light. Even as my fellow Clouds were whooping and clapping and stomping, even as the Athlete for Christ was shaking his clasped hands above his head like a champion, the last of my enthusiasm drained away, and I became an empty cloud. There on a folding metal chair next to Wyatt Reed, at thirteen, with my bangs stiffly sprayed, I smelled groupthink for the first time. Sheeplike clouds? Silver lining? My poster *made no sense*. And if my poster made no sense, what of the rivalry it symbolized? What of the whole Vacation Bible School? What of religion itself? Clouds, tornadoes, sins awhirl before some imagined but necessary altar—a Perfect Storm of jingoism! It was at that moment that I first grasped what Tennessee Williams meant when he mocked the tiny spasm of man. Gentle Wyatt Reed, trying shyly to touch my hand, fell into insignificance. Across the aisle on the Tornado side Aaron was raising his arms in ritual salute for Jesus. He was my brother, moving his hands, lifting his voice, a stranger.

That night as the closing cheers receded, I ran to the ladies' lounge to be alone with my troubling new discovery. I lingered there, slowly brushing out my hair, counting out a hundred strokes. I perched on the edge of the couch that nursing mothers used. In the mirror I saw my good-girl self, my clean dress, my tidy macramé purse, my white leather-bound KJV Bible. That image was no longer right. I had to wipe that look of polite accommodation from my face; I had to run away. I had to rethink every single thing that I had been taught. So I sprinted from the ladies' lounge, as from a thought too scary to think. And I collided abruptly with one of the Athletes for Christ. The hall was shadowy, and I hadn't seen him.

"Sorry!" I gasped, embarrassed.

"No problem." He backed away but stood looking down at me. This Athlete for Christ seemed off somehow. There was something wrong. It was as if he'd been *waiting* for me. "I was looking for you, actually."

Ah, he had intuited my sudden crisis of faith, my dark night of the soul! I was about to get called on the Christian carpet! I looked up at him and said, "Um." He moved a fraction closer. "I've been thinking. Would you like a visit some night? A visit from your Uncle Rodge?"

I stared as I digested his meaning. It took a moment to sink in, but then I turned and ran back down the hall to the foyer. Aaron was looking for me. "Where were you?" he complained. "Wyatt's mom has been waiting for ten minutes."

I followed my brother to Mrs. Reed's car, where I slid into the far corner of the backseat, holding myself rigidly away from Wyatt. Puzzled but polite, he withdrew into silence. "Did you have fun tonight?" asked Mrs. Reed.

"It was so cool," Aaron said. "The Tornadoes got the most points because I memorized Ezekiel 37. That's the one about dry bones. It has twenty-eight verses. I memorized all of them."

Mrs. Reed began to sing "Dem Bones." Aaron joined in, looking back over his shoulder to see why I wasn't singing along. Never before had a view of a crowded church parking lot been so absorbing. Never before had the cloud of witnesses seemed a rattling congregation of bones. Aaron's voice had already changed. His bass musically descended, a stairway going down, way down, beneath Mrs. Reed's soprano, as if these lyrics and this song could get to the bottom of everything I knew. "Hear the word of the Lord!"

With Aaron I knew I would never be close, but there was a moment in my adolescence when I thought that Caleb and I might become friends. Caleb was fifteen months younger than I. Despite his status as goofy kid brother, he was tall and cleanly coordinated at an early age. It must have pained him to see my clumsiness, because one day he offered to teach me how to play racquetball. Racquetball is a relatively easy game to pick up. You can go from zero to sixty in a couple of days. But what you need to imagine here is gangliness so inept, cerebral, and all-consuming that I had never successfully hit a ball of any kind—not with bat, nor stick, nor racquet. In my generation Mennonite parents did not encourage athletics for girls, and I had gotten used to the public shame of PE.

The very notion of trying to learn a sport had left me with a nervous sour feeling, as when one crosses Kierkegaardian dread with a trip to the dentist. Plus Caleb and I had no relationship whatsoever. He was science; I was English. He killed toads; I made pie. He got in trouble for sabotaging Donny Dorko's pants at Heartland Christian Camp; I got in trouble for spending my babysitting money on a black strapless bra.

I was skittery, therefore, when I first followed Caleb onto the racquetball court. I expected a hortatory condescension the likes of which Aaron delivered. But no. From the first moment when Caleb showed me how to shake hands with the racquet, he was the soul of kindness. Tender and patient, he made it his business to show me what I could do. What astonished me even more than my emerging ability to hit the ball was his generosity. It's not just that he was nice to me when I needed nice. It was that he freely gave some mysterious ingredient that created confidence. He was a brilliant instructor, perhaps the best I've ever had. Over my many years in school I've been exposed to some wonderful mentors, intellectuals at the top of their game, professors and Pulitzer Prize winners who challenged me. But Caleb would be the only one to call forth an excited faith in my own ability. He didn't make me think I was a better player than I was. He made me *love* the player that I already was. What a gift that was.

The moment we left the racquetball court, Caleb reverted to nose picker/sci-fi reader. But on court I adored him. Huge and stable as an Alp, he stood motionless in the center, reaching out a long arm to flick the ball with precision. "Yo," he'd say. "This one's gonna go in the front left corner. See what happens when I hold my racquet at this angle? Now you try." Caleb went on to become an award-winning science teacher, then an assessment director of science in secondary education. He makes a great living telling teachers how to be better teachers. Those afternoons on the racquetball court, long ago when he was still goofy and I was still scared, go a long way toward explaining his professional success.

Once when I was in town for the Fourth of July, my mother and I went to see Caleb and Staci's new swimming pool. It was a superdeluxe pool, with levels and lights and fountains and waterfalls and alcoves, the kind of pool that said, "Mennonite—who, me?" All the grandkids were splashing and shrieking inside it. This pool was a splendid homage to American excess. In every way it was the opposite of what my siblings and I had grown up with— namely, a sprinkler that raised a feeble mist from a sun-scalded hose. When my mother saw the Gatsbyesque scope of this pool, she grabbed my elbow and said, "Oh my! That looks expensive!"

Staci telegraphed for help, so Hannah said, "Didn't you ever learn how to swim, Mom?" This question forestalled any discussion of Christian stewardship for a good half hour. But Mom came right back trotting down that road to Rome: "That diving platform sure looks like it cost a pretty penny!"

I jumped in this time. "Speaking of pennies, do you remember when you bribed me a dime to jump off the high dive at the community pool?"

"You jumped off the high dive for a dime?" said Al, joining us, still in her underwater goggles. She held her thumb and forefinger to her forehead in the shape of a capital *L*. "Loooooser!"

Mennonite privation isn't what it used to be. My generation of Mennonites has made it different, as when my brothers find ways of giving their children what we were denied. I considered all this when I once again returned to the taboo of Mennonite dance. Having bid farewell to Hannah and Phil, I was back in California, and my parents and I were going to a dance recital.

Mennonite high schools still forbid dancing. Mennonite high school teachers are still often forced to sign contracts, pledging that they will neither drink nor dance nor have premarital sex while employed at a Mennonite institution. But some of the solid die-hard Mennonites are now letting their children dance anyway. Some of them even seem to be *encouraging* dance. My pretty niece Phoebe, my brother Aaron's daughter, trains seven days a week in tap, jazz, ballet, and hip-hop. At fourteen, she is already beginning to star in community productions—*The Nutcracker, Pinocchio*. Dance training like hers doesn't come cheap, and I knew that Aaron must find it hard to finance on his teacher's salary.

When we arrived, Aaron's wife, Deena, graciously insisted that

I take her own seat. "He's right down there in the VIP seats up front," she said, pointing.

"Where? I don't see him," I said, scanning the crowded room.

"He's right there, in those seats right in front of the stage," said Deena.

"Oh, there he is!" I said, but I was thinking "!!!!!" because I had been looking at Aaron all along. I just hadn't recognized him. Although I had seen him only weeks before at our family dinner, in that roomful of strangers I was seeing Aaron with new eyes: he looked like any other middle-aged, square-faced man with a cap of close-clipped salt-and-pepper hair. Authority was on him like a sportcoat. He had the air of a principal.

I imagine that Deena had thought that Aaron and I would welcome the chance to catch up. We sat in silence. Together my brother and I watched his daughter interpret the elemental concept of rippling water, her hair unfastened, cascading behind her like the sheer azure chiffon that clung to her slender form. When her partner swung her up into a lovely high arc, her chin tipped back, her arms seeming at once to stir and settle, I shot a glance at him. How did it feel to see your fourteen-year-old Mennonite daughter borne aloft in the arms of a man twice her age? Where were the man's hands during these liquid lifts—on Phoebe's waist, on her firm little heinie? Phoebe looked like a professional dancer up there on stage, all the softness of childhood stretched taut, all the roundness worn away to a flicker of muscle across her fierce slim shoulders, while Aaron sat immobile, opaque as a Buddha. But it spoke volumes that this man, who knew nothing about dance and who had probably never danced a step in his own life, was prepared to go without a second car so that his daughter could ripple like water.

# NINE

# Wild Thing

I was making myself a tuna salad for lunch in my parents' kitchen, draining the can of tuna into a small bowl. "Hey," I said, "are there any cats in the neighborhood who would appreciate this tuna juice?"

My mother looked at me as if I had entered the final stages of dementia. She swiped the bowl, chugged the tuna juice, and said, "*Schmeckt gut!* Tastes like tooooona!"

Then she asked me if I would run to the grocery store for corn on the cob and heavy whipping cream. You can never have enough corn on the cob and heavy whipping cream is what I always say, and it's a pleasure to provide them for a mother who does tuna shooters.

Rounding the corner from Produce to Dairy, I smiled as I passed the snack aisle: a man was bending over to shout in the ear of an oldster, "YOU WANT SOME BRIDGE MIX, DAD?"

"Eh?" said the dad. "What's that?"

"NUTS, DAD? MIXED NUTS?"

"I like nuts!" cried the old man.

"DAD, I'M GONNA GET YOU SOME SALTY NUTS!"

"Get the salty ones!" advised the dad.

The man tossed a can of mixed nuts into his cart. The dad grabbed his son's sleeve and suggested, "I like those salty nuts you got last time!"

"PLENTY OF NUTS, DAD," shouted the son.

There was something dear about a buff, shaved-headed rocker taking time out on a Thursday afternoon to take his old dad grocery shopping.

Later the man and his deaf old dad were in the next checkout aisle. The son had run into a church acquaintance and was saying something about prayer—ah, the rocker was religious. This promptly scotched my interest. I still thought he was dear for shouting about mixed nuts to his dad, but my rocker had suddenly joined the ranks of Sexy Men I Wouldn't Date.

In the snack aisle the man and I had exchanged a meaningful glance, as if to say, *Bridge Mix, $4.99. Shouting the same thing eight times in a row to your old dad—priceless*. This rocker and I had shared a few seconds of that delicious unspoken awareness that sometimes heats up the space between strangers. Thus I was not wholly surprised when I heard somebody pull up behind me in the parking lot as I was loading groceries into the trunk of my parents' Camry. The rocker pulled up directly behind me.

"Excuse me."

I turned, knowing it was he.

"Ma'am," said the rocker, extending a muscular arm from the window of his car. He was offering me a piece of paper. "If you're a single woman of God, I surely wish you'd e-mail me. That's my e-mail address. You can throw it away. But I hope you don't."

"Oh!" I said, stunned at the *Single Woman of God*. I put the paper in my pocket.

He went on, "I was noticing you in the store. And it was heavy on my heart to say something to you. It was like, *Go talk to her*, very heavy, three times. So I pushed myself out of my comfort zone, and here I am."

The old dad leaned over to the driver's side. "Is that the gal? Is she pretty?"

The rocker reached over and patted his dad's shoulder. "This is my dad, Albert. He's blind. And I'm Mitch."

We shook hands. "I'm Rhoda."

"Rhonda," said Mitch. "I surely hope you e-mail me. If you're single and all."

He drove off with his dad and his nuts.

The note was printed in hasty caps on Twilight Shores stationery. Twilight Shores was the assisted-living facility across the street from my parents' house. That sealed it. Who hits on a woman with a blind old dad in tow? I e-mailed Mitch the very next day and set up a coffee date. I wasn't exactly a Single Woman of God, but hey, I could quote scripture. There *had* been something unusual, even compelling, about this guy. Although I would never have suggested that a divine voice was urging me in his direction, I did understand what it meant to go with your gut. And my own gut was whispering, "Mixed nuts!"

The following week my heart sank when I approached the coffeehouse where Mitch was waiting for me at an outside table. Even from across the street I could see what he was wearing around his neck. A big-ass three-inch square-headed nail on a leather thong.

To the uninitiated, a nail necklace might seem like no big deal for a huge goateed guy with a hard edge; you might consider it the quintessential accessory for rockers and metalheads. But I already knew in my heart what this nail was.

This big-ass nail was a tribute to the agony of Our Lord and Savior.

Thousands of undereducated zealots had adored Mel Gibson's cinematic presentation of the Passion of Christ. Moviegoers had rushed out to pay $16.99 for "Authentic Nail Necklaces," fondly believing that the square-headed nail of the Turin Shroud ker-fuffle confirmed Christ's divinity. These were the same folks who, a decade earlier, had dared people with their eyes to ask them what their bracelet meant—WWJD, What Would Jesus Do? I was so embarrassed when I saw the nail that I couldn't even look at my new friend. Should I head back to my car and pretend that the Mixed Nuts Encounter had never happened? Should I go forward and tell him that this was a mistake? WWJD? WJSDAOL? (Would Jesus Sit Down and Order a Latte?)

That's what I did anyhow. And, wow, I liked him. The rocker, not Jesus. I liked his simple declarations. He'd been married twice; his daughter was dating a convict; God had granted his prayer for sobriety on March 12, 2001. He attended a church called Faith Now. Faith Now, I learned, had something called an Affliction Ministry Team.

I was immediately reminded of the Salem witch trials, when a group of adult men and women who called themselves the Afflicted alleged that they were suffering from various forms of demonic harassment. History makes much of the group of young women accused of witchcraft, but it was the Afflicted who always held my attention.

"Affliction Ministry Team? Really?" I leaned a fraction closer.

"The team is called in whenever there's a situation involving spiritual affliction," Mitch told me.

"Demons, you mean?"

"Demons, sure," said Mitch, "but also afflictions with sub-stance abuse. Or depression."

I smiled at the thought of the Affliction Ministry Team,

dressed in short-sleeved shirts and ties and carrying corduroy Bibles with pockets on the front cover, showing up on our doorstep to exorcise my husband's depression. Nothing could have made Nick destroy more furniture faster. And what a potty-mouth Nick had! He could swear up the bluest streak I personally have ever heard: "Jesusmotherfuckingchrist on a damn melba toast with a two-minute egg!" he'd shout. This outburst would no doubt have sealed the deal for the Affliction Team, more evidence that Satan's minions were abroad and active in the world.

"I gotta tell you, Mitch, I don't believe in an external evil entity like Satan."

"Why not?"

"I think Satan is a dodge," I said. "It gives us someone to blame for the evil that we create."

"Then who do you think is powering those Ouija boards?"

"What Ouija boards?" I asked, looking around, hoping for one nearby.

"Those Ouija boards you play when you're a teenager in Frankie Versalini's basement."

Tasty! "Tell me about that," I invited. As an obedient Mennon-ite, I had respected the injunction not to tamper with the super-natural. Even now at age forty-three, I'd never seen a Ouija board in real life. Here's what I've gathered from odd Ouija-related tid-bits over years of general reading: The Ouija presents as a board game printed with the alphabet and numbers. There's some kind of pointer device on which all players are asked to rest their hands. From there I imagine the game proceeds like a nineteenth-century séance: dimmed lights, a spooky feeling, an invocation to sum-mon supernatural forces or dead friends. The device is supposed to channel a disembodied element, which may or may not have an urgent message from the great beyond. If this supernatural entity does have such a message, it allegedly spells out the message using the letters and numbers on the board. Why it doesn't state its business out loud I do not know. Maybe it is shy. Maybe this supernatural entity is an introvert, passing us a note as in third grade.

Since the players' hands must physically rest on the Ouija board at all times, it would be impossible to tell just who is conveying the urgent message. Poltergeist? The spirit of Houdini? Your buddy across the table? Your own psyche? Following the pointer as it moves from one letter to the next must be an intensely slow, suspenseful process. A letter-by-letter spelling out of a ghostly message is a faithful reflection of the way we seek to impose meaning on chaos. Funny to have a board game, banned and censored for centuries, whose very punch line is the literal act of reading. You have to decode a message from the great beyond, the perfect metaphor for how we interpret those parts of ourselves that we cannot understand. Or that we don't want to understand.

"I'm sorry to say that me and Frankie played with a Ouija board," said Mitch, "and I've prayed that nothing bad stuck to me from it. I've prayed that prayer ever since I found the Lord on June 19, 2000."

"What would stick to you, for instance?"

"I don't know, and I don't want to know. Some bad vibe."

I tried to picture this. "A bad vibe that gets on you and stays on you, like a piece of toilet paper permanently trailing on your shoe?"

He frowned. "Except that a piece of toilet paper on your shoe isn't evil. It's just toilet paper."

"Touché," I said. Mitch's assertion had a ring of fresh truth to it, and I liked it so much I repeated it. "Toilet paper isn't evil."

"As Christ-followers, we're not supposed to even open the door to evil."

"Because evil might wedge its foot in there, like a fifties salesman?"

"You like to compare stuff to other stuff, don't you?"

"I'm a writer," I apologized.

"I will always remember the day when Frankie Versalini brought out his sister's Ouija board in his basement. The thing went wild. It moved around a lot, wildlike, all over the thing." Mitch shook his head at the memory of the thing going wild on the thing.

"Did it spell out a message?"

"No. But it sure moved around. Me and Frankie weren't doing it, I swear. You ever do anything like that?"

I liked the idea of the thing gone wild, of some kind of urgent longing to communicate coupled with an inchoate inability to do so. It had a message, dammit! But it couldn't quite articulate it! Or maybe the message was that there is some ineffable longing, some core need or pain, that can never be articulated. It spins our thing on the thing, and we are helpless before its frenzy.

This may have been my oddest first date of all time. Usually people exchange information about their careers, their families, their politics. Here we were revealing chinks in our spiritual armor. I was so floored that when Mitch suggested a walk down the street to a little café, I realized I couldn't not have lunch with him. This man and I were *destined* to have lunch. First the nuts and now the chink.

But here's the best part. As we began walking down the street, I suddenly spotted my friends Alba and Raoul having lunch at an outdoor café just ahead. We were going to walk directly past them, which meant that I would be forced to introduce them to Mitch. I hadn't seen this couple since the spring before in Bologna, when they were visiting Lola. Alba, like Lola and me, had grown up Mennonite, and although she had broadened her horizons, she still cherished her community of origin. Alba and Raoul had heard about the divorce; naturally they would be interested to see what kind of a man I was now with. Alba was a cognitive therapist who did trauma counseling in developing countries. Raoul was a plastic surgeon who traveled with Doctors without Borders to perform cleft-palate surgeries. This was going to be sticky.

We hugged. I introduced Mitch, mentally willing him not to inquire about the status of my friends' salvation. The four of us small-talked for five minutes. So far, so good. Just as I was exhaling a breath of relief, thinking we were going to emerge from the encounter unscathed, Alba focused on the big-ass nail.

"I have a nail like that," she said. "It's from my great-grandfather's barn. When we moved it onto our property, we saved some of the old nails."

"We made some groovy paperweights out of them," said Raoul. "That barn was originally built in 1850."

"1860," Alba corrected. "It was right after Garibaldi met with Victor Emmanuel at Teano." She turned to Mitch. "What's the story on *your* nail?"

This was where the demonic juju that had stuck to Mitch jumped to my own shoe, metaphorically speaking.

"My nail is the nail in the hands and feet of Jesus. He was crucified for our sins."

"Oh," said Alba, embarrassed.

"It's not the actual nail, though," said Mitch. "This nail is a replica."

"Right," said Raoul.

"Good to have run into you two!" I exclaimed brightly. "I'll be here for a couple of months. We should do lunch!"

∞

I saw a different side of California culture when I was with Alba and Raoul. Usually I hooked up with them in Europe; this was the first time I was seeing their new house in the States. Their son, Holden, was a big boy now, three years old, in the process of being promoted from Cub to Dragon at his expensive day-care facility.

When I arrived for an overnighter, Holden ran up to meet me and demanded a surprise. I proffered a sheet of dinosaur stickers, which he accepted with pleasure. These he laboriously affixed to the wainscoting of Alba and Raoul's 1912 Craftsman bungalow. The next hour, and every subsequent hour, Holden greeted me with the same question, "Rhoda, do you have a surprise for me?" I had planned three surprises for my overnight stay: the dinosaur stickers, a can of Silly String, and a magic washcloth. But I had no more surprises. And to tell the truth, I was beginning to find the whole demand-and-supply thing a little fatiguing. Holden always began to shriek and whine when I apologized that no, I didn't have any more surprises. To give, that is. Once I did receive a surprise. A kick to the shin.

Alba and Raoul, seasoned parents by now, were unperturbed by their son's behavior. If Holden's howling outburst was especially dramatic, they might observe conversationally to their boy, "Caro, sometimes people won't give you a surprise." Then they would turn to each other or to me and simply resume the thread of adult discourse.

Both Alba and Raoul had known Nick very well indeed, and they were united in their efforts to make me feel better. I'd been suffering from an ongoing sense of impaired judgment. Just why was it, I wondered, that an ostensibly self-aware woman had remained for fifteen years in a marriage with a man who didn't love her? Had Nick ever loved me? If so, when had he stopped? And why was it important to know that? Raoul said, "Hey, we were there too, remember? Of course Nick loved you. In his way. Bipolarity can be pretty damn charming. We fell in love with Nick, too. Don't beat yourself up over this."

"What you need," said Alba firmly, "is to get out there again. It's been eight months. Unless you count the guy with the Jesus nail."

"Not exactly eight," I said. I explained about the interlude with the pothead.

"The pothead doesn't count," she said. "That was just to show you that you still know how to kiss. What I'm talking about is really getting out there and meeting a guy you have something in common with. You know, a man who will appreciate you. A man you don't have to call the police on." Alba was remembering the time I had called the police on Nick: January 3, 2001. *I sound like Mitch,* I thought. *How lame is it that this date is etched so firmly in my memory?*

Alba proposed that I tag along to a couple openings and concerts. Between her and Raoul, they knew everybody.

One evening the four of us were going to an art opening. Alba and Raoul believed that children rise to the level of social intercourse we model for them; they insisted that children deserve exposure to the fine arts from infancy. If tots fill their pants, fuss, or throw raging tantrums in public, so be it. Thus they take Holden everywhere. Alba theoretically allowed Holden one sweet per day, and he had already had a chocolate-chip cookie earlier that afternoon. (By "one," I mean "four.") Yet Holden was pitching such a royal hissy that on the way to the gallery Raoul stopped and bought him some Pop Rocks.

At the opening, I was conversing with an artfully disheveled hipster: shaggy hair, intriguing stubble, Dries Van Noten pin-stripes, flip-flops. The hipster was name-dropping a list of bands and famous musicians whose cachet was lost on me for two reasons. One was that throughout my fifteen-year marriage my husband had been the one obsessed with music. He had seen it as his job to determine what we liked and listened to. At every dinner party it was he who decided what jazz, and when. The other reason was that, as a native Mennonite, I had so little knowledge of the 1960s, '70s, and '80s, that it seemed easier for everybody if I just backed out of music altogether.

I rarely approached the formidable wall of CDs, alphabetized in meticulous splendor. Most of the time I preferred the full sound of silence. Sometimes I hummed German hymns while cooking or cleaning, but very quietly, because Nick loathed anything religious, and he moreover wanted me to distance myself from what he called my Betty Crocker origins. But I like to cook and clean, and housework sometimes puts me in the mood for an old-fashioned hymn. Once a sympathetic girlfriend in grad school had given me an Andy Griffith CD of old gospel hymns. I kept it hidden inside a silicone oven mitt for long culinary projects when Nick wasn't home. Is it just me, or is there something richly satisfying about filling jam jars as you pick up the alto to "In the Sweet By and By"? Poor Nick—I always felt bad that I summoned so little interest in contemporary music.

So the hipster's name-dropping was lost on me. I had the sense that he might be a bit of a gasbag. Then again, he could have been a famous producer. What did I know? Either way, he wasn't particularly interesting to me. Beautiful people were gliding in random patterns, holding their pomegranate martinis. Suddenly, just over this man's shoulder, I became aware of Raoul among the glitterati. Raoul had a big blue Pop Rock clinging to the corner of his lip.

I made eye contact and brushed helpfully at my mouth. Raoul squinched his face as if to say, "Huh?" Okay, Plan B. I offered the internationally recognizable expression Dude, There's Something on Your Face. But this time he mouthed, "What?" Still pretending to listen to what Band Guy was saying, I whispered, "Pop Rock!" to Raoul, who finally took a tardy swipe at his lip.

But Band Guy thought I had been talking to him. All confidence and charisma, he said, "Pop Rock? Ahhh, yes, I heard them last summer at the Roxy. I had a backstage pass."

Don't get me wrong; I do love the cognoscenti. There's always a white scholar who identifies as black. There's always a cocktail with a retro ingredient such as Tang. There's always a conceptual artist whose preferred medium is her own menstrual blood. There's always an endive involving ginger chutney and a dance troupe that refuses to do any actual dancing. There's always somebody earnestly saying, "*Subjected*, like *productive*, is deceptive in that it can be quickly defined, but is not so quickly discussed because of the variant ways in which the definition can be interpreted." There's always a fashion-forward woman in a maroon dress, carrying a big matching Vidalia onion as an accessory. Then when you go home afterward, there's always a malapropistic nanny singing, "Row, row, row your boat, gently down the street."

These things are pleasures to behold. If I can't have a good time at such a function, I can at least laugh about it. But for some reason I couldn't plug in this time. I don't know why. Maybe it's because I too closely associated this world with my marriage.

One afternoon I was looking after Holden in Alba's courtyard. Raoul was in China performing cleft-palate surgeries, Alba was at Pilates, and the nanny was getting a pedicure. It was one of those perfect California late afternoons, warm enough to make me seek the shade of the jasmine-laden pergola. Holden was amusing himself with two drumsticks and an electronic keyboard that offered a choice of percussive rhythms. He had selected a techno beat, which was still playing at the loudest volume even when he left it on the step to approach me under the pergola. I dreaded what I knew was coming.

"Rhoda," he said with awful quietness, "do you have a surprise for me?"

"I'm sorry, Holden, but I don't."

His face reddened and squalled. Just like that, his cheer was gone. He began to sob, whacking his little drumsticks on the post of the pergola. "YOU DIDN'T GIVE ME A SURPRISE!!!" he wailed. He was twisting and whacking like a tiny Tasmanian devil, so I couldn't gather him up in my arms. "I WANT A SUR-PRISE!!!!"

"So do I," I admitted.

Poor Holden! Rhythm savant, whacker of sticks, kicker of shins! He bawled and twirled, and I just sat there. But a part of me recognized his dissatisfaction. On the steps the rhythm machine marched on, and I was catching techno snatches between sobs. Alba's heavy jasmine vine honeyed the air. How could a garden so beautiful be so filled with unhappiness, with a sense of loss for what we never had? "WHERE'S MY SURPRIIIIIIIIIIIIISE?" he shrieked, and as he churned there with fists balled and cheeks aflame, his pain swelled until he seemed the very incarnation of pathos. His whole body became a rigid whirling wild thing. He was the emissary of us all, we who felt we had not received our due, we who felt the late afternoon of our lives stung with fury and with sorrow.

## TEN

∞

# The Trump Shall Sound

My mother suggested a visit to a feeble senior who was recuperating from pneumonia. She proposed that we bring Mrs. Leona Wiebe a plate of fresh Zwiebach and my mother's own signature calling card, a miniature jar of homemade strawberry jam: "Just a taste, that's why the container is so small. That way they don't feel like they have too much food in their little refrigerators." My mother's garage freezer housed hundreds of these personal-sized jams. They rose in military towers. She single-handedly kept two assisted-living facilities in the jam.

When I first opened the door of her garage freezer and confronted the evidence of her largesse, I asked why she and my father needed so much jam.

"Oh," she said. "I'm a deacon."

"The position calls for jam?"

"Well, you want to bring something to cheer those old ladies up. Homemade jam reminds them of the old days before jam got so fake. Who would eat store-bought jam when you could have the real thing? You should come along with me to visit old Mrs. Leona Wiebe. She's eighty-six," Mom added, as if that might be extra inducement.

Actually, it was. I liked hanging out with the oldsters.

"Is she mentally alert?" I asked.

"Oh yes! She wears a wig!"

Note to self.

Old Mrs. Leona Wiebe greeted us graciously in her frosty wig and carefully applied makeup. We had called right before coming to give her a chance to wig up, and Mrs. Leona Wiebe had done a splendid job. My own makeup should look so fierce.

"Leona!" My mother gave her a shadow hug, careful not to squeeze those frail shoulders. "You've got your color back! When I saw you in the hospital, you were so pale. I thought, *She's not long for this world!*"

"God is good," said old Mrs. Wiebe. "I've got my breath machine. I'm supposed to do it every hour on the hour, but it's too hard to remember when I'm in the middle of something else."

"An incentive spirometer? Can you get the ball all the way up?" my mother asked, ever the nurse.

"No, about halfway. But I can hold it there for six seconds. A little at a time, praise God! I hope to be back on the track soon."

Behind Twilight Shores was the Mennonite university's track, a gorgeous facility. Finally healed enough to exercise, I ran there every morning. Under a flat blue California sky, that track invited dreamy distance, hot bright miles. I ran as if in a trance, loving the cry of peafowl from the nearby Havakian estate. It was my first sustained exposure to peafowl. They meowed portentously, like netherworldly cats. If I got there early enough, I'd meet Mr. and Mrs. Clarence Penner. Together they walked twelve slow laps every day, holding hands the entire time. The only thing that could have improved my experience on this track was to see old Mrs. Leona Wiebe clinging to the turf like a blonde spider.

We sat down on her floral couch.

"I just turned eighty-seven, praise God," she announced.

"Many happy returns!" said my mother.

I did some math in my head. "Calvin Coolidge was president when you were born," I said. "You must have been a young woman already during World War II. Sugar rations, boys in uniform."

"No, dear," said Leona, legs elegantly crossed in their taupe slacks. "I lived in China in those days. What I remember are fearful times under General Chiang Kai-shek."

I sat up straighter. "Oh! It must have been terribly dangerous for missionaries to be in China then!"

"It was. We feared for our lives. All of us kids were born in China, and we spoke Chinese before English, so we understood what people were saying in the village. Our parents didn't; they had a translator, who always made things seem better than they were. But even so, my parents were scared. My parents put food and water at one end of our compound and then they brought in a lot of mud bricks we'd made. My father's idea was to build a false wall inside and to hide behind it, so the soldiers would never know we were there. The soldiers who served under Chiang Kai-shek hadn't been paid or fed properly, so they were breaking away to prowl around the country. They would sweep into a village and steal all the food and attack the women. Those were dreadful times."

"Did the soldiers ever come into your compound?" I asked.

"Praise God, no. The Lord kept us from harm. But twice the soldiers terrorized the village, and we had to go into hiding. I remember once our security guard shouted down into our hiding place that we could stop praying. He said we were safe."

"Were you?"

"Well, we could hear a terrible ruckus coming up from the village, so we knew the soldiers were still there. My older sister Rebecca asked the security guard why he thought it was safe to

come out. He said"—she leaned forward, bewigged and earnest—
"that there were two angels on the wall." Her voice dropped to a
holy hush.

I had never actually met anyone who claimed an angel sighting, even a secondhand sighting. As far as I was concerned, angel
sightings were not unlike alien kidnappings or Ouija juju on your
shoe. Naturally Mrs. Leona Wiebe's story made me perk right up.
In fact I couldn't have been any perkier. "Really?" I asked, jaw
dropping. "Real live angels? *Two* of them?" Did they come in
pairs? Mate like swans for life?

"Two real live angels," confirmed Mrs. Leona Wiebe solemnly.

"Were they—"

"Well, we won't keep you," said my mother, frowning at me.
"I brought you some Zwiebach and a taste of strawberry jam."

"Thank you, my dear. I can't tell you how much I appreciate
your visits. You're an angel yourself. If somebody had to see me in
that state in the hospital"—she patted her wig—"I'm so glad it
was you."

Walking back home, I complained that Mom had cut me off
just when it was getting good.

"I don't think it's right to make fun of poor Leona," said my
mother sternly. "She's entitled to a couple of angels on the wall."

"I'd like a couple myself," I said. "I wasn't making fun of her.
I just wanted to know what those angels were doing up there on
the wall. Why weren't they down in the village, protecting the
Chinese?"

"Maybe the Chinese weren't praying."

"Mo-om!" I said, stopping smack in the middle of the sidewalk, horrified. "Maybe there's something wrong with a religion
that sends an angel to protect the Americans but lets the Chinese
fend for themselves! I wonder what they were wearing."

"The Chinese?"

"The angels."

"Old folks like Leona may be a bit literal in their beliefs, but God does work in miraculous and magnificent ways."

"Mom," I said suspiciously, "are you trying to tell me you see angels too?"

She laughed. "No. But there are powers and principalities. Speaking of cherry-plums, do you want to help me make *Pluma Moos*?"

My visit was drawing to a close, but my mother continued to surprise. One of the greatest surprises to proximate auditors was her contribution of hortatory flatulence. Loud and astonishing were her expostulations, like the speeches of Daniel Webster. These outbursts had become so frequent, yet so casual, that she no longer apologized. She treated them stoically, with great inclusivity and tolerance.

My friend Lola, who is also afflicted with intestinal turbulence, once reported that she had been deeply embarrassed at a cultural evening at a villa in Bologna. Two Italian artists had followed her to the kitchen, where she began to replenish a tray of appetizers. She broke wind suddenly, audibly, primordially, in front of these men. They froze, staring. Poor Lola improvised. She shrugged, laughed, and said, "Che posso dire? Sono americana!" (Translation: What can I say? I'm American!) I relayed Lola's story to my mother, suggesting that every time my mother was caught in a situation of similar social rupture, she could shrug jauntily and blame it on her nation of origin. She could murmur, "So sorry! I'm Canadian!" or perhaps, "God save the queen!"

One day in my last week in California we were at Kohl's

inspecting bundt pans. There in front of several shoppers and a seeing-eye dog my mother sounded the clarion call to all rogue farts—so rich, so specific, so thunderous, that really it was almost prophetic. This was the Moses of all farts, a leader of its kind. The trump shall sound! It shall rouse us to action! I could not believe that my own mother had produced such a remarkable acoustic effect. In public.

Mom always reminded me of the virtuous woman in Proverbs 31, the one whose worth is far above rubies. She had other things in common with that woman, too. "The Virtuous Woman," I remarked, thinking of Proverbs, "girdeth her loins with strength."

"I wouldn't talk," my mother said ominously. "You're half Canadian, you know." Then she added one more junior fart, as if for emphasis. She always gets the last word.

The Kohl's incident seemed curiously linked to my mother's interactions with frail bewigged Mrs. Leona Wiebe. Mom's stoicism regarding the body and all its functions was really almost *Christian* in its ideation of openness and transparency. What the rest of us considered malfunctions of the body—death, disease, crippling intestinal turbulence—she rather interpreted as functions of a *normal* body. She talked about death as she spoke about life, matter-of-factly, with that benign enthusiasm so out of place in this world. She had announced to Mrs. Leona Wiebe that in the hospital the latter had looked just awful. "Not long for this world" were her exact words. That would be among the last things I'd say on a visit to an invalid, yet from my mother's mouth these words seemed oddly comforting, as if there were indeed a time for all things under the sun. Likewise, the failure to excuse oneself for explosive gas is, to most Americans anyway, a shocking breach of etiquette. But in my mother this behavior adverted to an acknowledgment that the manners we seek are not necessarily the manners we have. There was a refreshing honesty about that . . . though I swear on a stack of corduroy Bibles that no matter how much I like the woman, I will not be emulating her behavior in Kohl's.

I spent some time reflecting on what it would mean to be a virtuous woman in this day and age. My mother, bless her, didn't really count; she was a virtuous woman from *another* age. Mary Loewen Janzen would have given the angelic nineteenth-century Marmee from *Little Women* a run for her money. Both Marmee and my mother healed the sick, clothed the poor, and took jam to the indisposed. Both offered free babysitting for struggling young mothers. Both called on their medical knowledge to minister and heal. Both went around in a shawl and a big cartwheel hat, if you count Friday mornings, when my mother volunteered as a docent at the Meux Home Museum. Both sewed, and sang, and served the Lord. Perhaps prim corseted Marmee did not pass whipcrack gas, or freeze a seeing-eye dog in its tracks, but in many respects she and my mother were similarly virtuous.

I suppose a sensible way to gauge virtue is to examine how the virtuous behave when things disappoint them. I'm sure my mother wishes—prays!—that I had a spiritual home in a church, even a non-Mennonite church. I'm thinking that she might even prefer a charismatic, tongue-talkin', faith-healin' gospel church to none at all. But, like Marmee, she has always backed her daughters up, always supported us, always welcomed us into her home with open arms, no matter what choices we've made. And we've made some strange choices, Hannah and I. That steadfast acceptance does seem to hark back to former centuries, at least to the hagiographic literature thereof.

What about virtue in the twenty-first century, however? I wondered if virtue, like virginity, no longer even existed in the conceptual realm. In the Western world, virginity has gone the way of butter churns and lard sandwiches. That is, virginity still technically exists in the form of folks who have not initiated sexual activity. But the old definition of *virgin* as a pure young woman, unsullied by knowledge of sex, is no longer with us. I may have been the last virgin. Nowadays even folks who are not sexually active know about sex. Virginity is therefore a changed creature altogether. Virtue is like that. Knowing what we know about human nature, would we even want to return to those days when we believed morality was simple, when goodness was something you learned at Marmee's knee?

Consider how impossible it is, for example, to aspire to the role of virtuous woman when professional commitments dramatically interfere with jam delivery to oldsters. Consider what happens when scholarship and education expose many of the assumptions of organized religion as intellectually untenable. Belief in literal angels, for instance, is something I am not prepared to endorse. Yet I cannot deny the genuine warmth my mother seems to radiate—indeed, that all these Mennonites seem to radiate. It's clear that this Mennonite community is the real deal. They really do try to practice what they preach.

It has been many years since I absented myself from the Mennonite church. I made lifestyle choices that would have been insupportable for this conservative community. Lord, if they had a problem with Mrs. Ollenburger's liposuction, imagine what they would have said about my marrying an atheist! Moreover, in addition to my marital defiance, there was the shocking fact that in my early twenties I declared myself free of body-related shame. This declaration translated to studded black minis, enormous hair, fuchsia lipstick, and preposterously high Manolos. I once wore such an ensemble to accept a senior award at a Mennonite college. It seemed an eloquent gesture at the time.

When I was a young woman, the Mennonites would have recoiled with fear and loathing before the thought of a female pastor, and even now I know of a Mennonite provost who very recently had to be "persuaded" to hire a female theologian as part of an academic faculty. There were those, like my father, who believed that the church would move forward in time. But in my opinion the Mennonite church was *already* a good fifty years behind the civil rights movement, and I wasn't in the mood to wait around. Nor could I stomach the Mennonite position on homosexuality ("Hate the sin, love the sinner!") or abortion ("Judge the mother, love the baby!").

The third deal breaker, as if I needed another, was Christianity's traditionally narrow definition of salvation. Buttressed with a black-and-white vision of heaven and hell as literal places, salvation was like an airline ticket sandbagged by black-out days. You could be saved only if you Accepted Jesus into Your Heart, preferably with tears, testimony, two weeks at Heartland Christian Camp, and a corduroy Bible with a pocket that you had embroidered with, let's say, Shasta daisies. Thus, in one dramatic assertion, all practitioners of competing world religions were damned. They had strayed onto the high arid plains of perdition. (Hence the collective Mennonite interest in the Chaco.)

My parents had always modeled commitment—to each other, to their word, to their church, even to the lane they had chosen to drive in. When things got sticky, did Christ-followers bail out and change their minds? That's nutso! When there was dissension in the church body, did they up and leave the church? In their dreams, maybe! In spite of my criticisms, I might have been able to treat church membership like a fifteen-year marriage with problems I'd really prefer not to address. I might have stayed, and stayed, and stayed. I might have shut my eyes to all that was not right. But something happened to chase me away.

I applied for seminary.

You may be thinking, *Are you profoundly retarded?* Or, if you are more tactful: *Are you partially retarded?* But hey, I was in my twenties at the time, fresh from my first master's degree. Applying to seminary may seem like a strange choice for someone who would later feel lasting pleasure in an alliance with a potty-mouthed atheist, but there was something deeply attractive to me about seminary. Oh, I never intended to become a pastor or a theologian, like my father. I was thinking of the masters of divinity as a luxury degree, the way writers today often conceive of a graduate degree in creative writing: two glorious years of reading and scribbling, with no guarantee of employment at the other end, and all for the bargain price of forty thousand dollars! I hadn't ruled out the existence of a God. I still don't. In fact, I'm gonna come right out and admit that I believe in God. I have always loved the beautiful, mysterious power of the Bible, its lethal history, its toxic charm. I adored the idea of learning Hebrew and Greek. I longed for sustained study with other students who were also humbled by the power of creation, by the ineluctable search for meaning in a broken world.

Anyhoo. After having done my homework on the various Protestant denominations, and after learning exactly where each stood on the hermeneutical issues most important to me, I decided to apply to a Mennonite seminary. Go figure: I ended up really liking the Mennonites' position on global peacemaking, though I must say that I was still uneasy about their unstated intention to evangelize the Chaco. Robert Frost would have loved me. There I stood at a crossroads. Down one path, and I'd become a full-on, flat-out Mennonite. There'd be prayer chains in my future, and ruffled skirts, and a perm, and corduroy Bibles, and children whom I would raise up in the way they should go. I would marry a man with bad hair, and we would pray before meals, and together we would advocate for "liturgical movement" during the worship service. Down the other path, and I'd never be able to look back. I stood there hemming and hawing, like Lot's wife, who sadly never got the chance to memorize the Frost poem for extra credit.

Seminary, dammit! I was on the cusp of dropping the S-bomb on all my friends when I received a letter from the one other woman who was then enrolled in the seminary. Being Mennonite, the seminary did not enroll many women. Although the Mennonites had not passed a rule against the study of theology by women, at that time there was still no future for women in church leadership. I never met the author of this letter in person, but she changed my life forever.

This woman, let's call her Esther, had heard that the seminary had admitted one other woman. Esther was excited! She was promising to work with me in sisterly solidarity! We would mentor each other! For six handwritten pages Esther took artless swipes at the patriarchy. She was like a sincere kitten ambushing your ankle as you walk by the couch—adorable! Sporty-fresh! She would lift me up in prayer! Then she signed off with a Bible verse and a smiley face, under which she had drawn a cute dove holding an olive branch in its bill. The word *agape* was used, an early Christian Greek term to denote brotherly—or in this case sisterly—love.

The next day I applied to twelve grad schools instead.

My father recently told me a story that probably appears in one of his sermons. He described two World War II buddies who had become great friends. When one of them was killed in combat, the other risked life and limb to bring his friend's body to a Catholic priest in a French village. But before the friend could be buried in the little churchyard, the priest had to ask him an important question. Was the deceased a Catholic? The soldier shook his head—"No, that is, I'm not sure. I don't think he was a religious man." The soldier had to leave but vowed one day he'd return to pay respects to his friend's grave.

Years later, the ex-soldier made his way back to the little village and found the old church. He wasn't a man of faith himself, but he had since understood that his friend would not have qualified for burial inside the churchyard. Burial inside the churchyard was for Catholics only. The churchyard fence had historically symbolized the boundaries of the Kingdom of Heaven. The ex-soldier therefore searched the perimeter of the churchyard, seeking his friend's grave marker outside the fence. But he couldn't find it. Finally he tracked down the same priest into whose care he had entrusted his friend's body so many years ago. The priest remembered him and led him to a gravesite that was surprisingly inside the fence.

"But my friend wasn't Catholic! I thought he had to be buried *outside* the fence!" exclaimed the ex-soldier.

"Yes," said the priest. "But I scoured the books of church law. I couldn't find anything that said we couldn't move the fence."

We all have our own ways of dealing with grief and pain. We might find succor in the thought of angels on the wall, guarding us, us especially, in our moment of travail. We might find comfort in the idea of comforting others, as my mother does. But what if there is no comfort? What if an angel atop the wall is the very last thing you'd imagine? If there was an angel on the wall, Nick's brother Flip never saw it. Flip dealt with his grief and pain by killing himself.

My in-laws didn't attend the funeral, interpreting Flip's suicide as a ploy for pity from a solipsistic slacker. By the logic of their brand of Christianity, Nick's parents didn't know what to do with a son who had committed suicide. They believed that suicides, like unbelievers, went to hell. (I recently learned that some Canadian Mennonite churches buried suicides outside the fence as late as the 1950s.) Nick and I could never quite wrap our minds around his parents' response to their son's death. Given the anguish that drives suicidal depression, how could anyone who has not suffered it wave a self-righteous banner of judgment and damnation?

Flip was Nick's closest sibling. Flip had made mistakes. He'd become a parent knowing full well that he was too depressed to be a good or even an adequate father. Wrapped in his own misery and despair, he was incapable of the simple practiced presence that love demands. Flip couldn't be there for anyone. He couldn't listen. He couldn't even communicate his own wants and needs to those who cared for him. Like so many people who suffer from severe depression, he couldn't keep a job; he couldn't stay on his meds. Bouncing from one bad job to the next, he lost everything along the way. He was fired once for some unprofessional behavior we were never able to identify. His wife left him; subsequent girlfriends left him. Finally, at age forty-two, he downed a bottleful of antidepressants, asphyxiating in a puddle of his own vomit, kneeling before a toilet in a cheap hotel. A man's life in one paragraph.

Nick and I were horrified when his parents accused Flip of selfishness. And we were stunned when the larger Christian discourse found Flip guilty of insufficient faith; we actually heard wellmeaning Christians say that if only Flip had been able to put his trust in God, the tragedy of his death could have been prevented.

One church leader went so far as to suggest that since Flip had elected to live a hell on earth, he had made for himself a hell in the hereafter. We were simply blown away by the idea that a man's psychic hell would follow him beyond the grave. Whatever Flip had done or failed to do, the very least he deserved was our compassion and love.

It was easy for me to show compassion and understanding for Flip's suffering, since Flip had never hurt me personally. But it is much harder to show compassion and understanding when we are the ones being hurt directly, when the wrecking ball of someone else's misery takes us down, too.

In the months before Nick left me, when his behavior became more desperate, I practiced neither compassion nor understanding. I went numb with shock. And the thaw has been a long slow business. It is tempting to make categorical, sweeping statements about Nick. He used me because he never loved me. He left me because he's gay. He cheated because he's cruel. All of these statements would let *me* off the hook for my own complicity in the failure of our marriage. Also, none of the above statements has the merit of being true. Nick loved me as much as he was able, while he was able. Nor did he ever conceal his bisexuality from me; I entered my marriage with full knowledge that Nick had dated a man before he moved in with Julia, the woman he was with for eight years before he met me. And anybody who's taken Psych 101 knows that cruel behavior is more often a symptom than a cause.

Like Flip, Nick did what he thought he had to do. Like Flip, Nick made a choice that resulted in an ending, maybe even a new beginning. Both choices reflected ways to conceptualize healing, born of desperation and unhappiness so great there was no adequate language to express the pain. I don't want to end up like Nick's parents, who blamed their son for hurting them with his suicide. And I especially don't want to end up like one of those bitter divorcees who can't forgive their exes for cheating. I know a woman who is still holding on to her feelings of betrayal after twenty-two years! Self-pity has hardened her face; even her eyes seem wary behind their Botox, like children peeking out of an empty house. This woman's world has been steadily shrinking, and now it's the size of a martini glass. What she wants to talk about after all these years is how badly her husband treated her two decades ago. He did treat her badly, no doubt about it. But her ex-husband has spent *his* twenty-two years learning and changing and growing. He has tardily become a good father and a loving partner while she keeps injecting her syringe of paralysis into the same wrinkle, over and over and over. Are there not other ways to process abandonment than through the lens of our own victimization and anger?

There's a sad suicide story I remember from Sunday-school days. A guy named Ahithophel gave King David some wise advice that the king ignored. Ahithophel was a big cheese in the world of political counseling, sort of like a Condoleezza to the king. Ahithophel had a sex bomb of a granddaughter, and she looked even better naked. The sex bomb granddaughter was named Bathsheba. In a nutshell, Ahithophel's advice to the king was: Back off Bathsheba. And P.S., Your Highness, don't go murdering Bathsheba's husband just so you can boink her. King David weighed this advice very carefully, but, being king, he chose to ignore it. This is a political pattern we sometimes see among presidents of large capitalist nations.

On the one hand, there was advice from a counselor who had proven trustworthy over the years. On the other hand, there was Bathsheba's really luscious bottom. When King David made his choice, Ahithophel tried to hatch a desperate but lame plot to kill him. Ahithophel even volunteered to murder King David himself. We nod at what comes next: yup, sometimes convoluted military coups have a way of backfiring. When the plot to overthrow the king failed, Ahithophel went home, put his house in order, and hanged himself.

Here's the punch line. We are told several times that poor Ahithophel was a *godly* counselor. Whenever he spoke, "it was as if God were speaking through him." What was a godly counselor doing plotting murder and treason, even if he had good reason? Even if he was hurt, grieving for his beloved granddaughter?

I think the answer is best phrased in the form of another question, as on *Jeopardy*: Who knows? Who knows how we can be both good and bad, both hurt and hurtful? The answer is that none of us knows how. None of us knows why. All we can agree on is the fact that the human condition is constituted by wild vacillations between altruism and nefarity, between kindness and cruelty. One moment we're opening our hearts and our wallets to hurricane victims; the next we're torturing prisoners of war and laughing about the photographs with our friends. Of course, when our badness breaks the law and infringes on the civil rights of others, we deserve incarceration, if only to keep folks safe from our depredations. But by and large most of our injurious actions do not break the law. No, most of them create the kinds of hurt that are legal: deceptions, betrayals, infidelities. And since even the most virtuous among us displays this adiaphorous morality, what if we agreed just to let people be who they are, since we can't change them anyway?

I used to think that virtuous people, for instance nuns, or even my mother, existed as a kind of Darwinian opposite to pederasts and serial killers. I suspected nuns were the recipients of a genetic gift basket featuring predetermined goodness, in the same way that some folks seem blessed with a natural aptitude for drawing in charcoal. Then, in addition to the genetic gift basket, the stars aligned in a confluence of beatitude, causing environmental forces to help out. Would my mother have been so nice if she hadn't been reared in a simple community, innocent and underexposed? God knows nuns couldn't have many distractions in a convent, where soothing rituals purged the world of temptation.

But I have come to believe that virtue isn't a condition of character. It's an elected action. It's a choice we keep making, over and over, hoping that someday we'll create a habit so strong it will carry us through our bouts of pettiness and meanness. Until recently I dismissed Niccolò Machiavelli's brutish philosophy that the ends justify the means, but lately I've begun to question that. If in the service of choosing virtuous behavior we need to practice some odd belief, where's the harm? Don't we all have our weird little rehearsals and rituals? Sure, from a ratiocinative point of view, the invention of angels on the wall seems an unlikely way to achieve virtue in praxis. Or take the case of the nuns. Insisting that you are the bride of Christ is pretty wacky, in my opinion. So is the bizarre corollary, giving up sex on purpose. Yet these choices, odd as they are, harm nobody. It seems to me that there are many paths to virtue, many ways of creating the patterns of behavior that result in habitual resistance to human badness.

And let's just hypothesize: what if there are angels on the wall? To be sure, neither you nor I have seen them. But does that negate their existence? I can imagine a counterargument that might retort, "Well, neither have we seen zombies, and most of us are pretty sure that the utter absence of documentation regarding the undead makes a persuasive case that zombies do not exist." True. Yet I'd like to assert an important distinction between angels and zombies. (Hopefully I am not the first to do so!) The existence of angels adverts to the person of Jesus Christ, a real, living, breathing historical figure; whereas the existence of zombies does not attach to any real historical figure, unless you count Calvin Coolidge.

At this stage of my life, I am willing to accept not only that there are many paths to virtue, but that our experiences on these varied paths might be real. We can't measure the existence of supernatural beings any more than we can control our partners. And anyhow, I don't want to measure supernatural beings or control my partner. What I want to measure, what I can control, is my own response to life's challenges. If my husband needs to dump me, fine. Let him. This is why I say: Let husbands ditch their wives for guys named Bob. Let Bob dump our husbands for reasons we still haven't heard. Let the angels promenade upon our walls. Let them sound the trump in public, crying, "Prepare ye the way of the Lord."

# ELEVEN

# And That's Okay!

One afternoon before I left for the Mennonite left coast, I was simultaneously cooking and talking long-distance to my friend Alba. Ready to sauté some shallots, I added a *Schulps* of olive oil to a skillet. Since the broken clavicle prevented me from clamping the phone under my chin like a normal long-distance cook, I had to pour with the right hand and hold the phone with the left. Thus when I reached over to replace the bottle of olive oil among its fellows, the difficulty of holding the phone shorted my reach. I had to replace the olive oil with the front facing sideways. "Hang on a second," I said automatically to Alba, as I set the phone down to straighten out the cattywampus bottle.

Then I realized what I was doing. Personally, I didn't care whether the front of the bottle was ninety degrees skewed. It was Nick who would have cared. And Nick wasn't there. I experimentally turned the bottle sideways again, to see how it felt to defy my husband's rage for order. Then I stared at the sideways bottle in brief but silent agitation. *I'll be damned*, I thought. I couldn't do it! Fifteen years cannot be rotated a quarter-turn to the left, just like that. I righted the bottle one more time. It was an eye-opening moment. For the first time I saw how very far I had been willing to go to accommodate Nick's anxiety. Since I liked things tidy, I'd always told myself we were in accord, we were thinking as one. But the nitpicky perfection he demanded was not what I would have aspired to. Whether Nick had been projecting his artistic eye on the minutiae of his environment or simply assuaging his anxiety by controlling me, all I now felt was a bemused sense of wonder at my need to accommodate. I had work to do, so much was clear.

As soon as my friends learned that Nick had ditched me for a guy on Gay.com, the self-help books started pouring in. Some provided wise counsel. Some offered strong therapy. Some triggered new insights. And then there was *The Language of Letting Go*. This book was organized into daily meditations, directed to persons recovering from situations of codependency or addiction. This author was all about affirmation, eager to include everyone in her program of self-acceptance and positive change. Her desire to be inclusive and upbeat emerged in passages that I might paraphrase like this: "Sometimes, we feel confused and broken. Sometimes, we have a hard time leaving relationships that are hurtful. Sometimes, we do the hurting. Sometimes, we do the leaving. Sometimes, we are left. Sometimes, we leave and feel bad about it. Sometimes, we leave and feel good about it. And that's okay!" No matter what the list of our putative faults and self-destructive behaviors, the conclusion would always be some form of "And that's okay!" I imagined this advice uttered in the poignant, sincere tone of Barbara Walters. I loved this book very hard and tried to apply its many useful lessons to my life.

Although I am not an addict, I am indisputably an idiot. Idiocy was nothing new to me. The breaking news on the self-help front was that I was also codependent. Over the years I had heard this term loosely and peripherally in women's magazines and on *Oprah*. But I had always dismissed it, on the grounds of overwhelming lameness. Now, I suddenly saw, I needed to give this word its due. Being codependent so surprised me that I was forced to consume an entire batch of chocolate-chip cookie dough with a salmon tartine chaser. And that's okay! It seemed clear that since I was now officially codependent, I could benefit from something like a twelve-step program. However, I had only a hazy idea of what a twelve-step program included.

RHODA.  Hi, my name is Rhoda, and I'm codependent.

ALL.  Helloooooo, Rhoda!!!

RHODA.  I love a man who left me for a guy he met on Gay.com. I've wasted most of my adult life caretaking his needs, paying his bills, and trying to meet his inhuman standards of perfection.

ALL, *scattered applause.*  That's okay!!

None of the books my friends had given me described the twelve-step process. Since it turned out that I was also a passive-aggressive blamer, I was content to note their omission and move forward, making up my own twelve steps.

## Step One:  Admit You Have a Problem

Nick had baldly announced that he no longer cared what I said or did, and he demonstrated this so often that I was eventually forced to believe him, despite my Herculean effort to convince myself that underneath it all, he would continue to love me if I could just ride this one out. Bob, the lover from Gay.com, would call our house at all hours. Once he called at midnight when Nick and I were asleep. The phone was on my side, and I sleepily picked it up.

"Hello?"

"Uh, can I talk to Nick?"

"This is Bob?"

"Yeah."

There it was: confirmation from the man of the hour. The man from Gay.com. In the flesh, ready to whack off, requesting the assistance of my husband. I handed the phone silently to Nick, who had tensed beside me. I rose, collected my tractable cat from the foot of the bed, grabbed my robe, and went downstairs to sob in the guest room. That was the last time we ever retired together to the same bed.

## Step Two: Sit Down at the Computer with Wild Medusa Hair

It's comforting, sort of, that during the marriage, the man made a mighty exertion to love me. Fifteen years is a long haul to be in a relationship when you don't feel good about your partner. And he must have really loved me once. I don't know when he stopped. It's hard to gauge because, even when he did love me, his bipolarity subjected him to fits of manic contempt, during which he'd say things like a child, unfiltered, whatever thoughts crossed his mind. "I don't love you, I hate you!"

One of the things that always mystified me was Nick's fault-finding, a chronic irascible nagging. He used to nitpick about so many little things, and then apologize, matter-of-factly blaming his overreactions on his bipolarity. He'd explode if I left a pair of earrings overnight on the bathroom counter; he'd rage if I sat down at the computer in the morning without having brushed my hair. We both agreed that these things should not be deal breakers in any relationship, but they galled Nick nonetheless.

I always assumed that bipolar folks were missing some crucial fuse in their anger-management system—that their inner thermometer was set a shade too high. Two years out from my marriage, I now have a more useful perspective. After Nick left, I eventually began dating a man I liked but didn't love, and I finally have firsthand experience in those little sparks of irritation that ignite impatience. I'd never minded the little things in Nick's behavior; I'd never even noticed them. It was after Nick had left me that I learned the lesson: it's when you don't love somebody that you do notice the little things. Then you mind them. You mind them terribly.

## Step Three: Hide the Bike

Let's say that you're dating the new guy, and you're about to give your first dinner party together. This man you're dating is a whimsical clutterbug, so you clear the clutter from his table and set it with the best stuff you can find in his antique sideboard. You fold the napkins just so, like elegant pup tents. You arrange a vase of gorgeous yellow forsythia for the sideboard. You bring in candles. Then you go upstairs to change because this man, a serious cook, has already finished the blancmange with honey and goat cheese. When you return, you note that your new guy has placed a miniature plastic bicycle smack in the middle of the tablecloth. Why this is you can't say. The plastic bicycle, about an inch and a half long, looks like a prize from a box of Cracker Jack.

Now, if you are a nonconfrontational Mennonite woman who has been trained to communicate her needs and requests in terms of covert passive-aggressive questions, you might ask, "Sweetie, what's the story with this little plastic bicycle?" If, on the other hand, you are a Mennonite woman who has been working very hard at trying to be more assertive, you might go a step further: "Mister, I object to this small plastic bicycle, no matter that you received it as a door prize at an office party twelve years ago." It's too bad, though, that whatever you end up saying to the new guy, you're still nowhere near being able to say this: "Mister, I'd like to love you, because you are everything that is good and kind, and you play piano like a dream. But I will date you for a year and then break up with you."

## Step Four: Hide It, I Say!

If I had loved this fabulous man, would I still have objected to the little bicycle? Probably. But the little bicycle would not have unleashed a tsunami of indignation, nor would it have seemed to affront the very foundations of dining etiquette. Now I know how poor Nick must have felt when I plopped down at the computer at 6:00 a.m., perfectly alert, with a cup of coffee. I had taken the trouble to press a pot of good coffee; I was chipper in the way of annoying morning people—why then would I neglect to brush my own hair? How could I so disrespect the aesthetics of domestic accord? It wasn't that I had tried and failed to brush my hair. It was that Nick had tried and failed to love me.

## Step Five: Get Some Colored Construction Paper

When Nick left me shortly after the midnight call from Bob, one of the first things I did was call my realtor. I knew I couldn't afford the mortgage payments on my own, and I had to put my house on the market. Agitated but too frozen to cry, I sat numbly in my realtor's conference room, sketching the situation. Annike and I had become personal friends—not intimate, exactly, but our relationship was warmer than a professional acquaintance. Her assistant brought in a tray of ginger tea.

When I had outlined the trajectory of recent events, Annike spoke slowly, out of the beautiful calm she always seemed to wear like a coat. "Let's not worry about the house for now. We're coming up on the winter months, and no one will be looking for a lake house until spring anyway. Just sit tight. Do you have an attorney?"

I nodded. I had filed for divorce the day before.

"What's her name?"

"Cora Rypma."

Annike nodded. "You're in good hands."

"I don't want to screw him," I said, just to clarify. "It's not like—"

"I understand," Annike said. "Of course not." She took a serene breath. "Rhoda, there's something you need to read." She got up and excused herself. "I'll be back in a minute."

I was expecting a legal document, or maybe a pamphlet on how not to be a dummy when filing for divorce. Instead, when she came back a few minutes later, she pressed into my hand a paperback book on feng shui.

I dutifully read and followed the book on feng shui. Why not? It couldn't hurt. If Nick had been there—the old Nick, I mean— I would have read him passages that would have made us both howl. Instead I obediently arranged my rooms according to the book's schema; I divided the lake house into color-coded *baguas*, each replete with its own cluster of shapes and symbols. It was either rearrange my house or stare in front of the fire with my cat on my lap.

The feng shui book urged me to scribble little notes to myself on construction paper of various colors. "I surround myself with healing vibrations!" "I no longer need and now release my love for Nick!" This went on through the weeks following my car accident, when I went rolling through my empty house on my office chair, battered and bruised. "I no longer need, and now release, this writhing mess of scar tissue on my legs!" "I no longer need, and now release, this piercing pain in my clavicle!" It was a long time before I found myself saying, "I no longer need, and now release, this book on feng shui!"

## Step Six: Grade Inflation

The first Sunday after the accident, my friend Carla called and deadpanned, "Okay, don't go anywhere. I'm driving out there. We'll just sit and grade papers together. You want me to bring you anything from town?"

"The *New York Times*. And some purple construction paper."

Carla brought her knitting and her own grading and sat with me in front of the fire for three hours that afternoon. She made it clear that she would set her work aside if I wanted to talk. But I didn't want to. I wanted to be silent forever. I sat on the couch with my broken bones and my cat and a big stack of papers to grade, and I graded, exactly as if my life hadn't just crashed down on me. But I gave all the papers upbeat grades and positive comments. "Terrific topic sentence! I'm with you!" "Is it just me, or is this the strongest paper you've written?" "You had me at *Since the dawn of time*!"

## Step Seven: Polish Your Floor with Your Ass

Because the lake house was forty-five minutes out of town, I didn't get many visits. Curiously, the isolation didn't bother me. For all my adult years I had been Urban Girl, and I was surprised that I wasn't scared out there in the middle of nowhere, in a sizable empty lake house. That year the first snows came heavily, big flakes falling into the lake like words into memory, heavy, irreclaimable. Even when my broken bones had healed enough for me to scooch down the stairs on my bottom, there was something mellow and tranquil about my painstaking movement through the house. I liked the deliberate way I had to negotiate the stairs, concentrating on not breathing too deeply, hunching my shoulder forward so as not to jar the clavicle. Roscoe, my cat, followed me everywhere on silent haunches, as if I needed a witness.

### Step Eight: Make Imprudent Purchases

Still thinking of the book on feng shui, I burned all of Nick's letters and cards. I deleted all his files from my computer, especially the pictures of male genitals freely posted on Gay.com. Those, dear readers, were not hard to let go. I paged through every old photo album, removing every picture of him. These I hurriedly stuffed into an envelope and sent to a Chicago address before I could change my mind.

Nick had always been opposed to framed photographs of loved ones as part of home decor, on the grounds that such photos were cheesy, low-rent, and sentimental. The one photo he let me display was a goofy little picture of me and Lola when we were kids. Now I saw a clear way to assert my independence. I wrote to Hannah and my mom, asking for copies of old photos, of family photos.

Right around this time I had some poems published in *Poetry*. Unlike most of the fine-arts journals, *Poetry* actually pays. I knew I should take the money straight to my savings account, or use it for the medical bills that my insurance wouldn't cover. But I didn't do that. Instead I blew up one of the old photos and had it expensively framed. It's an old black-and-white snapshot from 1949 in which my mother and her sisters stand in a long line, dressed in identical Mennonite white blouses and dark skirts, with arms about each other's waists. The seven of them look like typical Loewens, with their round homely faces, their wide smiles as fresh as hoop cheese. They are lined up in order of age. My mother, the youngest, stands to the far left beside a blooming hollyhock.

In the face of all that Mennonite sobriety, my mother had tied a wee white bow into her hair. None of the older sisters had bows. Just my mother. I studied that photograph for a long time, wondering if the essence of that little bow had come down to me in a genetic form. I inherited a flat ass, big hair, strong bones—why not a yearning to be pretty? The bow delivered an eloquent little argument: there had been a time when appearance was important to my mother. She had once wanted to be jaunty, different, even if only for a day. Over the years I and my siblings had settled into the inevitable acceptance of family roles. Aaron was the Smart One, Caleb the Athletic One, Hannah the Sensible One, and I the Vainglorious One. I was the one who majored in minor things. I was the one who spent time on foolish details. As a girl I had no way of knowing that Flaubert and van der Rohe had already argued what I secretly felt: God was in the details. I'd long acknowledged my debt to Flaubert, but now that wee white bow also suggested a debt to my mother. It was nice to think of her as a pioneer of aesthetics. She was Mennonite, but she was mine.

## Step Nine:  Consider the Autoharp

During those first weeks of crisis, Lola was e-mailing me every day, sometimes twice a day, from her seventeenth-century apartment in Bologna. Since my fingers were about the only part of me that felt fine, I briskly typed the entire narrative of the end of Nick's and my relationship, no detail left behind. My study looked out over a winter waterscape, a peaceful vista. The lake hadn't yet frozen entirely over, and sheets of ice would vanish into steel-gray holes in the middle of the lake. In the twilight the lights from the dam on the far shore would suddenly breathe life into the gathering gloom, and the tiny glowing pinpricks of light grew dear to me. They held a promise of succor and comfort, like Portia's candle in *The Merchant of Venice*: "How far that little candle throws his beams! So shines a good deed in a naughty world." At twilight I made sure to be in my study, typing to Lola and waiting for the naughty world to shine. Sometimes I whispered out loud, substituting Lola's name for the name of the almighty God, a snippet from the Holy Eucharist, "Almighty Lola, to you all hearts are open, all desires known, and from you no secrets are hid."

And when I had come to the end of everything I had to say about Nick, I asked Lola what she was eating, wearing, reading, singing. "Tell me about your invisible mustache," I urged. Or, "What do you do in Bologna when you're in the mood for potstickers?" She answered every question, no matter how dull. She reported on freckles, furniture polish, her husband's sister's dinner parties. She discussed deodorant, ironing boards, and double-sided tape. She described in detail the impact and trajectory of the secondhand autoharp my mother had purchased in 1971. Mom had been disappointed when Hannah and I had categorically refused to learn how to play this autoharp. In 1971 we knew in our bones that the autoharp, along with everything it represented, was the zenith of uncool. My mother strummed it alone and singing, until she retired it to the garage, going back to the piano of our youth. One day Lola tardily surprised my mother by asking for this selfsame autoharp. This was the last time Lola was in California, and my mother had joyfully passed it on to her. Lola took the forgotten autoharp back to Italy, where it seemed a thing of wonder to many an amazed Italian. In these stories and others, Lola's presence was so complete that I could hardly believe she was five thousand miles away. "Hey little Lola, play on your harp!" I sang.

## Step Ten: Branch Out from Borscht

My local girlfriends, most of them busy professors themselves, showed their support by leaving me treats in my office mailbox when I returned to work. I'd find the pile of grammar exams I'd ordered, but also a container of baba ghanoush. An article on American sexology circa 1912 came right on time, but there on top I'd see a stack of Tupperware bowls, each containing a different homemade soup. I found quirky recipes, bottles of oddly flavored vinegars, selections of Moroccan spices. New bestsellers, old favorites. Tickets for events that did not interest me. Candles in fragrances I would not have chosen. I gratefully read everything, lit everything, attended everything.

## Step Eleven: Reinterpret Student Sympathy

My students knew about the accident but not about Nick. I had told my girlfriends to wait until I was safely out of town for my sabbatical before they launched the catapult. Yet the students may have sensed there was more going on with me than broken bones, because they reached out in extraordinary kindness. Young women made me loaves enough to feed five thousand; young men brought me lattes and poetry. As I would leave my office to begin the slow trek to class, a gracious student would appear at my elbow, ready to take my briefcase and bag. For weeks I drifted about like an unmoored buoy; I couldn't even carry my own purse, let alone a briefcase weighted with books and papers. Strange how those familiar trappings anchor and define us! Because I couldn't raise my right arm, students sprang up to take notes on the board. If I hadn't been too numb to cry, I'd have shed buckets of tears at the hearty outpouring of support. I knew that my students were only being kind to a disabled professor, but their courtesy was easy to interpret as sympathy for heartbreak.

## Step Twelve: Visualize Patty Lee

Since I had supported Nick financially, he could have sued me for alimony. I don't know whether his sense of fairness stopped him, or whether he just didn't think of the legal possibility. At some level he must have regretted that he wasn't a stable provider, and that he was incapable of showing up for a job that took time away from his heart's true interest. He often made fun of me for doing just that, charging that my Mennonite workhorse habits bespoke both cowardice and a kind of underclass conformity. If I had any balls at all, he charged, I would walk away from academia and become a freelance writer! But beneath his scorn there must have been some degree of guilt, because he would often remind me that although he wasn't bringing money or stability to the relationship, he was bringing just the things I'd never known I needed: genius, insight, a view of the road not taken, a new heart for the people he affectionately called "the bungled and the botched." And it was true: Nick's abiding love for the severely mentally ill, the developmentally delayed, the homeless folks who wore six coats and made a beeline for him in the street, did much to change my worldview. I always admired his commitment to this population, which was another reason I had been okay with my own role as breadwinner. In the early years his caseworker jobs paid even less than I was making as a TA.

Then when he finally landed a job that far outpaid mine, he was as stunned as a kid in a candy shop. He spent his money on fancy stuff: a sportscar, a bike, guy gear. It was the first time in his life he was truly financially independent. His new toys were well earned, in my opinion, and I reasoned that after the reality of his higher income settled in, he would start prioritizing our financial future together as a couple. I figured that eventually he would start caring about and investing in our home, our retirement package, things that benefited us mutually and not just him. What I couldn't quite grasp, of course, was that the financial goals that were important to me seemed banal to him. Moreover, there was the matter of the sacrifice he had made for me six years earlier. A big-city boy to his toes, he still felt that he had gone over and above by moving with me to the Midwest so that I could take the job of my choice. He saw his increased salary as a long-delayed, much-deserved payback. Which it was.

I loved the lake house to which we had moved for closer proximity to his job, but the mortgage was exactly double what I had paid in our old rancho. There was simply no way I could afford it on my own. I knew it. He knew it. And we had moved in with the explicit agreement that this time he would *have* to pay his share of the bills and mortgage. In the last hideous days before he left me for Bob, he agreed to pay his half of the payments for three years, during which I would put the house up for sale and pray for a buyer.

I told my attorney that Nick was ready to do the right thing by me. She raised her eyebrows and said, "Well! Let's get him to sign his name to that before he flakes out on you!"

I knew that Nick wouldn't flake in the usual sense. He

wasn't one of those deadbeats who shrug off responsibility like a hangover—oh well, can't do anything about it, too late now, bummer, chil*lax*, man. He wasn't like that. But at the same time my belief in his fairness was destabilized by a faultline of doubt: how could he make the payments if he couldn't hold on to his job? The hospital administration position was a beauty, but I knew in my bones that he would quit within minutes of driving off with Bob. Nick quit everything; quitting was his special MO, the fullest flower of his bipolarity. He quit jobs, friends, karate, pets. He'd buy a brand-new Cannondale bicycle and sell it two months later. He'd paint in oils and abruptly switch to photography. The moment he had something, he didn't want it, a philosophy eloquently echoed in the platonic concept of desire, except that, as far as I know, Plato was not bipolar. By definition desire turns on something you want but don't have, and it follows that if you have it, you don't want it. In the fifteen years of our marriage, Nick had never held the same job longer than a year. If the best predictor of future performance is past performance, then I was in trouble. My heart sank when I received a terse e-mail from Nick a week after he had gone off with Bob. He had quit the plum administration job. There was a familiar note of panic in his e-voice.

Nervous, I asked my attorney what I would do if Nick stopped making his half of the payments. She was texting me from the courthouse, and she managed to raise her eyebrows electronically: "Bailng on u so sn? Find out whr he wrks. Grnish wges."

She didn't wholly understand the situation. You can't garnish wages if there are no wages to garnish. Nick would quit whatever new job he managed to land as soon as he dumped Bob, and then what would happen? If he went into a tailspin of depression, he wouldn't be able to hold a job. Hell, he wouldn't be able to *look* for a job.

About this time Lola gave me a stern lecture on positive thinking. "Hear me out," she said. "I know you're the queen of cause and effect, but what if you flipped the argument around? We don't know how the universe works. Maybe you've got the logic backward. On the one hand, you could say that people doubt Nick because he has a long history of being a flake. But what if it's just the opposite? What if he's a flake because people don't expect him to be anything else?"

"Is this some lame new-age hoodoo?" I said.

"You got anything else?"

"No," I admitted. "Go on."

"Well, has Nick flaked on the payments yet?"

"Not yet. He's threatened to, though. He's been sending frantic e-mails saying he just can't do this. He said he doesn't care what happens to his or my credit. He wants me to voluntarily give the house back to the bank, the way he did with that truck a while ago. He actually called me two weeks ago to tell me that the October payment would be the last one he could swing."

"So what you're saying is, he hasn't flaked yet?"

"Honey, aren't you listening?" I asked. "October is going to be the last payment. He said so. Into my ear. I *heard* him."

"It's you who aren't hearing *me*. Just answer the question. Has he flaked yet? As of now, this moment, today?"

"No," I said in my Voice of Condescension. "No, okay, he hasn't flaked yet."

"Here's what I think you should do. Take this whole financial thing with the house one day at a time. Don't worry that Nick won't come through for you. Instead just be grateful that he has made each and every payment so far. Just, you know, breathe in and focus on today."

I considered this a moment. "Lola," I accused. "Have you been reading *The Language of Letting Go*?"

"I have," she conceded. "And you know what? That's okay!"

Lola told me to get caller ID and not to pick up for Nick at all, ever, under any circumstances; I could not preserve a tranquil attitude if I was simultaneously listening to him spin his crazy web of negativity, like a spider run amok.

"But I'm worried about him!"

"Yeah, well, let somebody else take care of him for a change. You don't need fear right now," she said. "Not yours, not his, not anyone's." She suggested that I return polite, one-sentence e-mails. And that every day I write out the following message on an index card: "Nick makes timely, reliable direct deposits to my account!"

This I did, feeling like an idiot. Writing the message onto an index card profoundly embarrassed me, as when in a theater class your instructor asks you to come up in front of the class and act like a strip of frying bacon, and you either wriggle and hiss or get a C−, take your pick.

On the morning of November 10, the day when Nick's deposit was scheduled to appear in my account, I wrote out, "Nick makes timely, reliable direct deposits to my account!" on an index card, as if this day were like any other day. I marched the card over to the spot in my house that corresponded with the feng shui prosperity *bagua*, where I set it smartly on top of a growing stack of identical cards. Then I wedged the stack back into the wooden slats under my boxspring, which was where I was hiding it due to New-Age shame.

That same day I came home from school to discover the cards all over the floor beneath the bed. This freaked me out a little, because I had really wedged 'em in there pretty tightly, and I didn't see how they could have fallen out. But there they were, fanned out across the floor, a chorus of index cards shouting, "Nick makes timely, reliable direct deposits to my account! Timely! Reliable! My account! Nick!"

"Roscoe," I asked my cat carefully, "did you do this?"

He looked at me as if to say, "I like tuna."

It was past 6:00 p.m. I could make the call. "I am breezy and calm," I asserted out loud, fingers trembling. I punched in the numbers of my account, the security code. "Press one if this is a checking account!" I pressed it. So breezy! "Friday, November 10," said the dispassionate recorded voice. "A deposit of—"

It had gone in.

Reliable. Timely. Nick. I pulled the phone slowly away from my ear, tears of gratitude springing up where before there had been the breeziest panic.

This ritual, minus the fanned-out fallen cards, was to repeat twice a month for the next two years. Three months later I learned that Nick had sold the sportscar to be able to make a few more payments. After that he stopped e-mailing me altogether, so I had no idea where or if he was working. He had moved from that first Chicago address. I knew only that he was living somewhere in Chicago, making timely and reliable direct deposits into my account.

About a year after the divorce had gone through, I received a packet of legal papers summoning me to appear in court. Nick was challenging the judge's order that he pay half the mortgage and utilities for the three years, on the grounds that he was too mentally ill to keep working.

I wasn't ready to see him, but I had no choice. He rounded the corner as my attorney and I stood in the hall outside the courtroom. Cora, my attorney, was facing him. I sensed her posture stiffen, and I knew he must be somewhere close behind me. She had never actually met him, but I had described him, and his urban flair in this small-town city hall would have been impossible to miss. "Jesus, Rhoda," Cora leaned in to whisper, "You weren't kidding about his looks. Wow. He's pissed off. Don't turn around."

I had to sit beside him, inches away, while we waited for the court to call our docket. He was simmering with rage. Just as we all were rising for Judge Perkowsky, Nick delivered his one and only sentence to me: "I might have known you'd be here," as if there could be some surprise in my presence. Startled, my eyes flew to his: *Oh no. Oh noooooooooo.* He was not himself; he was not thinking clearly. "You subpoenaed me," I whispered. "You *made* me come here." He was so angry he was shaking.

Judge Perkowsky dismissed Nick's case in less than a minute, pointing out that Nick was not in fact paying spousal support, but a mutually agreed-upon property settlement. The judgment could not therefore be set aside. It was binding. When Judge Perkowsky's gavel sounded the verdict, Nick shot me a look of intense hatred, turned on his heel, and strode out of the courtroom. I clutched Cora's sleeve and took a couple of deep breaths.

"You see?" she said. "I told you that he didn't have a case. But I want you to do something for me."

"What's that?"

"I have to stay for another client. I want you to leave this room and go straight to the women's restroom and stay there for half an hour."

Her implication lifted gooseflesh on my arms. "Oh, but Nick wouldn't—"

"We're not taking any chances," she said brusquely. "You stay there half an hour, and then you go anywhere but home. You got that?"

I was hunting through my purse for a Kleenex. She handed me one, and I wiped my eyes, knowing that my mascara was a mess.

"Rhoda. You got that? *Don't go home.*"

"I promise," I said weakly, and fled with my briefcase to the bathroom. Inside a locked stall I sat down on the toilet, put on my reading glasses, and got out a stack of quizzes to grade. But I didn't grade them. Instead I sat in horror that Nick's ice-cold contempt had convinced my attorney that he might harm me. This man who hated me, *loathed me*, was Nick, my Nick, the same man who had once pledged to love me in sickness and in health, as long as we both would live. I leaned my flushed cheek against the metal wall, on which someone had scrawled, "Patty Lee sucks good cock!" I summoned an image of the invincible Patty Lee, sucking her heart out, living in the moment, doing what she did best. And I clung to this image for the next half hour, half crying, half needing this picture of tenacity and joy. "You go, Patty Lee!"

That was the last I saw or heard from Nick, but it wasn't the last picture I have of him. Including that day and every day thereafter, I have imagined Nick not as hateful or disturbed, but as timely and reliable.

And he has been.

The three years of court-mandated payments aren't up yet. Nor has my house sold yet. I know that inductive logic would point to Nick's failure to follow through, and indeed, as some of my more cynical friends have pointed out, there is still a strong likelihood that he will bail on me and that I will lose the house into which I have invested so much. Yet I no longer see the value of such logic. Some things are better than reason. Some things actually *defy* reason. Some things like faith.

And you know what? That's okay.

# TWELVE

# The Raisin Bombshell

I was sewing when Mom came in and offered to put on some music. Outside of car trips, she was rarely in the mood for music other than her own singing, so I said sure.

"What about the pan flute?" she asked.

I had to decline.

"How about some nice classical?"

I nodded, pins in my mouth.

A few moments later I heard the opening strains of Tchaikovsky's finale from *Capriccio Italien*. Not my first choice, but okay. Then suddenly I froze.

Was that . . . the distant cry of a *loon*?

Cresting over and above the music as if ministering with some essential relevance to the capriccio?

Ah, I was to hear much more from this amiable loon, in songs hushed and brisk, calm and martial. My heart convulsed in sympathy for poor, shortsighted Strauss, Mozart, Wagner, and Grieg, who had all collectively failed to predict what future centuries would demand in their easy-listening music. Who knew that two hundred years down the road audiences would crave the magnificent quaver of the loon? I can do no better than to quote the CD's dust jacket, which I made haste to examine: "*Classical Loon II* presents a return to the wilderness of loon country in classical style. You'll hear the hoots, tremolos, wails, and yodels of the common loon with the following selections . . ."

It struck me that the production of *Classical Loon II* implied a formidable predecessor, *Classical Loon I: The Early Bird*. Indeed, there might well be a whole family of Classical Loons, not to mention R & B Loon, Reggae Loon, Hip-Hop Loon, and Achey-Breaky Country Loon. And then—stay with me now—might we not envision for the future Scrub Jay Blues, Peacock Meditation, and Bald Eagle Techno? And why stop there? Why not Loon Books on Tape? I don't know about you, but I'd like to hear the words of our Lord and Savior enlivened by loon tremolos. Those long chapters in Leviticus are practically begging for a few loon yodels.

But I made my peace with the loons. I am the type of person who invariably finishes a book, no matter how much I have grown to hate it, or who stays seated right through the worst movie of all time. I always think, *Eh, it's not so bad. I can stand it!* Sitting there in the sewing closet, listening to *Classical Loon II*, which my mother had thoughtfully left on "repeat," I even got to the point at which I felt good about attempting my own tremolos now and then. A gifted loon impersonator I am not. But I think I deserve points for trying.

While I was experimenting with the most flattering way to situate the pockets on my flat ass, old Mrs. Cornelius Friesen telephoned.

"Mary?" she asked when I picked up the phone.

I recognized her voice. "No, Mrs. Friesen, this is Mary's daughter Rhoda." I remembered that Mrs. Cornelius Friesen was hard of hearing, so I raised my voice a bit. "Mary's gone to her Bible study. Can I take a message?"

"Bible study, hey? Bless her heart," said Mrs. Friesen. "Will you give her a message? You just tell her that I was hoping she had finished *The Cat That Dropped a Bombshell*. I want to give it to Cici."

My mother had agreed to read this book out of respect for Mrs. Friesen's advancing years. The titular figure was a literal cat, a Puss 'n' Boots detective that larked about as it solved crimes. My mother was by no means a literary snob, but she did have standards. Legal thrillers, okay. Mysteries, perhaps. But a cat that dropped bombshells was going too far. Thus my mother had expressed worry about how to refuse further loaners in the series. I was meanwhile encouraging her to read the entire collection of these books, especially if there was one titled *The Cat That Dropped a Bombshell and Buried It in Hard-Clumping Litter*. Mom had delayed returning the finished paperback because she wasn't sure how to extricate herself from the cat sequels.

"Mrs. Friesen," I said, "I happen to know that my mother is finished with your book. Would you like me to run it over?"

"What's that?"

"I'LL BRING YOU THE BOOK," I said loudly.

"Bless your heart, honey."

A few minutes later I was sitting in Mrs. Friesen's living room at Twilight Shores. Her snug apartment smelled strongly of cat box, ammonia, and patchouli.

"Sweetie," she said, offering me an old-fashioned butterscotch candy in a cellophane wrapper, "you don't look a day over twenty." Amazing that the older we get, the younger everybody else looks. "Don't you worry about being divorced. You have a nice shape, and your ma tells me you went to college. A lot of men like that."

"Here's your book," I said.

"Your husband wasn't very good to you, I hear."

Uh-oh. I had assumed that my mother would gossip about my divorce with her Bible study group, but I hadn't anticipated that the details would wend their way toward the likes of Mrs. Cornelius Friesen, who must be nearing ninety.

"My husband left me," I said simply.

"What's that?"

"MY HUSBAND LEFT ME!"

"Well, I'm sure it was all his fault." She leaned forward and patted my knee.

Hard to know how to respond to that one. I tried for a subject change. "HOW LONG WERE YOU MARRIED, MRS. FRIESEN?"

"Sixty-four years. Would you like to borrow one of these books? Your ma read one of them. This here is a cute book. It's about a cat detective."

"NO, THANKS," I shouted politely, "I'M GOING ON A TRIP."

"A trip, hey? Let me get you something for your trip."

She shuffled out of the room. In her absence a thin odorous cat appeared. It was white, and it wanted to purr on my brown lap. It would not be shooed.

Mrs. Friesen came back in and pressed a box of raisins into my hand. "For your trip," she said.

"THANK YOU! RAISINS ARE A HEALTHY SNACK!"

"Well," said Mrs. Friesen, "I have a grandson who went to college. He might do for you. He's a real steady young man. He has a good job and all. He's twenty-seven. How old did you say you are?"

"I'M FORTY-FOUR."

"Ain't that a shame," she said. "He'd probably think you're too old for him. But you look real pretty."

I rose to leave, brushing some of the cat hair from my skirt.

"PLEASE SAY HELLO TO CICI FOR ME. AND THANK YOU FOR THE RAISINS!"

"Well, I'll tell my grandson about you," she said matter-of-factly at the door. With her foot she prevented the thin white cat from egress. "But I expect he'll think you're too old. I'll tell him you have a real nice shape."

"I'D APPRECIATE THAT!"

Walking home, I congratulated myself on having escaped with no more Cats That Dropped Bombshells. That was a pretty good day's work for a sabbatical, all things considered. Plus I had made good progress on the pants I was sewing. And the raisins. There were always the raisins. Score.

The next morning I was topstitching belt loops, frowning through my reading glasses. Nothing makes you feel middle-aged like needing a new prescription for reading glasses. This I was prepared to discuss with my friend Eva, whose call I was expecting, and who had recently been itemizing her own catalog of veins, age spots, and lower-back problems. Making self-deprecating comments about the body is a chick thing, pure and simple. It makes us feel terrific.

The phone rang. "Rhoda?" It was a man's voice I didn't know. But my heart stopped for a second; the timbre was a little like Nick's, low and engaging.

"Yes?"

"This is Soren Friesen. I'm Emmaline Friesen's grandson—"

"Oh, heavens," I exclaimed. "This is taking filial duty above and beyond!"

There was a merry twinkle in his voice. "I hear you have a real nice shape."

"And I hear you have a real nice job. Do you always let your oma set you up?"

"She's the Yentl of our tribe," said Soren. "Actually, I already knew who you were. I've read your book. We know people in common." He mentioned the name of a writer at a well-respected MFA program in New England. This sparked a real conversation; it turned out that Soren had studied with my friend and had earned an MFA in screenwriting. After we'd chatted a while, Soren said, "How long are you in town? You wanna grab coffee sometime?"

"Soren," I said, "I know I have a real nice shape and all, but I'm forty-four, and that's just plain weird."

"I don't think it's weird to be forty-four and to have a real nice shape," he said earnestly. "I think it shows a positive self-image and good dietary habits. You probably eat a lot of fiber."

I chuckled. "What I mean is, it would be weird to be forty-four and go out with someone who is twenty-seven."

"Yes," he said, "but you're failing to take into consideration the fact that I have a real nice job. Oma advised me to mention that right away. C'mon," he urged. "It's only coffee. It doesn't have to be a real date. If it'll make you feel better, we can talk shop the entire time."

"Hm," I said, waffling. "I'll meet you for coffee on one condition."

"Name it."

"That you neither admire nor discuss *The Cat That Dropped a Bombshell*."

"But that bombshell has a real nice shape!" he protested.

It's strange to consider what makes a man sexy, is it not? I'm always surprised when women diddle around with things like chest hair or cologne or what kind of car a man drives. I have one girlfriend who looks for a guy with a nice tight butt. This mystifies me. If a man I like has a butt like an empty hammock, so be it. If his butt spreads like wurst on a cracker, God grant me the serenity to accept the things I cannot change. If his butt has hair on it, and maybe a big mole, and also a smattering of pimples, I focus on his pleasantly scratchy chin instead. Perhaps an alert reader might suggest that the flawed buttock is suspiciously easy for me to champion, given the fact that Nick's butt was a thing of beauty and a joy forever, especially in its last public incarnation on Gay.com. Yet I insist that a butt is not where it's at.

In my opinion, sexiness comes down to three things: chemistry, sense of humor, and treatment of waitstaff at restaurants. If the sparks don't fly from the beginning, they never will. If he doesn't get your sense of humor from the first conversation, you'll always secretly be looking for someone who does. And if a guy can't see restaurant servers as real people, with needs and dreams and crappy jobs, then I don't want to be with him, even if he just won the Pulitzer Prize.

With my exceptionally generous criteria for defining sexiness, you'd think that there would be a good chance that Soren Friesen could make the cut. Let's face it, my standards were pretty low. The unsexy characteristics that usually attend Mennonite men would theoretically not be barriers to me. By my own confessed standard, I would have no problem dating a man with beefy pink skin, or chins that skipped like rocks on a pond—one, two, three, kerplunk. I could even fall for a guy whose wallet contained an expired ten-dollar coupon for a bad chain steakhouse, at which the server would refuse to honor the coupon because it was a good six years out of date.

However, Lola and I had long observed a special Mennonite exemption clause. We had never met a datable Mennonite man. There were Mennonites who passed as good-looking, funny, kind, and sexy to the outside world. I had met some of these men. I had encountered Mennonites who wore good cologne and cashmere jackets. I personally had known Mennonites who could tell a Bacon from a de Kooning. But Lola and I sensed that a nameless shuddersome surprise coiled like a snake in the grass. Why did the idea of dating a Mennonite give us the willies? We couldn't say, exactly. But Mennonite men seemed too familiar. It wasn't just that they gave us a brotherly vibe; it was that they actively grossed us out in some curious, elemental way.

So my expectations were very low as I drove to the coffeehouse to meet the twenty-seven-year-old grandson of the granny who handed out bombshell books like candy. Soren was sitting at a small table, reading the *New York Times Book Review*. I knew it was he the moment I saw him, even though there were one or two other solitary thirtyish men about. Soren had the straight sandy hair of our people, and a ruddy goatee to match. He looked cheerful and attractive as he stood to greet me. He was tall. And I liked his glasses.

We shook hands. "Nice shape," he said.

"Don't think I won't drop a bombshell on your ass," I warned. "I can't believe I'm on a blind date with a Mennonite seventeen years younger than I am."

He had sunrise eyes, the kind that smile in a little fan of laugh lines.

"So which is worse," he said, "the fact that I'm Mennonite, or the fact that I'm seventeen years younger than you?"

I sat down, considering. "Honestly? The Mennonite thing is harder."

I watched him as he went to get my coffee. He had an international vibe, except that he obviously spent time in a gym. He didn't look Mennonite.

"You ever date a Mennonite?" I asked.

"In college. Maybe you know her. Sheri Wiebe Penner. She and her husband go to your parents' church."

"Sheri Wiebe?" I asked. "I babysat her! She used to give me the stinkeye for making her go to bed at eight o'clock. She had two monotone brothers who sang in the Mennonite Children's Choir."

Soren nodded. "I sang in that choir too." He sang a snippet of a song from a 1970s children's musical based on the Old Testament story "Daniel in the Lions' Den."

It isn't HOT in the furnace, man!
(repeat)
Man, this furnace is cool, cool, cooooool, yeahhhh!

I knew the lyrics and joined in on the last part. Soren licked his finger and made the "Muy caliente" gesture—"Tsssss!"

We both laughed reminiscently, as if those had been good times indeed.

"Is that where you met Sheri Wiebe? In the Mennonite Children's Choir?"

"No, Sheri and I go way back. We had playdates when we were babies. I grew up on the same block as the Wiebes and the Petcurs. Sheri and I went to different high schools and then met up again in college. We dated for a year when I was at Goshen."

I nodded. I had always liked Sheri Wiebe. "Once when I was babysitting, Sheri made a witches' brew out of bark, dog poop, and a carton of eggs."

"Doesn't everybody?" Soren asked. "So why are you so set against Mennonites?"

"I'm not set against them. I love them. I just don't know if I want to date them."

Under the table Soren shifted, and his leg brushed against mine.

"You prefer—?"

"I prefer atheists who ditch me for a guy they met on Gay.com."

He put down his coffee. "You wanna go for a ride?" he asked. "I've got a bike. And an extra helmet."

I looked down at my peep-toe flats, at the skirt of my sundress. They were wholly inappropriate for motorcycle wear. "Okay."

"Leave your bag in the trunk of your car."

"But what if we get in an accident and we're unconscious and they don't know who we are?"

"Babe"—he grinned—"that's what dental records are for."

Mennonite men usually drove like conservative dads, but Soren swooped and sped. On the back of the bike I relaxed against him, my skirt puffy and restless, like something with a mind of its own, despite my best efforts to tuck it in and down. I rode with one arm hooked loosely around his stomach, the other resting lightly on the tank between his legs. When he'd take a turn at a sharp angle, my grip would tighten on his stomach, and I'd feel his abs tense and gather. His torso was all hard rangy muscle. At intersections, he straightened his back briefly, leaning against me, resting his hands on my upper thighs as if by prior invitation. The day was warm, and we were starting to sweat. As we hit the open stretch before the foothills on the outskirts of town, Soren took the bike up to a hundred miles per hour. I clamped both my arms around his waist, clung like a limpet, and knew somehow that we would get where we needed to go.

# THIRTEEN

# The Therapeutic Value
# of Lavender

I was squeezing in one last evening with my friend Eva. I had known Eva Wiebe-Martens since we were little girls. Back when our fathers were both teaching at the same seminary, I had been better friends with Eva's older sister, who was my age exactly. Then over the years I had fallen out of touch with both sisters. They had been content to remain in the Mennonite heartland, while I had been on fire to leave. On this return to my parents' community, I'd been pleased to run into Eva once more, and even more delighted to find that she was busily living my life—my *other* life, the life I would have chosen had I not rejected the faith of my fathers.

Eva had graduated seminary, earned a Ph.D. in theology, and had stepped up to chair the local Mennonite university's religion department. In fact, it had been she who had replaced my father when he had retired. Eva was married to a man she'd met while studying at seminary, and she had two kids, Matea and Hazel. It was funny that even as I was having a little fantasy about Eva's life, she was keenly interested in mine. She said that long ago, if she had followed her heart's interest as an undergraduate, she would have chosen the path of literature, art, and travel.

So we had renewed our friendship—that is, we had gotten to know each other as adults over my months in California, and an intimacy had sprung up between us. Every Thursday night we met for jazz and drinks at a downtown bar, and we poured out our souls to each other even when we weren't talking. There was something deliciously simpatico about this woman. I loved her deep well of calm, which seemed to proceed from a deeply Buddhist sense that we live the lives we choose to lead.

Eva was going through a rough patch. Her father, also a minister and a leader in the church, had recently been diagnosed with Alzheimer's. The effect of his disease on a traditional Mennonite family had been far-reaching. I won't say much about that, because that is Eva's story to tell, not mine, but some of the illness-management details were heartbreaking. For instance, how do two Mennonite daughters intercede for a father who can't remember his own improvident financial decisions, and assist a mother who is incapable and unwilling to take the helm? Throughout her father's slow decline, Eva's grief had thrown out tendrils, clambering up her walls. Her father's situation had now reached the point at which there were new losses every day. And it was in spite of this grief—maybe because of it—that I saw the tranquillity blooming in her like a hundred years' hush. She always reminded me of Sleeping Beauty, eyes either about to open or shut.

Eva was the only one among my friends who wasn't slightly horrified that I was dating a man seventeen years younger. Poor Lola was practically apoplectic in Italy, but more because Soren was Mennonite. "Are you INSANE? Run before he ties your apron to the bedpost and makes you listen to a sermon on the importance of nasty procreative sex! And can you say MOMMY ISSUES?"

In the wake of incoming advice on Soren and on related matters of the heart, I had plenty of time to appreciate true friendship, and to feel grateful for rich, sustaining, tell-it-like-it-is relationships with women such as Lola and Eva. I had never been forced to make do with what sometimes passed for friendship among women. What if my closest female friendships were the kind I often observed at my college, where I acted as faculty adviser to a sorority of young women?

Although I had never participated in sorority culture when I was in college, I saw no reason why I should oppose it as a professor, especially since I had had no actual experience with sororities. My stereotype of them as the refuge for attractive but intellectually unimaginative young women was based strictly on hearsay. The trope of the sorority, which often figured in the quintessentially American bildungsroman, was altogether alien to my upbringing. Mennonites did not consider the Greek system an option for their virginal daughters; the sorority as a nurturing institution simply didn't exist on the Mennonite horizon. Mennonites would have neither approved nor understood any network that promoted social lubricities such as datability, popularity, or unquestioning institutional loyalty. That last quality would have seemed too much like mindless nationalism, and Mennonites, with their pledge to peacemaking, felt uneasy about promising loyalty for the sheer sake of loyalty. While they believed in loving and serving one's country, they reserved the right to question any institution capable of legislating war. Or lingerie parties.

Academics like to talk trash about Greek life. We roll our eyes and one-up each other's stories at cocktail parties, which makes us about as immature as the sororities and fraternities we're criticizing. Academics frequently observe that the Greek system is hopelessly anti-intellectual. Fair or not, we see it as a social organization, a dating network for women and an old boys' club for men. Many

Greek institutions do enforce minimum grade-point averages, but these grades often promote hoop jumping rather than learning. We've all seen Greek men and women demonstrate anxiety about grades; what we'd prefer to see is Greek men and women demonstrating real intellectual inquiry.

Fresh out of grad school, I agreed to be faculty adviser to a sorority whose members were commonly referred to as "the Campus Hotties" or, variously, "the Ones in Deep Doo-Doo for Trashing Four Hotel Rooms Again." I was not surprised when these young women turned out to be a troupe of impossibly pretty coeds who color-coordinated their outfits on important occasions.

One twelve-degree evening in February, when there was eight inches of snow under a layer of slippery drizzle, my sorority gals celebrated their fellowship by donning denim minis, pink tights, and stilettos. As their faculty adviser, I had been formally summoned to an event titled the Passing of the Brick, which would take place at 11:00 p.m. on a Friday. The Passing of the Brick was a tearful candle-lit ceremony at which the sisters declared undying love for one another as they passed a lace-wrapped brick from sister to sister around a Circle of Solidarity. I gave the brick a poke with my index finger as it passed, but I could discern nothing unusual in its shape or texture, except that it was dressed up in a little lace ruff, like Anne Boleyn. When it was a sister's turn to hold the brick, she solemnly received it into her arms and shared an upbeat message of trust and hope. Invariably the message went like this, with much sniffling and apology for smudged mascara: "You girls will be watching my back *forever*! Thanks, ladies!"

Would the heartfelt protestations of eternal friendship last longer than ten minutes after graduation? These women seemed to be figuring friendship solely in terms of what it could do for them. I never heard a sorority sister affirm any unique character qualities in the women who formed the Circle of Solidarity. I never heard anyone say, "You are the soul of grace and tact." "Your kindness is an inspiration." "Your passion for geology made me change my major." Instead the sisters declared they valued one another because they refrained from backstabbing: "Here's a gal who will not snatch my boyfriend! God, I love her!" "Here's a gal who will loan me her Jimmy Choos! BFF!"

I had never experienced a desire to Pass a Brick, or to dress it up, or to match my tights and shoes to those of my associates, but, overall, I came away from this sorority event more sympathetic than I had been. Also, I am grateful to my sorority for raising the whole question of What Not to Wear If You're a Brick. I had never thought much about how to dress a brick so as to bring out its best features.

---

_____ Yes, I think a brick looks adorable in lace, and perhaps a bonnet.

_____ No, I prefer to dress my brick in something more androgynous, such as a jumpsuit.

---

My new-old friend Eva, whom I had known in college but whom I was just now really appreciating, has one of those souls that run deep, a clear cool well whose depth keeps on surprising, like Lake Louise. Something about her makes me feel at home, at rest. She has a way of looking at you from sleepy, heavy-lidded eyes that recalls a marmalade cat drowsing in the sun. In fact, this cat metaphor is much better suited to Eva than my earlier comparison to Sleeping Beauty; while the latter suggests oblivion, the former implies a restful alertness, which characterizes Eva very well. She sees everything. When I told her about Soren, she asked if I wanted to bring him round to dinner. "Um," I hesitated. "Bring him to dinner? To your house? No."

She nodded and smiled, eyes heavy. From that one low-key question about Soren, I learned exactly how I really felt about dating a young Mennonite guy. He was funny and sexy, but there was no way I'd be able to bring him to dinner with anyone. I just couldn't do it. And anyway I wanted Eva all to myself. We'd reached the stage at which sitting around and discussing theology was more interesting than sitting around and discussing men.

It was funny that her daughters vibrated with simmering energy while she herself seemed so tranquil of spirit. Eva left Matea and Hazel largely alone. They tore through the house in April dressed in Christmas garland and tinfoil; they grooved to the beat of a Mennonite mandolin; they sang songs from the Opera of Life ("Lalalala, I cut this worm in HALF, lala! There's a HAIR on my toothbrush, lalalalala!"). Eva usually remained in the background, watching but not interrupting. So many parents feel that they must respond to every single word out of their children's mouths, even when the children are merely giving voice to unfiltered interior monologue. Eva's willingness to let her daughters play on their own seemed refreshingly like trust. She didn't neglect them or avoid them, by any means. They delighted her. But she exercised faith in the process of just being. My other friends had polyglot kids, equestrian kids, classical guitar kids. Eva's kids just ran around and did stuff.

Eva had phoned me to come over for grilled veggies and chicken. When I got there around 6:00 p.m., Matea was studiously avoiding me, using her arms and legs to act out all the letters of the alphabet. She was wearing a pink floral bikini. "When I told her you were coming over for dinner, she went and put on that swimsuit," Eva remarked.

"Gotcha. Hey, Matty," I called, sticking my head into the living room. "Groovy bikini!"

My compliment was what Matea had been waiting for. She felt affirmed, validated somehow. It is one of the mysteries of childhood that the opinions of people we barely know are of paramount importance. I've always loved the way children confide secrets to strangers or anxiously await a stranger's verdict on a pink bikini. After I had given the bikini the thumbs-up, Matty went and changed back into the outfit she'd been wearing earlier: jeans, a tutu, and a burnoose.

At dinner Eva and her husband, Jonathan, and I were discussing a spy-fiction class that Jonathan was putting together for his high school curriculum. Suddenly I felt a tug on my sleeve. I looked down. Little Hazel, four years old, amber eyes snapping sparks of pride, had some urgent news to share. "Rhoda! Rhoda!"

"What can I do for you, Hazel?"

She was throbbing with energy, her straight bob snapping her chin like a crisp red flag. "Rhoda!" She looked me in the eye and announced, "I wouldn't DREAM of pooping in my pants!"

"Neither would I," I said. Hazel's announcement struck me as something my mother might be tempted to confide at a dinner party, so I was unperturbed.

"I wouldn't poop in my pants," said Eva conversationally. She didn't even blink. She just helped herself to more zucchini.

"That makes it unanimous, then," said Jonathan. "There is nobody present who would DREAM of pooping in their pants."

Little Hazel nodded triumphantly and vanished into the living room, where she told her sister that her pants were free and clear of poop, now and forevermore.

That night I watched Eva and Jonathan put the girls to bed. This process involved two stories, two songs, and elaborate combinations of kisses among siblings, parents, and stuffed animals. As Eva and Jonathan harmonized a made-up song in the darkened bedroom, I found myself blinking back tears. It wasn't because this was a scene I would never know. I had no regrets on that front; I had made my decision, and I was at peace with it. It was more because I suddenly felt destiny as a mighty and perplexing force, an inexorable current that sweeps us off into new channels. Here was Eva, who could have made such different choices with her education and career path. Here was I, with my decades of restless travel, my brilliant but tortured ex-husband. And how sad it suddenly seemed to be buffeted by the powerful currents to which we had yielded our lives. So many years had passed. My childhood, my early friendships, my long marriage, all seemed to hang from an invisible thread, like the papery wasps' nest outside my study window. I had watched the lake winds swinging and tipping it, expecting it to go down, but it never did. Memory swayed like that nest—hidden but present, fragile yet strong, attached by an unseen force to perpetual motion.

I sometimes ask my college students if they think it's possible for a thirty-plus adult to experience saltatory ideological change. I tell them that I'm not talking about the kind of gradual mellowing that results from age. Nor do I mean the kind of abrupt character fissure that opens in the wake of trauma or suffering. Rather, I want to know what they think about the possibility of a profound, lasting change that emerges from an act of deliberated, conscious self-determination. I want to know if they think we can change our core assumptions about what we believe. About *how* we believe.

*Yes,* say my students, *absolutely! Of course we can change!* And then I marvel at their hope. My students carry optimism around in their backpacks like bright bottles of designer water.

Can a skeptic ever be anything but a skeptic? Can a loner ever come to cherish groupthink? It was sobering to think that Eva's and my lives, so similar in potential and core interests, had taken such different turns, and that the only place they could ever intersect would be in the liminal space of childhood, or in the theoretical no-man's-land of alterity. I closed my eyes and tried to imagine Eva in my world, Eva in a sexy-serious dress at an art opening, Eva laughing off some biting remark of Nick's that had landed and stung, like a black fly. The image didn't compute. Eva favored sensible shoes and a hankie. Eva would have never, not for one minute, put up with Nick's temper. The very picture of mental health and self-respecting balance, Eva would have told Nick in the first month of marriage, "If you can't make some changes in how you manage your illness, I'll be making some changes in how I manage this commitment."

But, then, Eva would have never fallen for Nick in the first place. His wracked misery, his anger at God, his creative brooding, were in some ways attractive to me. These qualities orbited me, too, like shadowy moons around Jupiter. Nick's dark distress mimicked my own perpetual waffling: my questions about organized religion, my chronic doubts, my cynical shrug when husbands left their wives for men they had met on Gay.com. I believed both the worst and the best about human nature. Reading the Edenic myth literally, my parents thought that God created us, and that we subsequently fell from grace. I believed that the fall from grace was a metaphor for how we inevitably fall short of our potential. And if we had been created, hadn't we also created God?

My mother and I were going to spend the day with the Mennonite Senior Professionals, a group of retired scholars, ministers, and sundry educated oldsters. They met twice a month for a gentle intellectual stretch. On the day in question my father couldn't attend, so my mother had asked me to accompany her. This was an all-day gig, a day trip to local valley farms, to learn about Mennonite agrarian history. Some of the Professionals were my old college teachers, and I remembered most of them as very conservative. For the occasion I had selected plain brown pants, Diesel sneakers, and a high-necked top.

"It's supposed to cool off later, so I can understand why you don't want to wear shorts today," my mother was saying. "But you didn't even at the barbecue last night. Staci and Deena were wearing shorts."

"Mom, I'm forty-four, for heaven's sake. There comes a time when you just resign yourself to not wearing shorts."

"I'm seventy, and I wear shorts in the garden."

"There comes a time, and then it goes away, and then it comes back," I amended politely. "But I haven't reached that third phase yet."

"You have good healthy legs."

"Not anymore," I said firmly. "People don't want to see a mess of scars."

"Nonsense," said this Mennonite matriarch. "I like to see a healthy pair of legs in shorts."

Mom's new sartorial pronouncements were a little surprising for a Mennonite. For example, she had recently suggested that the business world would be a better place if stockbrokers and executives would all agree to wear tank tops to work. Her pro-shorts stance was similarly surprising, given that I had not been allowed to wear jeans in my youth, on account of the fact that jeans belonged in the barn and God would not have been glorified. I'd have guessed that a glory-seeking God would have preferred the jeans to the shorts. At least the jeans covered blemishes. Cellulite, veins, and scars surely offered God limited glory at best. But, hey, who was I to predict the wardrobe preferences of the Almighty? It was a crapshoot as far I was concerned. God might even fancy a skort. I usually left speculation of this sort to folks like my mother, who seemed to know.

Now Mom frowned at my pants, which I had also worn to the barbecue the night before. "I think everybody wants to see your legs. I know I do. Yesterday it hit ninety. I got hot just looking at you."

I pulled up a pant leg. With the scars and the luminous gooseflesh, prickly and translucent, my shin was not a pretty sight. Added to that, I'd been living a scholar's life in a northern clime for seven years, and my shin was the color of new-driven snow— no, of reconstituted nonfat milk powder. For my morning runs I covered up in my karate pants. I couldn't bring myself to wear shorts, even on the track.

"Why all of a sudden do you want to hide your legs?" Mom pressed. "It doesn't make sense. Is it the scars? You wear your pants low, just like all the teenagers."

"That's different."

"No, it isn't," she insisted. "When we went on the church hayride, and we were sitting on those low hay bales, your jeans were cut down so far that I could see your panties."

"Good god," I said, suddenly queasy. "Do you think Elsie-Lynn and Walter could see my panties?" Elsie-Lynn and Walter had been sitting on the hay bale right behind mine.

She nodded peacefully. "They were bright orange and pink. The panties, not Elsie-Lynn and Walter."

Oh! The tardy humiliation! "I once wrote Walter a term paper on the Münstereich! I would so much rather show him my legs than my underwear! I bet they're both going to be there today, judging me for my inappropriate panties!"

"Don't get so worked up. When you get to be our age," said my mother, on behalf of Elsie-Lynn and Walter Hoeffer, "virtually everything is more interesting than the color of your underpants. Walter and Elsie-Lynn have grandkids. They've seen it all before."

Arriving a full fifteen minutes early for Mennonite Agrarian History Day, Mom and I were nevertheless the last ones on the bus. I scanned the silvery waves and gray beards; Mennonite punctuality was a testament to our German heritage.

Making our way to the back of the crowded bus, I experienced a pleasurable flutter, sort of, that I would be sitting opposite Abe and Arlene Kroeker. My mother automatically ceded me the aisle seat, since I needed the legroom. Thus I found myself sitting less than twelve inches away from Abe Kroeker. Abe Kroeker was the father of a boy I dated briefly in high school.

I'm going to take a risk and really put myself out there. Here is my confession. For the last twenty-five years my single most frequently occurring dream has been a feeble nightmare about my classmate Karl Kroeker. The nightmarish aspect never varies its stone-cold panic: Oh nooooo, my name is Mrs. Kroeker! Oh crap, I'm dating Karl Kroeker! Dammit, I'm walking up the aisle and the groom is—wait! No! Karl Kroeker! I'd like to make it clear that in real life Karl Kroeker and I never slept together; never shared adult joys or sorrows; never exchanged information vis-à-vis goals, ideologies, friends, or extracurricular activities. I'm not sure we even had a conversation. Once we inexpertly made out on a school bus.

Therefore it is mystifying that for years Karl Kroeker has belabored my dreams. I see Karl Kroeker as a nagging message from the unconscious realm. Like Glenn Close in *Fatal Attraction*, Karl Kroeker will not be ignored. However, it's not as if I dream of Karl Kroeker every single night. It's not as if dreaming of Karl Kroeker makes me wet the bed or anything like that! I mean, I'm not weird! I assure you that I dream of Karl Kroeker only often enough to make me glad that Karl and I don't know each other as adults.

I always wake in a cold sweat, mentally kicking and screaming from the cosmic compulsion that is forcing me to wed the second son of Abe and Arlene Kroeker. This is compounded by the strange fact that if I could handpick two people I would really cherish as in-laws, it would be Abe and Arlene. I've always loved them.

I'm no psychotherapist, but I have always assumed that for whatever mysterious reason, Karl Kroeker represents the sum total of my Mennonite experience, the essence of Mennonite manhood. He's the ur-Mennonite who personifies why I cannot appreciate "liturgical movement." He's the *Abromtje*, the frosty heart of the melon—supposed to be a treasure, but for some reason a little creepy, like a tumor that grows hair and teeth. Most girls think they've turned a corner when they get their period. With me it was when I started dreaming about Karl Kroeker. This happened long before I made out with him on the school bus. Although I was in junior high when the nightmares began, I recognized that they signaled some important change in my psyche, some rupture with tradition. My nightmares were telling me to run screaming from the Chaco.

This whole thing is very odd, because Karl Kroeker may be

(after me) the Mennonite Least Likely to Evangelize the Chaco. Karl Kroeker has made choices that have taken him far afield of the Mennonites. Now a successful cardiologist in Boston, Karl mainstreamed even earlier than I. While the rest of us Mennonite kids, shyly garbed in homemade clothes, were high school wall-flowers, savvy Karl Kroeker was a letterman, a tennis star, and president of the student body. Therefore Karl Kroeker is not an appropriate portent of doom. In real life, at least to hear Abe and Arlene tell it, Karl is smart, kind, humorous, attractive, and affluent.

So it was in a state of heightened alert that I settled down next to Abe and Arlene, who gave me detailed updates about Karl and his brothers. Karl, I learned, had married an Armenian with a close-knit family in Des Moines. This news unaccountably cheered me. Petty, I hoped that Karl's Armenian wife had to wax her upper lip or, like Yvonne, had to prioritize the management of a hirsute bikini region.

Abe Kroeker was a history professor whose august education often propelled him outside Mennonite circles. As a girl I had found this most impressive. Abe, like my father, was now retired. He seemed to have mellowed a teensy bit, and he even manifested a restrained expression of pride when Arlene was telling stories about their successful sons. Whenever I saw him and Arlene together in public, they replicated the marriage dynamic so often seen in our circles. As with my own parents, he was stern and tac-iturn; she, gregarious and warm.

Five years earlier, Arlene had heard of my interest in Mennon-ite history and had thoughtfully presented me with three special tulip bulbs, descendants of the same tulips cultivated by Menno Simons, the sixteenth-century father of the Mennonite faith. I told her that when I had moved to the lake house, I had dug up those Mennonite bulbs to take with me. She nodded soberly, as if I could have done no less.

The big bus had a bathroom. My elderly compatriots didn't use it. Mennonites don't want other Mennonites to see them walking down an aisle to pee, but I was too much my mother's daughter to mind. On my way back from the bathroom, I swayed as the bus driver took a sharp curve. The motion lurched me violently toward Abe. I fell into my own seat, just managing to snap my torso back from full contact. Abe didn't miss a beat. He spread his arms wide and teased, "Well, come on!" as if I were deliberately throwing myself at him. Arlene loved this. She clapped delightedly and made little jokes for the rest of the day about her husband's magnetic personality.

Here's the thing. I don't know if it was because of the strange connection with my dreamscape, but in that moment when Abe Kroeker's seventy-something eyes were twinkling at me, I suddenly experienced a powerful attraction. In fact, in a self-fulfilling prophesy, I *did* want to throw myself into his arms. Yikes. I even considered the thought that all this time I had been attracted to the father, not the son. Was it just me, or was there something deeply compelling about a scalpy Mennonite septuagenarian in comfy shoes and a sweater vest?

The last stop of the day was at an herb farm run by an ex-hippy farmer. She knew and understood Mennonite culture, having fled the community decades earlier. As part of her introduction to the majesty of herbs, she passed out the kind of rhythm instruments you play in kindergarten: sticks, tambourines, little clusters of jingle bells. Then she invited all the Senior Professionals to play them while she strummed a folksy song about the healing properties of sage and thyme. My mother, looking accidentally stylish in embroidered jeans and snakeskin jacket, sashayed her hips and smacked the bejeezus out of that tambourine. (One of our family's unsolved mysteries was Mom's gravitational pull toward animal prints. Perhaps this fondness resulted from a recessed gene. Once she made me a dress from fabric printed with realistic giraffes, lions, and antelope running and pausing on the high open grasslands. Mom knew too little of fashion to associate animal motifs with a bold sensibility, so it was delicious to see her appear in something as chic as a snakeskin jacket.)

All around me these beautiful people were good-naturedly shaking fistfuls of little jingle bells and whacking sticks, an ancient but enthusiastic percussion band. They knew the humor, of course—Mennonites don't do movement—but they had all reached the stage in their lives where God had relaxed enough to take a few jingle bells. I saw old Herman Froese, a retired organist, stomping his leg to the downbeat. There was sweet Doreen Hiebert swaying with Arthur's arms around her. Arlene Kroeker was singing along in her melodious alto, *en pointe* with a musical triangle, while Abe held several foolish bags from the gift shop. He wore the look of an owlish scholar who wants to purchase neither rosemary sachets nor clove tea, but who has done so because he loves his wife of fifty years.

From the valley came the scent of lavender. When I was little, my Sunday-school teacher Mrs. Lorenz, the same who had offered us cookies spotted with raisins, had once given me a prize for memorizing the Sermon on the Mount. The prize was probably something she had regifted, considering that I was only eight and it was clearly an object intended for a grown woman.

"What *is* it?" I breathed reverently when I unwrapped this prize at home after church.

"I'm not sure what it is," my mother said, "but I think it's a little old for you."

It was a pale blue silk embroidered envelope for hosiery, padded with light satin, beribboned and elegant. I didn't have any hosiery, being eight. This pale blue satin object had no real purpose; it would have been just as easy to safeguard one's pantyhose by wrapping them in a slip. But the object was as beautiful as it was frivolous. I rightly intuited that if Mennonite culture had an opposite, this thing was it. We didn't even know what to call it. This blue thing was peripheral to everything that we stood for. The pale embroidered envelope suggested the very essence of young ladyhood, and I imagined a time when I would wear white gloves and take tea and straighten the seams of my stockings. (Because Mennonites lived away from the world, I had no idea that young ladies had long abandoned the trappings of femininity portrayed in the books that came my way.)

I loved this satin object with all my heart, with all my soul, and with all my mind. My mother thought that we should put it away until I got older, but I begged so hard to keep it that she finally relented. Inside it I kept a single cotton handkerchief clustered with tiny lilac florets. One of my aunts had sent me this floral kerchief, perhaps assuming that children of my generation still carried starched hankies in their pinafores. And for my birthday that year Lola gave me a bottle of talc that smelled like lavender. Her Mennonite parents, who were more liberal than mine, allowed such things as gifts in her family. I dusted the hankie with the secret powder every Monday evening in a hazy beauty rite. I wasn't sure what elegant ladies did with floral hankies, so I'd unbraid my hair, brush it slowly and elegantly, and then touch the perfumed hankie lightly to my brow. "Why, thank you!" I'd whisper in the mirror.

"I feel so faint!" Then I tucked the hankie back into the pale blue satin thing, where it would fragrantly remain until the following Monday evening.

Ever since, the smell of lavender had reminded me of the beautiful embroidered blue thing into which I once folded all the inchoate desires of childhood. That lavender hankie was my silent pledge to learn the ways of the world, to sigh and dance the cotillion and wear lace underthings. Beneath the mysterious satin flap there was just enough room to tuck everything I longed for but couldn't name.

Now a swell of bamboo rustled in the spring breeze, and as I shook my bells, I drew my sweater across my shoulders. My eyes misted over a little as I considered these people, percussing and swaying and singing. Without my husband I had somehow drifted back to this point of origin, as if my turbulent marriage had been a long journey on dark waters that had propelled me away from everything known and safe. I suddenly had the feeling you get when, after a long sea swim, you touch bottom and draw a breath of relief: you made it, land ho, sharks from this point on extremely unlikely. The oldsters were singing and smiling and shivering in the breeze that had picked up, heavy now with the scent of lavender. Harmony rose like prayer in the cool of the late afternoon, and the music was gentle as a hand on the small of the back, nudging me forward—the sound of my heritage, my future.

# A Mennonite History Primer

If you're like most folks, you may still have some pressing questions about the Mennonites. I get these questions all the time. At the outset of this book you were probably thinking, *Whaaa—? Mennonites? Don't they drive around in horse-drawn buggies and wear doilies on their heads?* Or maybe, if you're a straight guy: *Hey, yeah, don't Mennonite chicks dress up as semisexy French maids, in black dresses with aprons? What are they wearing under all those layers, anyway?* Or, if you're a subscriber to interior decor magazines, *Aren't Mennonites the folks who make collectible quilts, many of which are now unaffordable on eBay?*

These are reasonable questions, and no Mennonite writer worth her salt would leave them unanswered. So the answers to these questions are, in order:

- Sometimes, depending on your congregational filiation.
- Keep your pervy pecker in your pants, mister. Mennonite gals do not put out, no matter how alluring we are in our bonnets and aprons.
- Granny panties. White as a flag, but with no surrender.

• I know of one that sold for $15,500—quilt, not panty. Though I'm pretty sure that the same guy who'd ask question number four would also be prepared to bid on a pair of Mennonite panties on eBay. Perhaps an enterprising entrepreneur should try selling Mennonite panties on eBay, perhaps even set up an e-store, for instance, MyMennonitePanty.com. Hell, I'll volunteer to get this chap started. I'll donate a pair of my own panties for free. Provided that I get to choose the panties.

Clearly the dominant American culture confuses us Mennonites with the Amish, who in fact began as an insurgent faction rebelling from the Mennonites. America's conflation is reasonable, since the Mennonites and the Amish have historically overlapped in many lifestyle choices.

But the Amish cut away from the Mennonites in 1693 because the rest of us were too liberal. That's rich, no? A liberal Mennonite is an oxymoron if ever there was one. So many Mennonite beliefs and practices are conservative that folks are perplexed by what they see as a curious dichotomy. On the one hand, the Mennonites resist change with their narrow doxy and their old-fashioned commitment to family values. On the other hand, those same Mennonites have actually identified with some leftist attitudes over the course of their near-five-hundred-year history. Because they are pro-peace, they are antiwar. Because they are nonviolent, they oppose the death penalty. Because they are anticonsumer, they promote a simple lifestyle that advocates for the environment. It's a curious collision of opposite forces that even today results in split political filiations among American Mennonite churches. Some are Republican; others lean Democrat.

While it seems laughable at first to think that the Amish broke up with the Mennonites because we were too liberal, it actually does makes theological sense. It nevertheless still tickles my funnybone to think that the Amish had a problem with the big bad carousing Mennonite lifestyle. "We'll have none of your worldly schnitzel, thank you! Come along, Esther! From now on we'll attend sing-alongs with our own kind!" Mennonite youth gatherings, no matter how enthusiastic, would never dream of spinning the bottle. If you think Mennonites do anything at a sing-along except sing, you are sadly mistaken! Mennonites don't party. We don't cut a rug. We *make* the rug, braiding it festively out of old rags, like the ancient rugs you sometimes see in museums dedicated to the life and times of Laura Ingalls Wilder.

Thus I'm not really sure what the Amish rebel Jacob Amman found to object to in our humble little religion. We Mennonites were pretty damn holy in the early years. For instance, we were the folks who got burned at the stake, like witches, but without the exciting element of sexual mystery. With witches, there was a trial that involved a strip search for a *witch's tit*, a devil's mark where Satan would come and suckle. In actual practice, the witch's tit was often any old mole or freckle, but the idea was that, due to the witch's consensual but unnatural suckling activities, she was one cold mama, and therefore you could shove a needle into the witch's tit and she would not flinch. This is where we get that expression *cold as a witch's tit*.

Not that Mennonites would say *cold as a witch's tit*. We don't hold with witches. Mind you, we haven't ruled them out. If Satan, or séances, or witches, or witches' tits, come up in casual conversation, as they inevitably must, a Mennonite might nod and murmur darkly, "There are powers and principalities!" This affirmation, a bromide descended peripatetically from Romans 8:38, I have always understood to mean something like this: "As an obedient Mennonite, I do believe in an external evil entity, and also in a literal hell, and damnation, and eternal punishment, and so on, but overall I prefer not to say the word *Satan*, because, all things considered, I do not want to sound like a nutter." After this Mennonite remarks that there are powers and principalities, she will almost certainly redirect the conversation back into more wholesome nonsatanic channels. "There are powers and principalities" is the Mennonite version of "It is what it is"—a polite way to simultaneously show that you are listening, but to indicate that you'd really rather change the subject.

An alert reader might ask the follow-up question: "But what is the Mennonite position on tits?" Good question! This reader has really been paying attention! In fact Mennonites neither say nor have *tits*. Hence in the seventeenth century at the trials of heretics there was no Mennonite strip search. No tit probing. At the Anabaptist trials, it went more like this:

BURGHER OR MAGISTRATE. Aganetha Janzen, do you hereby confess that you refuse infant baptism?

AGANETHA JANZEN. I do.

BURGHER OR MAGISTRATE. Then I hereby sentence you to death by burning. And if you sing God's praises, I'll have to shove this iron stake through your tongue.

AGANETHA JANZEN. Okay.

I can't speak for the witches, but the Anabaptists were so eager to die for their faith that they made it a point to refuse the optional little bag of gunpowder that was offered as a civil courtesy to most martyrs. You'd strap the bag to your upper shin, see, so that the dying would be over and done with lickety-split. When the flames flared as high as the knee, kaboom. But the

Mennonite martyrs waved away the gunpowder. They *wanted* the long drawn-out pain, on the theory that Jesus Christ's protracted suffering on the cross served as a shining example for us all.

Before all of the Mennonites in Western Europe could meet their Maker in this rather spectacular fashion, Russia's Catherine the Great saved the day in 1789 by inviting them to settle her weakest border spot, the land that would one day become Ukraine. They came; they saw; they planted. In 1817 they buckled down to business under the leadership of my favorite czarist dictator, Johann Cornies. I have personally visited this man's 25,000-acre holdings and his Ukrainian estate, Jushanlee. Although the man has been dead for 160 years, his passion for micromanagement lives on. Johann Cornies insisted on implementing a wide variety of agricultural innovations and on passing laws chillingly specific. For example, he legislated paint color—not just of public buildings like schools and churches, but of people's houses. Some call him a pioneer and a visionary. Okay, maybe that's just me. Such innovations! It was attractive paint, and durable! Merino sheep, animal husbandry, silkworms for one and all! And he was also the guy who introduced potatoes to the Russian clime.

Johann Cornies ruled the Mennonite *Kolonien* with an iron fist in a sweaty glove. From 1830 to 1848 ole Johann became more hands-on in his governing style, passing laws that progressively became more obsessed with lifestyle, sanitation, and ritual. He set up "model villages" for problem neighbors, such as the Russians and the Jews. He liked his *Judenplan*—the model Jewish *schtetl*—so much that he transferred the idea to the Mennonite villages, which soon became rigid utopias of sameness and hygiene. Cornies busily started making decrees about what the villagers should and shouldn't eat. Finally he even started enforcing daily menus, threatening to flog the noncompliant. For Monday, boiled potato dumplings! Tuesday, leftover dumplings! Wednesday, fat-back and fried dumplings! And so on. Woe to you if you're in the mood for a taco.

Johann Cornies's nickname was "Tree Devil," because, in a powerful vision for a new and improved Ukraine, he ruthlessly bullied the Mennonites into planting fruit trees at the rear of their property lines. They also had to plant a fruit tree in front of every house, in every village, by every road, thirty feet from every front door.

Naturally, some of the Mennonite villagers started bitching about the long arm of the Johann Cornies administration. The rebels came up with a surefire way to demonstrate their opinion of laws regarding trees. Here's what they elected to do by way of social protest, and you'll surely agree that this eloquent gesture presents Mennonite protest at its finest. They decided to plant the trees *upside down*. Since there weren't a lot of trees on the Ukrain-ian steppes at that time, these farmers could, if questioned by the Johann Cornies mafia, pretend that they just *hadn't known any better*. "Dude," they'd shrug, pointing at the apricot tree with its roots in the air, "we planted that sucker exactly like you told us. Thirty feet from the front door. Measure it."

I see this eloquent nineteenth-century gesture of subversion as brave, savvy, and intensely effective. It brings to mind similar ges-tures of defiance, as when, on *American Idol*, a rejected vocalist in her Princess Leia costume flips a turgid bird at Simon Cowell and shouts, "Your mother!"

So to sum up: Mennonites. Not the Amish.

For the entire Mennonite occupation of Ukraine, Mennonites thought of themselves as having been divinely called to lead the local Russians and Jews out of the darkness and into the light. It was as if the Mennonites thought the indigenous population was a lot of special-needs folks who just couldn't get there on their own. For hundreds of years Mennonites had a teensy ego problem. Well, who wouldn't? Let's face it, their hygiene was superb; their ovens, well-ventilated; their soup, full of savory prunes. They had a lot to be proud of. Did they live in mud huts like the Russian peasants? No, ma'am. Did they marry outside the extended family? By no means. Did they contribute the idea of the *Judenplan* for the ideal Jewish village? Sure! Whatever your village-planning problem, the Mennonites could solve it, particularly if your problem involved being Jewish, Russian, or Nogai! The Mennonite cheese stands alone. The Mennonites enjoyed three centuries of high-handed superiority. Is not a bit of self-congratulation pardonable, given the really good flavor of Mennonite sausage?

It's not that the Mennonites made a big push to *convert* the Russian peasants and the Jews; in fact, theologically speaking, Mennonites have kept pretty much to themselves throughout their four-hundred-year history. They haven't been evangelical in the sense of those freshly shaven young men in short-sleeved shirts who, clutching their corduroy-covered Bibles, ring your doorbell and ask earnestly if you've thought about hell at all. Mennonite superiority wasn't about what we believed. It was about what we did. It turned on demonstrable things like work habits and hygiene. It wasn't our fault that the entire native population was shiftless, unmotivated, and blighted by poor economic judgment, but we could fix that shit!

Allow me to illustrate my point. I was reading a riveting text titled *Heritage Remembered: A Pictorial Survey of Mennonites in Prussia and Russia.* After eighty pages of old-time photos of Mennonite farmers, preachers, and mill owners, the book suddenly offered a drawing of a Russian wagon. This Charlie Brown wagon looked like the sad fort my brothers built in the backyard when

Russian wagon, compare to Mennonite wagon on page 249.

they were eight and five, using the crappy wooden crate that the Nachtigalls' refrigerator had come in. Under the drawing, the Mennonite author Gerhard Lohrenz had written laconically, "Russian wagon, compare to Mennonite wagon on page 249." I have to say that I was a little surprised by the braggadocio of this caption. The Reverend Gerhard Lohrenz's tone was implying that the Mennonite wagon was the Porsche Boxster to the rusted Russian Pinto.

The Reverend Gerhard Lohrenz must have cherried out his own wagon, back in the day when he washed it in his driveway. But at the time that *Heritage Remembered* was published, the Reverend Gerhard Lohrenz was seventy-six years old, mature enough to live and let live on the whole wagon issue. *Dude,* I thought. *Mennonites aren't supposed to boast about their wagons. They're supposed to live simple and humble lives, earnestly thanking God that they've moved beyond horseback.*

But whatever. I obediently turned to page 249, where I was met not with one, not with two, but with *three* Mennonite wagons, all of which clearly kicked the ass of the lesser Russian wagon. Here are the captions. The first read, "A Mennonite covered wagon, unfamiliar among the Russians." *(Hey, Russians! You WISH you had a wagon like this!)* The second caption read, "Mennonite droschka. Every Mennonite farmer had one. Among Russians the droschka was unknown except when a well-to-do Russian citizen bought one from Mennonites." *(Too bad that your richest Russian is like the poorest Mennonite!)* Finally, the third caption cleared its throat with pride and said, "A Mennonite box-wagon. It too was unknown to the Russians but very much desired by them. The better-off Russian farmers bought such wagons as soon as they could." *(Say uncle, you sorry-ass-wagon losers!)*

The reason I bring all this up is that in a shocking historical reversal, the very Mennonites who were once the cool kids on the block became not fifty years later the überdorks of the universe, just in time for my childhood. History reminds us that there are highs and lows on any ethnic journey.

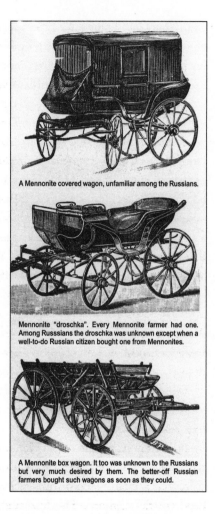

A Mennonite covered wagon, unfamiliar among the Russians.

Mennonite "droschka". Every Mennonite farmer had one. Among Russsians the droschka was unknown except when a well-to-do Russian citizen bought one from Mennonites.

A Mennonite box wagon. It too was unknown to the Russians but very much desired by them. The better-off Russian farmers bought such wagons as soon as they could.

With a nod to the prophet Isaiah, "Every valley shall be exalted, and every mountain and hill made low." Thus the wheel of fortune turned, and it was the Mennonites' time in the doghouse. Gone were the days of triumphant *Judenplans*. Gone the czarist kickbacks, gone the *Beisitzer* estates, gone the serfs who served your family loyally for three generations. Hello long skirts, tight braids, and Borscht in your thermos. While the Beatles were arriving and the rest of the nation was singing "Here Comes the Sun," I couldn't help noticing that the Mennonites, led by Connie Isaac, were singing alleluia.

This is the real dope on Mennonites, the good stuff that you won't find in the academic works by Mennonite scholars. Because I respect your time, I have organized this material under a list of helpful subheadings. Mennonites have a high threshold for boredom. As mentioned before, we can sit still for hours and hours on end in church, and on a wooden pew, with a flat ass, in a scratchy dress; it's a skill we learn from birth. But I am aware that not everybody has the Mennonite *Sitzfleisch*. Hence I offer an abridged version, a *Cliff's Notes* for the busy and the brief.

## Cannabis sativa

First, and most important, most Mennonites don't know what dope is.

Second, if you told them, they wouldn't know what to do with it.

Third, not only would they not inhale; they would chop it up like parsley and sprinkle it into a bowl of Borscht. When I finally overcame my Mennonite hesitation at age forty-three, I found that, like Bill Clinton, I too was incapable of inhaling. Unlike Bill Clinton, I wanted to. Something in my lungs just snapped shut. Lord knows I tried. I even got a friend to exhale a cloud of smoke in my mouth while I breathed in deeply, as in yoga. But no go. Which brings me to a tentative working hypothesis that Mennonites may be *genetically incapable* of getting high.

## Exemption from Military Service

The United States recognizes "membership in good standing" in the Mennonite church as a justifiable reason to bestow exemption from military service. Being a Mennonite is like having a note from your mom. This exemption is due to the fact that throughout their history Mennonites have defined themselves by their refusal to fight. Pick a war, any war, and the Mennonites have opposed it. In Mennonite doctrine, there is no such thing as a Just War. Moreover, we believe that violence leads inevitably to more violence. Thus we may say that in peacemaking activities Mennonites resemble Mahatma Gandhi. But the resemblance ends there. This may be just my personal opinion, but I don't think a Gandhi-style hunger strike would work with the Mennonites. Lay down their guns? Sure, no problem. Lay down their steady diet of potato dumplings? Not so much.

Sidebar for cynics and apostates: In the eighteenth century the peaceful Mennonites of Nieder Khortitsa were known throughout southern Ukraine as *Cherkessy met aufjebroakne Tjniefs* (Men of the Broken-Tipped Knives). The Mennonites had to fight with pocketknives because, as pacifists, they couldn't carry firearms. This brings me to a related point, which is that irony isn't a Mennonite strong suit.

Mennonites traditionally called themselves *Die Stillen im Lande* (the Quiet in the Nations)—meaning that civil resistance could be achieved through the twin activities of thoughtful active nonparticipation and farming. Both of these activities involve practical action. If it's worth believing, it's worth doing. Mennonites are big doers. In some respects Mennonites resemble Henry David Thoreau, who eloquently went to jail rather than pay a tax he thought was unfair. Mennonites have a sweet tooth for such demonstrations; they are very literal folks who enjoy a practical demonstration of what they believe.

For instance, let's say that you call your little brother a fool when you are six years old. There's a verse in the Gospel of Matthew that says, "But I say unto you, . . . whosoever shall say, Thou fool, shall be in danger of hellfire." Your mother may therefore seek to demonstrate an important lesson, namely, We Do Not Utter Un-Christian Words, Especially to Our Brother, Even Though He Has Just Floated a Semi-Deliberate Turd in the Bathtub. Your mother may believe that the best way to demonstrate this lesson is to scrub your mouth out with homemade lye soap. What happens to the turd is between your brother and God. Meanwhile, the lye soap is both participatory and practical.

Mennonites would rather do anything than engage in physical violence—lose a war, go to jail, perform six years of alternate service in forestry, you name it. Military conflict is thus for Cro-Magnon brutes and losers. Did Jesus lift a finger to fight back when they came to crucify him? No! Jesus preferred a lifestyle of homosocial bonding and potluck luncheons! So if you're thinking about studying karate or dating a Lebanese black belt, fuhgeddaboutit. You can't believe in peace if you're practicing war.

### Mennonite Dance

Who are we kidding? Mennonites don't *really* dance! Puh-lease!

### Intermarriage and/or Genetic Pinkness

Mennonites marry their cousins and second cousins. Mennonites all know each other instantly, on sight and by smell. Our last names are the same. We practically have a secret handshake. If you are a Mennonite, I think I can safely guarantee that you married my mother's second cousin. We're all eerily related, and thus the gene pool is shallow. Come in and splash if you must, but you won't get tan. We are ruddy Teutonic giants who wear plus-sized swimsuits.

Gotcha! We don't wear swimsuits! If we wore swimsuits, that would mean we would have had to get naked! We've got better things to do. Such as sitting attentively in church, and praying that God will not call us to become a missionary on the Chaco!

## *Multitasking*

North American Mennonites all used to grow up speaking Low German, using an outhouse, and shelling peas, sometimes all at the same time. This makes us ace multitaskers. My mother, one of seventeen kids, grew up with a two-seater biffy so that people wouldn't have to wait to use the toilet; they could enter in pairs, do their business, and get right back to work. The family that shits together knits together.

The outhouse behind the church where my father was pastor offered only single seaters, but that was okay by me. I liked going alone to the outhouse. I liked taking a big gulp of outside air and seeing if I could hold my breath the entire time. I never could, and I always ended up inhaling the prodigious stink. After about ten seconds, you got used to it: a simple, uncomplicated odor. I sort of liked it. And I liked to stare down the hole at the shuddersome waste and the big damp flies. There were full-bodied turds slightly misshapen by the fall; there were interesting dark patches that absorbed smeared paper. Once I saw a rat moving like a shadow in the decomposing twilight. I often remained in the outhouse longer than necessary.

I wouldn't have been able to explain it, but there was something satisfying about confronting the very worst that humanity could produce. What lay below the wooden seat presented a composite assurance that all the prim ladies of the church—Mrs. Franz Redekopp, Mrs. Heinrich Braun, Mrs. Jakob Liebelt—were, beneath their matronly skirts, not so prim after all.

But I digress. Perhaps when you're the seventeenth child you are merely grateful that there is a seat for you, that your crap is part of the larger crap. You learn to work hard and pay attention to the many simultaneous conversations around you. Even as you sleep four to a bed, you master the art of plurality. Performing five different tasks, for five older sisters, each of whom is also multi-tasking, creates a soothing sense of anonymity. Call us Legion, for we are many!

## The Sing-along

Mennonites may be unfamiliar with the pleasures of nudity, but we can all sing a capella, in gorgeous harmony, the reverent hymns of our youth. This is one of the reasons Mennonites have such big families. The parents are trying to round out the family choir. If they don't get a tenor, dammit it, they'll keep trying until they get it right. I am not at all gifted in the musical arena, though of course I can carry a tune and deliver an acceptable alto. When I first went to public school, I remember being astonished when my classmates in the Easterby Elementary school choir aired their rendition of the classic "Jimmy Crack Corn." They were more enthusiastic than tuneful, and nary a student knew how to harmonize, except Lola, who had a gorgeous voice even as a child. Poor Lola looked as if she'd break into tears.

Once, traveling as an adult with a group of Mennonite scholars,

I visited the Byzantine cathedral of Saint Sophia in Kiev. Our guide mentioned that the acoustics were spectacular. Spry Klaus Quiring, a retired music professor, was quick to turn to the rest of us, excitement in his eyes. He tried the opening bars of *"Grosser Gott wir loben Dich"* (Holy God, We Praise Thy Name). There wasn't a moment's hesitation. Suddenly the cathedral swelled with beautiful harmony. We all knew every word of every verse, and the hymn was so beautiful that the officials waited until we had finished the last note before they booted us out and politely requested we not come back.

Perhaps you have been wondering, *How can I join this attractive religious group?* Yet it would be only fair to be forthcoming about some of the social lubricities that Mennonites have jettisoned for carefully considered theological reasons. This list includes, but is not limited, to the following:

- Drinking
- Dancing (though let's not forget "liturgical movement," which is sort of allowed)
- Smoking
- Sex outside of marriage
- Sex inside of marriage
- Sex on television
- Sex in the movies
- Sex in the classroom
- Gay sex
- Straight sex
- Sex on the Chaco
- Higher education

- The Walt Disney Story of Menstruation
- Gambling
- Playing cards
- Foul language (i.e., the word *fool*)
- Ouija boards
- Slumber parties
- Cafeteria lunches
- Divorce
- Prada
- Atheist husbands who, after fifteen years of marriage, leave you for a guy named Bob.

On the other hand, Mennonites happily endorse the following:

- Public prayer, out loud, with bowed heads, especially in restaurants and at airports
- Mind over matter when it comes to dental hygiene
- Huge donations to charity (with the money you save by not going to the dentist)
- Potlucks (A-J bring a main dish; K-Z, pie)
- Sweater vests buttoned right up to the top, so that they nicely cover the short-sleeved poly-blend shirts beneath
- *Pluma Moos*, a hot fruit soup starring our friend the prune
- Can I just say here that *Pluma Moos* also contains *raisins*?
- Christian fish decals for the bumper, or perhaps a sticker depicting a cartoon girl and boy kissing each other in the name of Yahweh
- The scrupulous consumption, on principle, of any and every moldy leftover in the fridge. In the words of the 1970s naturalist Euell Gibbons, whom I like to think of as an honorary Mennonite, "Many parts are edible!"

Okay, I think my job is done here. The above summary of Mennonite culture is probably much more to the point than whatever's on Wikipedia. If you have paid close attention to the preceding pages, you are ready to meet Mennonites in real life. When you do, speak slowly and smile. If you play your cards right, I'm pretty sure they'll offer you some cabbage.

# ACKNOWLEDGMENTS

Special thanks to my editor, Helen Atsma, and my agent, Michael Bourret, for their role in shaping this memoir. I would have never thought of writing this story had not my svelte red-headed friend Carla Vissers pointed out that my e-mails from California were sounding a lot like nonfiction. I'm thinking of buying Carla a drink or something. And I never would have moved forward without the active encouragement of Anna-Lisa Cox. I'm grateful to Beth Trembley, Julie Kipp, Laura Roberts, James Persoon, and Jill Janzen for their insight, and to Joanne Jenkins for reading some of the chapters in early draft. Spirited nine-year-old Emma Jenkins had the pluck to dance an Irish jig in the lobby of a symphony hall, thus becoming my inspiration.

It is my parents who played the greatest role in supporting this project. They invited me to stay with them as long as I liked, and were perfectly good-natured when I asked them pressing questions about their Mennonite youth. Also, when I was out writing in their gazebo, sweating it out in the valley heat under a slow fan, my dad would sometimes appear in his long shorts and dress socks, puttering about the backyard. Eventually he'd come over to the gazebo, deposit a handful of ripe cherries, and silently go away again. How sweet is that? And my mom! For her I'd drink scrofulous buttermilk— though in all probability if it's scrofulous, she's probably already finished it herself. In buttermilk, as in life, she's my hero.

# etc.

extras...

essays...

etcetera

more author
**About Rhoda Janzen**

more book
**About *Mennonite In a Little Black Dress***

...and more

# Meet Rhoda Janzen

Shelley LaLonde

Rhoda Janzen holds a Ph.D. from the University of California, Los Angeles, where she was the University of California Poet Laureate in 1994 and 1997. She is the author of *Babel's Stair*, a collection of poems, and her poems have also appeared in *Poetry*, *The Yale Review*, *The Gettysburg Review*, and *The Southern Review*. She teaches English and creative writing at Hope College in Holland, Michigan. ◾

I had just returned to a conservative Mennonite community after an absence of more than two decades. In the recent past, my husband of fifteen years had ditched me for a guy named Bob whom he'd met on Gay.com. The same week I'd been in a nasty car accident. My heart was broken, my legs were scarred, and I just wasn't up for research as usual. So when my sabbatical rolled around, I went home to the Mennonites. It was therapeutic, almost soothing, to be back in the old stomping ground, browsing an antique mall with my seventy-year-old mother. At one stall she spied a country-fresh ceramic rooster and said, "Do you know Norma Franz? Conrad Franz's wife?"

"Sure," I said.

"Norma Franz has a thing for roosters," she said thoughtfully. Then, following some thread of logic that I couldn't quite trace, she added, "Her husband Conrad is a Butt Man. You know how some men like to focus on one body part? Well, Conrad Franz has a thing for bottoms. Once he took a picture of Norma's bottom. She was wearing beige slacks and she was bent over, like this." My mother obligingly bent over right there in the middle of the antique mall.

"Norma told you this?" I asked.

My mother nodded.

"Was Norma posing? Or did Conrad just sneak up on her?"

"She had something on her shoe," my mother answered. "And then Conrad wanted to frame the picture and hang it in the living room! Can you believe that?"

"Did Norma let him?"

"She did! She showed me the picture."

"How'd it look?" I asked.

"It looked like a bottom in beige slacks. That's not my idea of art."

"Mom," I said, "which would you rather put in your living room: a framed picture of Norma Franz's bottom in beige slacks, or this ceramic rooster?"

She snorted. "Oh, no contest! The rooster! But it wouldn't look good on the piano."

"Why do you need to put it on the piano? You could put it on the coffee table."

"No, the grandkids are too rowdy. They'd knock it over."

"In that case," I advised, "maybe you should revisit the picture of Norma's bottom. You could hang it above the sofa."

"No," my mother said decisively. "A picture of Norma's bottom would be problematic for Heinrich Groebel. He stays with us when he's in town for conference meetings. Those South American Mennonites are always so straight-laced."

Together my mother and I considered the Rev. Heinrich Groebel's shock and distaste upon confronting solitary gabardine patootie above the couch. We paused for a moment of respectful silence before moving on to the next vendor's stall.

In the days that followed I described this incident and others to my friends via email. They started pressing me for more email bulletins about the Mennonites. They wanted to know about my parents' church, their neighbors, their moral preferences. My friends seemed fascinated by my enormous extended family, many of whom wore tall black dress socks with shorts and sandals and a sweater-vest. In the same way that all of Los Angeles comes to a grinding halt when there's a high-speed car chase on TV,

> My friends seemed fascinated by my enormous extended family, many of whom wore tall black dress socks with shorts and sandals and a sweater-vest.

my friends were mesmerized by my parents' frugality and stern simplicity. There must be a universal need to explore why some people, for instance my father, elect to reuse their toothpicks. And I have photo-documentation of a parental teabag that flavored three separate cups of tea. It was finally my friend Carla who told me to start saving my emails. She said they were starting to smell like memoir.

As I reflected on my turbulent return to this community, I began to see resonant possibilities in the Mennonite world around me. Here were marital drama and profound failure, plucked out of an urban intellectual landscape and set down in the middle of a Mennonite no-man's land, where folks were charitable to ceramic roosters they didn't like, or, variously, to bottoms in beige slacks. I decided that healing was not only possible, but probable. And I began to write. ■

Your previous book is a collection of poems, Babel's Stair, and your poems have also been widely published in journals and anthologies. Was it difficult to make the switch from writing poetry to writing prose?

Fools rush in. I've been studying the craft of writing poetry my entire adult life, and my commitment to it has a serious edge that I blessedly don't feel when I write creative nonfiction. Because of my training, I'm *supposed* to know what I'm doing in poetry. But I've never studied nonfiction in a formal context, so it's easy to give myself permission to wing it. This is the beauty of ignorance.

What's up with those head coverings that so many Mennonite women wear?

My question exactly! The Mennonites would tell you that they wear them as a public sign of modesty. Mennonite women have a long tradition of not wanting to tempt men with their worldy beauty, you know. They used to wear ugly little capes like ponchos to hide their "womanly shape." But I suspect that the head coverings are just cheaper than hair products.

Where are you on your spiritual journey today?

So often we think of faith as the crutch of crisis; we turn to it only when our world bottoms out, as mine did when my husband left me. Weirdly, faith is becoming more important to me, not less. I'm still exploring issues of spirituality and theology, and I'm even regularly attending a church. Also, nobody's twisting my arm! I'm often amazed that an English professor prefers nonfiction to new fiction. . . . With a nod to Viktor Frankl, the books on my nightstand are all about man's search for meaning.

> You write briefly in your memoir about having chosen to not bear children. Was this a difficult decision?

Nick had a vasectomy the first month we were married. That was a joint decision. Given his misery, we felt that it would be irresponsible to risk passing on bipolarity. I do love children, and I've often wondered what kind of a mother I would have made. For us, though, the harder decision was not to adopt. We chose not to because we couldn't provide a stable parenting environment.

But I can't pin my decision solely on Nick's situation. You know what troubles me? The notion that we should reproduce just because we can. Seems to me we should be able to articulate some proactive, deliberated reasons for bringing a child into the world. When women cite their biological clock, I wonder if they've thought that out. Shouldn't human beings *assess* their biological urges as well as admit them? What if we're having babies to feel less lonely, more needed? If so, we're using someone to make us feel better about ourselves. That's a little creepy.

> Your mother is wonderfully, irrepressibly upbeat. Did her sunny outlook on life shape your terrific sense of humor?

Sure. She cracks me up. She sees the world through an astonishing parental lens. Recently I drove her to a family reunion and she sent along a picture of me that made me look like the love child of Menno Simons and Spiro Agnew—no comment, just, *Here, I thought you might like this hideous picture of yourself!* Then there was a picture of my sister with a pandowdy face and an underslung

7

chin, like a muffler dragging a bumper. What *is* it with moms? Have they no *sense*? I retaliate by taking pictures of her in hats. She has a global head and no neck, and yet she just peacefully stands there and lets me photograph her in any hat whatsoever, including an eighties shoulder pad I removed from her coat.

What memoirs have moved or inspired you? Did they influence the way you wrote your own?

One memoir I read late into the night was Kao Kalia Yang's *The Latehomecomer*, about the Hmong emigration to the United States from Laos. But I never seriously read memoir as a genre until I had written one. I was always too busy with poetry and with cultural criticism circa 1885. Now, though, I love curling up with a good memoir from time to time. Who doesn't love David Sedaris's deadpan humor, Jeanette Walls's submerged self-pity, Elizabeth Gilbert's discursive questing? Good stuff. ■

Truth is stranger than fiction, folks. I'm here to tell you that on the subject of shame-based foods, I've heard from readers all across America. Some have generously shared their own ethnic traditions—"In my family we serve beet soup cold, with horseradish!" Some have disputed my Mennonite labels—"I'll have you know that the Mennonites stole those cabbage rolls from the Poles!" Some readers even wanted to know how they could get hold of some of the damp persimmon cookies I describe in chapter six.

I'll never be accused of recipe hoarding. Nor will my mother, who cheerfully launched into prescriptive cooking mode when I called her the other day. The only recipe she had to look up was the one for persimmon cookies. She hadn't made them since we were kids. "You and Hannah never liked the raisins," Mom said. "But you should be over that by now."

Last night, with apprehension, I made the damp persimmon cookies. You know what? They're pretty good.

———

Warmer Kartoffelsalat

Persimmon Cookies

Platz

Cotletten

Onion Cream Gravy for Cotletten

Borscht

# WARMER KARTOFFELSALAT

## as told by Rhoda's mom

boiled potatoes, cut up (but I don't like it when you leave the peel on)

wurst or sausage

½ cup chopped celery

1 medium chopped onion

salt

pepper

about ⅔ cup of room-temperature water

1 tbs flour

2 tbs bacon fat

⅓ cup sugar

⅓ cup vinegar

Cook the onion in the hot fat, but don't let it get too brown. Add the flour and stir. Add sugar, salt, vinegar, and water, and bring mixture to a boil, stirring constantly. Pour over the hot potatoes and the chopped wurst. Sprinkle with pepper and serve warm.

# PERSIMMON COOKIES

## as told by Rhoda's mom

½ cup unsalted butter, melted

1 large egg

1 cup white sugar

3 ripe persimmons

1 teas baking soda

2 cups flour

½ tsp salt

½ tsp cinnamon

½ tsp freshly grated nutmeg

½ tsp cloves

1 cup chopped pecans, toasted at 375° for 7 minutes

1 cup raisins

Preheat oven to 350°.

Cut out the tops of the persimmons as if they're tomatoes. Spoon out the pulp and throw the skin away. Mix the teaspoon of soda into the persimmon pulp and set aside.

Cream your butter and sugar. Add the egg and mix. Now stir in the persimmon pulp. Combine dry goods and add to persimmon mixture.

Don't skip the raisins! They're good in this recipe! Plump them up in the microwave for 30 seconds and add them with the toasted nuts. Bake about ten minutes.

# PLATZ

### as told by Rhoda's mom

a slightly sweet yeast dough
tart cherry-plums or other fruit

Streusel topping:

   1 cup flour
   1 cup sugar
   ¼ cup butter

Roll out your yeast dough to the size of your pan and let it rise a little so that it starts to come. Now cut up your fruit. If you use cherry-plums, be sure to get the pits out. Arrange the cherry-plums on the dough.

Cut up your flour, sugar, and butter for the Streusel and sprinkle evenly over the fruit. Bake at 350° for about 20 minutes, until the crust turns a nice golden brown.

# COTLETTEN

## as told by Rhoda's mom

2 lbs ground meat

2 eggs

¼ of a big box of soda crackers

about 2 tsp salt

pepper

baking powder

1 small onion, chopped

evaporated milk

bacon drippings for frying

Crush crackers in plastic bag with rolling pin. In large bowl break 2 eggs. Measure salt in hand; add pepper so that it looks tasty. Add enough baking powder for the Cotletten to fluff up. Then stir in a good Schulps of evaporated milk. Add cracker crumbs. Now mix in the ground beef, but wet your hands first. Fry Cotletten in hot fat until brown. Turn and brown the other side. Serve with onion cream gravy.

### ONION CREAM GRAVY FOR COTLETTEN

small onion, chopped

heaping tbs flour

hot potato water

evaporated milk

Mince the onion and cook in 1 tbs of the remaining fat. Stir in the flour and add some hot potato water. When it starts to thicken, add some more evaporated milk.

# BORSCHT

### as told by Rhoda's mom

1 small pork roast

1 bay leaf

1 medium chopped onion

salt and pepper

cut-up potatoes

sliced carrots

1 small cabbage or ½ a big one, chopped and cored

parsley

1 can tomato soup

Simmer your roast for a long time, but near the beginning add your bay leaf, onion, and salt and pepper. When meat is tender, add some cut-up potatoes and at least four carrots.

Add the parsley with your cabbage. When potatoes are about done, I add a can of tomato soup. I know you girls like the old-fashioned way, with beets, but a tomato taste is just as nice and much easier. You can also use real tomatoes instead.

Serve with Zwiebach and sour cream, of course. Dad likes a little vinegar in his. ■

1. Rhoda's parents are deeply religious. What are some of the more notable ways their faith manifests itself? What qualities do they possess that you admire? Were you surprised by anything you learned about the Mennonite community?

2. Consider Rhoda's family gatherings on Christmas Eve and Christmas. How does their family dynamic work? Rhoda and her siblings are very different from one another—do they get along better than you would expect, or not?

3. Rhoda announces early on in the memoir that her husband left her for a man he met on Gay.com; however, as the book progresses, she slowly reveals that her marriage had been troubled for some time, and that she knew Nick was bisexual before they were married. Did this change your perspective of their relationship? Do you think these piecemeal revelations in some way mimic the way Rhoda comes to terms with the end of her marriage? Why do you think the book is structured this way?

4. To what extent is this a memoir about growing up? Rhoda humorously relates her embarrassment at having to eat "shame-based foods" at school as a child—but admits that as an adult, she enjoys them. Similarly, she looks back fondly on other experiences that were likely not very pleasant at the time—setting off a yard bomb inside the van she was sleeping in on a camping trip, for one. Are there other examples you can think of? Do you think this kind of nostalgia—a willingness to appreciate and poke fun at bad memories—is something that's indicative of maturity, of adulthood?

5. The Mennonites disapprove of dancing and drinking alcohol. Rhoda says that while growing up, radios, eight-track tapes, unsupervised television, Lite-Brites, and Barbies—among other things—were all forbidden. Does

her family gain anything positive by limiting "wordly" influences? Did Rhoda and her siblings lose anything in being so sheltered?

6. Some Mennonites disapprove of higher education. Do you think that a career in academia necessarily precludes one from faith? How does Rhoda reconcile the two?

7. Rhoda's mother is, as Rhoda puts it, "as buoyant as a lark on a summer's morn." Rhoda claims to be not as upbeat as her mother, but do you think that in some ways, she is? Given the seriousness of some of the issues explored in the memoir, did the humorous voice surprise you?

8. Rhoda freely discusses the problems in her marriage, and how poorly her husband sometimes treated her. Looking back on it, however, she thinks that she probably still would have married him regardless. She asks, "Is it ever really a waste of time to love someone, truly and deeply, with everything you have?" What do you think?

9. Rhoda and Hannah make a list of men they would refuse to date—it includes, but is not limited to: men named Dwayne or Bruce; men who have the high strange laugh of a distant loon; men who bring index cards with prewritten conversation starters on a first date. What qualities might you assiduously avoid in a romantic partner?

10. Rhoda's mother tells her, "When you're young, faith is often a matter of rules . . . but as you get older, you realize that faith is really a matter of relationship—with God, with the people around you, with members of your community." Is Rhoda's own relationship with faith an example of this?

11. Towards the end of the book, Rhoda remarks that she "suddenly felt destiny as a mighty and perplexing force, an inexorable current that sweeps us off into new channels." Do you believe in destiny? Can you really ever escape your roots or change your beliefs? ■